1,000,000 Books
are available to read at

www.ForgottenBooks.com

Read online
Download PDF
Purchase in print

ISBN 978-1-333-69912-3
PIBN 10537248

This book is a reproduction of an important historical work. Forgotten Books uses state-of-the-art technology to digitally reconstruct the work, preserving the original format whilst repairing imperfections present in the aged copy. In rare cases, an imperfection in the original, such as a blemish or missing page, may be replicated in our edition. We do, however, repair the vast majority of imperfections successfully; any imperfections that remain are intentionally left to preserve the state of such historical works.

Forgotten Books is a registered trademark of FB &c Ltd.
Copyright © 2018 FB &c Ltd.
FB &c Ltd, Dalton House, 60 Windsor Avenue, London, SW19 2RR.
Company number 08720141. Registered in England and Wales.

For support please visit www.forgottenbooks.com

1 MONTH OF FREE READING

at

www.ForgottenBooks.com

By purchasing this book you are eligible for one month membership to ForgottenBooks.com, giving you unlimited access to our entire collection of over 1,000,000 titles via our web site and mobile apps.

To claim your free month visit: www.forgottenbooks.com/free537248

* Offer is valid for 45 days from date of purchase. Terms and conditions apply.

English
Français
Deutsche
Italiano
Español
Português

www.forgottenbooks.com

Mythology Photography **Fiction**
Fishing Christianity **Art** Cooking
Essays Buddhism Freemasonry
Medicine **Biology** Music **Ancient Egypt** Evolution Carpentry Physics
Dance Geology **Mathematics** Fitness
Shakespeare **Folklore** Yoga Marketing
Confidence Immortality Biographies
Poetry **Psychology** Witchcraft
Electronics Chemistry History **Law**
Accounting **Philosophy** Anthropology
Alchemy Drama Quantum Mechanics
Atheism Sexual Health **Ancient History**
Entrepreneurship Languages Sport
Paleontology Needlework Islam
Metaphysics Investment Archaeology
Parenting Statistics Criminology
Motivational

D'AUBIGNÉ,

AND

HIS WRITINGS

PRIOR TO HIS

HISTORY OF THE REFORMATION.

D'AUBIGNÉ,

AND

HIS WRITINGS:

WITH A SKETCH OF THE

LIFE OF THE AUTHOR,

BY

REV. ROBERT BAIRD, D.D.

NEW YORK:
BAKER AND SCRIBNER,
145 NASSAU STREET.
1846.

Entered according to act of Congress, in the year 1846, by

BAKER & SCRIBNER,

in the Clerk's office of the District Court of the United States for the Southern District of New York.

S. W. BENEDICT,
Ster. & Print., 16 Spruce Street.

J. H. MERLE D'AUBIGNE,

BY

REV. ROBERT BAIRD, D.D.

In compliance with the request of many friends, who desire to know something of the family, life, character, and literary labors of the Rev. Dr. MERLE D'AUBIGNE, author of the celebrated "History of the Reformation in the Sixteenth Century," I furnish the brief memoir which follows.

John Henry Merle (or, as he is called in England and this country, *Merle d'Aubigné*) was born in the city of Geneva, in the year 1794. Consequently he is a little more than forty-eight years of age.

Although a Swiss by birth, Dr. Merle is of French origin. His family, like that of many of the inhabitants of Geneva, is descended from Huguenot ancestors, who were compelled to leave their native country because of their religion, and to take refuge in a city upon which one of their countrymen, *John Calvin*, had been the instrument, under God, of conferring the blessings of the Reformation.

The great-grandfather of the Rev. Dr. Merle d'Aubigné, on his paternal side, was *John Lewis Merle*, of Nismes. About the epoch of the Revocation of the Edict of Nantes (1685), this worthy man, who was a sincere Protestant, fled from his country, and took refuge in Switzerland, in order to enjoy the religious liberty which France, under the rule of Louis XIV., denied him.

His son, Francis Merle, married, in the year 1743, Elizabeth, the daughter of a Protestant nobleman, residing in Geneva, whose name was George d' Aubigné. Agreeably to a usage which exists at Geneva, and, I believe, in many other portions of Switzerland, by which a gentleman adds the name of his wife to his own, in order to distinguish him from other persons of the same name, Mr. Francis Merle appended that of *d'Aubigné* to his own, and was known as *Francis Merle d'Aubigné*. Since his day, the family have retained the name of Merle d'Aubigné. At least this was the case with the son of Francis Merle,—the father of our author,—as well as with our author himself.

George d'Aubigné, just mentioned, whose daughter Elizabeth became the wife of Francis Merle, was a descendant of *Theodore Agrippa d'Aubigné*, who left France, in the year 1620, on account of religious persecution. This Theodore Agrippa d'Aubigné was no common man. The old chroniclers call him *un Calviniste zélé, si oneques il en fut;* "a zealous Calvinist, if there ever was one." He bought the domain of Lods, near Geneva, on which he built the Château of Crest, which still remains. The old Huguenot warrior handled the pen and the lyre as well as the sword; and his *Tragiques*, a poem full of life and genius, drew a vivid picture of the court of the imbecile Henry III. of France, and his infamous mother, *Catharine de Medici*. His *Histoire Universelle de la fin du 16me. Siècle* had the honor of being publicly burnt at Paris, in the year 1620, by order of Louis XIII. He wrote also the *Confession de Saucy*, and several other works. It is related of him, that, at the age of eight years, he knew well both the Latin and the Greek languages. At the age of fourteen, he went to Geneva, to finish his studies in the "Academy," or University, of that city. Having completed his course in that Institution, he returned to France; whence, as has been stated, he was compelled to fly, in the year 1620. Upon establishing himself at Geneva, he became allied, by marriage, with the families of the Burlamachi and Calandrini, two of the most honorable families in that city, both of Italian origin; for Geneva was a "City of refuge" to persecuted and exiled Protestants of Italy as well as of France.

Francis Merle d'Aubigné had many children, one of whom, *Amié Robert Merle d'Aubigné*, was born in 1755, and was the father of three sons; the oldest and the youngest of whom are respectable merchants in this country—the former in New York, and the latter in New Orleans—and the second is the Rev. Dr. Merle d'Aubigné, the subject of this notice. Amié Robert

Merle d'Aubigné had a strong desire in his early years to consecrate his life wholly to the service of his God; and his parents allowed him to pursue the studies requisite for the right discharge of the office of the ministry of the gospel. But on his father's death, his uncle and guardian, "*par un caprice qui fit le malheur de ma jeunesse*"* (as he says in his memoir, written for his oldest son, William), caused him to give up his studies and embrace other pursuits.

The end of this excellent man was truly tragical and deplorable. In the year 1799 he went on an important commercial mission, to Constantinople and Vienna. On his return from the latter city to Geneva, through Switzerland, in the autumn of that year, he was met on the road, near Zurich, by the savage and infuriated hordes of Russians, who had been recently defeated by the French forces under the command of Massena, and by them was cruelly murdered!

His widow, who is still living in Geneva, in a vigorous old age, devoted all the energies of an active and enlightened mind to the care of her fatherless children; and now daily thanks God for having supplied her with the means of giving them a liberal education.

The preceding paragraphs will suffice to give the reader some knowledge of the ancestors of the subject of this biographical sketch.

The Rev. Dr. Merle d'Aubigné was educated in the "Academy"—or, as it is more commonly called by strangers, the *University*—of his native city. After having completed the course of studies in the Faculties of Letters and Philosophy, he entered that of Theology. I am not certain as to the time when he finished his preparations for the ministry; but believe that it was about the year 1816.

The Theological Faculty in the Academy of Geneva, when Dr. Merle d'Aubigné was a student, was wholly Socinian in its character. Whatever were the shades of difference in regard to doctrine, which prevailed among its professors, they all agreed in rejecting the proper divinity of the Saviour and of the Holy Spirit, salvation through the expiatory death and intercession of

* Through a caprice which rendered my youth miserable.

the former, and regeneration and sanctification by the influences of the latter. With these cardinal doctrines of the Gospel, others which are considered by all Evangelical Christians to be fundamental in the system of their Faith, were also renounced. Alas, the same state of things exists at this day, in the School which Calvin founded, and in which that great man, as well as Beza, Francis Turrettin, Pictet, and other renowned men taught the youth, who gathered around them, the glorious doctrines of the Gospel and the Reformation.

It was under such instruction that Dr. Merle pursued his studies for the sacred ministry. But it pleased God to send a faithful servant to Geneva about the time that he was completing his theological training. This was Mr. Haldane, of Edinburgh, a wealthy and zealous Christian, who still protracts a long and useful life, which has been spent in the service of his Master. This excellent man, deploring the errors which prevailed in the theological department of the Academy, endeavored to do what he could, during the sojourn of a winter, to counteract them. For this purpose, he invited a number of young men to his rooms in the hotel in which he lodged, and there, by means of an interpreter at first, he endeavored to teach them the glorious Gospel. In doing this, he commented on the Epistle to the Romans, at much length. God blessed his efforts to the salvation of some ten or twelve of them.

Seldom has it happened that an equal number of young men have been converted about the same time, and in one place, who have been called to perform so important a part in building up the kingdom of Christ. One of these men was the excellent Felix Neff, of blessed memory. Another was the late Henry Pyt. The greater part of them, however, still live to adorn and bless the Church in France and Switzerland. But none of them have become more celebrated than the subject of this notice.

Not long after his ordination, Dr. Merle set out for Germany, where he spent a number of months, chiefly at Berlin. On his way to that city, he passed through Eisenach, and visited the Castle of Warburg, in the vicinity, famous for the retreat, if not properly the imprisonment, of Luther. It was whilst gazing at the walls of the room which the great Reformer had occupied, that the thought of writing the "History of the Reformation" entered his mind, never to abandon it till its realization should put the world in possession of the immortal work whose existence may be said to date from that day.

From Berlin, Dr. Merle was called to Hamburgh, to preach to an interesting French Protestant Church, which had been planted by pious Huguenots, when compelled to leave France, upon the Revocation of the Edict of Nantes, and which has been continued by their descendants. In that city he spent five years, diligently employing his time in amassing information on the great subject upon which he had resolved to write.

From Hamburgh he was invited to Brussels by the late king of Holland, to preach in a chapel which he had erected in that capital, for Protestants who spoke the French language. At that time, and down till 1830, Belgium (of which Brussels is the capital) was united to Holland, and formed a portion of the kingdom of the Netherlands.

In the year 1830, a Revolution took place in Belgium, occasioned as much by religious as by political causes. The priests, in order to deliver the country from the Protestant influence which a union with Holland diffused in it, joined De Potter and the other "patriots" in their revolutionary measures. The enterprise succeeded. The Dutch were driven out; and all who were considered friendly to the king, or intimately connected with him, were in no little danger. Among those who were in this predicament was Dr. Merle. At no small risk of his life, he escaped from Belgium to Holland, where he spent a short time, and thence went to his native city.

The return of Dr. Merle to Geneva was most opportune. The friends of the Truth had been steadily increasing in number since the year 1816, and had begun to think seriously of founding an orthodox School of Theology, in order that pious Swiss and French youth, who were looking to the ministry of the Gospel, should no longer be forced to pursue their studies under the Unitarian doctors of the Academy. The arrival of Dr. Merle decided them for immediate action. The next year (1831) the Geneva Evangelical Society was formed, one of whose objects was to found the long desired Seminary. In this movement Dr. Merle took a prominent part, and was placed at the head of the new School of Theology. His intimate friend, the excellent Mr. Gaussen, so favorably known in this country for his *Theopneustia*, and in Switzerland for many other writings, took an equal part in this important enterprise, and was chosen Professor of Theology. Mr. Gaussen is one of those in Geneva who have had to endure much of the "shame of the cross," and he has endured it well. For the noble stand which he had taken in behalf of the Truth, he was, by the government, turned out of the Church of which he was for years a pastor. A man of fortune, as well as of rich gifts and attainments, he has devoted himself, without a salary, to the infant Institution which he and Dr. Merle, sustained by some distinguished laymen—among whom I may mention Col. Tronchin, Ch. Gautier, and M. Boissier—have been the instruments, under God, of founding and of raising up to its present respectable standing. Commencing with some three or four young men, it has steadily increased, till it has now forty students, including both the preparatory and the theological departments.

This Seminary has enjoyed the talents of other valuable and distinguished men. For several years, M. Galland was a professor in it. The late, and still much lamented Steiger, the pupil and friend of Tholuck, was a professor in it during some years; and, at present, it enjoys the services of Messrs. Pilet and La Harpe, who are worthy colleagues of Merle d'Aubigné and Gaussen.

The publications of Dr. Merle have been numerous. I will give the titles of the most important of them

1. *Le Christianisme porté aux Nations.*
    Christianity carried to the Nations—a Missionary Sermon.
2. *Célébration de la Cène.*
    A Discourse on the Lord's Supper.
3. *Confession du nom de Christ.*
    On the Duty of Confessing Christ before the World.
4. *Culte Domestique.*
    On Family Worship.
5. *Discours sur l'Etude.*
    Discourse on Study.

6. *Eglise appelée à confesser.*
   The Church called to maintain the Truth.
7. *Enfans de Dieu.*
   The Children of God.
8. *Etudes Chrétiennes.*
   Christian Studies.
9. *Foi et Science.*
   Faith and Science.
10. *Miracles, ou deux Erreurs.*
    Miracles, or two Errors.
11. *Voix de l'Eglise.*
    Voice of the Church.
12. *Voix des Anciens.*
    Voice of the Ancients.
13. *Liberté des Cultes.*
    On Religious Liberty.

Most of these publications are pamphlets of from twenty pages up to sixty or eighty. The last named is a volume of some 200 pages, and was called forth by the state of things in Geneva last year, and is alluded to in the Discourse on Puseyism, where the author speaks of his having played the part of Cassandra, in what he had said respecting the recent Revolution in his native Canton.

But Dr. Merle's great undertaking is his *History of the Reformation in the XVIth Century.* The first volume of this admirable work appeared in 1836.

Two others have, at intervals, followed. The author is now engaged on the fourth, in which he is well advanced.* It treats of the Reformation in Great Britain, and is expected with very different feelings, by different religious parties in England. Nor is its appearance anxiously looked for by people in England only.

It is not probable that the fourth volume will appear in French before the end of this present year, if even so soon. The fifth and sixth volumes—for it is Dr. Merle's intention to make six volumes instead of four, if God grant him life and health—will

The fourth is just issued from the press. 1846.

not be published for some years. It is no easy task to write a History of the Reformation upon the plan which Dr. Merle pursues,—that of making authentic documents speak for themselves. It is not my intention to write a *critique* on Dr. Merle's work. It needs it not. The world has learned and acknowledged its surprising merits. It may almost be said that the History of the Reformation was never written until his matchless talent, for judiciously selecting and skilfully arranging facts, and graphically presenting them to the reader's mind, was brought to the subject. With the art of a conjuror, if I may so speak, he causes scene after scene to pass before us, on which the *dramatis personæ* are brought forward with almost the vividness of the objects which are presented to the bodily eye. For the first time, vast numbers of readers will learn the true characters of Luther, and Melancthon, and Calvin, and the other Reformers. And for the first time, the Reformation, with all the various and boundless benefits which it has conferred upon the world, is beginning to be, in some measure, comprehended by mankind.

Three translations of the three volumes of this great work which have appeared have been published in Great Britain—those of Messrs. Walther, Kelly, and Scott—of which the first and the last are better than the second. Mr. Kelly's, however, has had a wider circulation in Great Britian than either of the others, because of the low price at which it has been published. Mr. Scott's translation is the latest of all, and is not only extremely faithful but is also accompanied with valuable notes. It is published by the Messrs. Blackie, at Glasgow, in twenty-two numbers, each for a shilling, and every second one is adorned with an admirable portrait of one of the principal personages who figured in the Reformation—Luther, Melancthon, Tetzel, Leo X., Calvin, the Elector of Saxony, etc. This edition would be called by the French an *affaire de luxe;* but no one who could afford to pay for it would regret the difference of the price.

It may be insignificant to remark—but it will answer some inquiries which have been addressed to me—that Dr. Merle d'Aubigné is a large fine looking man, of most agreeable manners; and *personally,* as well as mentally considered, he would be pronounced by every one to be altogether worthy to speak of Martin Luther, John Knox, and the other giants of the Reformation. Nevertheless, I am pained to say it, his health does not correspond with the robustness of his frame, nor the vigor of his appearance. He suffers much at times from complaints of the chest. I am sure that in making this statement, I shall secure the prayers of many a reader, that his valuable life may be spared many years to bless the Church and the world.

R. B.

New York, Jan., 1843.

CONTENTS.

I.
HISTORY OF CHRISTIANISM,..27

II.
THE CHURCH AND HER VOCATION,..............................49

III.
THE CHILDREN OF GOD,..67

IV.
CONFESSION OF THE NAME OF CHRIST,........................79

V.
CHRISTIANITY AND FOREIGN MISSIONS,.....................101

VI.
CHRISTIANITY AND PROTESTANTISM,.........................125

VII.
FAMILY WORSHIP,..145

VIII.
CHRISTIAN STUDIES,...159

IX.
FAITH AND KNOWLEDGE,...185

X.
THE VOICE OF THE CHURCH ONE,..201

XI.
A VOICE FROM ANTIQUITY,...223

XII.
LUTHER AND CALVIN,..245

XIII.
PUSEYISM EXAMINED,..273

THE STUDY

OF THE

HISTORY OF CHRISTIANISM,

AND

ITS UTILITY FOR THE PRESENT EPOCH.

TRANSLATED BY THOMAS S. GRIMKÉ,
OF CHARLESTON, S. C.

HISTORY OF CHRISTIANISM.

A DISCOURSE DELIVERED AT GENEVA, JAN. 2, 1832.

Gentlemen,

My design is to address you on the History of the Reformation in Germany—in the 16th century. Literature, the Sciences, the Arts, Philosophy, the Civil History of nations, have been successively in this city, and in the midst of you, subjects of instruction by men justly celebrated.

I invite you to a new field—the history of Christianism.*—I ought then to assign the reasons of my choice. I ought to disclose the advantages which I discover in the study of that history at this epoch.

You are, perhaps, at this very time, my justification.—That we should believe it possible to fix the attention of men in our day on the history of the Christian religion; that we should command an audience desirous of hearing it: this, Gentlemen, is a sign of the times. It proves that men of the world, absorbed until now in the exterior forms, the ornaments, the splendid dress of nations, and of their history, have at length begun to consider what is, what ought to be their heart and life.

And yet, who is it, who dares to venture on this new career? Who dares to follow so many men, admirable for genius, profound in knowledge, and skilful in the art of speaking; whose privilege it is to gather every winter in this city, an audience of every age, and of both sexes? Powerful indeed must be the motive, which brings forward one who has been called, it is true, to preach the everlasting Gospel; but who has never yet ventured to speak save in the Sanctuary, and with the aid of that holy office which exalts the humblest, and animates the most feeble.

This motive is the excellence of that study, to which I invite you.

There are in the life of each man in particular, and of nations in general, three great elements, *politics*, *letters* (comprehending, of

* I have used the word Christianism, instead of Christianity, throughout the translation, the former being the term in the original. It appears to be singular that Christianism in French should mean the Christian Religion and Christianity, Christendom or the nations professing it; whilst in English they signify the reverse, though the former has both meanings.—*Translator*.

course, the sciences, the arts, and philosophy), and *religion*. And it might almost seem, as though these three elements have appropriated to themselves the three great modifications of man. The political has engrossed his will and vigor of action. The literary, his intelligence, and all the variety of his imaginations and thoughts. The religious, his heart and the energy of his affections. But religion, enthroned as it were in the centre, extends over the whole man her sceptre of power.

There are then, according to these elements, three species of the history of man—the *political*, the *literary*, the *religious*. The History of Religion, it cannot be denied, is the least cultivated in our day. How zealously, on the contrary, do not men study political history, believing that they shall discover there, as augurs in the entrails of victims, the prognostics and the key of futurity? How many systems of history, now picturesque, now philosophical, are passing in review before us! How many eminent men, within our own walls, has not their narrative of national events immortalized! With what ardor is not the history of *letters* studied! Who has not read, again and again, the Lyceum of La Harpe, the works of Ginguené, of Schlegel, of De Staël, of Sismondi, and of so many others? Still more is done. Each fashions this history for himself: he approaches these documents, these materials, so formidable in the other two departments; he reads them, again and again, with delight, because they are the masterworks of genius. Every educated man examines, compiles, judges, creates an entire history of letters in his own mind.

But as to the History of Christianism, who is engaged in that? Who studies it? A handful of our contemporaries, if indeed so many. And yet, I regard it undoubtedly the most worthy of the attention of men: as that which, in our age, furnishes the most salutary lessons, and in whose prophetic entrails we shall learn correctly what is sought in vain elsewhere.

Perhaps this first sitting will be suitably employed in the endeavor, at the outset, to remove the prejudices entertained in our day, against studying the History of Christianism: and I shall afterwards establish the usefulness of this history, in the present age of the world.

One of the distinctive features of the past age, was a spirit of profaneness and mockery. The History of Christianism was affected by it. This imposing edifice, which appeared as the *work of ages*, was assailed with sarcasms, that confounded in one sentence of condemnation, Catholicism and Christianism, the Church of Men and the Church of God. The structure of Men, which might perhaps have resisted all serious assaults, soon crumbled with a loud crash, before the light breath of ridicule. But in its fall, it drew along with itself the power which had overturned it. Man passes not in vain through such a crisis. He acquired beneath the ruins a new temper. Baptized in blood, our age could no longer exist in the frivolous atmosphere of its predecessor. The profane La Harpe, in some respects the successor of Voltaire, in the office of President of the Anti-Christian League, came forth a Christian from the dungeons of the Revolution, into which he had been cast an unbeliever. The tempest of the Revolution has not, however, entirely swallowed up the impious spirit which roused it. Still does it subsist among us, although a stranger perhaps to the characteristic spirit of our age. The History of Christianism is still assailed by ridicule, in which you may perhaps discover, at times, some grains of the wit of Aristophanes and Voltaire. That ridicule must leave some impression on light minds, which may thus, for a season at least, become indifferent to grave and useful studies. It is not expected of me to answer sarcasms : one word suffices. Doubtless, ye scoffers of the age ! ye may find on this or that passage in the history of Religion, a brilliant quibble of heartless raillery ; but there is in Christianism and its annals, something beyond your reach. History exhibits it as an angel, bearing from Asia to Europe, from Europe through the whole Earth, and among all Nations, light and life: destroying evil everywhere in its course, and leaving everywhere, the incorruptible seeds of good. Whoever has met with it, has been healed by the salutary influence which it sheds around. Before such achievements of benevolence, the weapons of ridicule are impotent. The pointed shafts of the scoffer never can destroy the work of God. Childish arrogance only could attempt it: timid weakness only could fear it.

There are men of a graver cast, though not less incredulous, who attack with other arms, the history of religion. What, they ask, can the History of Christianism reveal ? Why do you thus unadvisedly ransack its annals ? What can you derive from them ? Christianism has been injurious to humanity. Man has been kept by it in swaddling clothes. Its influence on the civil and political state of Nations has been unfavorable. Such words afflict the soul by the deep ingratitude, the utter blindness from which they flow. We shall not even mention the blessings of Christianism in Eternity, though these are its chief object; but shall stand on the very ground to which our adversaries challenge us. " Take," will we say to them, " a map: lay before us a statistical view of nations. Where is light? and where darkness? Where is liberty? and where slavery? Do you not observe the shadows which rest on all the unchristianized States, and the light which covers Christian countries? What is it, that rends the black and polluted veil, which hung so long over the shores of Otaheite, of Eimeo, of Hawai? What but Christianism? Take now a pencil ; mark by successive shadows, the regions, where knowledge, morality, religion, prevail the most ; you will find but one progress, that of Christianism itself. Wherever the Gospel shines the brightest, there will you behold most abundant, the chief blessings of humanity. The United States of America, Great Britain, other Evangelical countries, where the light of the Eternal Word is shed in all its purity, will be at the top of the scale : and the transient shades which lead us from Christian to heathen regions, distinguish those portions of the earth, where, though Christianism

exists, it is stifled by the human elements commixed with it.*
But why have recourse to this geographical *coup d'œil?* The
history of Christianism will itself give the answer to your objections. There will it be seen elevating gradually from age to age,
the character of nations. Still more: it will there be discovered,
that even the corruptions of Christianism, those, against which
you contend the most strenuously, have been useful to humanity,
whenever they have retained the least element of the religion of
Jesus Christ. There will you behold those Convents (the just
objects of our reprobation) becoming, as it were, unconsciously,
depositories for the preservation of so many ancient monuments

* This passage recalls a similar one in my Address before the Literary
and Philosophical Society of South Carolina, delivered 9th May, 1827. It
is found at pages 23, 24, 25, of the volume containing my principal pieces
on Literature and Education, published at New Haven, April, 1831, by H.
Howe. It is as follows:

"My subject calls, however, for a free, impartial review of the character
of the Reformation, and of its influence on Science; nor is it possible to
examine the History of that period, in any point of view, however remote
from Religion, without a continual reference to the state of the Catholic
Church, in connection with government and society, both spiritual and
temporal—with the Arts and Sciences—with the fortunes and character of
nations—with the education and general welfare of the people. Considering the Reformation as matter of history and philosophy, it must be a chief
ingredient in every discussion, on enlarged principles, of the state of the
world for the last three hundred years, of its actual condition now, and of
its future prospects. Besides, the Protestants of these United States may
well believe that, without the Reformation, they would have been rather
like the South Americans, before the late Revolutions, than what they
now are, the wonder, and admiration, and example of the world. They
may well believe, also, that their Catholic brethren, fellow-heirs of the
same glorious and inestimable heritage of Religious, Political and Civil
Rights, never would have enjoyed, in any Catholic country, the full
measure of power and liberty, of property and happiness, which the
youngest child of the Reformation confers on the eldest daughter of the
Christian household. Under these considerations, and with these sentiments, I proceed to execute the task which I have undertaken; satisfied
that my opinions will be those not merely of a Protestant, but of an American, and of a Man, the lover of truth, the thoughtful student of historical
philosophy. In many of the following pages, I shall adopt the very language of Villers; especially in those pages which express the severe, but
deliberate judgment of that invaluable writer, as to the degraded condition
of the whole circle of knowledge, at the close of the fifteenth century.

" I have said that the Reformation only gave or could have given to ALL
LITERATURE, *not merely to the literature of Theology,* a decisive, permanent
character. To express it otherwise, my judgment is, that without the
Reformation, the revival of learning, which had commenced, would have
terminated as all others had, in public ostentation, princely patronage, and
the dazzling homage of Genius and Taste, still intent

'To heap the shrine of luxury and pride,
With incense, kindled at the Muse's flame.'

"But THE PEOPLE, THE PEOPLE would have remained almost, if not altogether, in the same degraded and miserable condition, as to civil, political,
and religious rights, as to education, as to social improvement, and indi-

of letters, amidst the deluge of Northern Barbarians, and when the flood had passed, again sending forth those treasures. But there, you will especially behold that illustrious Reformation, some of whose features I shall sketch, which delivered the human mind from the chains which had oppressed it, and which has become to the Nations, the dawn of a new day of light, evangelization, and life. In its history, Christianism is everywhere exhibited as the friend of human nature.

But, you must confess, say other men of the age, that the history of Christianity reveals to us many things, intrigues, wars and the like, which cannot but expose it, and diminish that respect, which you demand for it. This we deny. Christianism is a divine work, and of course perfectly pure. Whatever has flowed from itself is good. But, in descending from Heaven to Earth,

vidual welfare. To illustrate this opinion, let us advert to the actual state of Europe, before the French Revolution, bearing in mind the remark of Montesquieu, that Loyola would have governed the world, but for Luther and Calvin. He, in defiance of the Reformers, has swayed Italy, Spain and Portugal: they rescued from him and his Church, and have ruled Holland, England and Scotland. Ignatius has governed South America: Calvin and Luther these United States. Is there now an American, whether of the Reformed or Romish Creed, who would exchange the condition of the Protestant Countries which have been named, for that of Southern Europe or Southern America? Is it not obvious that Society has been comparatively stationary for 3000 years in these, while Protestant nations have been continually advancing? Look at the wonderful progress of Holland, Great Britain, and our own country, since the Reformation. Place beside them, Italy, Spain, and Portugal, and assign, if practicable, any adequate causes for the incalculable difference, except the principles of the Reformers. Every student of the philosophy of history, I feel assured, re-echoes the sentiment, THESE ONLY ARE THE CAUSES. If then, as I have already said, *Science and Art are nothing worth, unless they bless the people as well as adorn the State*, and if, in Protestant countries, they have thus blessed, as well as adorned, beyond all parallel; it becomes a question most interesting and momentous, how have the principles of the Reformers wrought this change in the use and application of the whole circle of knowledge? I proceed to attempt an explanation; though I believe that every improved mind already comprehends the development of my subject.

" The Reformers began with the fundamental principle, *the obligation and correspondent right of private examination and private judgment*. They admitted no superior to control and limit this duty and this right, save God and his Scriptures. Whatever uninspired man had done or could do, whether individually or collectively, was acknowledged as a guide to the understanding, but not as authority to bind the conscience and the judgment. The position was taken that Man not only had a right, in regard to his fellow-men, but was obliged by the law of God to study his Word, and by that standard, to examine the history of the Church; her doctrine, worship, and ceremonies; the acts of councils; the writings of the Fathers and the scholastic theology; and last, though not least, the authority of the Pope. THIS WAS, IN RELIGION, 'THE DECLARATION OF INDEPENDENCE'—and by its principles the Reformers did for the shackled mind, what the angel did for Peter in the prison; they did for the mind's eye, what Ananias did for Paul, when, at his touch, the Apostle received his sight."—*Translator.*

from God to Man, it has suffered alloy. Christianism in man, and even in the holiest of men, is not Christianism in God, that is to say, in Jesus Christ. Impute not to God, that of which man only is guilty. The water which falls from heaven is pure, and even the purest of all, for it has been distilled in the wonderful apparatus of God. And yet, scarcely has it touched the earth, when it is already defiled. How often, alas! will not the hardened heart of man suffer the life-giving waters of Christianism to penetrate his bosom? To those heavenly influences how obstinately is it closed? Man drives away religion from his heart, and is content to wear it without, as a cloak to his sins. And then, the vulgar dignify, with the name of Christianism, what is thus displayed to their eyes! History will rend this hypocritical mantle: and will reveal the passions which it hid, and which were the only moving cause in him, who had enveloped himself thus artfully. There will you see, for example, that those irreligious wars, called religious, sprang not from Christianity, but from the immediate influence of that very power of evil, which Christianism came to destroy. There will you discover, that those maxims of the Governors, of the chiefs of the Church, which you justly condemn as disgraceful, were directed *against* the religion itself of Jesus Christ; that this was the victim which they immolated, not the tongue which uttered them. History justifies Christianism, dissipates every cloud and every prejudice, and all the hatred wherewith man has been pleased to surround that sublime and heavenly image, which dwells in the midst of ages; and exhibits it to the admiration of men, in all its simplicity, innocence, beauty and glory.

If Christianism be innocent of all that is usually laid to its charge, at least, it will be said, the history of the Church is the most barren, the most destitute of life and emotion, and consequently the least interesting, which can be imagined. Councils and decrees of Councils, Popes and bulls, metaphysical doctrines, subtile distinctions, scholastic systems, are not these all that it offers? Doubtless, it would be strange that the history of this kingdom of God, which its founder said should be a living seed, that would become a great tree, full of sap, and casting all around its beneficent shade: or as leaven, which should leaven the whole lump, that is, should communicate life to the world; that such a history should abound in unfruitfulness and subtilty. Not so, for there are two histories. There is, if you please, what we shall call " the History of the Church," that is, of human institutions, forms, doctrines, and actions; and " the History of Christianism," which has brought into the world, and still preserves, a new life, a life divine; the history of the government of that King who has said, " the words which I speak unto you are spirit and life: " the history of that regenerative influence of Christianism, through which so many individuals and nations have experienced a thorough change in their moral and spiritual condition: the history of the first and second creation, which fashions a people for God upon earth: the history of that invisible Church, which is the assembly of the first born: Heb xii. 23. Most Historians, it is true, have hitherto presented only the barren history of the exterior Church; because they themselves were only the outward Man, and had scarcely even imagined the life of the spiritual Man. But is this a proof that it does not exist? Grant that human forms have destroyed this new dominion of truth, justice and love, which proceeds from the Father. Because you see at first only a dry and hard shell, will you reject the delicious fruit which is concealed under this homely covering? In seasons of barrenness and death, the Church could only have a lifeless and sterile history. But Life, while descending to the Church of our day, has descended also in its history. Reserve your objections for those who may continue to drag on in the barren field of rationalism and human opinions. The old man sees in the field of the Church but dry bones. The new man there discerns that spirit which blows from the four winds, and creates for the Eternal "an exceeding great army," Ezek. xxxvii. 10. There is then a new History of Christianism: that which we have undertaken to unfold and defend: and not the history of human forms and barrenness.

"Do you then imagine that you shall find in Christianism, life, elevation, generosity," says a gloomy philosophy, which pretends that the individual good of each man ought to be the noblest object of his life. "What an illusion! Those remarkable actions, that self-sacrifice, of which the history of Christianism seems to furnish examples, are but hidden passions, ambition, avarice, sensuality, envy, covered with obvious veils: an egotism, somewhat more refined than that of the multitude. The only difference between the grossest of men, and the heroes of the Christian history, is that these know how to disguise somewhat more ingeniously the passions which govern them. And if all be not thus explained, a deplorable fanaticism and enthusiasm will account for the rest." Such is the language that has been held, more especially of the history which I am called to lay before you, and of the most illustrious characters which it presents to your view. Gloomy and hideous system! which only taking account of the corruption of man, is ignorant of those pure and sublime inspirations which proceed from the Spirit of God: a system, which overturns the whole moral hierarchy, since the most dissolute and the most criminal of men would be at least sincere, by appearing such as they really are; whilst the flower of humanity, men of disinterestedness and self-sacrifice, would be a band of deceivers and knaves, whose only aim would have been to conceal the disgraceful motives of their actions. Seriously to refute such a system would almost be high treason against Divinity and humanity. The History of Christianism shall itself be, moreover, the most triumphant vindication. It will open to you the gates of a world, different from that inhabited by the natural man.. It will display to you a power, which a narrow-minded philosophy cannot comprehend. The majority of men comprehend nothing but materialism. Some, more enlightened, attain to rationalism. The history of Christianism will carry us still higher. It will disclose to us spiritualism, which is the true, the primitive life of man, of which he was deprived, and which Christianism comes to restore. It will constrain us to acknowledge that life to be more certain, more real, than rationalism, and even materialism. It will set before us, and we shall almost touch with our hands, a strength of faith, which is given from above to man, and which overcomes the world and all the passions of the heart. It will teach us to understand this profound thought, " The first man is of the earth, earthy; but the second man is the Lord from heaven. As is the earthy such are they also that are earthy: and as is the heavenly, such are they also that are heavenly." 1 Cor. xv. 47, 48.

"At least, however," it will be said, "it is certain and irrefutable, that the history of the Church most frequently presents us with controversies, agitations, quarrels, wars. What interest would you have us take in such things? How, indeed, could we esteem such a history?" Controversies, agitations, say you? And are such the motives for your contempt of the History of Christianism? But let me ask you, what beneficent principle, what fortunate conception for humanity has ever been established, without agitation, without a struggle, without a conflict? Philosophers! had not your Galileo a contest to maintain, whilst he was teaching the movements of the heavens, and do not you honor him the more for it? Literati! had not your Corneille to endure discussion and criticism, whilst he was creating the language and poetry of France? And you, ye Liberals of the age! who, perhaps, chiefly assail the history of the religion of Jesus Christ, was your Mirabeau without combats in the tribune? and when he blew the trumpet of new-born liberty, was the war, of which he sounded the signal, a short one? or rather, are we not now as between two armies of nations, in battle array against each other, brandishing with impatience the arms which must decide the victory? And Christianism, which attacks man in his dearest passions, though they are the very cause of his misfortunes, in his love of riches, his ambition, his vain-glory, in a word, in this inferior self, which man idolizes, and of which a sublimer self is the slave, shall this Christianism be alone exempt from struggles and contests? The burthened atmosphere is only purified by tempests: and the crisis of his disorder is deliverance to the sick. And, in like manner, that truth may possess the earth, she must combat hand to hand with error, But the end, the result of Christianism is peace. *Peace upon earth!* Such was the cry from Heaven, when the earth received its Saviour. We are marching onwards to peace—Let us then march onwards, if necessary, through the fire of battle.

But I am deceived if the history of the religion of Jesus Christ do not present to you far other objects than agitations and troubles It exhibits a phenomenon altogether unique, and to be found nowhere else. It offers to you peace, in the midst of trouble: meekness of spirit amidst the conflagration of the passions. It will lead you to the sanctuary of the men of God; and whilst around them, agitations, conspiracies, and terrible cries prevail, you shall behold them calm, cheerful, and full of a peace which passeth all understanding. Satisfied with having borne witness to the truth, they have committed their cause to the Eternal, and remain tranquil and at rest, waiting on him. Of this, the history of the Reformation and of that of Luther, in particular, will furnish you illustrious examples. The history of Christianism makes known the only real peace which has ever been upon earth.

Are not such studies, say respectable men, but of unsettled opinions, at least fitted to confuse us on religious subjects, to strip us of our faith, and to lead us into skepticism and incredulity? There is nothing, after the Word of God, better suited to save us from incredulity and superstition, and to attach us to true Christianism, than the history of the religion of Jesus Christ. Undoubtedly, if you take one Ecclesiastical Historian, who presents a Religion and the Church in Popes and Councils; or another who arrays them in a meagre natural theology, lightly shaded with Christianism, and in the barren instructions of human reason; or another still, who exhibits them through metaphysical dogmas or scholastic distinctions—such would undoubtedly disgust you with what each would call religion. But where is the great evil? Take, on the contrary, a historian, who presents to you the religion of Jesus Christ, such as it is in reality, "the light and the life of the world." Such a history, I feel assured, would make you love that religion. There is still more. If other considerations have shaken your faith, this study will strengthen it. The enemies of Religion, of Christianism, and of the Reformation, in particular, will perhaps exclaim, that craft, enthusiasm, credulity or incredulity, have accomplished these two great revolutions in the world. They will tell you that men had not time to examine: that they were accomplished by means of a commotion, from which mankind were astonished to find that they had come forth Christian and Protestant. Let us stretch forth the torch of history, and all these phantoms of a hostile imagination instantly vanish. Then do you see how everything has been examined, discussed, tried; how every inch of ground has been defended by the adversary. Abandoning the field of history, does he occupy that of reasoning? Are you gravely assured that Christianism is contrary to human reason? Are all those objections repeated, so much boasted of in our day, as the fruits of the advancement of the age, and aimed against religion itself, against the Divinity of the Saviour, salvation by grace, and the fall of man? History still has something to say. She teaches you that these are shafts, long since used and broken; the ideas of Greek and Pagan authors revived; for she will point you to them in Celsus, and Porphyry, and Hierocles, Greek and Heathen writers. On the one hand, history shows that all these objections, so vaunted in our day, were employed from the earliest ages, against truth and the Church, which is its depository: and, on the other hand, she shows you that very Church, advancing unceasingly amidst these assaults, growing, and extending everywhere its benefits. Fear not then; for these assaults will no more injure the Church and arrest its progress now, than they have hitherto. During eighteen centuries, the little prejudices of the human mind have accustomed it to these attacks; and with little or no anxiety on these subjects, the Church marches onward through eighteen centuries, to the triumph which her Head is preparing for her.

But is there not reason to fear, that the history of the Church, and of the Reformation in particular, may revive polemics, above all against the Roman Catholics, and may re-open the wounds of the Western Church, as yet but imperfectly healed? I believe the reverse. History will doubtless show us, in a general way, truth on one side and error on the other. But she will also show us good and evil mixed here and there; she will show us, on the side of the Catholics, many a true Christian, although in some respects certainly but little enlightened; and on the side of the Protestants, many a man unworthy of that name. She will show us Catholicism, adding without doubt many things to the Word of God, and preserving nevertheless most of the fundamental doctrines of Christianism, the depravity of man, salvation through the atonement, the essential divinity of the Redeemer, the indispensable work of the Holy Spirit in the heart. And to pass thence to the history of the Reformation—I shall be a Protestant—I proclaim beforehand—Yet not as a sectarian, but as a Christian. I desire not to be unmindful of the respect which is due to men, in whose ranks have shone the names of Laurence de Bibra, Sadolet, Borromeo, Vincent de Paul, Pascal, Fenelon. It shall not be my province to strike Catholicism with redoubled blows: that was the affair of Luther's age; it was done then, and is not the business of our age: but it shall be alone my object, if I can accomplish it, to invest with a touching influence the living principle, which produced in the sixteenth century a great religious regeneration, and which must produce the same in our day. I shall notice the evil deeds of Protestants when I meet with them. I shall notice the good actions of Catholics whenever I see them: and perhaps a favorable trait incidentally mentioned by a narrator (I cannot say by a historian) of the Reformation, will soothe the mind more readily than apologies for Catholicism, in the mouth of one of its priests.

But then it is lastly said, you must confess that the study of Christianism is advantageous to theologians only: but that we have nothing to do with it; that to us it is useless. I take the distinction: certainly it is not necessary to salvation: the knowledge of Jesus Christ is alone sufficient: and if we were addressing those who were indifferent to all history, we should perhaps be less favorably situated for a reply. But we address an audience, who have not neglected the literary and political history of Nations. We then say to you—Why should you reject that of Christianism? If this concerns only divines, assuredly political history is the province only of Magistrates and Princes. Whenever the members of Councils of State, and of some other bodies, shall be the only students of civil history, I may understand that only Ministers of the Gospel should devote themselves to religious history. If there be a history which you desired to study, ought not that of religion to stand first? Of the three great elements of history—politics, letters, religion—is not religion the most universal, and that which ought, above all, to interest each member of society? Had you not a soul and a God, before you had literary and political sympathies? Is not religion paramount in whatever is most dear and sacred in man? Let us grant that hitherto you have repelled religion as to yourselves, and that you desire to study that only which influences the destinies of man, is not Christianism the moving principle of political development, of intellectual labor? What but this has given, and still gives, the most powerful influence to the social life, to the literary genius of modern nations? The study of the History of Christianism *useless!* Is not this to say it is useless in a steam-boat, to study the machinery which communicates motion to the whole vessel; that it is sufficient to study the vessel itself, the planks and rigging, which that machinery impels. The religion of Jesus Christ is the machinery which moves the world.

But this very usefulness of that religion, especially at this present time, remains to be laid before you.

Jesus Christ founded, in the midst of men, a kingdom of God; and thenceforward the history of the human race, composed till then but of scattered, unconnected fragments, possessed a centre, to which everything might and ought to be referred. This divine kingdom gave unity to the Nations of the Earth, and to their history—and through it, isolated members became a body.

One of the noblest and most essential ideas of our age, as yet, perhaps but indistinctly traced on many minds, but which must continually become more and more the fundamental thought of those who reflect and believe, is that in the new period now opening before us, there will be no longer, so to speak, a personal history of nations, but a great history of human nature. Our age is the centre, where the numerous threads from various points are united, and thence issue in one cord. And what is this new period, but the fulfilment of the destinies of Christianism? Whilst some philosophers saw indistinctly, but yesterday, something of this vast centralization of the races of men, Christianism, opening the annals of a people, who had crucified their divine and eternal founder, exhibits there to the world the annunciation of this mighty event in the history of man, declared two thousand years before its occurrence, to Abraham the Chaldean, " in thee shall all families of the Earth be blessed," Gen. xii 3 : and proclaimed still more clearly two hundred years after, by an old man to his children, around his death-bed, when casting a prophetic look on the future, and announcing this Messenger, who was to issue from the midst of them, he adds, " Unto him shall the gathering of the people be," Gen. xlix. 10. Words of peace, which that mysterious person, when he appeared here below, repeats to his disciples in language still more striking, if that be possible, " There shall be one fold and one shepherd," John x. 16. The religions of antiquity rendered impossible this vast assembly of nations. Like the languages of Babel, they were so many walls, which separated nations from one another. The tribes of the Earth worshipped only National Gods—those Gods only suited the nations who made them. They had no points of contact, none of sympathy with any other people. Falsehood has a thousand strange faces, not resembling each other. Truth only is one, and this only can unite all the races of men. The idea of a universal kingdom of truth and holiness was a stranger to the ancient world. And if some sages had a vague and obscure presentiment of it; with them it was but a conception without the possibility of their even imagining what might be its reality. Christ came and immediately accomplished what the religions and sages of the world had not even been able to foresee. He founds a spiritual kingdom, to which all Nations are called. He overturns, according to the energetic language of his Apostle, the fences, the middle wall of partition which divided nations, and " hath made both one"—" for to make in himself of twain, one new man, so making peace." Eph. ii. 14, 15. Christianism is not like the ancient religions, a doctrine adapted to a certain degree of development in nations; it is a truth from heaven, which is able at the same time to act on man under every grade of improvement and climate. It bestows on human nature, whatever may be its rudeness, or the diversities of changes which letters and philosophy may have produced, the principle of a new and truly divine life. And this life is to be at once the great means of development to all nations, and the centre of their unity. With its appearance, commenced in the universe, the only real cosmopolitism. Citizens of Judea, of Pontus, of Greece, of Egypt, of Rome, till then mutual enemies, embrace like brothers. Christianism is that tree, of which the Scriptures speak, whose leaves are " for the healing of the nations." Apocal. xxii. v. 2. It acts at the same time on the most opposite states of society. It regenerates and vivifies the world, corrupted by the Cæsars; and soon after softens and civilizes the barbarous hordes of the North. And, at this very time, it produces similar effects on the citizens of London, Paris, and Berlin, and on the savages of Greenland, Caffraria, and the Sandwich Islands. The net is cast over the whole earth, and the day cometh when a heavenly hand shall hold captive in it all the races of men. Ye have perceived, men of the age, that we are passing out of the period of nations, and entering on that of human nature; but fashion not for yourselves a paltry standard for the union of nations. A new hierarchy, with its common frame, cannot be the bond of unity, nor political liberalism, which carries tempests and discord in its bosom. Christ is this ensign of which the prophet speaks, Is. xi. 12.; and around which " shall the gathering of the people be," Gen. xlix. 10.

But whilst many in our day hail, at this moment, the dawn of a new re-organization, others, on the contrary, behold in it only an epoch of dissolution. And these two opinions, apparently opposite, are perfectly harmonious; since dissolution must precede re-organization. The two great powers of man have been unable to resolve the problem of human nature. The hierarchy had undertaken it, but failed: and the iron arm of Rome was broken. Human philosophy rushed into its place, and said: I will accomplish it. But the disorder of the nations has increased in a frightful ratio. There remains the power of God, or Christianism, which already, while human power was making its trials, has laid everywhere the foundations of the new edifice. And it will succeed. Do you exclaim that, in our day, men walk in uncertainty: that all the doctrines for the welfare of nations are doubtful? It is true, that all does seem in our day to be dissolving. But, O man! listen to thy master, a master of eighteen centuries old, who has assisted more than once at the decline and elevation of nations, at the decomposition and recomposition of the world, and who has been the great organic principle of nations. Listen to what it has been, to know what it will be; and to what it has done, to know what it will do. Christianism is totally different from the religions of men. In these, it is man who gives strength to religion: in that, religion gives strength to man. Whilst the Republic was counting its days of glory, the gods of Rome shone with the greatest lustre. But when corruption had seized on domestic life, when personal ambition and venality had assailed public life, religion, worm-eaten at the base, decays and disappears with them. Jupiter falls, and is buried under the ruins of his own capital. Christianism, on the contrary, independent of man, remains firm amidst the fall of nations (their annals testify this), and renews the world by its power. When all the social forms of humanity are destroyed, as at the epoch of the invasion of the Barbarians, the religion of Jesus Christ remains upright on their ruins, and her hand scatters amid the chaos that seed, whence humanity shall rise anew. Fear not the mournful state of the world, at this time. History, and especially that which we shall lay before you, demonstrates that when corruption has extended its ravages the farthest over the world, the Divine power of Christianism, which has not its roots in the entrails of human nature, rises with the greatest power. The Spirit of God is moving on the chaos, and out of it he will bring forth a new earth.

But the history of Christianism will teach you, moreover, that this religion is the instrument which he has chosen to accomplish his work. It will exhibit her mode of action, not as a continued influence, but as a succession of struggles and combats. The essence of Christianism is conflict with the world. And thus the true Church of Christ hath appeared from the beginning, as "militant" amidst the nations. Already have two enemies successively assailed her, and been vanquished, however easily they promised to crush her. At first, she had to combat without against the idolatry and vices of Paganism. Paganism fell. But scarcely had this victory been gained, when the danger appeared in the bosom of the Church. Whilst men slept, according to the parable of the Divine and Eternal founder of Christianism, the enemy came and sowed tares among the wheat, Matt. xiii. 25. The evil continued to increase. The Church had been founded that man might seek for heaven in it, and there he sought only the world. Then the true Church shook off the dust of death. Arrayed as it were, in an instant, in the spiritual armor which God had prepared for her, she began a war, the most terrible, because intestine. Rome, vigorously assailed, tottered, and the crown fell from her head. This war we propose to lay before you. It remains for Christianism to obtain a final victory. An enemy, who is neither within nor without, as were the two first, or rather who is both at the same time, advances to the last assault. I refer to the incredulous, anti-christian spirit of the age. More powerful, more terrible still, than the two first adversaries, he casts upon Christianism that look of disdain, which the god of the capitol once cast on the citizens of Tarsus, in chains at their feet; and which, fifteen centuries after, Leo and the magnificent Court of the Medici cast, with a smile, into the obscure cell of an Augustin monk. Still more may be said. The anti-christian spirit of the world, now lifting his banner so high, does not suspect the enemy which is to vanquish him. And yet he will be conquered; and the formidable giant of the age, who defies the God of the armies of Israel (1 Sam. xvii. 45.), struck in the forehead, shall fall with his face to the earth, under the sling of the enemy whom he has despised.

Is the question asked, by what arms shall this victory be gained? Here, again, the History of Christianism will give the answer. It shows you that this religion has twice regenerated the world, at least partially, by doctrines entirely its own. To pretend that the religious system, which is to accomplish the grand solution, desired by all, consists of those general ideas of religion, to be found in Rabbinical Judaism, in Mahometanism, and even in Pagan Philosophy, is a strange error: for these ideas never have produced the regeneration of the people, who have known them. The power of Christianism lies in its peculiarity. It compels man to feel the astonishing contrast, between his whole life, and the law of its holiness. It produces in him the desire of deliverance from so miserable a condition. It reveals to him the magnificent work, which the mercy of a God has accomplished for his rescue, in the death of the Cross. It proclaims, by the command of the King of the world, an entire amnesty through all the world. Now, we maintain two things. *First*, that this news of a full pardon of a perfect amnesty proclaimed upon earth, that rebellious province of the empire of the King of kings, is alone capable of touching, of changing the heart of man, and of inclining him through love to obey the Sovereign who reclaims them. Ye politicians of the age, what advice would you give to a king for the establishment of peace and subordination, in the midst of a rebellious people? Classifications, conditions, scaffolds? or a generous amnesty without reserve, calculated to win all hearts? And we maintain, *secondly*, that the submission of the heart to God, the inward power of Christianism, is the only power which can now heal the diseases of nations. Every bond is broken. Selfishness and the spirit of censure are universal.

There are but two methods for the re-establishment of order and peace, among the rising and agitated masses: exterior and violent measures of compression: or the interior persuasive power of Christianism. What do I say? There is but one; for as to the first, all nations have shown its inefficiency. Three days have sufficed. By destroying selfishness, and planting in the hearts of all, the love of God and the love of man, Christianism alone will resolve the great problem, and establish liberty among the nations with order and peace.* These truths, taught by the nature of things, history will confirm. As to the *first*, she will disclose to us the unheard of powers of Christianism; she will prove to us that these doctrines can accomplish an actual second birth of human nature. And as to the *second*, contemporaneous history shall instruct us. Inquire of her in what nations order and liberty are the most closely united, and she will answer by pointing to the countries where the Gospel is the most openly proclaimed, the most universally believed. But above all, history will show that a power not of man hath produced these partial regenerations which are symbols and precursors of that universal regeneration, announced by Christianism. Call this power, God, or the Spirit of God, or even Providence—the name is of little consequence—the fact is certain, something hath descended from heaven. Such is the present state of the world, that whoever believes not in this power, as independent of the world, may well despair. But for ourselves, nothing terrifies us. "Give me," said Archimedes, "a place to stand on, and I will move the earth." Christianism is that point beyond the world, from which it shall be one day entirely displaced; and shall revolve on a new axis of

---

* These reflections of our author induce me to place in a note, two passages of the same Address, referred to in Note 3. They are found in the same volume, at pages 17 and 28.

" And do we not see that the total failure of the Greeks and Romans in political philosophy is due to the same cause, as their failure in morals? viz. an ignorance of the only true foundations of society and government, of the authority of public, and the obedience of private men, of the political and civil rights of the citizen? All these, according to the wise principles and experienced judgment of modern times, are laid in moral obligation, with God as its author, and Man as its subject. In a word, the code of public morals is founded on the code of private morals. Government is regarded as an institution for the good of society, and rulers but as agents; whilst the relative rights and duties of the governor and the governed are referred to the plain, practical sense, to the divine, yet simple wisdom, to the pure, the just, the immutable principles of Christian morals. *In fine, the New Testament is the moral constitution of modern society.*"

" The grand result of all the principles of the Reformation, and of all the considerations flowing from them, is worthy of such a cause, and of such champions, as the Reformers. It centres in two words—*duty* and *usefulness: Duty, as the only criterion of right; usefulness, as the only standard of merit.* In a word, the Reformation ordained, not only for its own day, and the communities of that day, but for all time, and for all nations, *that the New Testament is the only genuine moral constitution of Society, and its principles, the only safe and wise foundation of all civil and political establishments.*' —TRANSLATOR.

righteousness and peace. Then shall be poured out on all nations a mighty influence of the Spirit of God. Such are the most ancient promises. The Trojan war had just closed,* and Rome was not yet founded, when, in the midst of the people to whom God had entrusted the germs of religion for all the nations of the earth, these prophetic words resounded, " until the Spirit be poured upon us from on high," " and the work of righteousness shall be peace." Isaiah, xxxii. 15, 17.

Do you desire to know the obstacles which this renovation of human nature has to encounter, so that you may wisely remove them. The history of Christianism will point them out. They have been the same at all times. A wisdom, shall I say, or a folly, altogether earthly and carnal, which ridicules divine things, and would contract God and his kingdom to the narrow dimensions of its own scale; a priestly despotism, which claims alone the privilege of managing heavenly things, which turns a deaf ear to examination and research into the Divine Word, and materializes religion: a fanaticism, which opposes with all its might the knowledge of the truth; which, being hostile to liberty, would silence those who utter it; which labors to arm public opinion against Christianism and Christians,—whatever may be the name which fanaticism bears, such as Jewish, Pagan, Dominican, or falsely liberal and philosophic—such are the principal obstacles which the History of Christianism exhibits.

Do you ask with the Age for movement, for progress? History will show you that Christianism is the religion of progress: and that she calls man by continual advancements, to the liberty and the glory of the children of God. Let us carefully remark, that there are only two spheres, in which advancement can be made—viz. in the religion destined to renew mankind, or in man himself called to be renewed. The man of our Age ascribes this progress to religion: Religion—to man himself. Christianism came forth perfect from God, and is unchangeable as its author. Thou, O Man! art thus continually to advance: and in like manner that immense Christian Society, which the truth enlightens. The sun is not himself advancing to perfection; but perfectionates the shrub, which, receiving life from him, becomes a majestic tree. It is the same with Christianism and man. The Gospel places the goal,

---

* According to the usual chronology, the Trojan war happened at the very commencement of the 12th century (B. C. 1193) before the Christian æra. Isaiah prophesied B. C. 760, and Rome was founded B. C. 753; so that it seems very incorrect, to speak thus of an intermediate event (the prophecy) when it happened 433 years after the first, and only 7 years before the last event. And if we were to allow, with Sir Isaac Newton, " that the ancient profane history is generally carried about 300 years higher backward than the truth;" yet if we reduce the first date by 300 years, so as to bring it to 893 B. C., and reduce the date of the building of Rome by 106 years, according to Newton's principles (by allowing 18 or 20 years—say 20—for the reign of each of the Kings), to B. C. 647—still the expression " venait de finir" had just ended, would be incorrect, when applied to an event, 133 years before the days of Isaiah.

towards which that Christian Society ought to tend, beyond the veil which separates the two worlds. Thus, the Gospel summons society to a progress, incomparably beyond all that human systems demand, and assigns a task which can only be accomplished in eternity.

Will you speak of *enlightenment?* Will you say that we have reached an age too full of light for the triumph of Christianism? The History of Christianism will show you, that she fears not the light, though frequently a false one. I shall not speak of the present epoch, when she lifts her head with more energy than ever. This age at least ought to be out of the question. 1 shall not speak of the Reformation, preceded for a semi-century, by the great events which signalized the revival of letters—we shall soon attend to it. But consider what the History of Christianism records on its first leaf. The age of Augustus, when Jesus was born, is among the most brilliant in the annals of mankind. Christianism chose the noon-day for its appearance. A religious system, which had lasted as long as the nation, was crumbling under the assaults of the reason of the age: and, at that moment, Christianism presents itself to be, in like manner, examined and assailed. The raillery of the man of wit, the assaults of eloquence, the protracted warfare of philosophy and learning, it challenges all: it sustains the shock: and nothing moves it. On the contrary, it advances, it leads the thoughts captive, in obedience to the God whom it announces: and in celestial triumph on the theatre of human glory, it often numbers around its car those who had been the most formidable of enemies. Christianism is the true light; it is the sun which rises above all the lights of this lower sphere. " I am the light of the world," said Jesus Christ.

Lastly, will the Age speak of the *future?* Will attention be vouchsafed to a doctrine only so far as it relates to the *future?* The future belongs to Christianism. She claims it not to-day, or yesterday, like the ephemeral prophets of our day. She said so four thousand years ago. The seventeenth century was that of the past: the eighteenth is that of the present: the nineteenth is that of the future, and this belongs to Christianism. Men, if enlightened and sincere, can no longer continue strangers to the ancient promises of the future, laid up in the book of Nations. Following out in history the accomplishment of the Oracles of God, they will arrive at those which declare, that " the Earth shall be full of the knowledge of the Lord"—" his rest shall be glorious." Is. xi. 9, 10. Ever since the men, who were the heralds of God, uttered these words, all has been advancing, and all is now moving onward to their glorious fulfilment. Christianism is on her march, and she will never retreat. Her work is scarcely rough-hewn; but she will finish it. She will bring about a great revolution on earth, which shall change its very being. The times are not perhaps very distant, when its destinies will be accelerated. A new history commences. Christ opens to the world the gates of a new future. " Great voices" shall be one day heard, as a prophet tells us, saying, " the kingdoms of this world are become the kingdoms of our Lord and of his Christ." Rev. xi. 15.

These are my reasons for maintaining that the history of Christianism is the most important of all historical studies : not only in general, but particularly with a view to the present epoch. Christianism holds in her hands the future destinies of the world. She bears in herself the regenerative force that will renew the nations, the bond which must unite them. Here is that beneficent power which will spread over the earth and establish righteousness, liberty and peace. O ye men of the age! there only may you learn the direction which you ought to give to all your efforts and labors. Study in the past the history of that which must accomplish such great results in the future. Dedicate to this study your spirit of research and your profound meditations. Set the example of abandoning the beaten track of the world : and of seeking light, life, the future, where only they are found. Young people who hear me, be the first to comprehend the calling of the new generation : receive first for yourselves, the light which Christianism has kindled : then go forth the beacon fires of the Nations.

I am now to ask your attention to the history of the Reformation in Germany, or at least of the most important period of that history. Perhaps you will inquire what has led me to select that subject, and what circumstances have induced this narrative. I saw Germany, and loved her for the sake of this excellent work, which I propose as my theme, The Reformation, at the festival of its third centennial jubilee, welcomed me on the road, and in the Germanic cities, on my arrival in 1817. I recall (and not without some pain, when I reflect how far from them was the spirit of the Reformation) those bands of students, who flocked to the famous antique castle of Wurtzburg, where we shall one day, in the course of my review, behold Luther a captive. I love to believe that those youths were rather indiscreet than guilty! I well remember how the gates of that ancient fortress (to which those young Germans were ascending in solemn procession) opened immediately before me, at the name of Geneva, and the emotions revive which I experienced, when I found myself in the prison-chamber of Luther. I remember those melodious strains which, some days after, announced the festival within the walls of Leipsic, descending before the dawn of day, from the summit of the invisible towers of the churches, as though they had been music from heaven. Again, I met the Reformation in illustrious teachers at Berlin. I shall name only Neander, the father of the new History of Christianism; Neander, whose tender affection is so dear to my heart, and who has raised up in Germany that Christian instruction, to which other friends, his juniors, the Tholucks and the Hengstenbergs, now impart life with all the strength of their faith. Again I found it on the borders of the Elbe, in the midst of the kindred and friends of the simple, yet profound Claudius of Wandsbeck—and of the sublime poet of " The Messiah." Again, I found it in the ancient and Catholic Brabant itself, near the throne on which sat the descendant of the Nassaus, the heir of *the Silent*, that noble hero of the Reformation of the Low Countries. There the earth soon trembled beneath my feet. The throne which it bore, crumbled at the sound of the fall of another throne. A queen of cities became, during four days, the bloody field of horrible combats. There I was a witness, and nearly a victim of unspeakable calamities. I returned to our mountains, after an absence of fourteen years, desiring, if God should give me adequate strength, to speak amidst my countrymen, of those admirable things whose glory and influence met me everywhere. Perhaps those noble, correct, and liberal manners, whose charm I experienced in a foreign land, have not been found by me in all at home. Subject, however, myself to human frailties, I shall know how to excuse, and not to condemn them in others. I promise, then, a cordial welcome to all who are disposed to hear my simple narrative. We shall survey together the plains of Mansfeld, the cells of Erfurt, the halls of Wittenberg, the palaces of Augsburg, of Leipsic, and of Worms. You will behold the Reformation. You will examine all things. You will not suffer the yoke of man to rest on your necks. I have seen Wittenberg; I have seen the land where the despotism of Rome perished: let us not bow down before the despotism of the Age. A freeman myself, I seek after freemen; and I believe I have found them. May the divine blessing rest on my narrative! May words be vouchsafed to me, suitable to spread true light and true liberty! and, whilst I am relating to you the history of a great event in the kingdom of God, may the image of Christ, King of the Church, grow unceasingly before your eyes, and in your hearts!

THE CHURCH

CALLED

TO CONFESS JESUS CHRIST.

TRANSLATED BY M. M. BACKUS.

THE CHURCH AND HER VOCATION.

PREFACE.

MANY Christians at Geneva, as well as in the canton of Vaud and in France, and doubtless in other countries of Protestant Christendom, have felt, while they reviewed the actual state of the Church of Jesus Christ, that there was need of a further *manifestation* of that great and glorious unity, which exists among those who have been redeemed unto God by the blood of Jesus out of every kindred and tongue and people and nation.

They believe, that in the face of the combined efforts of Rome and of all anti-christian opinions, evangelical Christians ought to gather round their Captain and unite in the confession of their common faith. A proposition to this effect was made in a numerous assembly which met at Geneva, the evening of the anniversary (1840) of the Evangelical Society. Some friends of the Gospel took up the same subject more recently at the time of the annual gathering at Lausanne. We have frequently observed that it is only after the lapse of years, and even after numerous repulses, that the most useful ideas are perfected, modified, received, and at length fashioned into realities. This of which we are speaking may likewise encounter its obstacles; the proposition which has been made may not have a single immediate consequence; but whoever believes in the word of the Lord cannot, it seems to us, entertain any doubt of the accomplishment of this Christian thought at a period in the future more or less remote. "Wherefore God also hath highly exalted him, and given him a name which is above every name: that at the name of Jesus every knee should bow, of things in heaven, and things in earth, and things under the earth, and that every tongue should confess that Jesus Christ is Lord, to the glory of God the Father."

Some persons, for whose judgment the author entertains presume respect, have thought that under these circumstances the publication of the following discourse, pronounced in the chapel of the Theological School of Geneva, and bearing only indirectly on the thought to which we have referred, might perhaps prove of some service.

It is a common apology that a discourse is published at the request of its auditors. The author finds himself obliged to repeat this on the present occasion, in order to throw upon his friends a part of the responsibility of a production, the many deficiencies of which, as well as its numerous imperfections, could not otherwise be justified. Nevertheless, he believes with his friends, that the subject of this discourse is of some importance, and merits the attention of Christians at the present moment. For this reason, although these leaves were not destined for the public eye, he commits them to his brethren, commending them to the blessing of God.

A DISCOURSE

DELIVERED AT GENEVA, SEPTEMBER 27, 1840.

"Whosoever therefore shall confess me before men, him will I confess also before my Father which is in heaven. Think not that I am come to send peace on earth: I am not come to send peace, but a sword. For I am come to set a man at variance against his father, and the daughter against her mother, and the daughter-in-law against her mother-in-law. And a man's foes shall be those of his own household. He that loveth father or mother more than me, is not worthy of me: and he that loveth son or daughter more than me is not worthy of me. And he that taketh not his cross and followeth after me is not worthy of me. He that findeth his life shall lose it: and he that loseth his life for my sake, shall find it." MATT. x. 32–39.

THE words you have heard, were pronounced by the Lord in view of a day of trial. For three centuries to come, the Church was to be that woman, whom St. John in the Apocalypse saw, clothed with the Sun, even Jesus Christ our Righteousness, having on her head a crown of twelve stars, the crown of the Apostles, "travailing in birth, and pained to be delivered." It was necessary then, for Christ to strengthen her in the confession of her faith, that she might remain firm in the midst of her long and severe throes.

My brethren, we live in a period which bears some analogy, perhaps, to that in which these words were spoken. Many signs seem to indicate that the time draws nigh, in which the Church, long straitened in a narrow place, is about to be diffused throughout the nations of the earth; in which converted Israel shall be re-established in his dwelling-place, and the false Prophet of the East and the High Priest of the West shall see their power crushed. Statesmen, who know little of the prophecies, and the most incredulous of the public journals, already speak of some of these events. The Jews turn their eyes towards the Holy Land, the Turk in Constantinople feels the earth tremble beneath his feet; and, as a missionary once remarked to us, who had recently returned from Jerusalem, where he had been familiar with the first Mohammedan families, the rumor is spread throughout the East that Mohammedanism is soon to fall; that Jesus Christ will soon descend upon the summit of the great Mosque of Damascus, and incorporate Judaism, Christianity and Islamism in one single and primitive religion. Such are the presentiments of the people

But before these things take place, there must be many a struggle. Do we not in fact see the enemies of Christ strengthening themselves in bold systems of unbelief and pantheism, presumptuously placing themselves before the cross of Jesus; the power of Rome stirring over the whole earth, its convents rising again in

France, and the most devoted soldiery of the Papacy, a celebrated society establishing itself in all parts, and even in the bosom of our own confederacy? Do we not hear wars and rumors of wars? Is not the East already lit up and gleaming with the flashing lightnings, those precursors of the thunder? And are not the powers of the East and the West, at this hour, gathering together around the land of revelation—that Judah, which is already becoming the centre of the world, of whom it is said, Judah shall be saved and Jerusalem shall dwell in safety?

We do not pretend, my brethren, to know the times or the seasons; but if, on the one hand, we ought to have much discretion and caution in these matters, would it not, on the other hand, be willfully closing our eyes to the light, to maintain that both in a political and religious point of view, the world has not now reached a crisis, but that she is rolling on through a period of very ordinary tranquillity? I think then, that it is meet for us to meditate upon the words our Lord gave to his disciples, to strengthen them through three centuries of persecutions, and which are designed to confirm his people throughout all time.

In times, such as those of which we speak, the great duty to which Christ calls his followers, is that of a fearless profession of his name. It is, first, the duty of each Christian; secondly, the duty of the Church. Let us consider these two duties, and may the Lord assist us to discharge both!

I. Persons are frequently found (perhaps there are such in this assembly) who would gladly become Christians, converted Christians, without revealing the change to the church, and provided it might remain a secret between themselves and their Lord. These weak Christians have an excessive fear of everything which would cause them to be recognized in their true characters.

You will hear them advance, in their justification, that *the kingdom of Heaven is within us;* that Christianity is too holy a thing to be presented to the world. But (perhaps without their perceiving the fact) it is this very fear of the world which rules and restrains them. A celebrated and corrupt church has admitted this pitiful hypocrisy. There are secret Romanists in Protestant countries; there are still more in heathen lands. The numerous and pretended converts in China, of whom Rome so loudly boasts, conceal their faith in that empire and give themselves out as idolators; and there we find that Christianity without a confession of faith which many would see established in the bosom of Christendom.

The Evangelical Christian church rests upon principles altogether opposite, although there are even in our days those who would bend its nature in this respect. She declares with the Apostles that it is not sufficient to believe with the heart unto righteousness, but that with the mouth confession also must be made unto salvation, and instead of the accommodations and tergiversations of Rome, instead of the silence, the indifference, the fear and the respect to human opinions of some Protestants, who forget the Rock from which they have been hewed, the Evangelical church proclaims and fulfills the sure and sovereign word of Christ. " Whosoever therefore shall confess me before men, him will I confess also before my Father which is in heaven; but whosoever shall deny me before men, him will I also deny before my Father which is in heaven."

Yes, weak and timid Christians, it is not sufficient for us to imagine that we can belong to Christ in the depths of our hearts. If we have truly embraced Jesus Christ we shall make it known to all. What! saved by him from eternal death, shall we not praise him with our whole soul? Oh! that all might read in our life an epistle traced by the hand of Jesus, proclaiming his ineffable love.

Very true, you reply; but are we to be counted unfaithful, because we have had to endure nothing for Christ? It is mere exaggeration to maintain that one cannot be a sincere Christian without enduring persecution. Does not Christianity everywhere tend to produce harmony, benevolence and peace? How then can we be pursued with contempt and hatred since Christianity has raised us all above them? This might have occurred in the early ages, in the midst of Pagans, but at this time, in the bosom of Protestant Christendom, in our church, no one need be tempted through fear of persecution to deny Jesus Christ.

Think not, replies Jesus himself unto you, think not that I am come to send peace on earth; l am come to set a man at variance against his father and the daughter against her mother. Yes, if your conversion is genuine, if you truly confess Jesus Christ, think not to escape this universal rule.

Jesus Christ, doubtless, came not to bring the sword, but such however is the invariable effect of his coming whenever he appears. And how can it be otherwise? But what happens in the world? The Gospel has proved effectual upon a certain person of your acquaintance, (perhaps upon yourself!) It has effected a fundamental change, which is seen in the whole life of this new Christian. This change attracts the attention of his friends, it is inevitable; and in view of this work of God they are reduced to this alternative, either to submit to the same transformation or to condemn it in him. Not willing to undergo the former, they have recourse to the latter; they condemn the conversion of their friend as an irrational, enthusiastic, fanatical, methodistical thing. And if this new Christian (be he yourself or another) keep himself near them, then their irritation is constantly displayed in a growing measure; for the shame and hatred of the world which the faithful disciple draws upon himself, is partly reflected upon themselves; the condemnation they should pronounce upon their own heart, becomes the more vivid the nearer that Christian approaches; and there is a natural impulse to rally such men, and recall their reason, imagining that they are surely gone mad.

Undeceive yourselves then, my brethren: the confession of Jesus Christ may be a difficult task even in the absence of extraordinary circumstances. If you are upright and sincere in your profession, you cannot escape opposition; it is the ordinary course of the world. *A man's foes shall be they of his own household.*

Permit me, then, in this place to put to you a question suggested by your words. What will Christ answer to your excuse? Is not the reception which you have until this hour received from the world, a sure indication that Christ will one day reject you? No! you reply. Some prudence is certainly requisite in order to avoid opprobrium; we have made some slight sacrifices, and availed ourselves of some trifling accommodations. But what! If we have merely been guiltless of great offences against Christian morality, if our only fault has been the non-confession of Christ before our friends, in our families, as frequently and as courageously as we ought perhaps to have done, does it follow that we are not in Christ, that for so light an offence he will deny us eternally? Impossible.

Here again I will reply to you, not in my own words, but in those of the divine oracle. "He that loveth father or mother more than me is not worthy of me, says the Lord. He that loveth son or daughter more than me is not worthy of me." If through fear of a father or a mother, of an elder brother or a sister, if through love for your children, through a desire of not compromising the future prospects of a son, the establishment of a daughter, you have yielded on any occasion, and purposely hid your sentiments from your associates, are you, in the literal sense of the Master's declaration, worthy of Christ? With your conscience I leave the answer. Further; suppose you confess Jesus in the family circle, that you support even the reproaches of your mother or of your son, and that you walk faithfully in this way until the last extremity, but that in case of violent reproach, the deep contempt of the world, yea, I go even further, in case persecution and the stake should be presented to you, you should be astonished, should falter, should keep silence and turn your back on Jesus as did Peter,—then notwithstanding all that you might have done, Christ would have a strong reproach to utter against you. Why hast thou turned back, he might say to you; have I drawn back from thee? This cross which you have rejected have I not borne for you? For you did I not permit myself to be led to Calvary? Were not my hands and feet pierced for you? But you have loved your ease, your interests, your life, more than my kingdom and my glory, I know you not. He that taketh not up his cross and followeth after me is not worthy of me.

Why should we be astonished at this severity of the Lord, when we see that we act in regard to him, so totally different from the manner in which we act towards the world. Who among us would not submit to a painful operation, if certain that it would bring him some permanent benefit? And shall we not esteem eternal life worthy of a few brief trials?

Oh! there is not before you the cross, the sword, the scaffold; death I know is not before your eyes. But no matter, it is at this price we ought to accept Jesus Christ. No one is truly in Christ unless he is prepared, in order to confess him, even to give up his life. It is thus we must act to save our own souls. It is a deplorable thing, this same faith—if I may so term it—which is found in the Church, and which will certainly fail in the day of martyrdom. All are not called to confess Christ upon the scaffold, but every one ought to have the spirit to endure it. And this word that we preach to you is as true for tranquil times as for a time of trouble and blood. He that findeth his life shall lose it : and he that loseth his life for my sake, shall find it.

II. But we will take still higher ground: we will survey the whole Church, and say to her, That which is true for each individual is true for the Church. And, when I speak of the Church, the question is still of your duty; your duty, however, not as an isolated person, but as a member of an universal society, the Church.

The Church is called by her Master to confess him before the world. Why then is not the duty of each one of us the duty of us all? Is it because the obligation of a soldier to be faithful to his colors is not that of the whole army? And as God has ordered the movement of each star, does it not follow that the whole heavens should move harmoniously in its course?

Every false Church is hostile to this individual confession of Jesus Christ. "Whoever confesses that Jesus is the Christ," says St. John, "shall be put out of the synagogue," but every true Church confesses her Lord. The minister is called to confess him, not only as an individual, but as a minister and representative of the Church to imitate Timothy and like him to " make a good confession before many witnesses." The Church ought in all things to follow her leader. Christ has left us an example, says the Scripture, that we might follow in his steps. Jesus Christ says St. Paul before Pontius Pilate witnessed a good confession. And what is the eulogy Jesus passed, not on an individual, but on a Church, even that of a Pergamos, when from her midst the cruel Domitian took the faithful Antipas and caused him to be shut up in a brazen ox heated by fire, according to the acts of that martyr?* The glory of this Church, Jesus declares, was her confession of the name of Christ and her faith in the Lord. " I know thy works; and where thou dwellest, even where Satan's seat is : saith he which hath the sharp sword with two edges; and thou holdest fast my name and hast not denied my faith, even in those days wherein Antipas was my faithful martyr, who was slain among you where Satan dwelleth."

Such then, my brethren, is the duty of the Church; the Bible establishes it; and a Church that confesses not the great mystery of piety, *God manifest in the flesh*, is as unfaithful and guilty in her associated capacity, as is that Christian who fails to do it as an individual : these are the simple conclusions of sound judgment.

This is likewise what the Church universal has recognized. Yes, my brethren, it is not we who would arbitrarily impose this duty on the Church; on the contrary, the Church in her best days has not ceased to proclaim and fulfill it.

* Bollandi Acta.

She felt the necessity and duty of this confession, when, in the beginning of the fourth century, a deplorable heresy, the denial of the eternal divinity of the Son of God, began to spread throughout the world, and the church universal, assembled from the East and the West at Nice, A. D. 325, in the persons of its bishops, rejecting the errors of Arius, declared in the presence of the first Christian Emperor and of all the habitable world: "We believe in our Lord Jesus Christ, begotten before all ages and not created, very God, of the same essence with the Father, by whom all things were made, and who became man for our salvation.*.

The Church in Germany more than three centuries ago felt this same necessity and duty, when at Augsburg, in 1530, at the period of the revival of Christianity, in view of terrible wars and frightful persecutions which seemed ready to burst upon her, when commanded by Charles V. to suspend the preaching of the word, she replied through her organ, the Margrave of Brandenburg: "Rather let my head be severed from my body, than not confess my God and His Gospel!" and when the evangelical princes, being solemnly assembled in the imperial chapel, in the presence of that mighty emperor, who reigned over two worlds, of a multitude of sovereign princes, of bishops, of ambassadors, and of the mighty of the earth, in the midst of the glory of the age, the elector of Saxony and his brethren in the faith arose, the chancellors advanced, and the renovated church proclaimed for two hours, in a loud and intelligible voice, in the most profound silence and with the most powerful effect, her faith of great price, justification for the love of Christ, through grace, through means of faith.†

The Church of France felt this necessity and duty, on the 26th of May, 1559, when, not with a great splendor and royal pomp as at Augsburg, but in silence, in gloom, in disgrace, even under the sword of her adversaries, under the bloody sceptre of Henry II., and Catharine de Médicis, the deputies of all the churches then established in France assembled at Paris, "at Paris," says Theodore Beza,‡ because it was the most suitable city for the secret reception of so many ministers and elders;" when having penetrated into the capital through the arquebusiers of Henry II., these ministers and members of the church came four days in succession to a house in the faubourg St. Germain, by stealth one after the other from different quarters, and remained there for the confession of their faith, "in the midst of stakes and gibbets," says another historian, "which were raised in all quarters of the city;"§ when surrounded by the spies of the clergy, the emissaries of parliament, the lances of the king, obliged almost to hold their breath for fear of being betrayed, the Church of our fathers in France, protected by its humility, put forth that beautiful confession of faith which its ministers and elders carried into all their provinces and published in the light of the sun, in presence of the

---

* Θεὸν ἀληθινὸν ὁμοούσιον τῷ πάτρι. Symb. Nic.
† Fourth article of the Augsburg Confession.
‡ Hist. Eccles., page 109.
§ Hist. de l'édit de Nantes, Vol. i., p. 18.

satellites of Rome, and upon the ashes of the martyrs, saying, with a voice whose accents sound even to us: We believe that from this corruption and general condemnation in which all men are plunged, God receives those whom in his eternal and immutable counsel, he has elected by his own goodness, in our Lord Jesus, without consideration of their works. We profess that Jesus Christ, God and man in one person, is our entire and perfect purification, and that we have in his death full satisfaction to release us from our trespasses.*

Yes, my brethren, it is thus that in all times the Church has found courage to confess her faith, in obedience to her Master, and to make a good confession before many witnesses.

Shall not then the Church in our day do the same? Shall she remain silent? Has not Christ been crucified for her? or has she not faith enough to know she ought to proclaim it? More than a century has elapsed since the confession of faith in Christ—the God-Saviour has been destroyed in this Church of Geneva; a few months ago she again took up her abode in the Church of the Canton of Vaud. In almost all places the confessions of our fathers are overthrown or neglected. The Church is now in the midst of interminable rubbish. Ruins, ruins, everywhere ruins. Oh! while the enemies are so active to destroy, why should the friends of Jesus be so slack to build up? If they have gagged the mouths of our fathers, so that they should no longer speak of their ancient faith; if they have put them, so to speak, a second time to death, shall our mouths—our lips remain immovable and silent? What! because those arms, which presented to the world the confession of the "Word made flesh," have three centuries been stiff in death and sleeping in the sepulchre; because those eyes, which gazed with gentleness and boldness on kings and executioners, have for three ages been closed and wasted away; because those feet which ran when necessary to the stake rather than not confess Christ, are unjointed, broken and scattered; because those lips that cried in the midst of the mob and the flames, "Emmanuel! God with us!" are closed, fleshless, and for three hundred years have been mingled with the dust, shall we, in our days, shall we do nothing, confess nothing, say nothing! Oh, dry bones that we are! Let us renounce the name we have to live, since we are dead. Let us sleep in the grave since we speak no more than do its silent tenants. This Church which reposes in the bosom of the earth awaiting the cry of the archangel and the voice of the Son of Man, would start from her very dust if she could know the lukewarmness of the Church of our day. These courageous dead would rise from their sepulchres and address us. "We had arms to act and lips to speak with. Do you possess them to keep silence? Have you not heard then those august and fearful words, which make us tremble even in our graves: 'He who will not confess me before men, I will not confess before my Father which is in heaven.'"

My brethren, a confession of faith is necessary to manifest the

* Confession de foi des Eglises réf de France. Art. 12, 17, etc.

unity of the Church. Unity is a commandment which our Master has left us. We cannot throw it off from us. It is not, however, by an earthly leader, by a worldly hierarchy, by an uniformity of worship, of liturgy, by crosses, mitres, censers, it is not by all these things that the unity of the Church is manifested; she leaves to the world these miserable elements. The true Church of Christ has no other bond than the unity of her faith and her confession, in love and holiness of life. With her, all externals, which men regard of so high importance, are altogether secondary. All is free for her, saving her Jesus. When Rome points to her false and dead unity, the Church of Christ is to present a *true* and *living* unity; a UNITY and not an UNIFORMITY. Yes! to this dead uniformity of Rome, similar to the uniformity discernible in the parade of the armies of the kings of this world, let us reply by a vast and unanimous confession of the Lord our Righteousness, like that which angels make, prostrate before the eternal throne. The former is the unity of the children of this world, but the latter is the unity of the children of Heaven. What an admirable unity was that of the Church at her great awakening in the sixteenth century! It is not a servile uniformity; there is liberty in all things where freedom is proper, but there is likewise a sublime and imposing agreement in the confession of the truth, come from on high. Take the confessions of Germany, of Switzerland, of Belgium, of France, of England, of Scotland, everywhere the same faith, the same God, the same Christ, the same salvation. In the Church of Rome "the principal thing" is the men, the priests, the bishops, the pontiffs; and the unity consists in being united to them. In the evangelical Christian Church the principal thing is faith, the doctrine of Heaven, the truth of God, that is to say, God himself, and in her view unity consists in the unanimous confession of this truth. Every Church, which ceases to find her unity in the confession of the same doctrine, and makes it to consist in union with the leaders or the assemblies which direct it, may still bear the name of Protestant, but has clothed itself by these means with the essential and distinctive nature of the papacy. It is not walls which are soon to fall, it is not certain leaders, ephemeral beings who will to-morrow be in the depths of the grave, that are essential to the Church. The adorer of the virgin and of the saints in Spain or in Italy submits to the Pontiff, who by chance is found at the head of the most ancient Church of the west; and the Turk at Constantinople prostrates himself in the ancient porches of Justinian and Theodosius. Stones are nothing, men are nothing, Christ is all. To suppress the unity of the faith and the confession of Christ, is to suppress the Church. Doubtless there may be Christians scattered here and there, there may be walls, priests, ruins; but there is no Church; for there can be no assembly of God there, where there are only foreign, perhaps conflicting elements, without any divine and eternal bond to hold them together.

My brethren, a confession of the faith of the Church is needful, for by this confession the Church is led on to victory. What are its " weapons—mighty to the pulling down of strongholds," as St.

Paul says—what are these weapons? They are the confession of Jesus Christ. Behold the only strength of the Church! What will become of her, if the confession of faith is wanting? A fortuitous aggregation of certain societies almost civil, of which each follows its own good pleasure or the will of its masters; a tree, deprived of its common trunk, and whose branches separated, dispersed—are only ready to wither and die; a body, from which the head has been severed, and whose members are scattered to the four winds. How, in such a state as this, can she obtain the victory over her adversaries? Alas! this is too much the condition of the evangelical Church at the present moment; and it is this which gives us such lively alarm in view of the dangers which menace her. But let the Church revive and build herself up in her most holy faith, and, in her beautiful unity, let her clothe herself with the strength and life which should belong to a great community; let her join together the ends of the earth, to unite with one heart and one voice to confess Jesus her God,—these are the trumpets before which would fall down the fortresses of incredulity and the walls of Rome. "The people," says the Scripture, in the history of Jericho, "having shouted with a great shout, the wall fell down flat, so that the people went up into the city."

And will any of you, my brethren, repeat the worldly maxim, that there must be some bond in the Church, for without it she cannot exist (an acknowledgment, which it is well to remember); but that this bond is found in the commonly admitted principle—that the Holy Scriptures are the only source of our faith. "We have no need," says one, " of confessing any particular doctrine; the Bible—nothing but the Bible; behold our confession." Is, then, the Bible simply a certain volume of a certain binding, and of a certain form, in which are found only *blank* pages? The liberty of examination and progress, adds another,—this constitutes our Church; we have no necessity for doctrines,—each minister can have his own, and may preach them at will. Thus, then, my brethren, the poor Christian flocks will be delivered to every imagination which may pass through the brains of their ministers. Every church may be called to change her religion as often as it changes her pastor! When a new minister shall come into a curacy, a new religion will come with him into the village! One will preach Protestantism, another Anabaptism, a third Socinianism, a fourth Universalism, a fifth Roman Catholicism, and, in fine, what not?—a sixth Judaism, a seventh Mahometanism,—for Judaism has more foundation in the Bible than the most of these doctrines, and Mahometanism has a more explicit faith in Jesus than Socinianism itself. And all this ought to be for the advantage of the poor parishioners, obliged, as they are, with their children to assume all the doctrines of their masters in the same manner as valets assume successively the livery of the houses they serve. But at least the latter are obliged to change only their habits while in your deplorable system, that will be the true faith, —that is to say, the faith which saves unto eternal life—which must be for ever changing in the souls of the believers.

But is not the liberty of examination, proceed they, is not progress, is not research sufficient? Doubtless we need examination and progress, but we need sound ones, and such as produce the fruits of salvation and life. With you these are only phrases under which you conceal your indifference. What signifies, I pray you, your examination, which discerns nothing, and retains nothing? Of what consequence is your research, which, ever searching, never finds anything? What signifies your progress, if, like the traveller in the fable, you are for ever travelling and never arrive at the goal? For observe, that in this miserable system, although it may be enjoined on the Church to seek her true doctrine, it is forbidden her ever to find it. The moment she has found it, and consequently proclaimed it, that moment the system will be destroyed, for she will possess a doctrine and will enter into the truth of the Lord.

No, my brethren, it is impossible that the Church should have meditated during so many ages on the oracles of God, which make wise the simple, and should not yet know what is found therein. It is impossible that the Church should believe in the Scripture, and yet be ignorant of what the Scripture says. The Church knows from the beginning; she knows from Paul and Peter; she knows from Athanasius and Augustine; she knows from Luther and Calvin; she knows at this moment, everywhere, in all time, in every clime; what she believes, what she rejects, what she needs, "GOD MANIFEST IN THE FLESH." And if there are, alas! some doctors, some churches, who have withdrawn from this glorious and consoling confession, it is only men have fallen away,—the confession is lasting. The grass withereth and the flower thereof falleth away, but the word of the Lord endureth for ever.

Thus then, my brethren (and this is our conclusion), let a courageous confession of the Lord rise from the midst of the ruins heaped up in the field of the Lord, and let a mighty voice go forth living and faithful from the very bowels of the revival. But, you reply, do you then maintain that the Church in our day ought to confess in an authentic and universal manner its faith as she did in the 16th century?

And why not, my brethren? Are we then among those who think a commandment of God, obligatory in one age, is not equally so in another? I do not say that the form ought to be that of the 16th century; it may be quite another; not perhaps a confession made once for all, but frequent and repeated confessions; not perhaps confessions written with paper and ink, but living confessions made with the lips and in the life. "Every age has its peculiar mode of confessing Jesus Christ, just as every age has its peculiar mode of persecuting his confessors."*

I acknowledge with joy that some mouths have already spoken; that some mouths yet speak. But here I lay down this simple proposition, that the Church, everywhere in the earth, if she truly awaits her Leader, ought to confess with an unity and an

---

* Quesnel.

universality, greater than she has ever yet exhibited, that Christ is truly the Saviour to the glory of God the Father.

But you will still rejoin, this has reference to ministers; you should preach to them and not to us. What? Do the ministers constitute the Church? This is only true in the language of the Papacy. You are the Church, and your duty as well as ours is, to confess Jesus Christ. When the Church confessed her faith at Augsburg before Charles V., she did it only by her laity. Princes would not relinquish this honor to theologians. Will you now renounce the same honor? Be then, my brethren, confessors of Jesus Christ; first as individuals, as souls called from darkness into the marvellous light of the gospel, and who show forth the virtues of him who has bought them, by their words, in their lives and in all their actions.

Be confessors of Christ, my brethren, but let your confession be nourished in faith and in the life of the soul. Confession can be free and sincere without, only as sanctification advances within. A confession with the lips, without the renunciation of self, without life in the heart, is hypocrisy, is an abomination before God.

Be confessors of Jesus Christ, my brethren, but confess him with wisdom and charity, without a useless affectation of singularity, without placing too great an importance on secondary objects, without forgetting to watch with care over the dispositions of the heart. Your father or your mother perhaps demand of you an act of conformity to the world; you refuse; you do well; but if you do so, failing in reverence or gentleness towards them, you sin against the Lord.

Be confessors of Jesus Christ, my brethren, but confess him willingly with boldness, with joy, not with that timidity, that contrite and mournful air, with which Christians are sometimes reproached. There is joy in the harmony of an identical and universal faith, but there is sadness in the discord of human opinions. You have nothing to fear. " Whosoever shall confess that Jesus is the Son of God, God dwelleth in him and he in God:" and " He that is in us, is greater than he that is in the world."

Be confessors of Jesus Christ, and let each fulfil this duty in the situation in which God has placed him. Let the magistrate confess Christ in the council; let the mechanic confess him in the workshop, let the man of business confess him in the midst of his occupations, let the laborer confess him in the field, let the mother of the family confess him in her house, let the soldier confess him under arms, let each one, whatever may be his situation, regard it as a holy place, in which he is called to confess the Lord?

Young men, who have come hither from different countries, having quitted anew the paternal roof, to resume grave studies,* be confessors of Jesus Christ! Renounce the world and the flesh; be not disciples and servants of human masters, be not high in your own esteem; not only belong to Jesus but belong entirely to

---

* The students of the Theological School.

him; confess Jesus in your intercourse with this people, and one day as lights of the Church in the midst of the world.

But we hold, my brethren, to individual confession. Everywhere in the works of God we find union, harmony, and we see great things effected by them. In our mountains one drop of water detached from the glacier unites with another; streams join with streams, torrents mingle with torrents, and these united waters form those magnificent rivers which flow from afar through the plains, and bear life and fertility upon their bosom. In the morning of creation, when " the sons of God shouted for joy," a world came at the bidding of the Eternal to place itself near another world; " the morning stars sang together;" and the heavens began that harmonious course of the universe which fills the soul with astonishment and adoration. When the beloved disciple was ravished in spirit, so that he saw " a throne and some one set upon the throne, a voice joined to another voice, many angels around the throne united their accents, and they were many millions, and every creature which is in heaven, and on the earth, and under the earth, and such as are in the sea, and all that are in them replied, and all their voices united were as the voice of many waters and as the voice of a great thunder." Oh! should not we, the redeemed of the Lord, do the same! Let the voices of those who are here below, strangers elect and dispersed in the world, unite together in holy enthusiasm and holy courage to render glory to Jesus Christ. Let us for once go out of our petty individualities, let us not content ourselves with our feeble voices scattered here and there; that there may be upon the earth a mighty concert, a glorious harmony to celebrate Him who has redeemed us by his blood. Then would the world, which until now has been regardless of Christ, be constrained to listen, and the voice of the Church would become so powerful that all the kindreds of the nations should awaken and prostrate themselves before the Lord.

Oh! that my voice could reach beyond this narrow place! that it could be heard in the vast temples of this city in which in times gone by resounded the faithful voices of our fathers; if reaching farther on it could reach the church of Vaud, the church of France, the universal church of the Lord, and say to the great assembly, Let us confess the Lord as the Lamb who was slain, and who is worthy to receive power, and riches, and wisdom, and strength, and honor, and glory, and blessing.

Lord! I cannot do this; my weak voice must remain in this humble chapel, but thou canst accomplish it! Speak, Lord! speak, and may thy servants hear! Dispel the illusions, rend the veils, break with thy powerful hand the chains which bind generous souls whom thou hast called unto liberty; grant that none of thy servants, " consulting flesh and blood," may open their ears to the thousand voices of the world which insinuate themselves to put to silence thy confession, while they shut their ears to thy voice, which calls upon them to confess thee before men. The day advances, the time is ripening for the manifestation of thy salvation; call thy Church, cause each of our souls to hear thy awful voice, before that solemn approaching day, when seated on the clouds thou shalt say to many: "Father! they were ashamed of me, now I am ashamed of them." Oh! that this disgrace may never be ours, but rather may we be of those to whom thou wilt say in the day of thy glory: I have seen thy testimony, I have seen thy humiliations, I have seen thy fidelity, thy courage, the confession of my name which thou hast made! I declare them now before the assembled universe! Enter, faithful servant, into the kingdom of thy Lord! Amen!

THE

CHILDREN OF GOD.

TRANSLATED BY M. M. BACKUS.

THE CHILDREN OF GOD.

A DISCOURSE DELIVERED AT GENEVA, JULY, 1829.

" He came unto his own, and his own received him not; but to as many as received him to them gave he power to become the sons of God, even to them that believe on his name: which were born not of blood, nor of the will of the flesh, nor of the will of man, but of God."
—JOHN i. 11, 12, 13.

THE Lord had chosen the people of Israel in order to keep alive the knowledge of Himself and the hope of His salvation, while all other nations walked in darkness. He had brought them out of Egypt, established them in Canaan, preserved them distinct in the midst of other nations of the earth; and, when the appointed time was come, in which the Lord should humble Himself, and appear as a man among men, HE COMES at first, says the Gospel, unto *His own*—HE COMES into the midst of His own people, just as a man, arriving in a city, goes first to his own dwelling, and not to the abode of strangers. But His family would not recognize Him; *His own received Him not*, they repulsed Him, and *crucified the Lord of glory!* Yet there was a chosen remnant in Israel, who received by faith Jesus the Lord. Soon, from among the nations of the earth, an immense number cried Hosanna to Him who came in the name of the Lord, and all Jews, Greeks, Scythians, bond and free, were made *children of God. I have sanctified my king in Zion, the mountain of my holiness; I will give him the heathen for his inheritance, the uttermost parts of the earth for his possession.*

But does not the same thing still happen unto ourselves? Doubtless there are many who receive Christ the Lord and enter into the family of God; but how many reject Him? how many remain sadly without Him? Listen but to the conversation of men; open the writings which find the highest favor with them; contemplate the course of the world; above all, study your own heart. Have you there received Jesus Christ? Oh, my dear hearers! we would put forth a feeble effort to give you a better knowledge of the riches, that you have, perhaps, hitherto despised. We announce to you to-day, then, a fact, which has better claims on your attention than every other fact which is presented in the history of the world. Christ has come to establish, in the midst of all human families, *a family of God.* God, by one vast adoption, assumes all who believe for his *sons* and *daughters.* You can be accounted of this number; it is only necessary that you truly receive by faith Jesus Christ. Oh, man! my brother—thou mayest be adopted into the family of God, and thou wilt not! Let me unfold this important subject, presenting, as it does, Christianity in all its divine grandeur; and, above all, let us seek to dissipate the numerous errors in which it has been enveloped. Come, Lord! come unto us to-day by Thy word! Come Thyself to the door! Knock—and may we hear Thee, may we open to Thee, and may we receive Thee with joy! May there be many souls who will enter into Thy house, who may be reckoned in the number of the children of God, to praise Thee now and for ever, with all the kindred, who are named in the heavens and upon earth. Amen.

NECESSITY.

And first we address ourselves to you who, recognizing the Scriptures as the word of God, say: "God is the father of the human race. All men are His children, without exception, without distinction of religious faith, Jews, Christians, Mahomedans, Pagans—we have all but *one* Father, and we are *all* brethren."

Before refuting your opinion we ought to grant that it is grounded upon various foundations. It is true that God shows his paternal goodness to *all* men, and makes his sun to rise upon the good and on the wicked: it is true that we are all brethren in *Adam,* that is to say, we have all lost the holiness and primitive glory of our nature, and form by our birth but one family, exposed to sin, to the miseries of life and to death. It is also true that God has no respect of nations, of religions, the sect, or the visible Church in which one is born; and when a soul awakened by the sound of the good news of Christ *believes on Him that he might have life,* He receives that soul with joy whatever may be the standard under which he was born, whether of abominable idols, of the false prophet of Rome, or the glorious standard of the Reformation. *From my very soul I recognize the truth that God has no respect of persons.*

But Christ has actually been given to the world to create in it a *family of God* in quite another sense; in a sense much more intimate and true than it is of the human species in general. The word of God which is *the truth,* proclaims to us that to be *children of God,* is quite a different thing from being simply *children of Adam.* Turn to our text: *To as many as received him to them gave he power to become the sons of God.* Those, then, who have not received him, or will not receive him do not enjoy *this right.* The meaning of the Word is clear. Refer to the *twelfth* Chapter of Matthew. *For whosoever shall do the will of my Father which is in heaven, the same is my brother and sister and mother.* Whosoever therefore *does not* the holy will of the Everlasting Father, is not the *brother*, nor *sister* of Christ, and consequently, not the *child of God*. In the epistle to the Romans, chapter viii: *For as many as are led by the Spirit of God, they are the sons of God.* Those, then, who *are not led* by the Spirit of God, but by *their own spirit*, are not *his* children. It is impossible to receive the Word without receiving also its conclusions.

You well understand, in the interpretation of our human laws, that when the child of any man is his by *adoption* it is because he is not so by *nature*. Why not apply to the things of God, this plain common sense which directs us in the things of this world? Christianity proclaims to the sinner *who believes* a free and gratuitous adoption into the family of the God of heaven. Man is then, by nature, out of the family of the Most High, and he can enter therein only by an act of mercy and of love from Him, who would be his father. "God sent forth his son, made of a woman, made under the law, to redeem them that were under the law, that we might receive the adoption of Sons .... Wherefore thou art no more a servant but a son." Oh! if men by nature are children of God, what children, great God, are like thy children? Are those thy children in whom there is so entire a forgetfulness of their Father? We speak not solely of the nations who prostrate themselves at the feet of idols, but of ourselves by our own nature; do we not constantly forget the great God in all our actions, all our words, all our thoughts, and seek only ourselves and our own good? Are these indeed the children of God, having the nature of their Father, who are prone to pride, to envy, to hatred, to wrath, to covetousness, in a word, to SIN which God abhors? What family, Lord, should be like thy family? What! shall all this corruption, all these vices, all these crimes, all those abominations which one dares not even to name, which are found in the world, shall all these exist in *thy family!* A family so full of disorders would be disowned even by men; and should this be *the family of God!* thine, oh God! *who art of purer eyes than to behold iniquity.* No, my brethren, these fine words, that we are all the children of God, are the declamations of a carnal sensibility, but are not according to the truth; they are the words either of fraud or error. Yes, we are by birth children—but learn from the word of God himself *what* kind of children: CHILDREN OF DISOBEDIENCE, as says St. Paul to the Ephesians, *children of wrath*, he continues *disobedient, foolish*, says he to Titus, *living in malice and envy, hateful and hating one another.* There is no difference, we have *all come short of the glory of God.*

THE MEANS.

But here, my brethren, I discover among us other thoughts and another class of persons. You, my dear hearers, far from thinking so lightly of becoming a child of God, you imagine you can never become one. To be *a son, a daughter of God!* what a privilege, you exclaim! what a happiness! what a glory! but how dare we pretend to a relation so touching and so beautiful with the great God of the universe? Perhaps there are those who can thus aspire, but for *myself*, I cannot. I am too insignificant, too sinful—I remain afar: and I bow my head in the dust before the face of the King of kings. Who can abide in the day of his coming, and who can stand when he shall appear?

Oh ye, who are filled with such fear, haply the word of your God does not make the thing as impossible as does your own heart. You would have reason for such apprehensions if this privilege were to be *gained* by yourself; but know that this adoption into the family of God is a GIFT, a free gift which the God of Heaven makes by his beloved Son: To as many as received him, to them *gave* he power to become the sons of God:—gave, says the Word, not *sold;* given as a tender father makes a *gift* to his son, or as a rich man, powerful and good, makes the *gift* of adoption to the poor abandoned child, whom he thus makes rich by a simple act of his great compassion and of his great love. Why would you refuse to God the privilege of *giving*, of giving gratuitously such great blessings?

But how, you say, can I be assured that this pardon is truly *given;* that this salvation is truly acquired; that God adopts for himself a family on earth? How? Because God himself has spoken it; because He from whom such grace proceeds has caused it to be announced and published in all places; because he declares it to you by his ministers, by his sacraments, by his Word; by his *Word which is the truth.* Assuredly that which is spoken by the Eternal, the True, is well worthy of our belief. If some unnatural wicked children, having been banished from the paternal roof, loaded with a father's curse, should soon after learn the news of that father's death, with what trouble—with what anguish would the thought of that parent's curse fill their souls! But suppose that a friend should come unto one of these sons and should place in his hand a letter, a will written by that father, in which were written these words: "I declare unto my children, into whose hands these lines may fall, that before giving up my last breath I withdrew from them *all* my curses; I pardon them *everything*, and from my death-bed I raise my hands to heaven for them, to bless them and constitute them anew my children, my heirs." The child considers these lines; he exclaims, "It is my father's writing! it is his signature, it is his seal! it is himself who has said it! How can I doubt? I am blessed. I am saved. My father has caused me to attain unto this assurance. I am at peace. I believe the testimony of my father."

Unto you likewise I bring a letter, O my brethren! a letter written by Himself, furnished with his signature, and impressed with his seal: a letter which he has sent from heaven to earth; a letter of pardon: a letter of amnesty: a letter of adoption: a letter of peace. Listen! listen to that which is written in this letter by the finger of God himself. In this letter it is written,—I take the eternal word as witness: *Jesus saves his people from their sins. There is therefore now no condemnation to them which are in Christ Jesus.*—

Having been made perfect, Christ has become the eternal salvation unto all them that obey him. God gives eternal life, AND THIS LIFE IS IN HIS SON. HE WHO HAS THE SON HAS LIFE. *To as many as receive him to them gives he power to become the sons of God.* Will you not believe the *testimony of God?* This testimony written in a Testament which each of you possesses in his own dwelling, which you can read and read again. Will you refuse to believe a Testament dictated from the cross, sealed with the blood of its author? Alas! can you believe the testament of a father, and will you not believe that of God? a will which puts you in possession of so glorious an inheritance! "If we receive the witness of men, the witness of God is greater; for this is the witness of God, which he hath testified of his Son."

If, then, you have *believed this witness,* and have thus *received Jesus Christ,* you are become in God, my brother, you are become his child; already, here below, you belong unto him! And when He shall call you from this earth, it will be a father's voice to call you home to himself. You will enter then into the paternal mansion in the heavens. Oh what a glorious prospect! what happiness to you is given!

If you have received Jesus Christ, the God Saviour, who has borne in himself the curse of sin, and who has humbled and vanquished it by His divine power, why can you still doubt that you may become *children of God?* Do you speak of your sins? True, but Christ, who is now your Saviour, *has borne them,* says the Scripture, has *expiated* them on the cross: he has *scattered them as a cloud, he has cast them into the bottom of the sea.* And of them not the smallest part shall ever be brought to light.

Do you speak of your insignificance, of your nothingness, of the misery of this human nature which is your's? True: but Christ, the Son of God, has taken this humanity; he has become the *Brother* of man; the human nature has been glorified by the divinity of *Him* whom it has clothed. It may belong to God and enter into heaven. What is there in this which need astonish you? The *Son of God* is become *the Son of man:* cannot the *son of man* become then the *son of God?* He who was in *heaven* is become a member of the family of the *earth:* may not then he who is on the *earth* become a member of the family of *heaven?* And if the Son of God was not ashamed to call himself *our brother* in the midst of our misery, will he be ashamed to call us *his brethren* in the midst of all his glory and his immortal grandeur? *Behold what manner of love the father hath bestowed upon us that we should be called the sons of God!*

NATURE.

"Certainly," you say, my dear hearers, "certainly, we admit all these things; we are born in the Christian church; we believe in Jesus Christ: we think that it is through Him we can call God our Father." It may be so. Meanwhile, however, we invite you candidly to examine yourselves, to see if you truly possess the *faith* of which the Scripture speaks. You imagine that one can receive Christ and become a child of God by faith, without this faith producing any change in the heart. This is the third error that we would refute: for *as many as receive him*, says our text, *are born not of blood nor of the will of the flesh, nor of the will of man, but of God.*

The children of God *are not born of blood :* whatever the nation, the sect, the family in which they are born; whether of the seed of Abraham, the children of the holiest man on earth, tracing back their descent from generation to generation, to kindred the most distinguished for their faith, even all these cannot constitute one a *child of God.* The children of God *are not born of blood.*

They are not *born of the will of the flesh.* It is not our own wisdom, our own strength, that can make us the children of God. The flesh, that is, our fallen and corrupt nature, has neither the will n r the power to become such. *That which is born of the flesh is flesh.*

They are not *born of the will of man.* No man can assure the conversion of the dearest relatives, or of the most beloved friends. No minister of the Gospel can choose or even conjecture beforehand the souls, to whom his ministry will be blessed. The wisest advice, the powerful exhortations of men, will not avail, unaccompanied by other influences, to form a single child of God. *They are not born of the will of man.*

Of what then are they born? Our text says, *they are born of God.* There is something new-born in them, created by God. Adoption is not here, as is frequently the case in the world, a simple affair of titles and honor; but it is accompanied by a real change in those who are adopted. It may happen in the world, if a good man adopts a wicked child, that this adoption, under the divine blessing, may change the character of the child; but that, which in human adoption may or may not occur, always takes place in the adoption of God. The child of God receives, not only the *name*, but the *nature* of his Father. Every man, who is adopted of God, receives at the same time a *new spirit*, and becomes a *new man*. What shall hinder it? God, who in the beginning created out of nothing the heavens and the earth, can, doubtless, create in man a *new heart*, and make of him a *new creature*. *According to His mercy he saved us by the washing of regeneration, and renewing of the Holy Ghost.*

And why, my dear hearers, do you not feel that, if you ought to belong to the family of God, you ought also to have the *spirit* which animates this family, the holiness which is its nature, the filial confidence and the love, which are its sweet privileges? If a man of high rank in society adopts a child, educated in rude and coarse manners, he requires that it assume those habits and manners, which belong to the new state of life, into which it is introduced. If a very learned man adopts a child who has languished in ignorance, he will give it the instruction necessary to its new situation. If, then, a change is necessary in order to a reception into the families of men, is it a strange thing that it should be required of one when he enters into the family of God?

No, there must likewise be a change, but a change greater than that of outward habits and human institutions! There must be a new heart. There must be a new nature. There must be a first birth to enter into the family of man. There must be a second birth to enter into the family of God. *Therefore, if any man be in Christ, he is a new creature. Old things are passed away, behold, all things are become new. If any man have not the spirit of Christ, he is none of His. Verily, verily, I say unto thee, except a man be born again he cannot see the kingdom of God.*

DUTY.

But, when once the child of man has become, by an adoption, full of grace, and, by a new birth, a *child of God*, what ought he to do? What are the errors which those ought to shun, who have entered into their Father's house? My brethren, we may all understand these things of which we speak; *the spirit of adoption whereby we cry Abba, Father*, may have been shed abroad in our hearts. But, subsequently, under the seduction of *the sin which doth so easily beset us*, we have exalted ourselves because of our privileges, we have gloried in ourselves, we have lived *barren and unfruitful in the knowledge of our Lord Jesus Christ ; we have not brought forth fruit unto God, and have not given diligence to make our calling and election sure.*

This is the last error I have to notice. What remedy is there for such an evil? This is it: consider the right to be called *children of God*, as a high *privilege*, as being more than treasures, more than the glory of the world, more than perishable crowns. But apply your heart constantly and specially, to ponder the *duties* that this right imposes on you, and seek from Him, who works in us *both to will and to do*, the power to fulfill them

And what is your duty, children of God? It is to become *like your Father. Be ye therefore followers of God, as dear children,* says the Scripture. The imitation of vicious men and the corrupt world is forbidden to the children of God; the imitation of the virtues of the just is on the contrary recommended; but the imitation of the most sublime of models, of the primitive and perfect goodness of the most holy God, is the most excellent which the child of God can propose to himself. It has been said: The essence of religion is to imitate Him, whom thou adorest. Oh, my brethren! what signifies all our petty adoration, all our outward worship, if we strive not to attain this glorious conformity? The first impulse on looking at a child, is to seek in it some features of its parent. Oh my soul! shall some features of my Father be sought for in vain, in thee? *Christ is the brightness of the glory of God, the express image of his person.* Form thyself, my soul, after this divine model. A child resembles its father not only when there is a similarity of features and demeanor, but still more when there is a likeness in the heart and in the dispositions of the soul. Above all, we should bear this resemblance to our Heavenly Father *in our hearts*. When the spirit of God governs us, it sweetens our character and our disposition. Let us learn of Christ who *is meek and lowly in heart;* let us walk in love as Christ also hath loved us, and be holy, *for I am holy,* saith the Lord. The son who resembles his father, increases in that resemblance as he advances in years; if we are children of God, let us grow from day to day in his likeness. "But we all with open face beholding as in a glass the glory of the Lord, are changed into the same image, from glory to glory, even as by the spirit of the Lord."

What is your duty, children of God? If you are children, you ought in all things *to do the will of your Father.* Fathers! do you not exact this of your children? There are often many wills in an earthly family, but in the celestial and eternal family there is but *one will.* All the blessed inhabitants of heaven perform with joy and with a single heart the will of their Father: you can some day be united to them, only by doing on *earth,* what they do *in heaven.* Let us then apply ourselves to do it well. Let us be honest in our bearing towards all men. Let us be orderly in everything that regards our temporal interests, yet without the love of riches, without avarice, without vain glory. Let us carefully discharge all the duties of our station. Let us be active, obliging, useful, ready to render favors, *looking not only on our own things, but also on the things of others.* Let us be content in the lot which our good Father has assigned to us, patient in trials, giving him thanks in all things. Let us use with eagerness and joy, the means of sanctification that he offers us, praying with perseverance, reading the Scriptures, and offering to Him in our houses and in the bosom of our families, spiritual sacrifices; for why should we despise these gifts of our Father? We know, alas! that here below, we cannot do perfectly the will of our Father, that we meet obstacles without and within, and that we make but feeble progress. Notwithstanding all this, it is upon earth that this work must be begun: while it is yet day that it should be pursued: *Not every one that saith unto me, Lord, Lord, shall enter into the kingdom of heaven, but he that doeth the will of my Father which is in heaven. He that doeth the will of God, abideth for ever.*

Finally, children of God! beloved of the Father! it is your duty to think of your Father and of the riches unto which he has made you heirs. In proportion as you approach the great day in which you will be put in possession of your incorruptible inheritance, have more elevated, more holy thoughts, and become more desirous of heavenly things. One frequently sees a great heir before the period of his majority arrives, think very little of what he is to become, and entertaining feelings very little in accordance with the grandeur of his future state. But as he increases in years, he becomes more grave, and acquires the consciousness of what he is. Children of God! heirs of eternity! the hour of your entire redemption draws nigher every day. In an instant the thread of your life may perhaps be broken; a few hours may perhaps find you before the throne of God. Your majority approaches: the period of your emancipation is not far distant. Think of these things! *Let your affections be set on things above. Let your conversation be in heaven, from whence also we look for the Saviour, the Lord*

Jesus Christ. "The children of God," said a faithful pastor of the fold of Christ, "have three birthdays. They are born at first of a natural birth; they weep, but their parents rejoice. Afterwards by conversion, they pass from a state of nature into the life of God; then they often weep bitterly, but the angels in heaven rejoice. Finally comes that which we call death, and this the primitive Christians regarded as the true birth of the children of God: there is still much weeping and grief, but when all is accomplished, the joys of eternal life begin, and there are no more tears for the children of God."

We have all partaken of the first birth: have we had a part in the second? Are we children of God or are we not? This is the solemn question that the Word calls us to make. If we are not, God grant, we may become so this day! May we receive Jesus Christ! May we believe in his name, that we may have Life! May we be born again!

To you, who, hearing these words, may have been convinced in your hearts that you are not yet children of the adoption, and who ask us, how may we become such, we reply: take courage and assurance in the grace and in the love of Christ. He seeks your salvation; for it is He, who has already given you the desire to be saved. Since he has given you the *will*, will he not give you the *fulfillment?* Will he not complete that which concerns you? Oh, do not lean upon an arm of flesh; separate yourself from every hope of salvation founded in yourself, and cast yourself into the arms of the pure grace of Christ. Fear not lest he reject you, for *He is come to seek and to save that which is lost*, and He has himself said; *Whosoever cometh unto me I will in no wise cast out; and every one whom my Father giveth me, cometh unto me.* Go then to Him in the silence of your closet, thinking how important it is that you should meet Him and should find Him before death overtakes you. Go to Him in prayer. He comes himself to you, opens his arms and says: *Come, I will give peace to your soul!*

Then, when the King of terrors presents himself to you, fear not, children of God! Death will be for you a glorious birth. A child of dust dies to earth: a child of glory is born for heaven. A child re-enters His Father's house, *to receive the blessing of the Most High and the righteousness of God his Saviour.* "Oh death! where is thy sting? Oh grave! where is thy victory?" "Lift up your heads, ye everlasting gates!" To Him who has become the Author of our eternal salvation, and who has given us the power to become sons of God, heirs of God and joint heirs with Jesus Christ, be rendered the praise, the honor, the glory for ever! Amen.

CONFESSION

OF THE

NAME OF CHRIST.

CONFESSION OF THE NAME OF CHRIST.

"Whosoever, therefore, shall confess me before men, him will I confess also before my Father which is in Heaven."—MATTHEW x. 32.

It is now three centuries since the princes of Germany, assembled in imperial Diet within the city of Augsburg, boldly and solemnly confessed Jesus Christ and His word, before the emperor, the princes of the empire who still remained under the dominion of Rome, and the legate of Rome; and in the presence, as it were, not only of all Germany, but of the whole world. That day was, is, and ever shall be, till time is no more, one of the brightest days of Christianity. That day, therefore, all the evangelical churches of Germany, and some even of other countries, responding to the call of their princes and pastors, celebrate, with offerings of thanksgiving and praise, its third glorious centenary.

"May the commemorative festival," says one noble voice, in assembling all who are subject to his laws, "of the presentation of this testimony to the Christian faith, which still exists, and must for ever continue as true and firm as it was three centuries ago, and in the spirit of which I write with all my heart, contribute to strengthen and animate true faith in the evangelical Church, to inspire all its members with unity of spirit, true piety, and Christian love." *

Will not you also remember, Protestant Christians of France? Have you not participated in the blessings of that glorious day? Were you not born—do you not repose—are you not combating this very hour under the spotless banner of the gospel of Christ, which those noble men planted on that memorable day in the presence of their enemies? Is it not your belief which was then confessed before the universe by those illustrious princes and pastors; and do you not march with unfurled colors to the same holy war in which they then took up the powerful weapons of the word of God?

But, alas! no. We walk not as then they walked! Ours are "the hands which hang down, and the feeble knees;" and the heroic courage which formed, in those blessed days, the glory of the Church of Christ, seems to have forsaken her. Therefore, especially ought we to celebrate that day; so that seeing ourselves, as it were, surrounded "with so great a cloud of witnesses

* Order of His Majesty, the King of Prussia

for the truth, of magnanimous confessors of the cross of Christ," who "through faith subdued kingdoms," and "waxed valiant in fight," we, ourselves, may "fight the good fight of faith." Standing fast in one spirit, they strove together in that great day for the faith of the gospel, in nothing terrified by their adversaries.

Followers of Christ! you are called to do likewise. The times in which you live are not less remarkable than those; and the same courage is indispensable. Need I tell you, my dear hearers, that there is no allusion here to combats waged with carnal weapons? Need I tell you that we have nothing to do with contests inspired by violence or hatred? Doubtless, this is unnecessary; and were it not so, the example which is about to be offered to you would sufficiently enlighten you on that point.

As the events which the Evangelical Church celebrates this day are not sufficiently known, our design is to retrace them, and afterwards draw from them such instruction as they offer.

An historical discourse is contrary to our usual mode of preaching, but all that serves to edification is suited to the Christian pulpit; and, if we require precedents and examples, Scripture furnishes us with abundant and illustrious ones. Was not the sermon of Stephen, the first martyr, an historical discourse? Are not most of the discourses of St. Paul, in the Acts, historical discourses? What the Holy Spirit has adjudged to be good, *we* may not estimate otherwise. "These things," say the Scriptures, "were written for our examples." O, Holy Spirit! who didst animate in those days the heroes of the faith, kindle, we beseech thee, the same flame in our hearts!

The Emperor Charles V., whose dominions were undoubtedly the most extensive that any prince ever ruled—embracing a part of Europe, America, and other quarters of the world—and who, as has been said, never saw the sun set on his vast empire, having, in 1530, subdued his enemies, resolved to examine into the religious reformation which had taken place in Germany, and to stifle the, so called, heresy.

He caused himself to be solemnly crowned on the 24th of February, his birth-day, by the Roman Pontiff, and then remained for some time with him in the same palace. The Emperor there promised the Pope to annihilate Protestantism. He even pledged himself, as it appears, to use, if necessary, violence and extreme measures—this, at least, was the request made of him.

At this news, some advised the evangelical princes to meet Charles, sword in hand, at the foot of the Alps, and to prevent him from entering Germany until he should grant them full religious liberty. But this was mere worldly counsel, and the great reformer, Luther, whom so many are pleased to represent as a man of violent temper, succeeded in silencing these rash counsellors; "For the weapons of our warfare are not carnal, but mighty through God."

The Emperor, however, finding it expedient to try first the efficacy of pacific means, convoked an imperial Diet at Augsburg, and invited all the princes and states of the empire to be present. Several, recollecting the violence of the enemies of the truth, which had been exhibited, among other occasions, at the Council of Constance, in the torture of the early reformers, entreated the Elector of Saxony, the head of the Protestants, not to go in person to Augsburg. But the Elector determined to accept the Emperor's invitation; he desired to confess Christ in the imperial presence. He invited Luther, Jonas, Pomeranus, and Melancthon, four of his greatest theologians, to draw up for this purpose a confession of the faith of the evangelical party; and, having ordered prayers for a successful result to be offered in all his states, he set out, the 3d of April, on his journey to Augsburg.

Many princes, nobles, counsellors, and theologians accompanied the Elector. The same spirit animated them all in this solemn path. Luther preached frequently during the journey, strengthening, by his exhortations, the faith of these noble champions of the gospel.

At Weimar, they all partook together of the communion; at Coburg, the Elector parted from Luther, and ordered him to remain there during the session of the Diet. A castle, crowning the summit of a mountain was his home; twelve knights guarded it night and day, but the servant of God had a more secure defence, even the Lord, whom he praises in a beautiful hymn composed at that time, beginning with these words—

"How strong a fortress is our God."

The Elector was the first of all the princes to arrive at Augsburg, to the great astonishment of the many who supposed he would fear to present himself. Soon, however, the electors, princes, deputies, bishops, and a multitude of soldiers, crowded into this city, filling it with all the pomp of worldly splendor. "Why do the heathen rage, and the people imagine a vain thing? The kings of the earth set themselves, and the rulers take counsel together, against the Lord, and against his anointed."

In the midst, however, of all the tumult which surrounded them, the zeal of the ministers of the Word of God who accompanied the Protestant princes, relaxed not; they preached the Word, and shunned not to declare the whole counsel of God. Their preaching produced the effect which ever follows the Word, when presented in any spot for the first time. The Word of God is the cause of discussion, said Luther. "This is a hard saying, who can hear it?" Their discourses were complained of, though they declared in them only the simple truth without controversy. Letters on the subject were addressed to the Emperor, who still remained at some distance from Augsburg. In reply, he signified his opinion that preaching should be suspended until the doctrine was examined and approved. The Elector consulted Luther, and the reformer gave a fresh instance of his moderation, advising that the preaching should be discontinued if the Emperor persisted in his demand; "For," said he, "the Emperor ought to be master in his own city." The Elector, however, could not bring himself to accede to the wishes expressed to him. "It would be contrary to my conscience," replied he to Charles, "to forbid the preaching of the Word of God; especially in these times, when we so greatly need all the consolation and assistance which it offers." "Unless thy law had been my delight, I should then have perished in my affliction," said another prince, the royal prophet David.

In the meantime, while Melancthon, the friend of Luther, assisted by other theologians, was incessantly occupied at Augsburg in drawing up the confession, which was to be presented to the Diet by the Protestant princes, Luther was suffering greatly at Coburg, both in body and mind, and had already chosen in his *desert* (as he called it) a place for his grave. The Elector sent him some remedies for his malady, and wrote to him at the same time in words full of affection. Luther replied by a letter admirably suited to console this Christian prince, amidst the formidable combat in which he was engaged with the enemies of the Gospel. "Truly, without cause," he says, "you have graciously condescended to be so anxious about me; three weeks have passed so quickly, that they seem to me scarcely to have been three days. But it is your Grace who is now in a painful and dangerous position. Oh, may our good God, who is in heaven, succor you, so that your heart may remain steadfast and patient in the grace which he has so richly manifested to us. It must be only for the love of God that you endure so many trials and dangers, since all these princes and furious enemies can find no other fault in you than that of loving the pure and living Word of God, and acknowledge that, for the rest, you are a gentle, pious, and faithful prince. And it is certainly a strong evidence that God loves you, since he not only gives you His holy Word freely to enjoy, but accounts you worthy also to endure in its cause so much enmity and odium. It is this which sheds such light and peace over the conscience; for to have God for one's friend is better than to have the love of the whole universe."

Strengthened by such words, the Elector awaited the Emperor's arrival, which was postponed time after time.

At length, on the fifteenth of June, every preparation was made for his solemn entrance. The greatest magnificence was displayed on this occasion, doubtless with the design to impress the Protestant princes with an exalted idea of the power and majesty of the Emperor.

The electors and princes, with an immense crowd, went forth to meet him. When they had arrived within fifty paces of the Emperor, they all dismounted. The Roman legate seized the moment to pronounce the papal benediction. The Emperor, and all his followers, received it kneeling; but the Elector, and all the Protestant princes, remained standing—proving thus, in the very outset, their faith and their firmness. They resumed their route. On arriving at the Bishop's palace, where the Emperor was to lodge, all were invited to enter, except the noble Elector of Saxony and his generous brother in the faith. They suffered with all joy the reproach of Christ, and soon gave a new proof of their immovable courage; for, King Ferdinand, the brother of Charles, having required them, in the name and presence of the Emperor, to suspend the preaching of the Gospel, and to participate in the procession of the Holy Sacrament, which was to take place the next day, the Margrave of Brandenburg, standing forth in the name of all, exclaimed, " Rather would I kneel to receive my death-blow at your Majesty's hand, than to deny my God and his Gospel."

The Emperor having repeated his demand, by a deputation, the same evening, the Margrave and the other princes repaired the next morning, at six o'clock, to the Emperor's palace, and replied —" We will not sanction, by our presence, such impious human traditions, utterly opposed as they are to the word of God and the commands of Christ. So far from it—with one voice, we declare that we desire to see these doctrines of men utterly banished from the Church, and the yet uncorrupted members of the body of Christ sheltered from this mortal poison. Let not your Majesty be offended if I decline to comply with your wishes, for it is written that it is better to obey God than man. Wherefore, for the sake of confessing the doctrine which I know to be the voice of the Son of God, immutable and eternal truth, I am ready to face all dangers, and even death itself, with which, as I hear, those are threatened who believe in this wholesome doctrine."

Glorious courage ! noble renunciation of the world and self !—would that it might inspire our hearts also ! " He that loveth his life shall lose it: and he that hateth his life in this world shall keep it unto life eternal."

The procession took place, but none of the evangelical princes engaged in it. They displayed the same firmness with regard to the Gospel. " The Word of God," they said, " cannot be bound; to arrest it—to fetter it, would be a sin against the Holy Ghost. Besides, being only poor sinful men," added these magnanimous princes, " we need the preaching of this divine word to enlighten and console us. We cannot do without the daily nourishment of our bodies—still less can we bear to be deprived of the word of God ; 'for man doth not live by bread only, but by every word that proceedeth out of the mouth of God.' " Thereupon, Charles the Fifth caused a herald to publish, with the sound of a trumpet, in the city of Augsburg, that no clergyman should preach there any more, unless by special permission from the Emperor. There was no alternative but to submit. " Thus," wrote the Elector of Saxony to Luther, " our Lord God is commanded to be silent in the imperial Diet of Augsburg." Happy will the Church be, when, from the greatest to the least, all shall know the value of the pure and faithful declaration of the gospel of our Lord Christ ! " More to be desired than gold—yea, than much fine gold : sweeter also than honey and the honey-comb."

At last, the Diet was formally opened on the 20th of June. The opening address unveiled the hostile designs of Charles. It was, as it were, a declaration of war. Then was it necessary to " be strong in the Lord, and in the power of his might—to be able to withstand in the evil day, and having done all, to stand." On leaving the assembly, the Elector of Saxony invited all the princes, his brethren in the faith, to assemble at his hotel, and there exhorted them to stand steadfast in a cause which was that of God himself, and of the faith as it is in Jesus. The next day, very early in the morning, he dismissed all his counsellors and servants, and this pious prince passed the whole day in his chamber, drawing courage and consolation from the Psalms of David, and supplicating God to grant him His assistance and His grace for the glory of His gospel.

The Protestants obtained permission to read their confession publicly on the 24th of June, but on that day other affairs occupied the Diet too long. Their confession was demanded in writing. They insisted that it should be read in full assembly. The Emperor acceded to their wishes, and all awaited with impatience the following day, which, to all appearance, was to decide the destiny of the invincible truth.

In the meantime, Luther, at Coburg, took to himself the whole armor of God; he praised God without ceasing—he read His holy word, and was filled with courage, hope and joy. Not a day passed in which he did not spend at least three hours in prayer. He conversed with God, his servant tells us, as with his father. Once he was overheard praying thus in his chamber: " I know that Thou art our good God and Father; therefore, I am sure that Thou wilt destroy the persecutors of Thy children. If Thou dost not, the danger concerns Thee as well as us. The whole affair is Thine; we have done but what we ought to have done; and Thou, oh, kind Father, wilt protect us." Had I been in the place of our friends," said he to this same faithful servant, " I would have replied to our adversaries, 'If your Emperor will not suffer the empire to be divided, neither will our Emperor (the Lord Almighty) suffer the name of God to be blasphemed. Glory, then, if you will, in your Emperor; we, too, will glory in ours. We shall see who will remain masters of the field.'"

The wise, and gentle, and apprehensive Melancthon, at Augsburg, shared not the assurance of Luther; he was full of fears and anguish. His friend, Camerarius, often surprised him in tears. Luther endeavored to inspire his friends with the same confidence and courage that nerved his own soul. In writing to Jonas, from his desert (for thus he dated all his letters from Coburg), he said: " It is philosophy that torments Philip (meaning Melancthon), and nothing else! for our cause is in the hands of Him who can say, with the power of majesty, 'Neither shall any man pluck them out of my hand.' There I desire to leave it. I have had many affairs in my own hands, and have lost them all; but all those that I have confided to Him, I still possess securely; for truly God is our refuge and strength. 'Who ever trusted in Him, and was confounded?' So Wisdom speaks, and elsewhere says, 'Thou, Lord, wilt not forsake those who put their trust in Thee.' Let us defy our adversaries, strong in the might of the Lord Jesus, for since He lives, ' we shall live also,' even in death; and He will protect and bless the widows and children of those who confess Him at the price of their lives. Since He reigneth, ' we shall also reign with Him.' Already we have begun to reign. Oh! if I were summoned to Augsburg, how quickly, by the grace of God, I would be there! May His presence attend thee!"

Still later, he wrote thus to Melancthon: " Grace and peace be given you in Christ! In Christ, I say, and not in the world. Amen. Why wilt thou thus unceasingly torment thyself? If our cause is not good, forsake it; but if it is, why will we make God a liar, when he tells us to be tranquil and ' of good cheer ?' ' Cast thy burden upon the Lord, and He shall sustain thee,' are His own words; and again, ' The Lord is nigh unto them that are of a broken heart.' The issue of these events torments you, because you cannot foresee it. But I tell you that if I could foresee it, I would not interfere in it—still less would I have begun it. God has placed our cause in a place which you will find neither in your philosophy nor in your rhetoric. That place is called *Faith*, and there are found all those things which we can neither see nor understand. He who wishes us to *see* and *handle* things, as you do, has for his reward only tears and anguish of heart. If Christ is not with us, where in all the universe will you find Him? If we are not the Church, where then is the Church? Is it the Duke (of Bavaria), Rome, or the Turk? If we have not the word of God, who has it? And, ' if God be for us, who can be against us?' If we fall, Christ falls with us, and Christ is the Sovereign of the World. He has said, ' Be of good cheer, I have overcome the world;' and I know that it certainly is so. Why, then, do we fear the conquered world, as if it were the conqueror? Oh! precious word of truth! One would go to seek it on one's knees, even to Rome or to Jerusalem; and, because we have it and may use it any moment, we lightly esteem it. That is wrong. I know it proceeds from the weakness of our faith. Let us pray, then, with the Apostles: ' Lord, increase our faith.' ' Though an host should encamp against me, my heart shall not fear.' ' No weapon that is formed against thee shall prosper—saith the Lord.' "

At length arrived the memorable 25th of June, 1530—that day of triumph for the Church. At three o'clock in the afternoon, three centuries ago, all the electors and representatives of the empire repaired to the palace where the Emperor lodged, in the chapel of which the Confession was to be read, in order to avoid the concourse of the people. The Emperor commanded that none but the princes and representatives should be present, but, notwithstanding his orders, the palace-court was soon filled to overflowing. The two chancellors of the Elector of Saxony, strengthened by the hand of the Lord, outstretched to bless and protect them, advanced into the centre of the chapel, bearing duplicates of the *Confession*, one in Latin and the other in German. The Elector represented that, as they were in Germany, he hoped his Majesty would grant permission to read the Confession in the language of the country. The Emperor consented. One of the Chancellors then pronounced a short discourse in the name of the Protestants; and, at its close, the other began to read the Confession. This he did in so loud and distinct a voice that not a word of it was lost by the immense crowd in the palace-yard. The reading lasted two hours. Heard amidst the deepest silence, it produced a most powerful effect. No one had expected to hear such words as then met their ears. We cannot now repeat them to you, my dear friends; there are one or two principal points, however, among them, which claim especial attention in our day, when so many have lost all recollection of what that faith is which was " once delivered to the saints."

" We confess and teach," said the evangelical princes of Germany, in the presence of this assembly of kings, who listened to them attentively, " that there is one God, and in this single and same divine Being, three persons, God the Father, God the Son, and God the Holy Spirit, a divine and eternal essence, infinite in wisdom, goodness, and power, the Creator and Preserver of all things visible and invisible.

" We confess and teach, that, since the fall of Adam, all men are born in sin—that is, from their birth, they are filled with evil desires and inclinations, and can have, by nature, no true piety, no true love of God, no true faith in God. We maintain that this inbred sin is an actual sin in them, and certainly condemns, and consigns to eternal death, those who are not born of water and of the Holy Ghost.

" We confess and teach that God the Son became man; that he closely united the two natures, human and divine, in one person, which is Christ—very God, and very man—and who, being truly born, crucified, dead, and buried, was a sacrifice, not only for the inbred sin of man, but also for all other sins, and thus satisfied divine justice.

" We confess and teach that this same Christ, having descended into hell, on the third day arose from the dead, ascended into Heaven, and sat down at the right hand of God, where He ever lives and reigns over all creatures; that he sanctifies, by the Holy Spirit, all who believe in Him—that He purifies, strengthens, and consoles them; gives them life, and all manner of graces and blessings, and protects and defends them against sin and the devil.

" We confess and teach, that men being born in sin, not obeying the law of God, and being incapable by nature of loving God, we cannot merit the pardon of our sins by our works or by any satisfaction, and are not justified before God on account of our works, but are justified for Christ's sake by grace, through faith, when our conscience is appeased by the promise of Christ, and believes that remission of sins is truly given unto us; that God is favorable to us, and gives us eternal life, for the sake of His Son, who reconciled God unto us by his death.

" We confess and teach that such faith must bring forth good fruits, and produce good works; that we ought to do all the good works which God has commanded from love to God, without, however, trusting on them for justification, for when we have done all things, we still must say, 'We are unprofitable servants.' "

"This," added the Chancellor of Saxony, before proceeding to the enumeration of the abuses of the Church of Rome, "this is the summary of the doctrine preached in our churches, for instruction and consolation, as well as for the sanctification of believers."

After having finished this memorable reading, the electoral chancellor went forward to place the two copies in the hands of the imperial secretary. But the Emperor, who had not once lost sight of them, extended his own hand, and received them. The Protestant representatives then returned thanks to Charles, to King Ferdinand, and all the other princes, for the attention with which they had listened to their memorial.

A solemn act was terminated. The adversaries, and even several of the bishops, were struck with the admirable exposition of the Christian faith which they had just heard; and who knows but that the impression which it made on Charles may have been revived in the convent of St. Just, and surrounded his dying bed with unspeakable consolations? Copies of the Confession were immediately sent to all the Courts of Europe, and thus a knowledge of the evangelical faith and the seeds of divine truth were scattered abroad even to the most distant lands.

As for the heroes of the faith who had so boldly confessed Christ and Him crucified, from this hour a new sentiment animated them, a new feeling filled their hearts. They had confessed Christ before men, and felt happy in the blessed assurance that He would "confess them before His Father who is in Heaven." "The spirit of glory and of God" rested upon them. They had conquered—they had put to flight all the hosts of the enemy; an everlasting joy was upon their heads. From that day, the destiny of the evangelical Church was secured, and the Lord proclaimed over it anew, "The gates of hell shall never prevail against thee."

Such was the confession of the name of Christ in the sixteenth century. Shall not this glorious name be confessed in the nineteenth with the same boldness and fidelity? Oh, my dear hearers, shall the adversaries of Jesus, who could not prevail in that day, triumph over us now, while Christians remain silent? This same voice of the son of God which the heroes of the faith heard, when, three centuries ago, they carried off the palm of faithfulness and victory, speaks still in our day to His people, and proclaims, "Whosoever shall confess me before men, him will I also confess before my Father who is in Heaven."

But can all now confess the name of Jesus Christ? In order to confess Him, we must know Him, and all know Him not. The day which we commemorate presents to us an assembly in which were two entirely distinct classes of men; and Jesus, in the discourse from which our text is taken, declares to us that there are those who confess and those who deny Him. A grand distinction, a wide separation exists then between men. This is the first lesson to be learned from the picture placed before our eyes to-day. This separation which existed in the times of the Apostles, existed also at the time of the Reformation, when on one side we see those who made this noble profession of the truth, and, on the other, those who wished to crush it—and it exists still. We would not dwell now on the distinction established by varied forms of discipline and worship, for God is no respecter of persons; but on that which is found in all nations and in every denomination, between those who reject the immutable truth which the Apostles and Reformers professed. It is an axiom universally recognized, and proclaimed by every philosopher, that, as there is good and evil, so there must be good and evil men, the just and the unjust, saints and sinners; or, as the Scriptures emphatically express it, "the children of God, and the children of the devil."

Christianity does but separate these two classes more widely, while declaring that they actually exist before God, and will receive their reward. Him that confesseth me, I will confess—and him that denieth me, I will deny. And what saith the Saviour of the world, who is the TRUTH, as to the relative number of each of the classes, which the word of God and the day we celebrate present to us: "Enter ye in at the strait gate, for wide is the gate and broad is the way that leadeth to destruction, and many there be that go in thereat: because strait is the gate and narrow is the way which leadeth unto life, and few there be that find it." These words were true three centuries ago at Augsburg, and they are yet true over all the earth. So, then, if there is now, as in the times of the Apostles and Reformers, a doctrine rejected by the world, by the lovers of the riches, honors, and pleasures of this life, a doctrine which the many refuse to embrace, which is considered a strange thing, and is abandoned to a despised few, it is a strong presumptive proof that this doctrine is the truth. And if there is a mode of life which is considered too strict, too severe, which cannot be assimilated to the customs and tastes of the multitude, but is ridiculed and given up to a few, it is probable evidence that it is the true one. And if there is a Christianity against which all take up arms, which is rejected by all who are wise in their own eyes, and seek glory from men, and not that which cometh from God only, it would be reasonable to conclude that this was the gospel.

If I go with the multitude, if I think as everybody thinks, if I do as all do—well may I tremble! for those are proofs that I am in the broad way which leadeth to destruction.

"There are few that be saved," says one prophet; "One of a city, and two of a family," says another. Oh, my soul! thou art with God, or thou art far away from Him! Thou art converted, or thou art not! Thou dost either confess Christ, or deny Him! One of these two sides thou hast taken, and which is it? Art thou in the narrow path of life? or art thou in the broad way to perdition? Oh, my soul! this is **worth** consideration. Examine thyself; prove thyself; seek, and ascertain clearly what thou art. "Examine yourselves, whether ye be in the faith."

Dear hearer! you, whose conscience witnesses, this hour, that you do not confess Christ—you do not know Him—you are still in the broad way—why will you not now be saved? Why will you not this day be transported into the path of life, where the "fellow citizens of the saints" and confessors of Jesus Christ are found? One thing alone prevents you, and that we declare to you; it is your want of faith in the powerful, the life-giving name of Jesus. So long as you do not believe in this name by which alone there is salvation, your sins separate between you and God, and it is impossible for you to confess a name which has no glory in your eyes. But believe the word; this is what it tells you (and in comparison with its teachings all else is darkness and error), "Christ who is the brightness of the glory of God, and the express image of his person, and upholding all things by the word of his power, *when He had by Himself purged our sins*, sat down on the right hand of the Majesty on high." Understand well what the word of God here declares to you. Christ has, not by an angel, or by any of the heavenly intelligences which He created, but by Himself, purged the sins of all who believe in Him; which is to say, He was purified, redeemed, and delivered them from their sins, as effectually as if they had never committed any. At the moment when Christ expired on the cross, being "made sin" for all, all the sins of his people, of every age and every nation, were blotted out. What! could you believe that the Lord Christ himself took the trouble to purify His people from their sins, and that there still remains something in them which defiles and hinders them from seeing God? To use an illustration within the reach of all—if a mother has bathed her child in pure water, and has said to him, "Go, now, you are clean," her child believes her and goes to his play; but if, to assure himself that it is so, he should go to behold his natural face in a glass, according to an expression of Scripture, he would be insulting his mother, by thus admitting the possibility that she could speak falsely. Well! Christ himself, Jehovah, Jesus, says to the believer, "Go, thou art made clean—I have purged thy sins by myself, I have made an end of all transgression; he that believeth on the Son hath everlasting life." And we will not believe this eternal word of truth! we would make our Lord a liar! Oh, my dear brother! do you truly believe that Jesus is the Saviour—do you believe it in your heart, and confess it with your mouth? Then do I declare to you from the everlasting gospel: "You are clean." All your sins are forgiven. You have found grace in the sight of God. "There is no more condemnation" for you, says St. Paul. "You, who in times past were not a people, are now the people of God; you, which had not obtained mercy, have now obtained mercy." Listen, then, to the voice of the Lord. He summons you to quit the standard of error, that you may range yourself under that of truth. Go forth from the camp of His adversaries, and enter into that of His children and friends. Unite yourself to the holy band of His prophets and apostles—to those illustrious princes and doctors, who, in the days we celebrate, confessed His name so nobly. There is not one of you who cannot do it, and that, too, this moment; the door is open, wide open, for all. Oh, why will you prefer the sullied and perishing banners of injustice and unbelief to the pure and immortal standard of Christ? Behold, "the fashion of this world passeth away;" already its grandeur is fading, and soon will be no more. What will then remain to you? "Wherefore, come out from among them, and be ye separate, saith the Lord, and touch not the unclean thing; and I will receive you, and will be a Father unto you, and ye shall be my sons and daughters, saith the Lord Almighty."

But, if you have ever known Christ, my beloved brethren, if you have enlisted in the army of the living God, what lessons the events of this day teach you! Soldiers of Christ! who fight under His eternal banner—all ye who know the Saviour—children of God—strangers, as the Apostle calls you, scattered throughout the world! listen to the words of a poor, despised Man, who had not where to lay His head, but whom you will soon recognize, by the majestic authority of His language, as your Lord and your God! "Whoever shall confess me before men, him will I also confess before my Father which is in Heaven."

The confession of the name of Christ is, perhaps, still more necessary and more difficult in our time than it was in that of the Reformers. There was then but one adversary, fanaticism, or superstition; but God, who willeth that all the enemies of His Church shall manifest themselves, that it may gain over them all a brilliant victory, has permitted a new and not less formidable adversary to spring forth from the age succeeding that glorious period: materialism or infidelity. Its deadly atmosphere is widely diffused, over the lowly as well as the lofty places of the earth, in the institutions of learning, in the workshop of industry, abroad in the country, at home in the fire-side circle; it has mingled its poison with the very springs from which the people have been accustomed to draw refreshment and life. Satan displays in our day the whole of his imposing army. With fanaticism as leader of his left wing, and scepticism of his right, he aims at full victory over the high places of the earth, and the establishment of an undisputed empire. Who shall withstand him but you, scattered children of God, who have this promise from the Captain of your salvation, "The God of peace shall bruise Satan under your feet shortly." Therefore, we summon you, on this anniversary of a great victory, to one more glorious still. "Be of good courage," we say to you, as did the leader of the armies of Israel on the eve of a battle with the children of Ammon, "and let us play the men for our people, and for the cities of our God; and the Lord do that which seemeth Him good."

"Does not all that is passing around you tend to animate your courage? What if the enemy of God does multiply his forces, so long as Christ, the Head of His Church, the Captain of your salvation, lifts up still higher his standard against them? The soldiers of the adversary fill the air with cries of extermination, but the masses which they had heaped up to crush Him against whom they wage war, recoil upon their own heads, and "the Lion of the tribe of Judah" crouches down in triumph over their ruins. Have you not countries under your own eyes, in which, a few years ago, no single tongue confessed the name of Jesus, now filled with His glory? "There shall be an handful of corn in the earth upon the top of the mountains; The fruit thereof shall shake like Lebanon, and they of the city shall flourish like grass of the earth."

The distant isles of the ocean are awaking, and stretch out their hands to you: there is a sound of life throughout the whole earth, as of some one collecting his hosts, and marshalling them for the battle.

> "Lord, in thy power's triumphal day,
> Thy willing people shall obey;
> And when thy rising beams they view,
> Shall all (redeemed from error's night),
> Appear more numerous and bright,
> Than crystal drops of morning dew."

Content, then, oh children of God! by confessing the name of Jesus. Oh, brothers, well beloved! after having been saved by the Lord Jesus, it is our duty, as well as our highest joy and greatest glory, to be faithful to Him and to confess Him openly before all men. Doubtless, you are not called to so solemn a confession as that which we celebrate to-day; it is not to a pitched battle that the trumpet summons you; but each one of you is to confess the Lord, in the peculiar circumstances amidst which God has placed him. There is an essential difference between the two periods that we are contemplating. At the time of the Reformation, a few great names seemed to fill the whole field of battle; but, in our day, the armies of the living God have no earthly commanders; names are lost in a happy obscurity. One Captain alone appears at our head—and he is Christ. Oh, my brethren! realize the responsibility which this imposes on you. You cannot now rely on a few illustrious leaders; every one must fight at his post, as if on him alone depended the victory. It is not perhaps by great battles, but by a thousand private combats, that the King of Zion purposes to establish His kingdom. To the hands of each of you he commits a portion of its destiny. "God hath chosen the weak things of the world to confound the things which are mighty; and base things of the world, and things which are despised, hath God chosen, yea, and things which are not, to bring to naught things that are, that no flesh should glory in His presence." If God has placed you among cottages, confess Him among cottages. If He has placed you in the dwellings of the rich of this world, confess Him in the midst of abundance and prosperity. If He has placed you in the sanctuary, lift up your voice there fearlessly. If He has given to you the seat of the mighty, confess Him even upon the steps of the throne, as did in those days the princes of the earth within the palaces of kings. Suffer no opportunity to escape you of faithfully confessing Christ in the heart of your family, in your daily life and conversation. "Sanctify the Lord God in your hearts; and be ready always to give an answer to every man that asketh you a reason of the hope that is in you, with meekness and fear." This is all that Christ asks of you, as one of his soldiers; this is your armor for the glorious combat. His name alone, without any human help, gains the most noble victories; His name alone overturns the empire of darkness, and scatters afar the powers of evil. "God hath given Him a name that is above every name; that at the name of Jesus every knee should bow, of things in heaven and things in earth, and things under the earth."

Disciples of Christ! the truths by which you are to gain the victory over the world, and bring many captive souls to God the Saviour, are the same that the Apostles confessed, the same that the Reformers and illustrious princes confessed so courageously three centuries ago. Men change, but "Jesus Christ is the same yesterday, to-day and for ever." The Christ whom Paul, Peter, and John confessed, the Christ whom Luther, Calvin, and Beza confessed, is He whom you are to confess. Say, as they did, "We are sinners, and in ourselves condemned." Say, as they did, "We are saved by grace alone, by Christ through faith." Say, with them, "Except a man be born again, he cannot see the kingdom of God." Bear witness with simplicity and gentleness to all the truths contained in the Word of God, for it is the testimony of God himself. This is confessing Jesus Christ. It is not a doctrine of yesterday—it is an eternal truth which you confess. Human doctrines have been ever changing, and scarcely any two of those floating around you are consistent with each other; but the truth of God is unalterable. You must expect that the Christ whom you confess will be still, as in ages past, to the world "an unknown God." Some around you will say, "These are old superannuated doctrines;" others, "These are strange novelties." Yes, it is an ever ancient truth which you proclaim, for it existed in the council of God before the creation of the world. And yet it is a truth ever new, for each time that it is manifested to the heart of the sinner, he begins to see things of which he had no conception before. Do not allow yourselves to be hindered by vain clamors such as these. Ever old, yet ever new, twice already has this same truth saved and renewed the world: it has proved itself, if I may so speak. Let us stand firm: a third time it will save it, and I hope for ever. "I know that my Redeemer liveth, and that He shall stand at the latter day upon the earth."

Forward, then, soldiers of the God of armies, and fight fearlessly! In our day, we must have resolution, strength, devotedness, and entire self-renunciation; for, if the weapons which the world uses are more delicate and subtle than in the times of the Apostles and Reformers, they are so much the more formidable. The coldness and contempt of those who surround us, sometimes even our dearest friends, consume the heart with a keener anguish than that inflicted by the flames of martyrdom; and human opinion, the fear or the love of the world, has made more infidels than the sword of the executioner.

Be strong, then, and steadfast, fixing your eyes on the certain triumph of the Lord's cause. The leader whom you follow has already conquered all His enemies—"He has spoiled principalities and powers, and made a show of them openly, triumphing over them, in the cross." The conversion and subjection of the whole world to Him is the subject of promise. "Yet have I set my King upon my holy hill of Zion. I will declare the decree: the Lord hath said unto me, Thou art my Son; this day have I begotten thee. Ask of me, and I shall give thee the heathen for thine inheritance, and the uttermost parts of the earth for thy possession." Already the King of the Universe is preparing all things for the accomplishment of this promise. Already do the Gentiles seek the root of Jesse, which shall stand for an ensign to the people. Already does the Lord "set His hand again the second time to recover the remnant of his people" Israel. Already, in the bosom of our fallen churches, the Lord Jehovah is everywhere forming for Himself a "willing people," and the "Bright and Morning Star" is rising to cast its holy beams over the earth long wearied of the dark and fearful night. Soldiers of Christ! fight, then, the fight of faith with cheerful courage, knowing that the work in which you are engaged is God's own, and that He has prepared a full and glorious triumph as its consummation before the foundations of the world. Let your hearts be filled with holy zeal. Be vigorous and energetic, "for God hath not 'given us the spirit of fear, but of power;" and "he that overcometh shall inherit all things, saith the Lord; but the fearful and unbelieving shall have their part in the lake which burneth with fire and brimstone: which is the second death." Believe, and hope, if need be, even against hope; it is by faith that we obtain promises, subdue kingdoms, or stop the mouths of lions.

Nevertheless, beloved friends, remember that the combat to which you are called is that of eternal charity. It is not by bitter zeal that you can promote the interests of the kingdom of God. What is the object you have in view? Is it that you may be instruments in God's hands for saving souls? And how can you save souls, if you do not love them? Remember how Christ, your leader, walked on earth, in whose footsteps you are to follow. He walked in love, and it is by love that he overcame the world and saved His people. "When he saw the multitudes" about Him, "He was moved with compassion on them, because they fainted, and were scattered abroad as sheep having no shepherd." He "went about doing good." Oh, if we had more love in our hearts, what noble victories we should gain over the prince of the world! How many souls would be saved from death! Let us, then, oh, my brethren, love souls as Jesus loved them! Let his spirit be our impulse and example. Never may we cry, "peace, peace, where there is no peace:" but let us beware, also, of all narrowness of mind—of all bitterness, contention, domineering, and condemnation of others. Let us beware of trusting to ourselves; but let us abound in confidence in the Lord Jesus, who is love. Let truth be, as it were, the body of the *athleta* of Christ, and charity his garment; for God hath not given us the spirit of fear, but of love.

And, finally, let us remember, in our confession of the name of Christ, that the war which we wage is that of sovereign wisdom. It is not by precipitancy, or natural zeal, that we can advance the Lord's kingdom, as " novices" may fancy, " being lifted up with pride," and therefore, says the Apostle, they may not bear the office of bishop in the Church of Christ. What an example of wisdom our illustrious predecessors of three centuries past, have given us. Let us distrust ourselves. Whenever we go forward in our own strength, our own zeal, or our own wisdom, we injure the cause of Christ. Before taking the first step, always ask counsel of God. Be willing to wait, for this is a lesson which every servant of God must learn. Have a sound judgment in all things; and endeavor to choose always the noblest end, and the most prudent and proper means for attaining it. " Let us not fall into the condemnation of the devil" (or calumniator). Let us have " the wisdom that is from above," which is not " earthly, sensual, devilish," but " is first pure, then peaceable, gentle, and easy to be entreated, full of mercy and good fruits, without partiality and without hypocrisy ;" for again, as says the Apostle of the Gentiles, " God hath not given us the spirit of fear, but of a sound mind."

Ministers of the word of God! you who are, in the strongest sense, my brethren, to you and to myself I would first of all address the word of exhortation. May we be found faithful in this combat of eternal love, to which we are called! Oh, my brethren! let us pray, much for ourselves, and much for one another. Let us be girt about with truth and charity. Let us " hold fast the form of sound words," which we have heard. Let us proclaim fearlessly the Divine testimony, declaring the whole counsel of God with clearness and fidelity ;. " for," saith the Scripture, " if the trumpet give an uncertain sound, who shall prepare himself to the battle ?" Watchmen of Zion! let us blow the trumpet when we see the sword coming, that the people may be warned, and that the sword take not away their life.

Pastors of the Lord's flock! let us lead them to feed on the plant of renown which has been raised up for them, that they be no more consumed with hunger in the land. " Let us reprove, rebuke, exhort with all long-suffering and doctrine," for, in doing this, we shall save both ourselves and them that hear us.

Elders of our churches! all you, who are called to labor with us—and you, earth's mighty ones! follow the example of these illustrious princes whose fidelity and glory have been this day recalled to you. Learn from them that the doctrine of the truth is not the exclusive property of the ministers of the sanctuary, but that it belongs to you as well as to them, and that you, as we,

CONFESSION OF THE NAME OF CHRIST. 95

are called to be its defenders. " Be not (ye), therefore, ashamed of the testimony of our Lord," but confess Him, as did this assemblage of princes, before the world. And, as they were the strong support of the ministers of the Word, grant us also, i every occasion, your love, your sympathy, and your prayers. one in defence of the doctrine of the truths which God has e. trusted to our churches. Value the gift of a faithful minister as a very precious privilege. "We beseech you, brethren," says St. Paul, " to know them which labor among you, and are over you in the Lord, and admonish you, and to esteem them very highly in love, for their works' sake. And be at peace among yourselves."

And ye all, disciples of Christ, of every age, sex, and condition, walk worthy of the vocation wherewith ye are called! Confess Christ in your words, with all humility and modesty; but, above all, confess Him in your life. Comfort the feeble-minded, support the weak, be patient toward all men. If thine enemy hunger, feed him; if he thirst, give him drink. Ever follow that which is good, both among yourselves and to all men. Rejoice evermore, showing forth thus the praises of Him who hath called you out of darkness into His marvellous light; and let your light so shine before men, that they may see your good works, and glorify your Father which is in heaven

The day shall come when the Lord's promise to you shall be gloriously fulfilled. He will come, with all His holy angels, and then will He say unto you, " Come, my brother, my sister, fear not; thou hast confessed me (on earth) before men, now will I confess thee before my Father which is in heaven. Oh, my Father! he is mine—I have redeemed him—he is my friend, my brother. He has made a covenant with me by sacrifice. He has confessed me amidst the scorn of the world; now do I confess him before Thy glory. Give unto him a white stone, and write upon him the name of my God. Ye everlasting doors, give way! Enter thou into the joy of thy Lord!"

9

is
and
fear

CHRISTIANITY

CARRIED TO THE

NATIONS OF THE EARTH,

OR

THE DUTY OF CHRISTIAN NATIONS.

TRANSLATED BY M. M. BACKUS.

TO THE COMMITTEE

OF THE

AUXILIARY SOCIETY OF BRUSSELS

For the Propagation of Christianity in the two Indies.

THE AUTHOR.

Brussels, March, 1830.

A MANUSCRIPT copy of this discourse falling into the hands of a friend of missions in Holland, he translated it by the author's consent, and published it in the Dutch language.* The author did not at that time think of publishing it in French. The work that it recommends having been established in a more regular manner at Brussels, by the formation of a Society for the propagation of Christianity in the two Indies, auxiliary to the two Evangelical Missionary Societies, established, the one at the Hague, the other at Rotterdam, the author thought that this discourse might perhaps contribute to enlighten the friends of Christianity and of humanity, concerning the end proposed by the new Society; and it is consequently published in the language in which it was pronounced. That the Lord may make use of it, whether in our own or foreign countries, to kindle the zeal of some in favor of the best work which man can undertake, is the wish and prayer of his heart. The facts alluded to in this discourse, are drawn from the most authentic sources; many have been extracted from the *Letters upon India*, by the missionary Ward, which have recently been translated into French. Some passages in this sermon were not pronounced in the pulpit, for fear of occupying a longer time than is usually accorded to the preacher.

* *Het Nut van Evangelische Zendelingen ouder de Heidenen, en onze Verpligting om deselve he Bevorderen*, in octavo, Amsterdam, by Saaks, 1828, and more recently in 12mo. by the same publisher, under the title of *Predikt het Evangelium allen Creaturen*.

CHRISTIANITY AND FOREIGN MISSIONS.

A DISCOURSE DELIVERED AT BRUSSELS.

"And Jesus said unto them: Go ye into all the world, and preach the Gospel to every creature."—MARK xvi. 15.

THE work of publishing the Gospel among all the families of the earth, is the greatest and most glorious work which has ever been or ever will be undertaken. While many deep shadows still obscure the tableau of Christian society, and while the reign of selfishness is still far from being over among men, yet we must acknowledge that the present is distinguished for its love of public good and for its humanity. Numerous associations have been formed in different countries, for objects of general utility. But all the associations, all the enterprises of the age, are but trifles in comparison with the magnificent undertaking of carrying the Gospel to every creature. The friend of humanity, before engaging in this, can make but feeble efforts; but when he enters upon this chief work, he pays the debt he owes to his species, and has the glory of bearing in his hand one of the stones destined to raise the temple of the living God in the world.

Is there anything called great among men, which the work of publishing the Gospel to every creature does not infinitely surpass? Is it an association intended to release some unhappy beings who are pining away in dungeons, or under the pressure of some other misery? That were a great work; but the work of which I speak announces to a captive world *the opening of the prison and the oil of joy for mourning.* Is it a conquest, having for its end the deliverance of a people from the oppressors who desolate them, and their restoration to their legitimate sovereign? This were indeed a noble task; but the work of which I speak is intent on conquering *all the nations of the earth* to their true and eternal King. Is it the giving to a whole people a legislation which will establish it in peace and prosperity? But the work of which I speak bears to all nations the charter of the human race, the fundamental law of its happiness, a celestial legislation which alone can give them *righteousness* and *peace*. The work of Evangelical Missions is the most stupendous of all the works of benevolence in which men can engage, for it embraces the whole world; it is the noblest, for the benefit which it confers is, of all those which man can bear to man, the most in harmony with the immortal nature of which our bodies are but the mortal tabernacles; the most generous, since those to whom we send such gifts are unknown to us, differing from us in manners, in color, in language; who can never testify their gratitude in person, whom we shall never see but before the eternal throne, whither the preaching of the Gospel may have brought them. Why does this restless age, which is so busy in a thousand different ways, take so small a part in this labor of love? Why, when they lavish money in so many useless expenses, do they reserve nothing to assist those who would carry to Pagan nations the salvation of the world? Some object that this work is not necessary; we will reply by showing the magnitude of the *evil*. Others pretend that they do not know what remedy to apply to so great misery; we will present to them the *means*, ordained of God from the beginning of time. Others again object that they have no hope of success in this work; and we will show them the *success* with which it has already been crowned.

The Saviour, when he pronounced the words of our text, was standing on the Mount of Olives, after his resurrection from the dead. Beneath him was the earth which he had saved; around him his weeping disciples, above him heaven and its glory, of which he was about to take possession in the name of his redeemed. At this solemn moment, the last he was to spend on earth, he embraced, in the glance of his love, the world and the millions of people and generations whose eternal chains he had come to break, and giving to his disciples his last will, he established them perpetual executors of his love: "*Go ye into* ALL *the world, and preach the Gospel to* EVERY *creature!*"

Lord! grant us hearts attentive and obedient to thy Word, to meditate upon its holy obligations! Amen.

THE EVIL.

And first, some say: "It is not necessary to send missionaries to Christian nations; they are as well off as we are, and are likewise just as happy. Would to God we had their innocence, their sweet and gentle manners!"

It is not necessary! It is impossible that it is *a Christian* who utters these words. Judge of this: the population of our earth is estimated at about ten hundred millions, of whom only two hundred millions are Christians; one hundred millions are Mahometans; and nearly seven hundred millions are Pagans. Thus, every thirty years, eight hundred millions of souls, immortal as our own, leave the earth without having known the true God, He who has said: *I am the way, the truth, and the life; no man cometh unto the Father but by me.* Thirty years again roll round, and eight hundred millions more have followed the former to the grave—and thus generations on generations, millions descend sadly to the sepulchre, in the midst of a dark and lamentable night. What truly Christian soul, after this solemn reflection, can inquire: "Is it necessary?"

But the state of the unchristianized world is such, that the friend of humanity, whatever may be his faith, ought to be the friend of the work which I commend. Everywhere, in the absence of Christianity, the earth is filled with barbarism, with ignorance, with horrid superstitions; for Christianity is not only the salvation of individual souls, it is also the strength and prosperity of nations. Among all these nations, is there one of which a false philosophy would undertake the defence? Do they speak to us, for example, of China? We will reply by showing them nine thousand children annually exposed, in the capital of this empire, to the most sorrowful death. Would they exalt Islamism, which unites the belief in the unity of God and the immortality of the soul, which they imagine sufficient for man? We will show Islamism *extended like a corpse, for several centuries*, over the finest regions of the earth, changing, by its impure breath, these countries to a desert, and starting from its slumber only to scatter furiously around it fire and sword, and to spill in torrents the ancient and generous blood of the defenders of the Cross.

No, my brethren, *mild* and *simple* manners are not found among Pagans!

Let us make the tour of the world, and see what is the condition of the people among whom the evangelical missionaries labor, in whose behalf we to-day implore your alms and prayers. Do not fail to discover the horrors which appeal to your charity.

What do we behold, if, leaving Europe, we first pass along the western shores of Africa, from whence are transported, with all their superstitions and terrors, those poor West Indian slaves, to whom our missionaries bear the law of true liberty? We shall see negro kings celebrating cruel feasts, which they crown by the massacre of their prisoners of war and of their own subjects. A king dies at Akim: they break the limbs of three hundred and thirty-six of the females of his harem, then bury them alive. Do ambassadors desire an audience of these kings? they must approach the throne by filing across long rows of still reeking human heads; such is their method of displaying their magnificence, and of making their glory to shine forth. A king dies in the kingdom of Ashantee, on the Gold Coast: his *orams*, or servants, to the number of one hundred, are immolated on his tomb, and a great number of his wives submit to the same fate. The reigning king has recently lost his mother, and he testifies his filial grief and mourning by three thousand human sacrifices, to which each of the large towns are obliged to contribute a hundred victims, and the smaller ones ten; and, in these unhappy countries, the manners of the subjects are always in keeping with the manners of their rulers! The Bushmen, of South Africa, live only by murder and robbery, and deliver themselves to the commission of the most horrible crimes. There, the mother, the tender mother herself, forgets her child, and, like the beast, forsakes it. In moving about from place to place, these people frequently abandon, in the desert which they quit, their aged parents and relations: placing near them a little food and some shells filled with water, they salute them—and soon these unhappy beings die of hunger, or become the prey of ferocious beasts. I would ask you now, my brethren, is it *necessary* to go to the assistance of beings like ourselves, who cover with horror this earth, which is our common patrimony?

But leaving Africa, let us visit those countries of Asia in which some of our missionaries are found. What a spectacle is offered to us in *India*, the *mother of civilisation,* as she is frequently called! What ideas have its inhabitants of the living and true God? We see them bowing down before three hundred and thirty millions of idols. In the multitude of this army of idols, they know not in whom they ought to trust, whom they should obey. They kneel now before monkeys, and now before serpents, and again before vain shadows. Soon they fall down before the wives and daughters of their cruel and licentious priests, adoring them with abominable ceremonies, not fit to be described by a Christian tongue. Finally, when they have nothing else, they make divinities of their holy books, and prostrate themselves before their *vedas* and their *shasters;* "Everything is a God for them, but God himself!" Wretched people! your gods are monsters, your priests seducers, your holy writings codes of indecency, of fraud, of vengeance, of murder, your heaven itself an infamous house of prostitution!

And how do they wash away their sins? At the close of the day, numerous bands precipitate themselves into the river Ganges, persuaded that its waves will purify from all evil; while others, to obtain the pardon of their sins, occupy themselves day and night for years, in repeating the names of their protecting deities. But in the midst of all these useless names, there is not heard THAT ONLY NAME *given under heaven whereby men can be saved!*

But perhaps the domestic sanctuary will offer more inviting scenes to our hearts? No, and this is a solemn truth: the domestic circle, which gives to life all its charms, does not exist aside from Christianity. Mahometans, Pagans, are alike ignorant of it; and the most unnatural sentiments supply its place. Full one half of the human race, that which God created to be a companion of man, is degraded to the condition of slaves, and even lower still.

Among many of those nations, the birth of a daughter is a family misfortune. Among one of the tribes of India, the *Rajapoos,* girls are put to death by their fathers soon after their birth. On one occasion, a father, less barbarous than his fellows, could not resolve to destroy his tender infant; he hid her in a house, where she grew up until the age of ten or twelve years, which is usually that of marriage. At length, on a festival day, he brought her forth. But the sight of a girl was a sight so strange in the house of a Rajapoo, that no father would take the unhappy child as a wife for his son. The distracted father, pursued, terrified by the threats of his friends, and by the shame which oppressed his house, fell into despair, and beside himself, he went mad, and raising his hand against his young and innocent daughter, he destroyed her.

But if in other tribes life is allowed to the young females, their fate is still no better: they drag out their early years in the most languishing idleness, in the most barbarous ignorance. Disquieted by the most abject superstitions, they frequently wander forth on the longest pilgrimages. One day, sixteen young girls, with as many priests, embarked on the Ganges. Each of the victims bore a vase, fastened to her shoulder. Soon, leaning upon the hand of one of these cruel pontiffs, they cast themselves one after the other into the river, and floated, until the vases filling with water, plunged and kept them firm beneath the rolling flood! They believed they had taken the direct road to heaven; the priests gloated over the frightful spectacle; the multitudes on the shore shouted forth their plaudits, and not a single eye wept for the wretched victims! Oh Thou, who, in ascending Golgotha, wept over *the daughters of Jerusalem*, Thou at least, beholdest from thy seat in heaven these frightful miseries, and anew Thou soundest in our ears the words, " Go ye into all the world and preach the Gospel to every creature."

But let us consider a little further the lives of this half of the human race, the most interesting because the most dependant. Does a Hindoo die, a funeral pile is erected to consume his body ; his widow is dragged thither bound ; her eldest son approaches to kindle it with a parricidal hand! Sometimes these unhappy women break their bands, escape from the burning scaffold, and cast themselves into the river, to extinguish their funeral garment already in flames: but the barbarous priests bring them back, and the child replenishes the fire which is to consume her upon whose breast he has been borne!

Are there some castes who bury their dead, in place of burning them? The fate of these victims is still more frightful! The widow is conducted with great ceremonies to the tomb, and seated in the trench, holding the body of her husband in her arms! The relatives and children begin to throw slowly upon her the earth which is to cover her; she remains immoveable; the earth is gradually heaped up around her body ; soon it reaches her waist and neck, her lips; suddenly they cast a great heap upon her head—the earth chokes her—her children rush upon her and tread her under their feet, and the poor mother soon breathes her last!*

See, my brethren, what is still occurring ; in the single province of Bengal two hundred widows annually suffer this dreadful fate. Mothers and daughters of Christian Europe ! do you not hear the cries of your sisters issuing from the flames, and the stifled sighs uttered by these living corpses from the depths of their tombs?

If such is the fate of the wives, what is that which they frequently cause their children to experience ? Alas ! the spirit of darkness in these unhappy regions exercises his empire over all

---

* The English government has at length enacted a law against these sacrifices, but it can be enforced only in that part of Bengal where there are English troops. In the remainder of India, especially in the provinces submitting to tributary princes, the propagation of Christianity alone can abolish the abominable superstition.

sexes, all ages, all estates. A mother has perhaps consecrated, even before its birth, her child to some cruel divinity; when it has attained its third year she leads it to the border of the river, and exciting it by her gestures to enter, in order to bathe its delicate limbs, she leads it by the hand, until reaching a certain depth, the river washes and bears it away. Then, seating herself upon the bank, the mother listens to its plaintive cries, and contemplates its last struggles with death. Others cast their infants to ferocious crocodiles, and look on with astonishment as these river monsters dispute their prey until one of them has swallowed it up! Children, poor little children! you to whom the Saviour of the world has said with so much tenderness, *Suffer them to come unto me, and forbid them not, for of such is the kingdom of heaven:* you whom he took in his arms and blessed, placing his sacred hands upon your head, this is not the fate reserved for you by the gospel of Jesus Christ!

And what is the destiny of the old man? As the end of his days approach, he is dragged to the banks of the Ganges, or some other sacred river. They constrain him to drink abundantly of its purifying water; they cover his breast, his forehead, his arms, with the slime of the river, they fill with it his mouth, his eyes, and his ears, and before his soul has left his body, they cast it into the homicidal waters. So dies the old idolator. How different from the death of that Simeon, who desired to depart in peace, since his eyes had seen the salvation of God!

In what manner do these people adore their horrible divinities? Let us come and assist at the annual festival of Muha Deo (the great god). Here, some, after plunging iron hooks into their loins— cause themselves to be swung in the air, by means of cords attached to high see-saws; there, others run upon points of sharp iron, and give themselves mortal wounds with a knife, and all end the festival by dancing with naked feet on burning coals! Or, come to the festival of Juggernaut: while a great number of worshippers with difficulty drag along the immense car of the horrible idol, multitudes cast themselves in the road over which the murderous car is to pass, and being crushed by its heavy wheels; sacrifice their lives in the midst of dreadful torments! Word of the Lord! resound throughout those distant countries, and say to those unhappy nations: *God is a spirit, and those that worship him, must worship him in spirit and in truth!*

But let us approach the vast Archipelago of Lower India, to which our missionaries are especially destined! Alas! we shall but encounter the same spectacle, stained, perhaps, with still more barbarism and ferocity. The god adored by a large portion of the inhabitants of Java, is the crocodile. The neighboring islanders regard it as their father, and the stem of their species. In the Moluccas the inhabitants appear to recognize a superior divinity, but instead of serving him, they worship the devil. Their manners are grossly corrupt; adultery and debauchery are not regarded as sins; idle, false, treacherous, liars, abandoned to all vices, they are terrible when offended, and revenge themselves only by murder.

In the Island of Borneo, whose immense extent we possess, while possessing but a slight knowledge of it, there are found tribes in which no man can marry without having committed two or three assassinations. These islanders place themselves at the sides of the highways, covering themselves with branches, skilfully disposed, and remaining as motionless as if fastened by deep roots in the earth; the victim who thinks he sees only a grateful shade, approaches without distrust, and at the instant he passes by, these murderous trees spring up, cast themselves upon their prey and destroy him?

In the mountains of Java are cannibals, who ascribe a principle of love, as they say, to horrors which human language can scarcely relate. Is one of their friends sick? They call a soothsayer. Does he announce death? They kill the sick man: coolly cut his body in pieces; then the relatives divide it among themselves, and devour this flesh!

Oh, horrible scenes presented by the idolatrous world! oh, darkness, which covers the people, upon whom the *Star in the East* has not yet arisen! How lovely thou art, religion of Jesus, and how our affrighted eyes have need of repose in thy mild light! What, evangelical Christians! Do you think that it is not *necessary*? that it is not your duty to come, each according to your means, to the relief of so much misery? Is this a state of *innocence*? Are these *sweet* and *gentle* manners? Is not the evil sufficiently *great*, or shall it become still worse before our charity can move? Are better days never to rise upon the earth? Must darkness, superstition, cruelty, brutishness despair, continue to cover, from age to age, the greatest part of the globe we inhabit? It is easy, in the midst of all the charities, of all the tranquillities of life, to say: *it is not necessary.* But, do you not hear the voice of these victims which, from those distant regions, resounds even to you? If you send away this voice without listening to it, I declare to you, that it will go to accuse you before the throne of God! Yes, all these nations, who are sitting in the horrors of superstition, with their horrible attendants, arise and present themselves before you, as that man of Macedonia, who appeared in a dream to Paul at Troas; and, surrounded by all their griefs, they beg you, they address to you, as did that Macedonian, the urgent prayer: Come over and help us.

THE MEANS.

"It is true," perhaps you may now say, my dear hearers; "the wants of these people are pressing, but what remedy can be offered to so great misery? What means in our possession sufficiently powerful to change the state of nations, and the face of the earth?"

Yes, the evil is great, but the remedy is greater still. The evil has arisen from the power of darkness, who has involved our race in his rebellion; but the remedy emanates from the sovereign

God, who created the heavens and the earth. It is not man who comes to the help of man; it is God who advances into this arena, wherein such terrible battles are to take place. You are right, all the philosophy of man could effect nothing. Socrates and Plato, with their admirable reason, and by the power of their eloquence, have not converted a single village from its vain idols to the God whom they knew. He who causes herbs, for the healing of our bodies, to spring up in the fields, cannot forget the malady of our immortal souls.

THE PREACHING OF THE GOSPEL OF JESUS CHRIST AMONG ALL NATIONS, preceded, accompanied and followed by those things, which it usually draws with it, the founding of numerous schools, the propagation of evangelical knowledge, light and virtues, the introduction of a peaceful, active, social—in a word, of a Christian domestic life; such are the MEANS that God has proposed, and for the execution of which He has given to the world a Saviour; He has *planted*, as the Scriptures express it, *on either side of the river* of human generations, *a tree of life, whose leaves are for the healing of the nations.*

It is many ages since God began to dispose everything for the accomplishment of this work. He has gone before us, if we may so express ourselves, and nations no longer exist, until he has already with a wise hand laid deep the foundations of their salvation.

About two thousand years before the great epoch, which in giving a Redeemer to man, has made *all things new* here below, the sciences and arts began to spring up among the people, ideas became more distinct, and they began to classify them under certain heads; each nation was occupied in cultivating the wisdom, the industry that Providence seemed to have assigned for its part. The sciences appear to have found in Egypt and Babylon the soil favorable to their development: the arts in Greece; commerce in Phenicia. The knowledge of God reclaimed his people. It was necessary that religion which, infinitely more than anything else, contributes to the welfare of man, should have a proper soil in which to deposit its seeds, in which it might increase, and in time might spread its branches over the face of the earth. What it thus required was granted it. God chose and called from among the nations a man named *Abraham* to be the father of the people from whom should one day spring the founder of his everlasting kingdom. *In thee shall* ALL FAMILIES *of the earth be blessed.* Such was the motive of the alliance formed with the son of Terah. Isaac, Israel, the twelve patriarchs, succeeded Abraham. The Israelites became a powerful nation, but neither Abraham nor Israel thought of encompassing the whole earth, nor of converting *the families of the earth.* It was not then for immediate action that God called Abraham; he must have had in view some future institution, which preparing itself in silence, should, at the appointed time, pour out upon the nations the greatness of its benefits. Gradually there was found in the distant future, an image at first indistinct, upon which the eyes of the Patriarchs were fastened with respect, to which each passing century added some new feature, which promised to humanity a mysterious benefactor charged with fulfilling the promises of eternal love. Jacob on his death-bed had a glimpse of it, and saluting it by the name of *Shiloh*, explained that unto him should the GATHERING OF THE PEOPLE BE!

David, seizing his sacred harp, begins with a song of grief. He sees a just one persecuted. He speaks even of the crucifixion. His garments are parted among his enemies. They cast lots upon his vesture. But he ends in a voice of praise and glory, announcing a reign in which ALL THE ENDS OF THE WORLD, ALL THE HUNDREDS OF THE NATIONS, SHALL TURN UNTO THE LORD, *and shall worship before him* whose ineffable griefs he beheld. Isaiah, at the very period when the ten tribes were already led away into captivity, when the glory of Judah was darkened, when her ruin, the destruction of the city and of the temple, her exile, her dispersion and her great shame, were already prepared, announced to her the most brilliant destinies: he saw in the future the tender plant clothed in a dignity altogether new; the Lord gave him for A LIGHT TO THE GENTILES, *to be his salvation* UNTO THE END OF THE EARTH! Arise, he exclaimed to the people of God, *for the glory of the Lord is risen upon thee.*

Daniel, in the bosom of the court of Babylon, saw, in the future, the fall of all the power and splendor which surrounded him, and discovered four kingdoms which should succeed it, and then give place to *another kingdom*, created by the *King of Heaven*, and established by the *Son of Man*, whose kingdom is an everlasting kingdom, and all dominions shall serve and obey him. This sound of deliverance, of salvation for ALL NATIONS, pervades all our revelations like the distant rolling of thunder, whose sound increases in proportion as it approaches; and when the appointed time arrived—when the earth gave birth to her Saviour—when the *desire of the nations* appeared, the aged Simeon exclaimed, " *Mine eyes have seen thy salvation, which thou hast prepared before the face of* ALL PEOPLE." The son of Zacharias made the desert resound with the words—ALL FLESH *shall see the salvation of God.* The son of Abraham, and of David himself, whose glance pierced futurity, made to the earth, divided between a thousand superstitions, this touching promise: *There shall be one fold and one shepherd.* And finally, at the moment of his ascension, he left to his disciples the testament contained in our text, upon which the words we have quoted are but the commentary: *Go unto* ALL THE WORLD *and preach the gospel to* EVERY CREATURE.

Do you believe, my dear hearers, that a method, prepared so many ages beforehand—prepared by God himself, shall not be sufficiently powerful to attain the end for which it was designed? A work decreed in the *counsels* of the Father, for which he has formed a people to himself, has raised up prophets, has filled Israel from age to age with so many mighty promises, shall this be a work for which there is no method of accomplishment? The blessing announced four thousand years ago to the sons of Terah, on the plains of Haran, shall it not now spread over *all the earth?* That which man designs, so far as he has strength, he executes; shall it not be the same with God? When he has gone forward, shall he turn back; after having spoken, shall he keep silence? No; THE TRUTH did not *lie* unto the Patriarchs; THE FAITHFUL does not now repent of that which he then promised; *God is not a man, that he should lie; neither the Son of Man, that he should repent;* HATH HE SAID, AND SHALL HE NOT DO IT?

But, do you still ask, is this way decreed of God so many ages in advance? is it really appropriate for the end it was designed to accomplish, and capable of causing the abominations of the people to disappear? Since it is God who established it, God who knows the heart of man, can we doubt it? But let us investigate and admire how admirable and proper the means are to destroy even the principle of idolatry, and thus to pull up the tree by its roots. From whence has idolatry arisen? Man bears within him a conscience: this holy voice cries out that he is guilty. Dreading an angry Judge, he seeks everywhere for some support, for some intercessor. The angels, the stars, imaginary beings, men, shall I say, beasts, trees, stones? become to him so many secondary divinities, so many mediators, to whom he addresses himself to be reconciled with the supreme God, and before whom, alas! the same terrors soon come to assail him. *Your iniquities have separated between you and your God.* What shall be done to ruin from their foundations all these systems of polytheism, immensely different, but all having the same origin?

Fear has given birth to idols; love would re-establish the throne of God in the heart. It is necessary that this consoling voice should penetrate the depths of the heart of man: "God has pardoned thee! God has loved thee!" This voice has been heard! It sounded eighteen hundred years ago on Calvary; for eighteen hundred years it has resounded in the world; and it is now borne to all the inhabitants of the universe. At the moment when the Son of God, bearing our griefs, expiated our sins, satisfied eternal justice, reconciled the world unto his Father, uttered a loud cry upon Golgotha, fulfilled all things, and bowed his divine head, this astonishing mystery was made known to man— GOD IS LOVE! Nations of the earth! tremble no longer before your bloody idols? GOD IS LOVE! Cease your sacrifices! reject all your vain practices! Despise all your powerless mediators! That which God has already done, you need no longer do. *Jesus, the only mediator, has died, the just for the unjust. God has reconciled the world unto Himself.* GOD IS LOVE! At this new voice, which resounds throughout the world, the heart of the people is astonished. My brethren, their fears are dissipated; they abandon their Gods of blood, and cast themselves with tears into the arms of God their Saviour! "Nothing in the whole Gospel surprised me so much," said a converted African, "as the news that GOD IS LOVE. An inexpressible joy then filled my heart, and I broke my idols." "I have tried," said a Hindoo to a worthy missionary, who had asked him why he wished to become a Christian, "I have tried, in all the ways my countrymen know, to calm the troubles of my heart; I have bathed in the Ganges; I have visited holy places; I have made presents to the Brahmins; I have repeated all the names of our gods;—but all this has not given peace to my soul. Latterly I have learned that Jesus Christ became a man; that he died for us, his enemies, to take away our sins. This must be the true way of salvation, and therefore I would become his disciple."

Yes, Lord, it is thy death which must convert the people. *To the Jew a stumbling-block, to the Greek foolishness*, it is *the wisdom of God and the power of God;* and for eighteen hundred years it has not failed to accomplish this word of thine: *And I, if I be lifted up from the earth, will draw all men unto me.* But what were yourselves, my dear hearers, before the good news of Christ was borne to you? Decipher on the ancient monuments the names of the idols whom your fathers adored, seek in the deep forests for the bloody altars upon which your Druids immolated their victims, and you will form some idea of the *power* of this good news of the love of God in Christ, to destroy the superstition of the Gentiles.

Nations of Europe, to what do you owe the light you enjoy, the knowledge of the true God, the civilisation, the institutions of society, the blessings of domestic life, and the many foundations which come to the relief of human misery? To what, if not to the Gospel of Christ? And why will you not do now for other nations that which was formerly done for yourselves?

But does not that which we now see in our midst sufficiently attest the power of the cross of Christ to convert idolatrous hearts? I have seen the worldling converted; I have seen the unbeliever convinced; I have seen him who had sacrificed to criminal passions become holy unto the Lord; and it was the cross of Christ which effected these miracles! Do you think, then, my dear hearers, that the heart of man may be more capable of resisting it under one zone, than under another? Do you believe that those idols of gold and silver, before which these people prostrate themselves, have chains more difficult to break by the strength of God than the thousand idols of our lusts? No! *the laver* in which our members have been healed is accessible to all nations, and its water is powerful for all nations!

Think, then, my brethren, of your responsibility, and of the fault of which you are guilty, if you do not give to the world the powerful remedy which is found in your hands. If a town was ravaged by a contagious fever, how guilty would that man be who, possessing an infallible remedy, should refuse to make it known? Oh! the mental plague of the soul, which desolates idolatrous nations, is a thousand times more terrible than all the plagues of the body. We have in our hands the means which can destroy it, the Gospel of Christ—and will you refuse to bear it to them?

God has planted upon the earth a tree, which springing, said the Saviour, from *the least of all seeds*, is to shelter under its grateful shadow everything under the heavens. Christians of Europe! why do you arbitrarily cut off its branches? why do you permit them to cover only your own dwellings, and why do you hinder them from spreading over the most remote nations? God has decreed a temple to be raised in the earth, and from the beginning has traced its design in such a manner, that it shall hold within its enclosure all the tribes of earth—who has given you a right to contract its borders, and to narrow *the curtains of its habitations?* The Son of God has given up his life for the fulfilment of this counsel, and you, by your indifference, oppose it as much as in you lies; you render useless the blood of the Son of God, and you lose those for whom *Christ had died.* What, are not the nations of Asia, of Africa, of America—are they not those FAMILIES OF THE EARTH, who were to be blessed *in the posterity of Abraham?* Christian souls! you are now the depositories of the healing of the nations, and if you *bury it in the earth,* instead of trafficking with it, you will hear, in the day of God, these words, *Cast the unfaithful servant into outer darkness.* These unhappy nations think not as you do. With loud cries they demand of you this remedy. "For a long time," said a Hindoo to the European Christians, "for a long time you have had this glorious book, this book of the nations; for many ages you have known its truth, it has made you free: it has given you peace; and for us?—you have left us to languish in the darkness, in the slavery of superstition, of sin and of death." "*Woe is me,*" exclaimed the first missionary among the heathen, Paul of Tarsus, and we ought also to repeat it after him, "*Woe is me if I preach not the Gospel.*"

THE SUCCESS.

Yes, my brethren, the work of publishing the Gospel throughout the world, is the great work designed of God. "But," perhaps some one may say, "why may not even the greatness of the misery of the heathen discourage us? What hope can we entertain of changing all this? What a multitude of obstacles? It is an impracticable thing."

We will begin, my brethren, by a partial recognition of the truth of what you say. Yes, there are and there will ever be a multitude of obstacles. We shall find some nations who will appear resolutely attached to their superstitions; we shall encounter some who, bearing the name of Christians, will, through different motives, oppose this admirable work; we shall sometimes, perhaps, be deceived in our missionaries, who will not always be equal to the work; and other obstacles still will accumulate. But, though those obstacles should rise as high as the heavens are above the earth, we ought not for an instant to hesitate; for, notwithstanding all these obstacles, our business is still with the work of God, with the work of man's salvation. What good enterprise is there on earth in which obstacles are not found? What one is there, which would ever be accomplished, did we allow ourselves to be thus discouraged?

What should we have become, the nations of Europe, if the missionary Paul of Tarsus had lost all hope when he saw himself in the first European city to which he carried the Gospel, seized, dragged before the magistrates, cast into prison, and his feet put into the stocks? And when, in the second city to which he came, he raised against himself such a terrible tumult that his friends were obliged to set him without the walls by night, what would have become of us, if, frightened by these obstacles, he had ended his mission, had quitted Europe, and returned to Asia? Ignorant and barbarous, we should have still continued to sacrifice in our forests human victims to bloody divinities! But he feared no obstacle; he advanced intrepidly on his way; preached at Athens *the unknown God*, leaving to all ages an example of courage, which ought for ever to animate the disciples of Christ.

Let not obstacles, then, discourage us, but let them rather redouble our zeal! When the pilot finds himself on a stormy sea, he does not allow the bellowing waves which beat on all sides of his vessel, to check his course; but he looks at the compass, and holding with a firm hand to the helm, he ploughs the furious waves and stretches for port. My brethren, the compass to which you should look is the Word of God; there are the promises of God, God himself, who is true, and who will not fail you—look to Him and go forward. He knows that he gave a difficult order, and that the courage of his disciples would often waver. He who said to them in my text, "*Go ye into all the world, and preach the Gospel to every creature;*" likewise said to them immediately before, "ALL POWER IS GIVEN UNTO ME IN HEAVEN AND IN EARTH;" and immediately after, "Lo! I AM WITH YOU ALWAY, EVEN UNTO THE END OF THE WORLD." These two sayings are as two columns which support, on the right and on the left, the work to which we call you. Fear not! let not your courage falter for a moment! Friends of the publication of the Gospel of peace upon the earth! preachers of righteousness to the distant races of Shem and Ham! it is not your strength, but *the power of Christ* which is to accomplish all this. You fight under the standard of a master to whom ALL POWER has been given in heaven and in earth! He holds in his hands the hearts of all kings and people, and from the stones themselves, he can if he will raise up children unto Abraham! Fear not! "*He is always with you, even unto the end of the world.*" It is his work and not yours that you are to accomplish, and he is himself there to perform his work. *O, thou afflicted, tossed with tempest, fear nothing! says the Lord. Behold they shall surely gather together but not by me; whosoever shall gather together against thee shall fall for thy sake. No weapon that is formed against thee shall prosper.*

So, my brethren, even when we cannot see the least success, we ought to walk by faith. But is it thus? No, *the voice of rejoicing and salvation is in the tabernacles of the righteous: the right hand of the Lord doeth valiantly! Who are these that fly as a cloud, and as the doves to their windows? Thy Church, oh Lord, shall suck the milk of the Gentiles, and shall suck the breast of kings!*

Never, since the first propagation of Christianity upon earth, has the preaching of the Gospel been crowned with such success: this work is accomplished from the ice of one pole to the ice of the other, and the sun in his whole course does not cease to shine upon it. In the utmost limits of the north, Greenland has seen barbarism and the vices of savage life fly, and the icy desert *blossom like the rose*. A little lower, in Labrador, four Christian stations are gradually gathering around them these wandering savages, and transforming them into children of God and civilized tribes. "One has only to see an Esquimaux," said a venerable Missionary to us who had labored thirty years in these ungenial climates, " to discover in the peace and love which shine in all his features, or in his stern and ferocious glance, whether he is or is not a Christian." Let us descend to the islands and towards the continent of the West Indies, everywhere the unhappy negro slaves are called to the glorious liberty of the Gospel ? We have seen in the house of our colonists at Paramaribo, the negress converted by the Moravian missionaries, display all the Christian virtues, and act as a mother to the children of her masters. Do the miracles of Otaheite and the neighboring isles salute us ? Otaheite become a Christian church, a Christian state; Otaheite, where horrible debaucheries and human sacrifices have ceased ; Otaheite filled with the Word of God, an object of astonishment to navigators ;* a habitation of light, from which are constantly sent forth a number of native preachers, to bear to other isles the benefits of the Gospel; Otaheite, whose king, now deceased, gave to a European seaman, in place of any other present, a New Testament in the Otaheitan tongue. Shall we visit the Sandwich Islands, a few years ago covered with darkness ? We shall hear there, on Saturday evening, a public crier passing through the villages, saying : " Inhabitants ! cease from your labors ; the Lord's day approaches." Schools are multiplied ; polygamy is abolished ; children are no longer destroyed." " This," said a father, carrying a bamboo filled with oil, designed for the use of the Missions, " this is for my child ! if the Missionaries had not come, my child had lost its life like many others ?" And the powerful queen, *Keopulani,* raising herself on her dying couch, found strength to say to the chiefs who surrounded her : " The Word of God is a true Word ! I have no desire to return to the gods of Hawai : they are all false gods ; but I love Jesus Christ, and I have given myself to Him !"

Do we reach even New Zealand ? Undoubtedly the Gospel has not yet obtained there such glorious victories ; but it has already commenced to soften the cannibal inhabitants. The chief *Banghi* has forsaken his god *Atna,* invisible eater of men ; for he has found Christ, and at the point of death, he exclaimed : " There is great light within me."

Traversing the vast ocean, passing beyond South America, upon which still rests darkness, let us greet the southern part of the African continent. A continually increasing number of truly Christian and civilized communities are formed and are still forming among the Hottentots, the savage Bushmen, the Caffres, the Namaquas and other tribes. The stupid Hottentot, emancipated by

---

* See among others the despatch addressed to his excellency, the Minister of the Marine of France, by M. Duperrey, Lieutenant, commanding H. M corvette the *Coquille,* in the *Moniteur* of the 1st of April, 1824.

the Gospel, builds asylums in which are received his poor, his infirm, his aged; all the arts of civilisation are spreading in these countries, over which the philosophy of ages had pronounced its powerless curse. Upon the western shores of Africa, some colonies of free negroes present miracles of humility, of faith, of Christian charity, along with order and industry, and the Children of the burning sands include all Christianity in their touching summary: " Bad heart, very bad ; but Saviour good, very good."

Some Swiss missionaries are found on the frontiers of inaccessible Abyssinia, and one of them, whom we have the happiness to know, saw before he had crossed its limits, one of the most influential Abyssinians converted to true Christianity. Cairo, ancient Alexandria, echo to the steps of the preacher of the Gospel. The Greek, who is awakening, will awake, we trust, a Christian; Thessalonica already renews the spectacle she presented to the eyes of the missionary Paul. Children, young men, old men, a great number of Greek priests, all ask with eagerness for the Holy Scriptures in modern Greek ; and a poor gardener, who lived only by the produce of his little garden, deposited at the feet of the Missionary a basket of fruit, all his wealth, asking in exchange the Gospel of Christ.

The ancient and fallen churches of the East begin to stir and to awaken. The sons of the New World hasten from the banks of the Ohio to preach Christ crucified to the inhabitants of Jerusalem. The New Testament is liberally scattered among the dispersed Churches of Syria and Armenia, even in the midst of the ruins of Aleppo; a confused sound, as of a corpse that gathers together its bones, is heard throughout these countries. Some American families, protected by the Muscovite standard, have gathered in crowds upon the soil of their ancient country, from which have fled the subjects of the Crescent. Islamism, whose downfall is announced by more than one event, and one prophecy, begins to receive the gospel of the Nazarene. The Kurds, the Calmucks, the Burgates ask for Missionaries, and receive them. At Ceylon more than ten thousand children are found in schools. The ancient priests of Buddha announce the Gospel of Jesus Christ; they are seen in numerous groups, advancing towards the baptismal font, clothed in their sacerdotal habits; then casting them aside and confessing Jesus. The high priest, Nadasis, who had built sixty pagan temples, and who maintained three hundred and fifty priests, is converted to the Gospel—employs all his influence to spread it, and replies to those who ask him what he thinks of the religion of Jesus Christ: " The religion of Buddha is the light; but the religion of Jesus Christ is the sun." The Burman Empire, object of the most admirable devotion, begins to receive the rays of the sun of righteousness. The missionaries have penetrated into *the Golden City*, and before the *golden face* of the King. They are cast into dungeons; they see themselves robbed of dear companions,* but they remain firm in the faith;

* We refer particularly to the death of Mrs. Judson, whose memoirs have been published in America.

soon they elevate with more boldness than ever, the standard of Christ, and "hail," say they, "the period not far distant, when, like the Otaheitan, the Birman shall break the chains of superstition and idolatry, and shall join those nations who adore the one true and living God." But let us direct our step towards India, whose horrors we have described; they are not yet converted like Otaheite, Eimeo, the Sandwich Islands, the south of Africa; but already on all sides these countries begin to open to the Gospel; say the missionary societies of the Low Countries, "we now hear of young girls at Chinsurah, in Bengal, seated under trees, sheltered from the burning rays of the sun, reading aloud from the Bible, and relating to each other some of the extracts of our sacred books. Wives, in place of being only miserable slaves, sometimes contribute to the intellectual culture of their husbands, often teaching them to read, after having learned to do so themselves, and both coming to offer themselves to the missionaries as instructors of the rising generation. The poor children, instead of being thrown to the crocodiles, are received into an infinite number of schools. A little girl of nine years, born in Europe, restricted her food, in order to contribute towards procuring the benefits of instruction for children of her own age! ".We cannot describe," continue the respected men of whom I have spoken, "the progress that Christianity is making in these countries! Oh! if the women of the Low Countries, could, through love to the Saviour, take to heart the salvation of their sisters in Bengal! We who are here, cannot cease to supplicate our friends in Christ to come to our aid by missionaries, by prayers and by contributions."

And what touching scenes are laid open to us in India! Here we see a Brahmin who has made a vow of perpetual silence: when he passes through the streets, the richest Hindoos cast themselves at his feet in adoration. This mysterious personage wears a necklace of serpents' bones; he seems no longer to have anything in common with humanity, and believes himself a god. But a Christian work, in the Bengalese tongue, causes light to shine through the barriers whose perpetual silence surrounds him: his eyes are opened: he casts himself at the feet of Jesus Christ; he renounces his caste, receives baptism, and becomes an humble disciple of the Saviour. Here I see a man, for a long period the leader of a band of singers, who repeated heinous hymns in idol temples; now I hear him in a Christian temple, a minister of Christ, conducting with tears the song of thanksgiving of the disciples who are about to partake with him of the supper of the Lord. There I discover an aged Hindoo, who for a long period of his life submitted blindly to his priests, and who at six several times has yielded to the torture of swinging in the air. Now he has become a Christian and his death approaches. The horrible thought of having to pass through the bodies of sixty millions of animals before again becoming a man, does not trouble his soul at this solemn moment. *Old things are passed away.* A missionary visits his death-bed; he asks him if, in the midst of his sufferings, he still feels the presence of his Saviour; and the old man placing his hand upon his breast says : " *He is here, he is here, I feel that he is here !*"

Let us likewise come, my brethren, to Java and the neighboring islands, submitting to our august and beloved sovereign, and on which our missionaries are laboring at eleven stations. In the voyages made by our missionaries, multitudes press around them, desiring the words of the good news of Christ, like a thirsty soil awaiting the rain from heaven. Heathen princes themselves contribute to the maintenance of Missions; others call upon the missionaries to establish a Christian school in their island. Temples consecrated to the worship of the evil spirit are destroyed; the eagerness of these islanders for the Word of God is such, that the missionaries, not having a sufficient number of the sacred books, are obliged to distribute leaf by leaf, fragments of their own Bibles; the grace of God works in their hearts, everywhere they are asking for instruction, and the melioration of manners, and industry among these people, furnish striking proof of the progress they have made in the truth. We will show you a Chinese widow, long a disciple of Confucius, who having taken refuge in one of our islands, fell asleep shortly after in the Lord: " No, I fear nothing more," said she, on her death-bed, to the wife of one of our oldest missionaries in the East Indies, " I am not afraid of death itself, for *I know in whom I have believed*, and my Saviour is powerful to forgive all my sins !" The very night of her departure she said : " Now I feel that God is reconciled with me, and his peace is diffused throughout my soul." Shortly after, calling to the persons who watched near her bedside, she said: "Now you may go to sleep, for I shall soon go to rest." Then she slept sweetly in Jesus.

How can we better complete our survey than by greeting China herself, who believes herself to be as unchangeable as God, but whom the Word of the Lord has already begun to shake ? Our missionaries of the Eastern Archipelago, in the advanced posts of Christianity, are in the presence of this dreaded enemy : the Word of God translated into Chinese, is liberally scattered wherever it can find access. One of our missionaries, whose hand we have more than once clasped with fraternal pressure,* is unwearied in distributing it upon the Chinese vessels and upon all those that can penetrate our courts. Already *Keutenching*, a Chinese converted by his countryman *Leangafa*, has made the shores of *the Celestial Empire* resound with this touching confession: " My brother said to me ; man, though his sins are as weighty as great mountains, if he sincerely repent and trust in Jesus, the Saviour of the world, shall obtain complete deliverance from his sins and the blessing of eternal life !—I opened my heart; I believed ; I received baptism, asking the Holy Spirit to implant within my heart the root of holiness!"

Thus the pretended everlasting bulwarks begin to tremble. Thus *all flesh* begins to *see the salvation of God*. Thus from one end of the world to the other, the knowledge of the Lord and His

---

* M. Gutzlaff.

Anointed begins to fill the earth. O God! of a truth thou hast set up thine ensign for the nations!

Now, my brethren, we come to solicit you, in the name of God the Saviour, henceforth to take a lively and sincere interest in the great and admirable work of Evangelical missions among the heathen. Nations of Europe! We have long enough, through our avarice and licentiousness, borne misery, debauchery, discord, and slavery to distant nations. Boast of your civilisation, people of Europe! and these nations will reply, by presenting to you your errors, your depravity and your crimes! Such are the influences, which for ages have issued from a corrupt Christianity. We are indebted to these people, my brethren; we have many faults to expiate. Our fathers have left us a debt which we must discharge: new counting-houses must be erected upon all the shores of India, peopled with new merchants, circulating new treasures.

Europe, my brethren, is like a volcano which often keeps silence without, because it is stirring up within its destructive fires; but at certain periods it casts forth its flames and its burning lava. Europe cannot contain all the life that is enclosed within her. Three periods in modern times have already succeeded each other, in which she has cast her power without. Once stirred by a warlike spirit influenced by religious fanaticism, she placed herself in arms under the standard of the Cross, to seek by fire and sword, the conquest of the land once sanctified by the steps of the Prince of Peace. Later, a spirit of discovery spread along all the European shores; vessels followed vessels, Europe crossed the seas and discovered with astonishment a new World, peopled by inhabitants of whose being she had until now been ignorant. At a still later period, when her discoveries were secured, a mercantile spirit seized the same nations; they cruised for gold and silver, and everywhere established their counting-houses.

Now, my brethren, a new period commences. Europe, in peace, has a new necessity for carrying her strength without. Let the spirit of discovery continue, let mercantile relations be multiplied. It is well; but meanwhile there are new enterprises to be formed with which it is our business to be informed. All the evangelical nations of Europe feel religious activity kindling within their bosoms. This period must be marked by a new character and by a more noble zeal than all those which have preceded it. Let us bear to the nations who are our brethren, sprung from the same blood with us, and redeemed also by the same blood, let us carry to them the knowledge of God, civilisation, the Christian virtues, private and public peace, peace on earth, eternal peace!

Christians! think of those who have borne Christianity to you! Think that if Amand, Elige, Wilfried, Ewald,* and many others, had been so indifferent, neither you nor your fathers would ever

---

* *Amandus* spread the Gospel in Flanders about the year 635. *Elizius*, in Friseland and Flanders, about the year 640. *Wilfried* preached also in Frise about the year 680. *Willebrod* and *Ewald* came from England, preaching in Friseland, at Utrecht, about the year 690.

have become Christians. You owe a tribute of gratitude to those ministers of the Gospel, who first bore into these countries the news of salvation: pay it to their successors! And if these generous men were so devoted in diffusing the light, which the errors of men had already begun to obscure, what zeal ought not you to manifest, now that God has placed it in your hands in its primitive splendor?

Evangelical Christians! Has not the Lord transmitted the Gospel to you in all its purity? It is not without design that God has given the empire of the seas to evangelical nations. Remember those Missionaries of the truth whom the Lord raised up, three centuries ago, in the midst of slumbering Europe, and send to others the blessings they have borne you.*

Ye are the light of the world. Neither do men light a candle and put it under a bushel, but on a candlestick; and it giveth light unto all that are in the house, that is, in the world.

Christians of the Low Countries! show yourselves worthy of your ancestors! To them it was given to form the first evangelical Missions! It is nearly three centuries since, when they had but just broken a double yoke and formed themselves into a nation, under the glorious standard of Orange, that they proposed to propagate in the Indies at the same time with their commerce, *the glory of Jesus Christ.* There were some pastors who, renouncing all temporal advantages, went to preach the Gospel in Java, Ceylon and other countries. A Mission Institute was founded in that city of the northern provinces, celebrated by her magnanimous defence.† What! my brethren, have the times so changed? The standard of Orange is always the same; as it has not ceased to be that of true glory, so it has not ceased to be that of the Gospel, and to cover with its powerful and protecting shade the generous efforts of all who labor to spread among the nations the blessings of Jesus Christ! Christians of the Low Countries! hear the voice of your countrymen in the Indies who yet worship idols!

All evangelical nations now rival each other in zeal. Opulent England consecrates to the Lord the tenth of her increase, the speed of her navy, and the influence of her power.

Reformed France, issuing from her mourning, her long poverty, from her protracted trials, bears onward with joy the first fruits of the new life which animated her.‡ Switzerland listens from the bosom of her mountains, and though distant from the shores of the sea, hears the plaintive cries its waves waft to us. Old Germany, always faithful, when the words *light, truth, humanity,* are sounded, gives her sons and daughters in abundance, and makes

---

* This sermon was preached the 30th October, that, is on the evening of the anniversary of the Reformation.

† *Leyden.* See the history of the efforts of the United Provinces for the propagation of the Gospel, since the year 1602, in the islands of Ceylon, Java, Formosa, Amboyna, etc., in the *Journal of Evangelical Missions* of Paris, first year, page 289.

‡ The first three Reformed French missionaries departed from Paris in the summer of 1829 for the south of Africa.

them slaves unto slaves, in order to convert them to Christ. America, youngest in the ranks of nations, springs up with the ardor of youth, and carries the breath of a new respiration to the languishing countries of Asia, the primitive source of life, and the mother of nations. The love of Christ now embraces the nations; all evangelical communions stretch out their hands from the four quarters of the world, and march to the same battle under the same standard. Christians of the Low Countries! let this universal movement arouse us! We were formerly the first, be so still at the present hour. Let us rally around those noble men, who have founded in our country the best institutions that grace it, and let that comprehensive charity, which is the token of the strength and greatness of our nation, enlarge all hearts.

"But," you will perhaps say, "we cannot go, we have our business, our relations." True, my brethren, but we do not ask you to go; here are those that would go. Eleven young missionaries* await upon your shores for your offerings, that they may go, *in the name of God, taking nothing of the Gentiles,* and carry the glad tidings to those who know it not. Give, then, my brethren, give abundantly! Let each give according to his means. Give! all that you possess is from the Lord. He is it who has given it to you; He asks of you only a small portion of that which is His. Give! Think of the incomprehensible and eternal treasures of the grace of Christ, which have become your portion, and give him in exchange your silver and your gold.

Do not listen to that secret voice of your heart which counsels you to diminish your contribution, and do not bring to the Lord's altar worthless copper instead of silver and gold. *Give me to drink*, said Jesus to the woman of Samaria, at the side of the well. *Give me to drink!* he still says to each one of you by the mouth of those who languish and die for the want of that *water* which *whosoever drinketh of it shall never thirst!* Give! but above all bring to this work the contributions of your prayers: nothing can ever be effected in the Pagan world without the prayers of the faithful. Pray, then, that God will send the great, the only missionary, His Holy Spirit, who alone can change *the parched ground into a pool, and the thirsty land into springs of water.*

But I must pause, in conclusion, and ask if I am not myself a missionary, and if there are not in this assembly some souls to whom I ought to announce the good tidings from heaven as if they had never heard them. Listen, my brethren, to a prophecy of the Lord, and tremble: *Many shall come from the east and west, and shall sit down with Abraham and Isaac and Jacob in the kingdom of heaven, but the children of the kingdom shall be cast out.* I am seized with fear while contemplating these words; seeing how they have been fulfilled to Israel, I tremble lest they may be again accomplished in us! Oh! you who have grown up in the midst of the privileges of the house of God, have you understood, have you believed the good news, published through the world, as

---

* They have since gone forth, but others are preparing to follow them.

they are understood and believed by those blessed souls in our days, who have been called from the east and the west? Alas! I fear that the constant repetition has only hardened your hearts! I come to you now as if I were a missionary, arriving for the first time in a country where the sound of the Gospel had never been heard. Listen, sinful and guilty souls, to the great and heaven-descended news I bear. God saves the world: he makes peace with his people: he opens the gates of his grace and his glory. Christ gave himself a ransom for all, which has been testified in due time. Listen to this testimony as if it were the first time you had heard it, and seek to understand and believe it. Yes! eighteen centuries ago, oh soul that believest that Jesus is the *Son of God, the Saviour*, thy ransom was paid. Already has thy debt to God been discharged, and discharged at an immense price, at the price of the life of the Son of God. At that moment when Christ said upon the cross: *It is finished!* the salvation of all the children of God, who have been, who are and who will be upon earth, from every people, every tongue, every tribe, was finished, was perfected, as he said those words. Christ is now the RANSOM FOR ALL: he is the ransom of Europe; he is the ransom of Asia; he is the ransom of the distant isles; he is the ransom of the world; he is thy ransom, oh soul that believest in the Son of God! He who is the salvation of the universe is mighty for thy salvation. He whom the Hindoo, the savage of Labrador, the negro of Africa, the islander of Tahiti, joyfully proclaim as their Saviour, is thy Saviour, by the same title as theirs: *For as in Adam all die, even so in Christ shall all be made alive. There is therefore now no condemnation to them which are in Christ Jesus.*

Oh! what glorious tidings! Shall we say it to others without repeating it to ourselves? Shall we scatter far from us the precious gold of faith, and shall we ourselves remain empty and poor? Shall we open to others the gates of glory, and shut them against ourselves, "without entering in?" Let us believe UNTO SALVATION; let us believe it for ourselves; "Let us bring forth fruit for repentance." "Let us become the children of God!" let us become "new creatures;" and may the celestial spirit, which makes "the solitary place to blossom and flourish like the rose," vivify our own hearts and cause us to "bring forth fruit unto God."

Lord! Has this preaching of the Gospel which I would carry to the heathen, been received and believed in my own soul? Repentance and remission of sins, which I would proclaim to distant races, have they been preached in my own house? And has thy kingdom, which now extends to the ends of the earth, been established in my heart? Lord, MAY THY KINGDOM COME; may it reign within, may it reign without! Amen! Amen!

CHRISTIANITY AND PROTESTANTISM,

ARE THEY

TWO DISTINCT THINGS?

TRANSLATED BY M. M. BACKUS.

CHRISTIANITY AND PROTESTANTISM.

FROM THE "ARCHIVES DU CHRISTIANISME," August, 1827.

It is time.—Psalm cxix. 126.

THERE has arisen, in process of time, a new adversary against the Church of Jesus Christ. There sprang up in the last century, a kind of Protestantism, with which neither the Luthers nor the Calvins, neither the Drelincourts nor the Dumoulins, neither the Mornays nor the Claudes, have ever been acquainted: a bastard, generated by that union, which erratic spirits have pretended to effect between the Gospel and the philosophy of the eighteenth century. By an able stratagem, they seek to substitute this feeble and counterfeit child of an unbelieving age, for the healthy and powerful doctrine which issued forth for the salvation of the world, from the times of the Apostles and Reformers. If we do not approve of the substitution, if we do not recognize this intruder for the religion bequeathed us by our fathers, its patrons cry out intolerance, mysticism, enthusiasm; or what more?—perhaps innovation!

Neither the Reformers, nor any of those who have walked in their illustrious steps, have ever known any other Protestantism than Christianity; but the fathers and protectors of the system that we notice, think not so; we speak it with sentiments of deep grief, but we can no longer keep silence on a subject which everywhere presents itself to our minds. Instead of allowing Protestantism to be Christianity, all Christianity, and nothing but Christianity, they have made of it a separate being, which is neither this nor that, neither religion nor philosophy, neither faith nor incredulity. This pretended Protestantism issues forth from the camp of Jesus Christ, and raises an independent standard; an unfaithful deserter, it still pretends to mingle the colors of the Prince of Life with those of this world's wisdom; but it is only under the latter that it rallies, the other being found there only for convenience and by mistake. In its hands Protestantism becomes a separate idol, to which they offer the homage due only to the Lord, drawing thus upon the work of its hands and itself the adoration which belongs only to God. We do not fear to say, that this kind of view is a revival of the errors of Rome; it is Papacy under other colors. With what do we reproach Roman Catholicism? With having left Christianity and formed a new being. The same thing is repeated. To the idol of Rome another idol is opposed; idol for idol, the one may be worth a little more than the other; but certainly, we do not think we have gained much by the change. " And we know that the Son of God is come, and hath given us an understanding, that we may know him that is true, and we are in him that is true, even in his Son Jesus Christ. This is the true God and eternal life. Little children, keep yourselves from idols."*

Besides, there is nothing astonishing in all this; we ought to expect it. If Phariseeism has taken a body under the triple crown, Sadduceeism, the second vice of human nature, ought also to seek to assume some form ; but we shall do our duty, we shall not leave it to rest quietly in our midst; we shall raise our voice so that it may be constrained to fly and hide far from our churches its shameful infidelity.

Our business now is not with those who are in error, but with the errors themselves. As to the defenders of those errors, we recognize among them not only many of distinguished and undisputed talents, but we also believe their intentions are much better than their system. They do not suspect the mortal blows which they are giving to our churches; they do not know that the dry wind which arose in the vast desert of the eighteenth century, and whose breath appears so agreeable to them, will cause vegetation to cease, and will strike with barrenness the whole field of the Lord. Their views are perhaps limited; their intentions are perhaps praiseworthy ; they are urged on by that unfortunate desire which has already worked so much evil to the Church, while desiring its good, and against which Jesus with such earnestness has warned his disciples ; the desire of reconciling the spirit of the world with the spirit of the gospel—the spirit of the age with the spirit of immutable and eternal wisdom. They think that by harmonizing the wisdom of the world and the wisdom of God, the great secret will be discovered; they regard themselves as called upon to accomplish this great design. Doubtless they think in this way to effect good for the *world*, and good for *the Church ;* but what happens? They strongly resemble him who, in order to cure a person attacked with a fatal malady, should pretend that he must begin by communicating to the physician the disease of the sick man, instead of making the sick man take the remedy of the physician. What would be the result? *They would both die.* These are quite different proceedings from those revealed to us by the Word of God ; it knows nothing of the petty expedients of human wisdom ; it says :—I will destroy the wisdom of the wise, and will bring to naught the understanding of the prudent. Where is the wise?' Where is the scribe? Where is the disputer of this world? Hath not God made foolish the wisdom of this world?† Those who do not fear these words, and who wish to comprehend them, may comprehend them.

Is Protestantism anything else than Christianity ? Is it a *modified*

---

* 1 John v. 20-21.   † 1 Cor. i. 19, 20.

Christianity, having certain attributes not possessed by primitive Christianity? Perhaps this question is not quite plain. We would ask you, then, do these words, *Christianity, Catholicism*,* *Protestantism*, cause three distinct ideas to arise in your mind? It is probable they do. In this case, in our opinion, you are wrong; these *three* words are only *two* things,—*Christianity* and *Protestantism* being two expressions to signify the same thing. Properly speaking, there is no Protestantism; Christianity is sufficient for us. Protestantism is *revived* Christianity—but revived absolutely such *as it* was. We do not see why, after his resurrection, one ought to be re-baptized. Lazarus was, and called himself, Lazarus after, as before his resurrection. It is unfortunate that a new denomination was given to the reformed religion in the sixteenth century; we think it would have been better to have called it simply *Christianity*, or even Catholicism, in opposition to the Church of the Pope. But as names are only names, and words are only words, we will leave them as they are, and will content ourselves with protesting against the idea—against the thing.

We declare, then, with all the reformers, that Protestantism is *Christianity*, neither more nor less; all, that tends to make of it anything else, with particular colors, with principles which are peculiar to it, and still more strange doctrines, are the *unnatural*, since these remove it so far from *Christianity*, that is to say, from itself.

Is it necessary to cite here passages from our reformers to prove that they never pretended to form a new Church, but simply to re-establish the old one? I think we all know, that this would be to cite their whole works, for this is the principle which they constantly set forth. Ought we to be astonished, however, if the powerful hand of these great men of God is impressed, perhaps a little strongly, on their works, in such a way that human traces are to be perceived by the side of divine ones; and if the reformed churches have somewhat forgotten, if not during the lifetime of the Reformers, at least shortly after, that they were anything but a continuation, a repetition of the first churches of Jesus? Glory be ascribed, notwithstanding, to the Protestant Churches, or rather to Him who preserved them, this tendency of derivation was imperceptible; they were truly redeemed Churches. But the evil which has been suppressed shines forth, especially in our days; in our days the abomination has been introduced into the sanctuary, and an idol has been made of Protestantism. But as Paul and Barnabas rent their clothes before the pagans who wished to sacrifice to them, so Protestantism rejects with indignation these sacrilegious honors: it declares that it is nothing in itself, and attributing all honor to that Gospel which is the power of God unto salvation to every one which believeth, it exclaims—Salvation to our God which sitteth upon the throne, and to the Lamb.

We think the period has arrived, in which the slight human

---

* We use the word *Catholicism* not in its true sense, but in the narrow sense, which is usually given to it in conversation, meaning the Church of Rome.

foot-prints, necessarily imposed upon the work of the reformers, ought to be effaced; in which Protestant Churches ought everywhere to become solely *Christian* churches, placing themselves *above* Rome, not simply *opposite* to her, seizing the sceptre of *catholicity*, and banishing popery into the obscurity which belongs to it. Protestant Churches! let us seat ourselves on the twelve thrones of the apostles; let us proclaim and show ourselves the hereditary Churches of the Apostolic Churches of Jerusalem, Antioch, Ephesus, Philippi, Rome. Let us seek our armor whence Apostolic men drew theirs; that arsenal which is of so much more avail than that of the philosophy of the world. The time may not be distant when the Saviour will gather together the people: let us stand forth, as did our primitive brethren, to be the instruments of his mercy; this is a greater, a nobler task, than to form an imaginary mixture of the faith of the Gospel and of the unbelief of the present age.

Perhaps some one may say, It is erroneous to pretend that Protestantism is anything but Christianity; it is undoubtedly Christianity, but Christianity with a protest against Rome; it is under some points of view a thing by itself; this new situation gives it a new character, new duties; in a word, renders it, in some respects, decidedly different from primitive Christianity.

To this we reply; if Protestantism is nothing else than Christianity, then Christianity has been nothing from the beginning but Protestantism. Has it not always protested against Rome, and is not this one of its essential features? Has there been an age in which the Church was not filled with *Protestants?* Was not St. Paul a good protestant, when in a prophetic tone he wrote to the Church of Rome, *If thou boastest thyself thou shalt be cut off!** or when he wrote to Timothy: in *the latter times some shall depart from the faith, giving heed to seducing spirits and doctrines of devils; forbidding to marry and commanding to abstain from meats,* etc?† Was not St. John a *Protestant,* when, seeing *the woman seated upon seven mountains and arrayed in purple and scarlet,* he called her, " the great Babylon, the mother of harlots and the abominations of the earth."‡

Was not Polycarp, bishop of Smyrna, the disciple of St. John, a Protestant, when he refused to celebrate Easter like Anicetus, bishop of Rome,—placing before him the example of the beloved disciple, who served him as a guide?§ Were not all the churches of Asia Minor *Protestant,* when, caring little for the proud pretensions of Victor, bishop of Rome, they quietly opposed to him the doctrines established in their apostolic seats, *sedes apostolicæ?*‖ Was not Irenæus, bishop of Rome, a *Protestant,* when he rebuked Victor,—reproaching him with his anti-Christian proceedings, which were unknown to his predecessors?¶ Was not Cyprian, bishop of Carthage, a Protestant, when he established, with so much force, the independence of the bishops, and accomplished

---

* Romans xi. 20–22.   † 1 Tim. iv. 1, etc.
‡ Rev. xvii. Rome is built, as everybody knows, upon seven hills.
§ The year 162. ‖ The years 190 and 196. ¶ Eusebius, Lib. 5, cap 24.

that which he thought right, in spite of the opposition of Rome? When writing, in his own and in the name of the synod, to Stephanus, bishop of Rome, concerning a point in which he differed from him, he spoke to him as a colleague, possessing the same right and dignity with himself, saying: " By virtue of *the honor which is common to us*, and of the love we have for thee, we have thought it our duty to communicate to thee these things, believing that that which is conformable to truth and piety will please thee in like manner, agreeably to thy love of truth, very dear *brother!* Besides, we well know that there are those who do not wish to cast away opinions which they have once received, and who do not readily change their sentiments, but who, without prejudicing the bonds of peace and concord, which ought to unite colleagues, preserve certain things that are peculiar to themselves, which have been once established among them. We do no violence, and give no laws to persons in such things; " for whosoever is set over a Church, of his own free will, need render an account of his actions only to God."*

And after the violent declarations of Stephen, was not this same Cyprian a *Protestant*, and as much of a Protestant as Luther or Calvin, or ourselves, when, chiding the errors of the Roman bishop, whom he accused of sustaining the cause of *heretics against Christians*, of saying *contradictory things*, etc. (*quo lecto magis ac magis ejus errorem denotabis, qua hæreticorum causam contra Christianos et contra Ecclesiam Dei asserere conatur. Nam inter cætera vel superba, vel ad rem non pertinentia, vel sibi ipsi contraria, quæ imperite atque improvide scripsit, etc.*), he adds respecting that which Stephen called *Roman traditions:* " From whence does this tradition come? Is it derived from the words of the Lord, and the authority of the Gospel? Does it proceed from the doctrines and epistles of the apostles? What obstinacy and presumption to place *human tradition before the divine commands*, and to think that God is not angry whenever human tradition destroys the divine precepts, as the Saviour has said in the Gospel. " For laying aside the commandments of God, ye hold the traditions of men." The usages which are introduced among some, cannot hinder truth from prevailing, and bearing off the victory; for usage without truth is only a worn-out error (*nam consuetudo sine veritate, vetustas erroris est*); therefore forsake error and follow truth, knowing that truth will achieve the victory, as it is written: *truth dwells, and lives for ever.* If we but return to the source and origin of the divine tradition, human error ceases. If an aqueduct which formerly gave water in abundance, suddenly fails, do we not go back to the source to discover the cause, to see if the veins have been dried up, or the source itself has been exhausted, or, if running from the source as freely as before, to see if the water

---

* *Quâ in re nec nos vim cuiquam facimus, aut legem damus: cum habet in Ecclesiæ administratione voluntatis suæ arbitrium liberum unusquisque præpositus, rationem actus sui Domino redditurus* (Cypr., Epist. 71 ad Stephanum). It is to the bishop of Rome that Cyprian writes, no one need render an account of his actions only to God! *Utinam ubique!*

has been stopped in its course? And if it happens that the aqueduct drinks up the water, or that it is broken in the centre, is it not immediately repaired, so that the water may flow in its channel, for the use of the town, as abundantly as it flows from its source? We see in this the duty of the ministers of God, charged with the preservation of the divine precepts. . If the truth has been corrupted, and has wavered in anything, let us return to the origin of the Lord, and of the Gospel—to the tradition of the apostles, etc.* We despair of finding the principles of Protestantism more clearly expressed in the writings of Luther and of Calvin, than in this passage of Cyprian. Who can say after this, that Cyprian was not a *Protestant?* Finally, was not the bishop Firmilian of Cæsarea, in Cappadocia, a Protestant, who accused Stephen, the bishop of Rome, of rending the unity of the Church by his conduct—full of ambition and bitterness; and who opposed to the pretended tradition of the Roman Church, the tradition of the most ancient churches, and likewise many dogmatic proofs; and who showed that the Romans did not retain the primitive tradition, and appealed in vain to the authority of the apostles, since in so many things they departed from the usage of the Church of Jerusalem, and of other ancient apostolic churches? Is it necessary to quote here all the *Protestants* of following ages, who increased in numbers and strength in proportion as the usurpations of Rome multiplied? Yes! since Protestantism is even now nothing but Christianity; so, likewise, it has never been anything else than Christianity. We do not wish to be better Protestants than John or Paul! We do not think we have dwelt too long on this point, for it is equally important to prove this point to the Romanists, and to the innovators: both must know that there is not a Christianity and a Protestantism, but that they are *one and the same;* that truth is not divided into many distinct beings, but that she is, from the beginning of time to the end of the world, one and indivisible.

Further, it must be observed, that this new Protestantism, which seeks to be introduced in place of the old, is in effect different from Christianity; in some respects, it is even totally opposed to it. It has preserved but a single feature of true Protestantism; but making Protestantism to consist almost exclusively of this feature, it has, in so doing, rendered it not easily recognized. Freedom of examination, which we have sufficiently defended on all occasions, and are still ready to maintain against and towards all, is the feature to which we allude. This imprescriptible right of man and of Christians, which is absolutely necessary to attain religion, but which (in the present age it ought to be proclaimed on the house-tops) is not *religion itself,* but is the Gospel of this new sect, is the burden of all their writings, and they speak of it with as much enthusiasm as ever St. Paul spoke of *the cross of Jesus Christ.* They take the scaffolding, necessary to the construction of an edifice, for the edifice itself—the disputed right of those who wish to enter into the kingdom of God, for the precious and eternal privileges of those who are already within it.

* *Cypr., Epist.* 74 *ad Pompeium* contra *Epistolam* Stephani.

No! in vain would they build this new Protestantism on the ruins of the old Protestantism; no one would recognize it as the true one. It is not sufficient to take a part of the antique and venerable temple, whatever trouble they may give themselves to adorn it with new ornaments; it must be taken *entire.* If they have only a part, they have nothing. What would be said of persons who, wishing to construct a new house, in place of another which appeared to them out of fashion, should erect only a door, only an entrance, and then exclaim: come and see with what skill we have constructed a beautiful edifice in place of the old house, which was only fit for an ignorant age! Yes, is the reply, but we could seat ourselves in the old house, but in yours there is nothing upon which to repose; the old house afforded us a shelter from the wind and rain, but, alas! you have provided nothing to protect us from the tempests. So is it with this new religion; its façade is superb; philosophy and literature are exhausted for its embellishment, but behold all! Oh ye who are weary and heavy laden! there is nothing here to give rest to your souls; Oh ye, who are pursued by the shadows of life, you will not find here that refuge which is necessary for you, the secret place of the Most High, where one shall dwell in the shadow of the Almighty.* We are reminded of that faithful soul, who, on going out from listening to the discourse of one of the adepts in this new religion, said: *I was hungry and you gave me no meat, thirsty and ye gave me no drink.*

And after all, what is this liberty of investigation, concerning which there is so much boasting? Certainly it is not of the genuine stamp, and we do not see that it can even lead to much good. As far removed from Christianity as is the Church of Rome with its insupportable authority, so far removed is the pretended Protestantism that we oppose, with its examination, in which it takes away all means of examination. God who knows man, his nature, his wants, the limits of his intelligence, has in his infinite love provided for his weakness; he has aimed to come to his assistance; he has declared that he himself would be his guide, his interpreter, his light, his true friend in the examination of the Holy Scriptures. There is no promise more clear, more consoling, none dearer to the children of God in the divine Word. How many are there now among *men of letters* and among the *unlettered*, of whom the prophet Isaiah speaks in the 29th chapter, 10—12, saying: " For the Lord hath poured out upon you the spirit of deep sleep, and hath closed your eyes; the prophets and your rulers, the seers hath he covered. And the vision of all is become unto you as the words of a book that is sealed, which men deliver to one that is learned, saying, Read this, I pray thee: and he saith, I cannot; for it is sealed: And the book is delivered to him that is not learned, saying, Read this, I pray thee: and he saith, I am not learned!" Thus there are always men in all ranks, of different degrees of mental culture, who have well turned and re-turned, and examined on all sides the Holy Scriptures; they do not understand

* Psalm xci. 1.

them because they are as a sealed book to them. But ever blessed be the God of our salvation! He has declared that he himself will unseal this book, and will open the eyes of the humble and the poor, so that whosoever will address himself to *Him*, shall see; he shall see that which he never would have seen, had he remained alone. *And the deaf* (adds the prophet in the same chapter, 18— 19) *shall hear the words of the book, and the eyes of the blind shall see out of obscurity, and out of darkness. The meek also shall increase their joy in the Lord, and the poor among men shall rejoice in the Holy One of Israel.* Especially are these promises of assistance to men in their search after truth, and for understanding of the Scriptures, repeated in holy Scripture. The Lord said to the Messiah in the same prophecy: *I will give thee for a covenant of the people, for a light of the Gentiles;* TO OPEN THE BLIND EYES. *And I will bring the blind by a way that they knew not; I will lead them in paths that they have not known:* I WILL MAKE DARKNESS LIGHT BEFORE THEM, *and crooked things straight; these things will I do unto them and not forsake them.* Jeremiah announces the nature of the new covenant that he predicts: " I will put my law in their inward parts, and WRITE IT IN THEIR HEARTS, and will be their God and they shall be my people. And they shall teach no more every man his neighbor, and every man his brother, saying, Know the Lord: for they shall all know me from the least of them unto the greatest of them, saith the Lord "

The Saviour of the world himself says: *Ask, and it shall be given you; seek, and ye shall find; knock, and it shall be opened unto you. If ye then, being evil, know how to give good gifts unto your children,* HOW MUCH MORE SHALL YOUR HEAVENLY FATHER GIVE THE HOLY SPIRIT TO THEM THAT ASK HIM?* In St. John, he renews these promises in the most positive manner: *The Comforter which is* THE HOLY GHOST, *whom the Father will send in my name,* HE SHALL TEACH YOU ALL THINGS.† But when he, the Spirit of truth, is come, HE WILL GUIDE YOU INTO ALL TRUTH. *He shall glorify me: for he shall receive of mine, and shall show it unto you.* In the Gospel, we see Jesus himself acting upon his disciples, who had been with him already three years, to enlighten their minds yet darkened, as are the minds of men by nature, that they might understand the Scriptures: *Then opened he their understanding, that they might understand the Scriptures.*‡ And the apostle Paul, who had experienced with the faithful at Corinth, the efficacy of these precious promises, in speaking to them of the things of salvation, of the counsels of God, contained in the Scriptures, and whose search ought to be the object of Christian examination, said: *Eye hath not seen, nor ear heard, neither have entered into the heart of man, the things which God hath prepared for them that love him.* But GOD HATH REVEALED THEM UNTO US BY HIS SPIRIT; for the Spirit searcheth all things, yea the deep things of God. Now we have received not the spirit of the *world, but the Spirit which is of God;* THAT WE MIGHT KNOW THE THINGS THAT ARE FREELY GIVEN TO US OF GOD. But *the natural§ man receiveth not the*

---

* Luke xi. 9—13. † John xiv. 26. ‡ Luke xxiv. 45.
§ Our French translations appear to me to be very defective here; they have adopted the interpretation of the Vulgate, which translates *animalis*

things of the Spirit of God: for they are foolishness unto him; neither can he know them, because they are spiritually discerned; but he that is spiritual judgeth all things.

Now this new Protestantism passes by the illumination of the Holy Spirit; it is ignorant, or feigns to be ignorant, of all these promises of our God—constantly calling upon men to examine with their reason *alone*,—with its imperfections, its limited faculties, its ignorance; without dependence on and invocation of the Spirit of God. It does not perceive that reason is a glass, which it is necessary to employ, it is true, but it is a glass dimmed by the breath of sin, and that it must first be made clear before we can see well by its means (*that God may* ENLIGHTEN *the eyes of your understanding*, is the expression of St. Paul), and that God, the Father of our Lord Jesus Christ,—the Spirit of wisdom and of revelation, can alone do this. Thus it deprives the faithful of the succor that God, in his infinite wisdom, had designed for them; it separates them from their God; it isolates them; it leaves them in their weakness;—in their darkness; it exalts that pride which should be destroyed. What shall I say! Oh! blindness, which causes the Christian soul to tremble! It lifts itself up against the holy doctrines of the Bible, and calls the promises and commands of our God enthusiasm, mysticism! " *They be blind leaders of the blind,*" says the Saviour, " *and, if the blind lead the blind, they shall both fall into the ditch.*"

What would result from this, but that man, left to himself, would fashion a doctrine entirely different in effect from Christianity?

We shall not pause here to pass in review the different fundamental doctrines of the Christian religion, by dwelling at length on each one of them. We have before us the assurance that there is not one of these doctrines which this new Protestantism has not either corrupted or rejected; many of its doctrines it has even attacked with enmity; and a rapid glance will suffice to show that the Protestantism which exists apart from Christianity, differs, in fact, entirely from it.

homo. I prefer the English and German translations, which render it *the natural man.* "Ο ψυχικος, says the Greek: that is, literally, *the man of the soul;* that is to say, man with his soul and the faculties with which it is endowed in its natural and unregenerated state; and the man, ψυχικος, is put in opposition to the man πνευματικος, that is to say, the man enlightened by the πνευμα, the Spirit of God, *the spiritual man.* The word *animal* being doubtless derived from the Latin *anima,* soul, the French translation may have appeared the most literal. But the word *animal* is taken in so different an acceptation in the French language, that such a translation involves a great error; this is proved by the blunder made by the Academy in its dictionary. "*Animal,*" it says, "in the language of Scripture, signifies carnal, sensual, and is the opposite of spiritual, *L' homme animal ne comprend pas ce qui est de Dieu.* But the Greek word rendered here by *animal,* ψυχικος, is as different from *carnal,* σαρκικος, as in French *âme* is different from *chair*. The three scriptural expressions, ὁ πνευματικος, ὁ ψυχικος, ὁ σαρκικος, designate three classes of men entirely distinct; and nothing can be more erroneous than to make *one* of the *last two.* A distinction, definition, etc., etc., of these three classes, would give us the scriptural philosophy of human nature. We may, perhaps, return to this subject hereafter.

With regard to the fundamental doctrine, not only of religion, but, we might almost say, of all true philosophy—the doctrine of *the corruption of man*, the existence of evil within us,—we know how the new Protestantism treats the passage on this subject, and that it does not hesitate to say that the declarations of Scripture on this point are *but the figures of lyric poetry*. This idea of seeing images and figures everywhere is, of all modes invented up to this time, the most expeditious for putting aside Christianity. There are those among the new Protestants of Germany, who see, in the resurrection of Jesus Christ, only *a figure,*—an *image*. We must acknowledge that *our* new Protestants, through the restraining grace of God, have not yet gone so far.

Concerning the real divinity of Jesus Christ, and the worship of God the Father, the Son, and the Holy Ghost, one God, blessed for ever, that foundation of the Christian faith, we know what these new Protestants believe, and the pretended absurdities which they, in common with all unbelievers, find in this holy and glorious doctrine.

Justification by faith in the powerful merits of the great Victim of expiation, offered up for the sinner who repents and believes, is to this one-sided Protestantism a scandal and a folly. It maintains, with the Romish Church, the merit of works; not knowing that truly good works can proceed only from a heart touched and regenerated by the grace of God, and full of gratitude and love, and that, consequently, the best method of rendering all good works impossible, is just to hold that man is not saved by grace alone, but partly by his merits, partly by the works of the law.

Concerning the doctrine of *regeneration*, of the new birth by the Holy Spirit, they would introduce into our Reformed Churches their images and oriental figures; a *terra incognita*, of which its patrons understand less than did Nicodemus when Jesus taught him this fundamental truth of the kingdom of God; so that we might say to some of them, as Jesus said to the Pharisee, "Art thou a master in Israel, and knowest not these things?"

How shall we give even a passing notice of the crowd of errors which flow from this new religion, and which are sought to be thrust upon Protestants as great truths? This is especially manifest in that which regards the doctrines of the Church; it is there that they move in thick darkness. We will attend for a moment to a single example.

Unity in the Church of Christ, is not only one of the fundamental doctrines of the Gospel, but likewise one of the greatest benefits promised by the Saviour to his people. Jesus himself, in his sacrificial prayer, had invoked this unity among his own, and announced it unto them with the same breath; this could not have been a unity to exist only for the Apostles, but likewise for all who, in whatever place and in whatever age, should believe in Christ through their words. "Neither pray I for these alone; but for them also which shall believe on me through their words: that they all may be ONE, as thou Father art in me, and I in thee, that they also may be one in us: that the world may believe that thou hast sent me. And the glory which thou gavest me, I have given them, that they may be ONE, even as we are one; I in them, and thou in me, that they may be made perfect in UNITY." And would not this request of the Saviour, made at the solemn moment when he was about to make his voluntary expiation for the sins of the world, be accomplished? The Apostles speak continually of this *unity* of the true people of God: of all those who are *truly*, and not in *name* only, members of the body of Christ. *So we*, say they, *being many, are* ONE BODY *in Christ*. For, they add, by one Spirit are we all baptized into one body, whether we be Jews or Gentiles, whether we are bond or free. *There is neither*, they still further say, *Jew nor Greek, there is neither bond nor free, there is neither male nor female, ye are all* ONE *in Christ*. Endeavoring to keep *the unity of the spirit in the bond of peace*. *There is* ONE *body and* ONE *spirit, even as ye are called in* ONE *hope of your calling,* ONE *Lord,* ONE *faith,* ONE *baptism,* ONE *God, and Father of all*. These words are explicit, and we could cite many others equally so. Now, how does this Protestantism, which is distinct from Christianity, treat this unity demanded by the Prince of life himself for his Church, which he has promised, and which the holy Apostles have proclaimed? It says, that *unity* is a *philosophic invention;* it speaks of the *folly*, of the *thirst*, of the *fury* of unity; it adds that despotism, fanaticism, tyranny, exclusiveness, arbitrariness, are species of unity, or forms of unity, or means of unity, and that the most forcible objections which human reason can conceive may be urged against unity: that it is absurd, fatal, impossible; such, according to it, is the doctrine of Protestantism.

Having placed the words of the Lord and his Apostles side by side with those of the new Protestantism, there remains nothing but to keep silence. The stones, if they could, would cry out. We cannot conceive how it is possible so entirely to put away the Gospel, and to substitute for it the vain dreams of the imagination. May the time be far distant when these shall be the doctrines of *your* Protestantism! True Protestantism, however, casts it far from her. To THE LAW, AND TO THE TESTIMONY! if they speak not according, it is because there is no light in them,—and they shall look unto the earth; and behold trouble and darkness, dimness of anguish; and they shall be driven to darkness. Thus it is, that the Romish Church on one hand, and Neology on the other, seem to be skilful in wandering, the one to the right, and the other to the left, from the path of truth and life, trodden by the people of God. The Romish Church hears *unity* spoken of; and forgetting that the words of Jesus are *spirit* and life, that his reign is in the heart, that the question is concerning a *unity of spirit*, she invents an actual unity of appearance, a patched up unity, a unity of uniform and parade; provided its recruits all wear, whether good or bad, the same dress, the same cockade, and that at the same word they all turn their heads at the same moment, this is all that is necessary; the *heart* is not her domain; they may differ in *spirit* as far as the heavens differ from the earth; no matter! her concern is with that which *appears to be*, and not with that which *is*.

When we think of the infinite number of different opinions inclosed in the body called the Romish Church, is it not laughable to see this unformed mass baptized by the name of *unity?* It is the unity of *chaos,* and darkness is on the face of the deep. For, provided you carry a torch in a procession, or still more, provided you yield to importunities and mark your last moments by a few ceremonies, whatever else you may think *in your sleeve,* the Romish Church will acknowledge you as her child. But neology goes by a still easier reckoning, and needs not observe so many forms; it proclaims itself an army without standard, and a people without any common law; it declares that all its agreement consists in agreeing upon nothing. The unity of the Romish Church is the Prussian drill; the unity of the innovators is a Cossack band, each one moving as it pleases him. People of God! such is not your life and your unity! *Those whom he predestinated, them he also called; whom he called, them he also justified; and whom he justified, them he also glorified;* and those who have been the objects of this eternal grace, are *one* in heart at the foot of the cross; *redeemed unto God by the blood of the Lamb,* washed, sanctified, justified, by the name of the Lord Jesus, and by the Spirit of our God, built upon the foundation of the Apostles and prophets; Jesus Christ himself being the Chief Corner Stone, out of every kindred, and tongue, and people, and nation; they are *the true Church of God upon earth;* they are the true body of Christ, and they are *one,* as their Master has promised. Oh, ye, who may perchance read these lines, whatever language you speak, in whatever country you have had your birth, whatever may be the external confession to which you belong, I call you to witness that we are but *one!* We are but *one body,* we have *only one spirit, one hope, one Lord, one faith, one baptism, one God and Father of all, who is above all, and among all, and in all*. We are *one* with the Church which is in Heaven, and with that which is still upon earth. Let those who are without, reject with contempt the *unity* that our Saviour and our God has promised to his people; but as for us, we guard it as a precious jewel, and it constitutes our joy and glory!

There is, without doubt, a great error in that Protestantism which places itself *out* of Christianity. Perhaps we may take, as a ready example, another, and in some respects still more important one, which introduces into evangelical Christianity one of the most dangerous vices of Rome, and threatens to rob the Church of its liberty, its glory, its greatness, and to drag it down to shameful chains. But who will not feel the dangers that would encompass our Churches, if this philosophic-religious system, the child of the past century—if this Protestantism which is distinct from Christianity, could prevail therein? The necessary consequence would be to take away all life from the evangelical Churches. They will turn aside the river that waters the roots of this beautiful tree, causing it to yield its fruit in its season, and a dry and barren soil will quickly cause it to cast its foliage. Our Churches must be more strongly rooted in Christianity, in the Gospel; it is only from them they can receive life. Transplant them into the soil of worldly philosophy, as they pretend to do, and you will soon see them perish. What is it which has revived them? Is it not divine grace, evangelical sermons, the Bibles of the Bible Societies, the living spirit of the Missionary Societies? This is the way in which it must walk. The Protestantism, which is Christianity, is the spiritual lever of the world; it has received a commission to diffuse light and life throughout the families of the earth. The Protestantism which is not Christianity, is only good as it is the occasion of a little wit, and to give birth to some pages which amuse the ennui of their readers. Let us then plunge our roots in the spring of living water, and let us not, alas! plant the tree of our faith in broken cisterns which hold no water.

It is not only Protestantism considered as Christianity, which has to fear this new direction; it is likewise Christianity considered as Protestantism, that is in its struggle with Rome. In this exigency, the best method of obtaining strength, is to be vivified by the vital doctrines of faith. The best, or rather the only ground, on which we can meet and oppose to advantage the usurper who has established his camp, with all his hosts, on the seven hills, is that of the Apostles and Reformers. How would the branches be able to offer their fronts to the wind and battle with the tempest, if their roots did not derive from the depths of the earth their strength and their life? And what would become of soldiers who should fight continually without ever partaking of food or rest? They would soon become wan skeletons, which the least breath could overthrow.

We would ask, in closing this article: Is it a shadow we have been fighting! Pastors of our Churches! you know. Do you find among your flocks any error more general and more opposed to the propagation of Christianity, of the true Christian life, than that which consists in believing that, provided one is called *a good Protestant*, all will go well; that if he rejects the superstitions of Rome, her images, her processions, her saints, in a word (to use the happy expression of a French Christian universally distinguished by his birth, his talents, and his piety), if he is a *negative* Protestant, he is on the way to heaven. Is there an evil which strikes more directly and deeply at the root of piety?

If there are some shepherds who do not find this evil in their flocks, we rejoice and bless God for it; but we have heard the complaints and sighs of many, and this has induced us to lift up our voice in the Churches, that, weak but faithful sentinels, we might announce the danger which threatens Zion.

Faithful, beloved brethren! raised in the bosom of this Evangelical Church caused by the Lord to spring up in the midst of darkness, to lead many souls to light and life, it is not sufficient for your salvation that you are called in ordinary language *a good Protestant*. There is no Church which saves; there is no more salvation in the Protestant than in the Romish Church; salvation comes only *through Jesus Christ*. Neither is there salvation in any other; for there is none other name under heaven given among men, whereby we must be saved. Do you not perceive, my dear friends, that this is exactly the error of the Roman Catholics? Their capital crime is to put the Church in the stead of Jesus Christ, and to declare it is she who saves. And shall we commit the same fault? Consider that it is not necessary that this error be acknowledged in doctrine, as is the case in the Romish Church; it lives in our souls, if it renders us satisfied with ourselves, if it stops us in the way of life, if it hinders us from going as poor sinners to wash ourselves in that *fountain opened* on Golgotha *for sin and uncleanness*, and which alone *cleanseth us from* all sin—this will ruin our souls! No, no! neither the communion of Luther nor of Calvin, and still less of this or of that neology, can save us any more than that of Pius VII. or of Leo XII.; it is the communion of *Jesus* which saves. That which we have seen and heard declare we unto you, that ye also may have fellowship with us, and truly our fellowship is with the Father and with his Son Jesus Christ. Negative Protestantism is a comfortable cushion upon which we can quietly repose and slumber; we would that we were at this moment able to withdraw it from under the heads it pillows, even though it were a little roughly, so that falling naked to the ground they might awaken and seek that true point of support, which alone can give us peace of soul for time and for eternity. Friends and brethren! *These things I say, that ye might be saved;* God knows, and our conscience bears us witness. Oh! that every one to whom these leaves may come, would ask himself: I am a member of the Protestant Church, but am I a member of Christ? I hold communion with those who have separated from Rome; but do I hold communion with God? I have separated myself from the abominations without, from the worship that is offered to creatures; but have I separated myself from the corruption within, from that worship which makes *self* my idol? Is there in me an energetic Protestantism against myself, against sin which dwelleth in me, against the world and its lusts, against the devil and his works? This is *the Protestantism which affords salvation!*

Friends and brethren! Negative Protestantism is a first step, and we rejoice that you have taken it; but would you stop here? Alas! you will lose the fruit of your first efforts. Is it sufficient to pull down an old and tottering edifice, and to remove the rubbish from its foundations? This is the work of negative Protestantism. Shall we not also construct in its place a new building full of strength and bloom? This is the work of positive Protestantism; and these two Protestantisms, united, form alone Christianity. We beseech you, then, by the eternal compassion of God, to go to *the blood of Jesus*, there to wash away your sins, and there to find peace for your souls. Do not rest until you have proved for yourselves the import of these words of our Saviour: "Except a man be born again, he cannot see the kingdom of God." Then will you be true Protestants, then will you be true Christians, then you would have, together with all the redeemed Churches, whether that which now triumphs in heaven or that which still struggles on earth, " one spirit, one faith, one baptism, one Lord, one Father."

Pastors of Evangelical churches! the task which has been allotted you is a great one. Our voice has been but the echo of yours; and, if you have taken cognizance of the evil, you will the better know where to apply the remedy. Tender guardians of your flocks, you should zealously labor to guard believers against error, which, if not combated, would wither and destroy our Churches. We do not simply say that you should endeavor to make your hearers better Christians, still more firmly *rooted and grounded in Christ*, knowing that this is the only way of rendering them also better Protestants; because for a long while you have done this. But perhaps you may still judge it expedient, carefully to avoid everything which might improperly nourish, in your hearers, pride in the name of Protestant, without producing anything better. Undoubtedly you may incite them to consider the greatness of their advantages; but you should hasten to add, that in proportion to the magnitude of these advantages are their tasks and obligations, and this should be the point upon which you should insist. You must proclaim from the eminence of the pulpit, that Protestantism is nothing else than Christianity; that there is no Protestantism aside from Christianity; and that to be a good Protestant is only to be a good Christian, such as were the primitive disciples at Jerusalem, at Antioch, at Philippi. Perhaps you will also think proper to devote some particular meditation to the development of this important truth, and in refutation of the errors which are opposed to it, so that from one end of our Churches to the other, the standard of Christ alone may be lifted up, and that every new standard should prostrate itself before that of the Prince of Life, and hide in the dust its false colors. But what need is there of our words, venerable leaders of our flocks! God himself has implanted in your hearts the welfare of our Churches, and this flame, which already diffuses its genial warmth and rejoicing light, will not be extinguished. You have, so to speak, sent the words that we have uttered; our voice has been only your voice; our cry is only your cry. Destitute ourselves of wisdom and life, to pretend to convey unto others what we have not received ourselves, will end in ridiculous and powerless attempts.

Let silence then succeed to our word, and all listening to the voice of the Master who is in heaven, but who now speaks with so much power to the angels of his Churches, let us labor together with God, not only to strengthen the walls of Zion, but also to multiply in its bosom, abundance, life and peace.

Have we been severe? Determined not to go beyond this, have we confounded men with their wickedness and faults? We think not. We have avoided all personalities; our concern is with things and not with individuals. If we have contended against systems which appeared to us dangerous, we are ready to tender the hand to those who entertain them, as to brethren descended from the same Father with ourselves. How great would be our joy could we see talents that we appreciate, employed in that which can alone bring prosperity to our Churches! Friends, we trust you possess in your hearts the same desires as ourselves. Do you not perceive that every period of revival in the Church has been effected by its vital doctrines, by the spirit of power and of life in the Gospel, and not by the efforts of reason or of human philosophy? Have we not heard you sometimes joyfully declare that it is in these doctrines alone the Church can find her hopes of salvation? Why then at another period do you oppose these doctrines? Are you not delighted, do you not boast as Protestants, of the admirable labors of England and America, of their Bible Societies and their Missions? All who compose those Societies are *one* with us; the same principles that we maintain and have mentioned, are those that animate them. Why then should that which is the subject of your praise beyond the sea, be on this side the object of your attack, of your blame, perhaps of your ridicule? How can you praise the *effects* at a distance, and combat the *causes* near at hand? How can you present the labors of our British and American brethren as a model, at the same time that you rob your brethren on the Continent of the only means, the only power by which they might become their imitators? No! no! you are doubtless deceived, and we call upon yourselves to be better informed of yourselves. There is, it is true, a great temptation in this walking in accordance with the reigning worldly spir, d efending Protestantism as a species of ecclesiastical liberalism, and even in being praised by the organs of public opinion. But are you not called to resist and to overcome this temptation? Public opinion may be of some value; we approve it. But evangelical Christianity has received a nobler vocation than that of following in the *suite* of the world; it is at the *head* she must walk, strong in her own principles and borrowing from none. He, who walks only in the track of the multitude, may render a few services to humanity; but he who remains immoveable in truth, opposing a brazen front to the course of the world in everything that is wrong, obliging it, by his perseverance, to turn aside from its sinuous paths into the straight path of rectitude, allowing threatenings, injuries, violent language, and ridicule, to blunt their darts against the buckler of his faith; he will gain the crown and will have fought the good fight. Such is our vocation; friends, shall it not be yours?

It is this vocation to which you look forward, pupils of our Churches! Levites, who are growing up in the shadow of the sanctuary, and who learn in our schools what is the *wisdom*, the *righteousness*, the *sanctification*, the *redemption*, that you are one day to proclaim to the people, to know Jesus Christ and Him crucified, remember, that if you walk in the doctrines of faith, you will follow in the footsteps of the greatest and the noblest of the human race; in the path of Abraham, of David, of Isaiah, of John, of Paul, of Peter, of Polycarp, of Ignatius, of Justin, of Cyprian, of Origen, of Chrysostom, of Augustine, of Bernard, of Wickliffe, of Waldo, of Huss, of Luther, of Melancthon, of Calvin, of Zuingle, of Favel, of Knox, of Mornay, of Malbranche, Drelincourt, Claude, Bossuet, Fenelon, Bacon and Newton, Pascal and many others who have all believed the same that we believe; and above all, you will walk with Jesus Christ who has taught them. But should you abandon these doctrines for those sought to be substituted in their stead, you will drag along in the shameful steps of some pretended philosophers, with some obscure neologians of different countries, who are only known for their extravagances and for the evil they have wrought to the Church of the Saviour. Be ye not deceived; the vain objections they may offer to you are only the trifles of wits and sciolists, of superficial minds, who fall back before the steps of truth. All their pretended wisdom is only foolishness with God; the gifted, the choice spirits of the world, not allowing themselves to be deterred by these vain sports, have embraced eternal truth as it is revealed in the word of God, and as our Churches have professed it from their birth. Repel, then, a poisoned blow, which will not only convey death to your own souls, but also to the flocks over which you shall be established overseers. Ascend the pulpits, to proclaim from thence the powerful Word of Truth; be the noble instruments of God's mercy, and not the repeaters of man's inventions! Find grace before God for your own souls; your faces shall be enlightened by it, and you will reflect upon your brethren salvation and peace. Fear not the world. "He that is in you is greater than he that is in the world. Ye are of God, little children, and have overcome them." Christ says, "Lo I am with you alway, even unto the end of the world, and all power is given unto me in heaven and in earth."

Oh God! save thy church. IT IS TIME

FAMILY WORSHIP.

TRANSLATED BY M. M. BACKUS.

FAMILY WORSHIP.

As for me and my house, we will serve the Lord.—JOSHUA XXIV. 15.

Let me die the death of the righteous, and let my last end be like his. We have said on a former occasion, my brethren, that if we would die their death, we must live their life. Doubtless there are some cases in which the Lord manifests his grace and glory to man, on his death-bed, saying to him, as to the thief on the cross: *To-day thou shalt be with me in paradise.* The Lord, from time to time, gives such examples to the Church, thus to demonstrate his sovereign power, by which he can, if it please him, subdue the most hardened hearts, and convert the most alienated souls, causing us to see that all depends on his grace, and that he has mercy on whom he will have mercy. But these are only very rare exceptions, upon which you cannot absolutely count; and if you would have a Christian death, my dear hearers, you must have a Christian life—a heart truly converted to the Lord, truly ready for the kingdom, which, trusting only in the grace of Christ, desires to walk near Him. There are many means, my brethren, by which you can prepare yourselves during life, to obtain, one day, so blessed an end. To one of the most efficacious of these we would lead you to-day. This means is *domestic worship;* that is to say, that edification which, day after day, a Christian family receives at the common altar. " As for me and my house, we will serve the Lord," said Joshua to Israel. We desire, my brethren, to present to you the *motives* which ought to lead you to this resolution of Joshua, and the necessary directions for its accomplishment.

THE MOTIVES.

Domestic worship is the most ancient as well as the most holy of institutions. It is not one of those innovations against which one is easily prejudiced; it began with the world itself.

It is evident that the first worship, which the first man and his children rendered to God, could be no other than family worship, since they were then the only family existing on the earth. Then began men, says the Scripture, to call upon the name of the Lord. Domestic worship must have been for a long period the only worship rendered in common to God; for as the earth increased in population, each head of a family establishing himself alone, *a priest unto God* in the place in which his lot was cast, presented to the Lord of all the earth, with his wife, his sons, his daughters, his men servants and his maid servants, the homage which was His due. It was only when by gradual increase men had infinitely multiplied, that different families dwelt near each other, and then came the idea of offering to God a common adoration, and *public worship* had birth. But domestic worship had become too precious to the families of the children of God to be abandoned by them, and if they united with strange families in worshipping God, how much stronger reasons had they for persisting in adoring Him with their own families? So, when leaving the cradle of the human race, we transport ourselves under the tents of the patriarchs, we find there also this household worship.

Go with the angels to the plains of Mamre, when Abraham sits at his tent-door in the heat of the day; enter there with him and we shall see the patriarch, with all his house, offering a common sacrifice to God. "I know," said the Lord, speaking of the father of the faithful, "I know that he will command his children, and his house after him, to keep the way of the Lord,—to do that which is just and right." Public worship is established by Moses; he gives many ordinances;—a magnificent temple is to be raised. Will not domestic worship now be abolished? No; by the side of this temple, and all its magnificence, the meanest house of the faithful is to be filled with the Word of God. "These words which I command thee this day," said the Lord, by Moses, "shall be in thine heart; and thou shalt teach them diligently to thy children, and shalt talk of them when thou sittest in thine house, and when thou walkest by the way, and when thou liest down, and when thou risest up." Joshua, in our text, declares to the people that they, if they will, may adore idols, but that he will not mingle in their profane feasts, but withdraw into his own dwelling,—*he and his house will serve* the Lord. Job, rising early in the morning, *sanctified his children*, and offered burnt offerings according to the number of them all, saying: "It may be that my sons have sinned!" David, whose whole life is a continual adoration of God, and to whom a day passed in the courts of the Lord was better than a thousand days elsewhere, neglected not the domestic altar, when he exclaimed, "The things that our fathers have told us we will not keep from our children." Transporting ourselves to the times in which our Saviour appeared, we find domestic instruction in all the pious families of Israel. It is thus St. Paul was enabled to say to Timothy: "From a child thou hast known the Holy Scriptures, which are able to make thee wise unto salvation. I call to remembrance the unfeigned faith that is in thee, which dwelt first in thy grandmother Lois, and thy mother Eunice; and I am persuaded that in thee also." Jesus, during his ministry, laid the foundations of domestic worship among Christians, when he said: "Where two or three are gathered together in my name, there will I be in the midst of them." St. Paul recommends it by saying: "Rule well your own houses, having your children in subjection with all gravity; speaking to yourselves in psalms and hymns and spiritual songs, singing and making melody in your hearts to the Lord; giving thanks always for all things unto God and the Father in the name of our Lord Jesus Christ." Yes, my brethren, if we penetrate into the humble dwellings of the early Christians, after having been under the tents of the patriarchs, we shall find there also, this same family worship offered to the Lord, we shall hear in the distance those songs, which may have revealed the existence of the disciples of the Crucified to their persecutors, which they caused to ascend with joy before the throne of their Saviour, because they feared him rather than men; we shall see them gathered together around these sacred books which they hide so carefully, lest they fall into the hands of those who would destroy them.

An illustrious father of the Church, Clement of Alexandria, about the commencement of the third century, recommends to Christian wives to make common prayers and the reading of the Bible their daily morning employment; then, he adds, "The mother is the glory of her children, the wife is the glory of her husband; both are the glory of the wife, and God is the glory of all." And another father, not less celebrated, Tertullian, gave a little while before, this admirable description of the domestic life of a Christian pair: "What a union is that which exists between two faithful ones, who have in common the same hope, the same desire, the same manner of life, the same service of the Lord: both as a brother and sister united according to the flesh, and according to the spirit, cast themselves together on their knees; they pray and fast together; they teach, they exhort, they mutually support each other with gentleness; they are together in the church of God, at the table of the Lord; they partake of pains, of persecutions, of joys; the one hides nothing from the other, the one avoids not the other; they visit the sick, they succor the needy; psalms and hymns are heard resounding among them; they strive to see which shall sing most fervently in the heart to God. Christ has joy in seeing and hearing these things, he sends them his peace. There, where two like these are found, he is found also; and where he is no evil comes."

Leaving the humble dwellings of the primitive Christians, it is true that we find domestic worship becoming gradually rarer; but with splendor did it re-appear at the time of the Reformation. And what an influence did it then exercise on the faith, the manners, the intellectual development of these nations who returned to primitive Christianity! The period is not very distant in which it was found in all evangelical families. If our fathers have been deprived of its light, our grandfathers at least knew it. It flourished especially in the evangelical provinces of this kingdom, and we trust that numerous and precious fragments may yet be found.

My brethren, such has been in all ages a life of piety. Shall we be such Christians or shall we not? Do we wish to invent a new species of piety which shall agree very well with the world, or do we wish to retain that which God has ordained? Beholding this worship, which passed from the tents of the patriarchs into the dwelling of the first Christians, and at length established itself in the households of our fathers, shall we not say, "As for me and my house, we will serve the Lord?"

But, my brethren, if the love of God is in your heart, if you feel that, being purchased by a great price, you ought to glorify God in your body and spirits which are His, where will you delight to honor him, if not in your own family, in your own house? You love to unite with your brethren in rendering public homage to Him in his temples: you love to pour out your hearts before him in your closet. Shall it be only in the presence of the person with whom he has associated your life, and of your children, that you do not wish to be employed with God? Will it be precisely there, that you will have no thanks to give? Will it be precisely there, that you will not have some favors, some protection to implore? You occupy yourself with everything in your intercourse with them. Conversation turns upon a thousand different objects; cannot your tongue and your heart find a word for God? Can you not lift up your voice in your family for Him who is the true father of your family; can you not converse with your wife and children of Him, who may one day be the only husband of your wife, the only father of your children? The Gospel has produced a domestic society, which did not exist before it and cannot exist beyond it; it would seem then, that this society, full of gratitude to the God of the Gospel, ought to be especially consecrated to Him; and above all, my brethren, such unions as families, who call themselves Christians, who have even a respect for religion, and where there is never a question raised concerning God. What is the condition of immortal souls, who have been united, who never ask themselves who has redeemed them, who has united them, what is their destiny, their future, their end? What is the condition of those, who, seeking to aid each other in everything else, never think of assisting each other in "the one thing needful," of having a single conversation, of reading a single line, of pronouncing one prayer, which has reference to eternal interests! Christian partners! Is it then only in the flesh and for time that you desire to be united? Is it not in spirit and for eternity? Are you then beings who have met only by chance, and whom a new chance, that of death, will soon separate? Do you not wish to be united by God, in God, and for God? Religion would unite your souls in immortal bonds! But do not reject them; every day increase their strength by the devotions of the domestic circle. Passengers, whom the same ship encloses, discourse of the place whither they go; and you, voyagers on the same vessel towards an eternal world, can you not speak of that world, of the route which conducts you thither, of your hopes, your fears? "For many walk, of whom I have told you often, and now tell you even weeping, that they are the enemies of the cross of Christ," says St. Paul; "for our conversation is in heaven; from whence also we look for the Saviour, the Lord Jesus Christ." But if you ought for yourselves to be employed for God in your dwellings, ought you not for those of your household, whose souls have been entrusted to you, especially for your own children? You are much concerned for the prosperity, the temporal happiness of your own; but will not all this care cause your negligence in regard to their eternal prosperity and happiness to appear in the stronger light? Your children are young trees which have been confided to you; your house is the nursery in which they ought to grow; you are the gardener. Alas! would you plant these young and precious shrubs in barren sand? And yet this is what does happen, if there is nothing in your house which causes them to increase in the knowledge and love of their God and Saviour. Will you not prepare a favorable soil, fit to give them sap and life? What will become of your children in the midst of all the allurements which surround, and would lead them to evil? What will become of them in this restless age, in which it is so necessary to strengthen the soul of a young man by the fear of God, thus giving to the frail bark the requisite ballast before launching it on the boundless ocean? Parents! in whose families your children find the spirit of piety, take pride, then, in adorning them with all manner of outward gifts, in introducing them into the society of the world, in granting all their whims, in allowing them to walk according to their own desires, and you will see them vain, proud, idle, disobedient, impertinent, extravagant! They will treat you with contempt; and the more fond the indulgence you have bestowed, the less will be the regard they will exercise towards you in return.

It is such conduct as this, which is too often seen: but ask yourselves if you are not responsible for their bad habits and their wicked practices, and your conscience will reply that you are; that you eat of the bread of bitterness which you have yourself prepared. May you learn from this, what has been your sin in neglecting the means in your power for acting on their heart, and may others be warned by your misfortune and educate their children in *the fear of the Lord!* Nothing is more healthful for this end than domestic piety. Public worship is often too vague, too general, and not sufficiently interesting for children; they know not how much of the worship in particular they are to take to themselves. Lessons properly recited, if they are alone, will perhaps easily induce them to regard religion as a study similar to that of foreign languages or of history. Example here as elsewhere, and even more than elsewhere, will effect more than precept. It is not sufficient to teach them by means of elementary books, that it is their duty to love God, but we must also show them that we love him. If they see that no homage is paid to that God of whom they are told, the best instructions become useless; but by means of family worship, these young plants will increase as a tree planted by the rivers of water, that bringeth forth his fruit in his season; his leaf also shall not wither: your children may quit the paternal roof; but they will recall in distant lands the prayers offered under that roof, and those prayers will protect them. If any one has children or nephews, let them learn first to show piety at home, says the Scripture. But if any provide not for his own, and specially for those of his own house, he hath denied the faith, and is worse than an infidel.

What gentleness, what peace, what true felicity, will not a Christian family find in the establishment in its midst of the domestic altar, and uniting together in sacrificing to the Lord! It is the employment of the angels in heaven; and blessed are they who anticipate these pure and immortal joys! "Behold how good and how pleasant it is for brethren to dwell together in unity! It is like the precious ointment upon the head, that ran down upon the beard, even Aaron's beard; that went down to the skirts of his garment: for these the Lord commanded the blessing, even life evermore." Oh, what kindness, what new life, piety spreads throughout a family! In a house where God is forgotten, there is harshness, ill humor, ennui. Without the knowledge and the love of God, a family is but an aggregation of individuals, having for each other more or less of natural affection; but the true bond, *the love of God our Father in Jesus Christ our Lord*, is wanting. Poets are full of beautiful descriptions of domestic life; but, alas! the reality is often very different from their pictures! Sometimes this arises from want of confidence in the providence of God, sometimes from the love of riches, sometimes from a difference in characters, or an opposition in principles. Oh! what troubles, what miseries in the bosoms of families! Domestic piety will prevent all these evils; one can draw from it a perfect confidence in the God who "feedeth the birds of the air;" we can draw from it a *real love* for all those with whom we are called to live; not an exacting, suspicious love, but a merciful love, which excuses and forgives, like that of God himself; not a proud love, but a love humble, and accompanied by a feeling of its own faults, of its own misery; not a changing love, but a love as immutable as eternal charity. "A voice of singing, of triumph, and of deliverance, resounds in the tabernacle of the just." When the hour of trial comes, that hour which sounds sooner or later, and oftener more than once in the dwellings of men, what powerful consolation will domestic piety afford! Where are trials experienced, if not in the bosom of families? Where then but in the bosom of families ought the remedy for trials to be found? What grief is there in an afflicted family which has not this consolation! The different persons who compose it, mutually increase their sorrow. But if, on the other hand, the family loves God—if it is accustomed to invoke in common the holy name of God, from whom proceeds every trial, as well as every excellent grace, how the bowed soul will be lifted up! The remaining members, the fragments of the family, gather together around the table upon which is found *the Book of God*, that book in which they read of the resurrection, of life, of immortality, in which they find the certain pledges of the happiness of him who is no longer of their number, of their own hope. The Lord is pleased to send them in abundance *the Comforter*; the spirit of glory and of God rests upon them; an ineffable balm is poured into their wounds, and spreads there great sweetness; hence peace is communicated from heart to heart. They taste in some moments of a joy almost celestial. "When I walk through the valley of the shadow of death, I will fear no evil, for Thou art with me, Thy rod and Thy staff shall comfort me. O Lord, thou hast brought up my soul from the grave: For his anger endureth but a moment; in his favor is life; weeping may endure for a night, but joy cometh in the morning."

Who can tell, my brethren, what an influence domestic piety may exert over the whole face of society? What encouragements to this duty cannot all find therein, from the highest officer of state to the most humble artizan! If all would accustom themselves to walk in this way, not only in the sight of man, but in the eye of God, how would each one learn from it to be content in the station in which he is placed! Good habits would be formed; the powerful voice of conscience would be strengthened; prudence, decorum, talents, the social virtues would develope themselves with a strength altogether new. Behold what we may expect for ourselves and for society; "righteousness has the promise of the life which now is, and of the life which is to come."

DIRECTIONS.

If you would profit by all the benefits of family worship, what ought you to do? It remains for us, my brethren, to give you some directions on this subject.

And first, as far as it is possible, these exercises of domestic piety should not be destitute *of the spirit, of truth and of life;* they should not consist merely in reading certain books, or in reciting certain formulas in which the heart has no share. A total absence of domestic piety would perhaps be better than such mockery. These dead forms are too often found in families. But in this age, when the Church is everywhere striving to arise from her ruins, and when the wind, of which Ezekiel speaks, is everywhere breathing upon the dry bones, that they may have life, it is necessary that we should return to domestic worship, and should revive it, not in its perishing and dead state, but in a state of strength and life. What shall we do to effect this purpose? Let us engage in the offices of domestic piety; not so much as a pious work which we ought to fulfill, for there we may fall over the stumbling-block we have noticed, or into pride; but let us rather engage in them as poor creatures, who would have better riches; as those who hunger and would have nourishment for that which is the noblest part of them. Perform it as a duty, if you will, but the rather as through necessity. The little child knows very well how to ask for a morsel of bread, or even for milk of its mother; shall we not know how to ask of God for his spiritual and pure milk? "Blessed are they who hunger and thirst after righteousness, for they shall be filled."

A second rule that we would give you, my brethren, is this, that you should not attach yourselves too exclusively, too servilely, to some particular form. Establish, in the first place, such a worship as is suited to your own wants, and to those of your household; entire freedom: one day perhaps in this manner, another day in that; sometimes long—another time short. Perhaps it would be best that this exercise should not at first embrace all the individuals of the house, but should take place in a narrower and more familiar circle; in this way you would secure greater facility and edification. Follow these different impulses; the principal thing is, that God be not forgotten under your domestic roof. "Keep yourselves firm in the liberty wherewith Christ has made you free, and submit no longer to the yoke of bondage." But with what, then, ought the moments devoted to God, to be occupied?

In the first place, and as it is very natural, *the reading of the word of God;* occasionally, perhaps, that of other Christian works. In how many families has this admirable book, this book of the nations, been in all ages, and still continues to be, the most precious treasure! In how many dwellings has the Holy Bible diffused righteousness, peace, and joy in the Holy Ghost, and submission to every authority constituted of God. The different books composing the Bible, are almost every one of a different kind; it would be difficult to enclose a greater variety in the same volume, yet everywhere partaking of the same spirit of God. This circumstance renders it singularly fit for the nourishment of families; and thence it happens, that so many poor and obscure families among Protestant nations, with this book in their hands, so readily outstrip all others, and are brought by it not only into the possession of eternal life, but still more to a remarkable development of intelligence. The child, the old man, the woman, the man, find alike in it, that which interests and raises them to God. There is something in it suited to every situation in life. What abundant consolations may not all agitated and afflicted but faithful souls, draw from the psalms of the Prophet-king! It is convenient to read an entire book in course, but it is not necessary to follow the order in which the different books are found arranged in the holy Volume. On the contrary, it would perhaps be better to pass from the New Testament to the Old, from the Old to the New; from one of the Gospels, for example, to one of the Prophecies (how sublime is that of Isaiah, and how he reaches the depths of the soul!), from the Prophets to the Epistles of the Apostles, and then to one of the historical books of the Old Testament. It is desirable that the reader should make some application of that which he reads. You know how to speak of other things which you have read; here alone, shall sentiments and words fail you? Can you find nothing in it which is applicable to the state of your heart, to the situation of your family, to the character of one of your children? Always read this Book, not as a history of past time, but as a word written for you, addressed now to you; you will ever find in it something to benefit you. If, however, nothing is given you, be satisfied with asking the Holy Spirit to cause His word to bear in the heart, those fruits which he has promised. "For, as the rain cometh down and the snow from heaven, and returneth not thither, but watereth the earth and maketh it bring forth and bud, that it may give seed to the sower and bread to the eater; so shall my word be that goeth forth out of my mouth; it shall not return unto me void, but it shall accomplish that which I please, and it shall prosper in the thing whereto I have sent it."

A second act of worship should be *extemporaneous prayer*. There are doubtless good written prayers; but would you not know how to pray yourself with a loud voice? You know very well how to speak to a friend. Why would you not know how to speak to God? It is so easy to approach Him when one draws near in the name of Christ crucified! "Thou art God, very easy to be entreated," said David. "He hears us," said he, "before we yet speak." If you pray in a low voice, would you not also be able to pray aloud? Be not so careful about your words: "prayer requires more of the heart than of the tongue, more of faith than of reason." How can the influence be other than salutary, when the father or mother of a family, for example, prays aloud to God in the presence of their children, entering into the details of their faults before God, and asking for his assistance and his favor? And when is a family not in a position in which it is not called upon to raise its prayer to God for deliverance, for succor, for consolation? "You shall seek me, and shall find me, after that you have sought me with all your heart," is the promise of God.

A third act of worship, which, if it is practicable, ought to make a part of domestic devotions, is *singing*. Man has now associated song with his labors, and above all with his pleasures; but to praise God is certainly its first appointment. It was to this that the Prophet King consecrated it. Shall we not devote it to the same? If they sing so many secular songs in the household, why can they not sing to the honor of God, who has created and has saved us? "Speaking unto each other in psalms, and hymns, and spiritual songs, singing and making melody in your hearts unto God."

But, does some one ask, *what time* shall we think thus on God, and *when* shall we draw together towards him? I reply, at the time that you wish, the time which will best suit your convenience, which will derange your affairs the least. Usually this is in the evening; perhaps, on account of the fatigues of the day, it would be better in the morning, or rather both morning and evening. After you have taken your morning meal, or even while taking it, could you not consecrate the time that is usually employed in silence, or in useless trifling, to reading or hearing read some words which would lift up your thought to God? I am about to commence the day by the first function of animal existence; but thou, my soul, a spiritual and immortal existence, wilt thou do nothing, wilt thou receive nothing now? I am about to nourish my body with that which God has created; but thou, my soul, awaken thyself and be fed by the Creator! Oh Lord, thou art my portion for ever! Oh God, thou art my strong God! in the morning I will seek thee! What a blessing, my brethren, would such a commencement shed over the whole day, and to what happy dispositions would it dispose us! And to you, Christian parents, the evening of the Sabbath, that time which the children of irreligious parents devote to dissipation, ought to be especially precious and sacred. Instruct then your children in *the way of the Lord*, and your instruction at this moment will be more especially blessed, if they see that you are truly serious in the work in which you are engaged.

To all this, my brethren, add the main thing,—a life in agreement with the sanctity of the worship which you offer to God. Be not different men before the altar of God, and in the world, but be ever and everywhere the same. Let your conduct throughout the day be a living commentary on what you have read, heard, or spoken, in the hour of devotion. Put in practice the Word, and be not hearers only,—deceiving yourselves with vain words,—for the sacrifice of fools is abomination in the sight of God, but he is well-pleased with the entreaties of the righteous. Such is domestic worship. We have reminded you, my dear hearers, of the motives which ought to hasten its establishment in your families, and we solicit all, but particularly the married, the fathers and mothers, to put their hands to the plough.

But do you exclaim, "this would be so strange a thing?" What, my brethren? is it not still more strange, that a family, professing Christianity,—professing to have a firm hope for eternity, should advance towards that eternity without manifesting in its midst any sign of this hope, any preparation, any conversation,—perhaps, alas! without even a thought on these things? Oh! how strange is conduct like this!

But, do you say again, "It is a thing of low repute, inglorious in itself, and kindled with a thousand indignities?" And who is then the greatest;—that father of a family, in patriarchal days, who was also a priest of God—who supported his own paternal authority, and imparted to it a divine unction by bending his knee, with his children, before his Father and their Father, or that man of the world, in our day, whose mind is only occupied with vain pursuits, who forgot his own and the eternal destinies of his children, whose house is without God? Oh! what a reproach!

But do you further object? "*Different ages,—different manners:* these things were well enough once; but now everything is changed!" It is just because everything is changed that we must hasten to set up again the domestic altar in the bosom of families, lest the weak bonds, which still preserve these families, should be dissolved,—involving, in their ruin, both Church and State. It is not until after disease has spread with great violence that remedies become useless, and before despairing of a man's life, we give him at least the most powerful preservatives.

You, who by the grace of God have with good resolutions, and good dispositions, already made the attempt, do not be discouraged; make another trial still; have recourse to God in prayer; ask Him to guide you, to sustain you, to make you united; ask Jesus to be with you, for *where two or three are gathered together in his name, he will be in their midst.*

But, my brethren, before an altar can be raised to God in your households, there must be one set up in your hearts! And is it found therein, my brethren? Oh! if I could draw aside the veil; if I could now penetrate and read the hearts of those who listen to me, what should I behold? Or rather, Lord! what seest thou in our hearts, thou for whom there is no veil, and before whom all is naked and uncovered? In your heart, my dear hearer, I discover an altar raised to pleasure and worldliness; upon it you offer your morning sacrifice; and the smoke of your evening sacrifice ascends even throughout the night, filled with intoxication and stupefaction. In your heart, my dear hearer, I find an altar to this world's goods, to riches, to mammon. In yours, my dear hearer, I see an altar erected to yourself—you are your own idol, which you exalt above everything else; for whom you desire all things, and at whose feet you would see the whole world prostrate itself! My brethren, is there an altar in your heart raised to the living and true God? Are you *the temple of God,* and *dwelleth the Spirit of God within you?* So long as there is no altar erected in your souls to God, there can be none in your families; for what participation has justice with iniquity? And what connection is there between light and darkness? What concord has Christ with Belial? And what agreement has *the temple of God with idols?*

Be converted then in your hearts! die unto the world, unto sin, and above all, to yourselves, and live to God in Jesus Christ, our Lord. Immortal souls, Christ has redeemed you at a great price! He has yielded up his life on the cross for you; and know that if one died for all, it was that they who live should no longer live unto themselves, but should live in newness of life unto Him, who died and rose again. Depart, therefore, from idols, and touch not any vile thing, and I will receive you, and I will be to you a father, and you shall be to me for sons and for daughters, saith the Lord God Almighty.

Oh! my brethren, happy is that family which has embraced that God, who has said: "I will dwell in the midst of you, and will walk with you, and ye shall be unto me for sons and for daughters." Happy for time, happy for eternity! How can you hope to meet your children with Christ, in Heaven, if you do not seek with them Christ, on earth? How can you meet again your family on high, if you do not concern yourselves in your families below, with the things which are above. But the Christian family who have been united in Jesus, will be joined together around the glories of Him, whom they have loved, not having seen. It will but exchange its mean and perishable tabernacle for the immense and eternal mansion of God. Instead of an humble family of the earth, united by the same bonds with all the families in the Heavens, it will have become *one glorious family which no man can number.* She, with the hundred and forty-four thousand, will encompass the throne of God, saying, as she said upon earth, but with joy, and with glory: "Lord, thou art worthy to receive glory, and honor, and power!"

Oh my brethren, if there is now a single father or mother, who will resolve to assemble together around the Lord! if there is but one person not yet sustaining domestic relations, who has resolved, when he shall have formed them, to raise an altar to God in his house, and in future years shall put his resolution into practice, causing abundant blessings to descend on him and his; then will I render thanks to God for having spoken. Oh my dear hearers! may the Lord so have touched your soul, that you will now exclaim: *As for me and my house, we will serve the Lord!* AMEN.

CHRISTIAN STUDIES:

OR

FRAGMENTS GATHERED FROM A COURSE OF PRACTICAL THEOLOGY.

TRANSLATED BY M. M. BACKUS.

"Viderint theologi, ne si solitis vel quibuslibet viis immaneant ⋰ . ⋱ ., quod omitti non possit sine damno, a negotio eorum, qui a nobis instituendi sunt, malè secludant, vel ad iniquam exiguitatem condemnent."—
C. J. Nitzsch, Observat. ad Theologi. Practic.

CHRISTIAN STUDIES.

FROM THE "EVANGELICAL GAZETTE"—FIRST PUBLISHED IN 1833.

FAITH.

In nothing has there been a greater variety than in the ideas which have obtained on faith,—and as there is something of truth in all that has been said on this subject, it seems to be the cause of interminable disputes. One considers it only in its principle, another looks merely at its effects. Yet another believes the same elements of invariable and infallible trust to be divided between them;—St. James and St. Paul do not seem to have been at all understood. It has happened now according to the saying of Paul writing to the Corinthians, that men have *sought out many inventions* and have "*ten thousand masters in Christ*"—notwithstanding, the unity of faith is not a chimera. *There is one faith*, as there is one only salvation of which it is the object, and only one Lord who imparts it.—What means have we for reconciling all this? In our opinion the following:—

It is necessary simply to put each part in its own place. Do not let us invert the natural order of divine operations; let us not place the end before the beginning, the effect before the cause, the fruit before the plant by which it is borne, nor the plant itself before the root from which it is to germinate—(Rom. xi.18.) Let us have respect unto the Word, and its divine pages will reveal all, explain all, and satisfy every reasonable curiosity.

At the first enunciation of the term *faith* there arises before the mental vision an unique and complete picture of that light which a knowledge of evangelical doctrines bestows on man, as well as of the convictions which the proof of that trust engenders in the mind, and of the sentiments which that species of conviction awakens in the soul, and which are its inseparable companions—a picture, in fine, of the deeds to which faith stimulates us; of the fervor it imparts to the will, of the life it communicates to our zeal, and of the constancy it confers on the obedience of the Christian. It is, in a word, the entire life of the believer. We can dignify with the title of true faith, only that complete outline of zeal and efficient Christianity which alone was that of the primitive disciples of Jesus, and that which alone has never belied the excellence of its origin. Is this demonstrable? Beyond all question; the Scriptures are rigorously definite upon this point, and reject without mercy every *phantom* of faith, all empty *appearance*, all purely nominal profession, and all unfruitful pretensions to its gifts.

As a consequence of this, all treatises, religious systems, and nicely adjusted catechisms, give themselves ample latitude on the subject. It has not been deemed sufficient to define faith as a strong belief, it has become necessary to reclothe it in numberless new characters, by which it should acquire cleanness, depth, fervor, efficacy and life.

What has been the consequence? They have mingled with it some show of faith, yet so little, that it is impossible to offer it as a resource to those who are destitute and ready to perish; they have made it a by-path to those who have neither the time nor inclination to travel the long and difficult road of obedience.

How can one *be saved* by it? I dare not say he is *sure* that he possesses it; no one would be so rash as to testify of himself that he had really acquired it, so full is it of forms and of conditions; it would be necessary to any degree of assurance in the matter, to have first obtained perfection itself, to have become a *sainted* disciple, and who dare to give himself out for such? Humility seems to forbid it, till at length it has become a point of modesty among Christians, an element of security as I have already said, that strong assurance, that one *cannot know* positively that he possesses faith.

Was this the primitive design—the end of the preaching of faith, which should conduct by a certain way, which the law had failed to attain? Who could justify *the circumcision by faith, and the uncircumcision* also *by faith*? I dare to make the assertion,—no one; and I add, moreover, that men have completely lost sight of the primitive types of that faith and its most striking examples—that faith which our Saviour dignified with the title, and commended, with the highest praises, seeming, at the first blush, to expect nothing else. Faith, such as duties and human works have made and described it, is no longer that which was conspicuous in the Canaanite woman, who said, "if I may but touch his garment I shall be whole," or the centurion of Capernaum, who said, "but speak the word only and thy servant *shall* be healed;" and which then animated so many simple minds, destitute of all that is now supposed of such essential importance to true believers.

Without misapprehending, therefore, the effects and tendencies of faith,—all the developments it can receive or furnish, and all the riches which it is able to disclose, and the entrance to the possession of which it opens to its votaries, it concerns us, in my judgment, to have recourse to some very simple idea—the very commencement of the *way*, in fact,—for it is but one,—namely, the *way* of God. It is not an end to reach, but a road, a route, a path to follow. From the moment that the foot is truly planted in it, the believer has but to take one step, and he is *in the faith* which he has begun to exercise.

Faith is defined by the Apostle Paul, just as we define sentiments, by its results, rather than by its essence. *Faith*, according to him (Heb. xi. 1), is, to him who possesses it such, that he already *has* to a certain degree the good that it promises; and its subject lives always in the presence of God and eternal realities, and is no longer under the influence of sensible objects.

But what is it, we would ask here, what is this principle, the effect of which is so powerful as to give a reality to things as yet invisible? What is faith in its foundation—in its first act?

Faith, in its first elementary act, is belief; the taking, the laying hold of the soul upon the Word of God. If the truth of God is imparted by instruction, then faith receives it in the Word which contains it—it seizes, apprehends, and comprehends this living seed. If the truth of God assumes form in facts and promises, then faith accepts and embraces them, not in a *passive* manner, which would be dead and indifferent, but in an *active* manner; it fastens itself to them, it attaches itself to them, it submits to their influence, and adopts whatever consequences they may lead to. If this truth is a commandment, faith becomes an obedience—called the *obedience of faith;* if it be a doctrine, then faith becomes a profession: " obey the doctrine," says St. Paul; " obey the truth through the spirit," says St. Peter (Rom. vi. 17.; 1 Peter i. 22).

Faith thus receiving this truth of God, communicates through it to man a knowledge of divine things. It is the illumination of which the Evangelist speaks (John i. 7.; 2 Cor. iv. 6.; Eph. i. 18).—But it gives something more than light and knowledge, it affects the whole man. Like the sun, which at once imparts both life and heat, it is also a resuscitator as well as light to the soul that feels its influence. Like the fire which purifieth all things, *it* purifies the heart,—" God has purified the hearts of the Gentiles through faith" (Acts xv. 9). It is the introduction of a new principle, which renovates the entire man.

Faith, if we may so speak, takes God at his word—receives the truth instantaneously, and *lays hold on eternal life* the moment it is offered (1 Tim. vi. 12).

Thus conceived, it is *unique*, and the same throughout the whole extent of the Bible. The faith of the elders (" for by it the elders obtained a good report," Heb. xi. 2) is only that of the New Testament. To the one as to the other, to the first equally with the last, it is an overture, an entrance of the divine principle into the soul, which has operated everywhere uniformly when it has operated unto salvation. It is a hold which God has had upon every species of soul, whatever may have been its disposition. It is a handle by which to rescue them from the seductions of the world, and the engrossing cares of life. By this the Lord, who knoweth them that are his, chooses them *from the world, that he may keep them from the evil thereof.* God has done it all through faith; by its influence only does he operate on man, and through man, as there is nothing accomplished in the world but by his sovereign power. And as the influence of God upon men is attributed to men themselves, according to appearances, the men (of God) have done it all through faith, and through its influence alone. Here, then, is the secret of the eleventh chapter of Hebrews, otherwise inexplicable; but thus comprehended, it becomes the key of the Scriptures, the chain of revelations, the summary of divine dispensations.

Beautiful unity of faith! Misunderstood by the world, and by philosophy! "*They are all dead in faith.*"

For its operation in all time, notwithstanding the diversity of eras, and upon every species of person, of character, of qualities, and of different forms, God has given but *one way*, simple and independent of these varied accidents. Otherwise, that which has happened to one, would not have happened to another; and the same salvation would have been applicable only to men placed in analogous situations, or assimilated by a common education. But no! the faith of Abel is the faith which is yet preached in the Church as in an eternal school; the faith of Jairus, the leader of a synagogue, that of the Syro-Phœnician, who came from without, and that of the Roman centurion, although a Gentile, are not different in capacity or object; for all lay hold on a truth which penetrates them, a reality which strikes them, a promise which wins, rejoices, and consoles them, a succor which relieves, and a divine power which, for them, clothes Nature with a new aspect, and all attain their end on the very spot where they stand: so that the chain of true disciples is continued uninterrupted to the end of time; so that He, who should be most stringent in the act or form of faith, inasmuch as he cannot misapprehend it, and cannot be imposed on, approves, commands, and testifies of them. "Be it unto you according to your faith." "I have not found so great faith, no not in Israel." Who, then, shall dare to say that this is not faith in its simplest, clearest, and most powerful form? when the Master himself has said that this is the virtue of faith, and that at bottom it is nothing else. It refers beforehand to Him future; subsequently to Him present; and once absent from the earth, it refers to Him past and to come, with entire submission. "Whom having not seen ye love; in whom, though now ye see him not, yet believing, ye rejoice with joy unspeakable and full of glory, receiving the end of your faith, even the salvation of your souls."

On the other hand, the regenerative power of Christ acts wholly spiritually—every one receives the simplest definition of faith in regard to worldly matters, why not then in spiritual? It is justifying righteousness which becomes its object; it is not a mere healing of the body, but a blessing shed on the entire soul of man. "We believe from the heart to obtain righteousness," says St. Paul; "for therein is the righteousness of God revealed from faith to faith, and reigns in all, and over all who believe." Who, then, will refuse to believe it in this its fullest, richest, and most obvious meaning?

The unity of faith thus apprehended is admirably perfect, because it is a *unity* in every sense—an historical unity—a unity of cause and effect. We can truly say of it, *here is one faith.* We can thus speak of it independently of time and circumstance, ineident to different ages. There has been a progress in all other things, but none in faith, or rather there is a progress in the faith of every believer, an onward progress from " strength to strength;" but there never can be any increase in the nature or essence of faith, for God is unchangeable. Man goes on to perfection; he believes; he goes on from faith to faith (if indeed he has commenced this divine life): but faith never changes from century to century—never becomes other than that it always has been. Abraham will always be the type, the model; and those who have the faith of Abraham, are and ever will be his children.

He whom God has called, like Abraham, will obey; he to whom Christ has said, as to Levi, "follow me," will also walk in his footsteps. Every Christian feels the force of the Centurion's words and faith—" I say unto this man go, and he goeth; to another do this, and he doeth it." It is thus God would have us believe and live; and this faith, so simple, childlike, and yet instantaneous, is supported by that cloud of witnesses who have already attained to its full fruition—" of Moses who left Egypt, not fearing the anger of the king, of Gideon, of Barak, of Samson, &c. It is the faith of the learned Nicodemus, of the just man, Joseph of Arimathea, of Zaccheus the publican, and of the simple-hearted Mary. All else is only opposition, doubt, blind groping, or vain pretension, false and faithless. All who have ever believed, " *the multitude of those who have believed*" (Acts ii. 42), all continuing faithful in the doctrine of the Apostles, will ever be a cloud of witnesses to show what kind of faith we should exercise.

We seem to have taken at least one important step in our day towards the truth—that of valuing useful knowledge above every other consideration. It is but a few years since evangelical truth was refused, because unsupported by mathematical demonstration; and failing to see all that appertained to faith, of prompt discernment and confident profession, reduced to the form of an equation, they have pronounced it a string of abstruse definitions, vain, incorrect fables, powerless to persuade. Let us be thankful that we do not now live under the influence of these ill founded prejudices—this superficial judgment. No! faith is the instrument by which God saves man, and man may lay hold on God; it is the channel, the medium of communication between the visible and invisible, the natural and supernatural, the human and divine; faith, as an immediate and transcendent faculty, shall go on conquering and to conquer, till it shall be received by all who are truly wise, as that alone embodies the highest elements of reason.

REASON.

It is necessary to commence here, since our concern is with an instrumental faculty, or rather with all our faculties taken together. To say that religion should enlighten man, that it should be his guide, is only saying that he should be guided by reason, for reason properly is the entire mental part of man, the means by which he acquires all knowledge. But if, in place of the vague term religion, we substitute that of Christianity, the Gospel, and if the Gospel preaches, recommends, inspires faith, as a primary means; if Christianity is a religion of faith, our theme then is enlightened and guided by faith, which thus becomes its master and schoolmaster, whose science, object, and study are the Gospel.

Speaking thus, we assuredly do not wrong reason—it is without dispute the master faculty of man; his head or rather his eye, placed as a sentinel on the height of this moving tower, to watch the dangers which threaten him, and avoid the snares which surround him. It serves both as a light and sentinel while the night lasts, and even when the day breaks, it is a day which only makes clearer those objects it faintly observed—the first rays which bring the pure light. It receives and profits by them, and only gains knowledge *through* them. This comparison involves the principle of an irrefragable demonstration.

In the ministry of the reconciliation of the Gospel, it is to the reason of man that all appeals are made. But for this it is first necessary to form an accurate estimate of its capacity. To the rightful exercise of its privileges, we must not exaggerate or abuse them, much less turn against God the sovereign *reason* (otherwise called the WORD, λογος) he has given us to submit to him. How can he who has never humbled himself before God, nor surrendered the weapons of his unrighteous warfare, lead others " to the way of peace" by the path of reconciliation? To such a spiritual guide St. Paul says in vain, " Submit yourselves to God, resist the devil (or the rebellious spirit), and he will flee from you."

How can he triumph over rebellious men "who obey not the truth," who remains himself a rebel and gainsayer of the Gospel of the grace of God? How can he lead captive souls to Christ, who has not first given himself to him? How can he spread in the world this victory which is our faith, whose weapons are yet carnal, and who fights not with the sword of the Spirit, but with vain reasonings (James i. 22). Now this is the case of a large number of divines or spiritual guides, who cherish the most false ideas both with regard to their own reason and that of those to whom it is their duty to speak of the things of God. If there be a subject on which they are in error, it is certainly this of reason. After all that has been given us for the exercise of reason in matters of faith, how is it yet misapprehended?

Do not think that we have come before you to declaim against one of the holiest prerogatives of men. No—let us rather determine its true province, and thus assured, facilitate and perfect its highest aim. You say that it is reason which distinguishes us from brutes; we will place it still higher. But we add, that it places us far below men, if it does not raise us to God himself, and receive the impress of his divine Spirit; for alone and dependent on itself, it can only lead us in blind paths, precipitate us in the most frightful errors, down hideous precipices, while the brutes, unable to pass beyond certain limits, have consequently a fixed, imperfectible, determinate nature, which never deceives them.

Reason is the eye of the soul, and not its torch. For the eye is not the light: it is merely the organ by which light enters—an organ to the body is as a faculty to the soul.

There is, however, a light. It shines forth from the Gospel, not vague and indefinite, but positive, determined—even personified. (See John i. 8.) So much the more efficacious is that light. "The light manifests all things. All hidden things are made manifest by the light. Has any one regarded it? We are all enlightened by it. In thy light we see light. I am the light of the world, of all men who come into the world." (Who shall except himself from this rule?) Purify yourselves, that you may also become lights. Formerly you were darkness, now ye are the lights of the Lord. Such is the theory of faith. It is entirely philosophical.

That this light may be effective, it must be received, admitted, till it penetrate the eye of the soul—its organ of vision, of intuition; that so it shall reach the depths of the soul, its most secret sanctuary. With the best eyes, it is plain one can see nothing in a dark room. At midday it will be night in a house closely shut. It is not therefore the eye which makes light—but is made light. Or if we say it enlightens in its turn, we do not speak correctly. Material light is that which enables man to see and to read—it is a space, a medium between him and exterior objects, by which he acquires the idea of their existence—their presence or approach is revealed to him. Much more then is this true of the divine light. It reveals, it demonstrates, it opens, it instructs; and here we come back to the definition of faith: " the evidence of things not seen." Thus Christ, Light of the soul, Reason even of reason, wishes to be received. It is upon *those who have received him* that he has conferred this right of divine adoption. [This is the cause of condemnation and also of error, that " the darkness received not the light," as there would be an endless night to the world if the sun never rose upon it, or if an impenetrable cloud hung over it which intercepted its rays. These are no metaphors—they are realities—ideas almost mathematically true.

Light has only to appear, and shine upon the organ to which is appropriated and given. It is its own demonstration. It does not prove its own existence, it simply offers itself to the eye, and seeing is evidence sufficiently strong—like the definition of the word evidence—that which is so plain and stands forth so boldly that it cannot be proved. The internal evidence of the Bible, therefore, particularly of the gospel, is more powerful to convince the soul than the whole assemblage of external evidence. If a light is held before me, do I need one to tell me it is a candle? I see it: it shines upon me. Thus the evidence, the illumination of the truth of Christ is brighter, and goes farther than all these proofs, which should, say they, precede it. By this short, rapid, and perfect way is a system of faith formed, so clear that one would only become confused who should endeavor to simplify it.

Thus we see how one may commence the study of the Word of faith with a preconceived opinion. This disposition toward faith will assist, much more will it lead farther, than the system of philosophical doubt many have instituted in the research of truth. It will be one thing to reason along with faith, or to look with an eye which sees perspicuously; and quite another to search for the reasons of faith with a reason which sets out with refusing to believe.

Thus apprehended, the words of Christ are easily understood. It is a clear light itself, or which promises to become one, as the Saviour has said: " The eye is the light of the body; if therefore thine eye be light, thy whole body shall be full of light." These words contain the most valuable information. How can one see clearly with diseased eyes? How can one make a right use of a perverted faculty? How dare one pretend to be enlightened or judge of His Word, which judges not only himself, but *the thoughts and intentions of the heart*? Would it not be better first to heal his diseased organ, to recover his reason? And in order to recover his reason, should he not, like the staggering invalid, learn to walk step by step, foot by foot, or rather after the infallible guide which is given him?

From that time, the character, the design, the capacity of reason is marked. We say in two words, that one should become scholar and not master, should learn to be reasonable, not a reasoner. It is said of the true wisdom, that it *cometh from above*, and that it is not cavilling. Yet it is, without doubt, right that one should be able to judge for himself, to defend-himself, as is recommended in the Holy Scriptures. " Are you that are without able to judge of the least things?" " Judge yourselves, whether it is right before God to obey you rather than God." But, at the same time, take heed how you judge. " Judge not according to *appearance*, but judge *righteous judgment*." " *Prove* the spirits." " Examine all things." " Inquire *carefully* what is the will of the Lord." " I speak as to *wise men*; judge ye what I say."

And here let us rectify a common prejudice. Vain is that application which is used without distinctness, according to the apparent sense of these last words. It concerns a sincere Christian here, to be assured of his faith and of his doubts in this true light. Faith is this *wisdom*, which St. Paul calls *spiritual*, as given by the *spirit of revelation in the knowledge of Christ*. It testifies of believers that they are happy; they are enriched; it asks yet more for them with the most fervent prayers. The proof that this intelligence is nothing else than faith, is, that Jesus called his disciples a long time *men without knowledge*, and these words are equivalent to *men of little faith*. He explains this thought by adding, " Slow of heart to believe all that the prophets have said " (Luke xxiv. 25). It was this, consequently, which deprived them of a higher degree of knowledge, of discernment concerning the most important, simple, and obvious truths. The absence of this principle of light held their minds in total darkness, as we speak of those whom Christ has not enlightened by his Spirit, or who have turned back after receiving a knowledge of the truth.

Let us inquire what St. Paul means when he speaks of the *natural man* (1 Cor. ii.) It is not the purely natural man of which the other writers of the Scriptures speak, *abruti;* it is the man with his soul, as he actually exists, ανθρωπος ψυχικος, even the psychology of the soul. How few are they who give it any attention! And yet this natural man comprehends not the things of the Spirit of God, because they are *spiritually* discerned. Πνευματικως (spiritually) expresses a species of spirituality widely different from intelligence. Speaking according to the Word of God, *spiritual* cannot mean *intellectual.* One may, perhaps, be very intelligent, and yet have only a carnal understanding with regard to divine things. Observe the particularity with which St. Paul distinguishes the precept on which this discernment rests. " Now we have received, not the spirit of the world, but the *Spirit* which is of God, *that we might know the things* that are freely given to us *of God.*" Let us mark carefully the words, when, in speaking of the same things, he adds, " Which things also we speak, not in the words which man's wisdom teacheth, but which the Holy Ghost teacheth; comparing spiritual things with spiritual." Thus are the words of Christ made manifest, " his words are spirit and life," that " flesh and blood hath not revealed these things;" that no one could discern, or teach, or comprehend them by his own intelligence; and thus is the wisdom of God folly in the sight of the world, and, in return, the wisdom of this world folly before God.

Having named the doubt, we say that it is erroneous and foolish to desire this unceasing discussion, without holding anything as received or established, as if every man, entering into eternal life, must tear down and rebuild the edifice which has furnished him a sanctuary and a shelter. He might as well call in question his own nature or the existence of his body;—too happy if, like Descartes, he can return from it to the simplest exercise of thought. God protects his servants from this foolish distrust, which is only a confidence in the works of their own hands. If you can only believe in the God you have made for yourselves--that you have consecrated,—which shall come out of the crucible of your own weak imagination, if you cannot certify, publish, or offer anything better to your contemporaries, you do not give them much that is worthy their acceptance. How can you convict them for your penury? Proud in their own strength, which after all is only a created power that destroys more than it edifies, the men of our day, destitute of the erudition of the giants of past ages, reject, with contempt, the traditions which, though perhaps confused, are rich from centuries which are no more. Ungrateful, they misapprehend their benefits, and yet make no preparation to leave to succeeding generations the treasures they have themselves amassed.

Truly this is strange folly and presumption to desire to prove all things, and yet believe nothing—accept nothing with confidence.

Try not to prove all things, you who desire salvation! Be not so foolish as to make everything depend on your *proofs!*

Acknowledge intrinsic excellence without these—independent and irrespective of these antique verities; and do not offer your proofs in comparison with the testimony of reiterated experience, —of accumulated evidence, as if your happiness depended on adding yet your testimony. Believe, therefore, and, above all things, wear the air of belief, that Christianity may be able to live and extend its roots; that it may teach you it has need of nothing else; that, while it offers you a refuge, it asks nothing for itself in return. Consequently, if you neglect this salvation, you shall be the first punished, the first to complain, and all that you have known, or desired, or deemed advantageous, you shall regard lost, &c. Therefore, in place of this endless disputation, open, rehearse, search, repeat divine things; but the echo—the echo of this misapprehended verity, understand it for yourselves—yea, search to the very foundation.

Let not this century, already so vain of its acquisitions, behold you in pain, in labor—destitute of the everlasting gospel,—of an eternal Saviour. Let it see rather that you desire him for yourself, and treat it as a criminal, as it will appear in the presence of its judge, according to the words of our Lord: "*Now cometh the judgment of this world,*" and with it that of reason also.

We sympathize, therefore, with the great apostle who had attained the highest point of knowledge, and knew well how to appreciate human success. "We preach wisdom not of this world, nor of the princes of this world that come to naught—a wisdom which none of the princes of this world knew,—a wisdom among them that are perfect."

Among other strange mistakes incident to human reason is that of taking the effect for the cause; and *vice versâ*—many who would shrink back with horror from speaking of the grace of God, the will of God, and His sovereign power as first and last cause of all things, speak affectedly of nature, and personify it as it were, a creator rather than a creature. It is Nature who has done this, who has done that! Because God moves in man, and by the admirable efficiency of his continued power ever sustains and directs him, they have come at length to think it is man who acts for himself, and who finds in himself his origin and design. The first steps of salvation are revealed to him, and those things give him all the merit of its acquisition. How can reason, strict and severe, allow itself to forget the only hand which can guide unfailingly, the only piercing eye that can foresee the issue, *God* who *worketh in us to will and to do according to his own good pleasure?* Ah! this only shows too plainly that it has lost, even by the manner in which it addresses itself to man, the means it uses for his conversion. Instead of preaching, that is, of publishing, of proclaiming that it is *God who gives grace,* who converts, who touches, who strikes, who breaks, who subdues, who awakens, who animates, who changes, in short, who begins and ends his work, also in a God who temporarily enriches and impoverishes, who abases who exalts, who is the first and the last; it reduces to a mass of ruins the honor of belief, hoping itself to rise from the midst of the ruins, and elevate itself upon them even to the highest heaven.

Because there is necessarily something human, terrestrial, *material* in the Bible, since it is a book) and has a natural correspondent action), they forget, they lose sight of its only object, namely, to bring the soul in contact with the divine nature, only influencing, only powerful in itself; that the grand design is to furnish a point of meeting, of incidence, which once found regenerates the soul. (A simple analysis of the Parable of the Sower will enable us to comprehend this readily, and we may therefore return to it) The eyes, the hands, and the feet, are all necessary to the body, so, wit, memory, the attention which compares, the judgment which concludes, are necessary to the perfection of the mind. But after all, what has it for its final end, if it be not to place the soul in communication with this *lively* or *living* word which *regenerates*, which *can save* the soul, yet which can do it alone through the Eternal Spirit, ever the same, who operates on the minds he has formed !

Thus, therefore, speaking simply, giving heed and examining the Word, without desiring to find one meaning rather than another, without endeavoring to avoid anything—without adding or subtracting therefrom, this is the right, sincere, and correct design of reason, equally with the pastor as with the simple believer, and even he who does not possess this humble, docile spirit (which Paul calls *the same spirit of faith*), as well as the first, will be governed by it. For this spirit is not natural to man; they have it not who make the greatest pretensions; they who really possess the largest share see their ignorance, it can with difficulty enter a proud heart. Christ himself is the *Master* Sovereign, *the Shepherd of the sheep*, and manifests his willingness to impart this spirit to those who desire it. " Learn of me, for I am meek and lowly of heart; according as it is written of me in the volume of the Word; Lo! I come to do thy will, O God !"—*It is written!* comprehend it well! and this is the substantial WORD which refers to the Scriptures! What obedience of faith! What fidelity! What docility! Eternal, uncreated reason, the Logos, who has only to speak of divine things, teach us therefore to listen meekly while it is said—*Hear ye Him.*

But what difference, after all, is there between our exposition of the Scriptures, and that of those who explain it only by their reason, since we both agree that reason is only the medium by which we see the light placed on that candlestick, or the eye by which we read it there?

The eye sees undoubtedly in the Bible, as in any other book, characters traced, and from them forms words and phrases, and as the mind apprehends the meaning seizes finished or isolated passages, otherwise limited and dependent on that which precedes or follows. This is the natural process, and the same for all works. But how different the result! The disciple can never exceed his prescribed bounds, and God says to him as to the sea, " Thus far shalt thou go and no further." *The mouth of the Lord hath spoken*, Give ear, O heavens, and keep silence, O earth; hearken, my people, and I will speak. We have heard these marvels from our fathers, and we will tell them to our children and to our children's children, and generations yet to come shall praise the Lord. Let us not shrink back because they are mysteries. This is the mystery of God our Father and of Christ, and concerning the things of Christ, these are they hidden from the foundation of the World, but now revealed to those who believe: for "eye hath not seen, nor ear heard, neither hath it entered into the heart of man to conceive the things which God hath prepared for those that love him." "The secret of the Lord is with them that fear him and He will show them his covenant." Let us look at it in this light, at all times. God speaks to man generally and to the individual soul particularly, *to give it to know* his designs and the riches of his grace. It concerns us, therefore, O man! to read, to listen, to receive it!

And what can be more reasonably simple than to enter and take a seat, if you please, in the school of one Tyrannus (Acts xix.), where Paul disputes with his disciples. What can be better added to your faith, to make it reasonable, or even to transform your reason into faith, than this sure foundation, not on the uncertain, variable knowledge of man, but on the power of God—than to rest on the foundation of the Apostles and Prophets, Jesus Christ being the head stone of the corner? This is spoken concerning the WORD: but this word alway remains; for it is written: "Whatsoever things were written aforetime, were written for our learning" (Rom. xv. 41—1 Cor. x. ii.). While we read, therefore, and admit all that we find in agreement with the analogy of *faith*, of an unchangeable faith, a faith more open, which existed before it was thus called, our belief is confirmed by the testimony of a great cloud of witnesses—all receiving the Bible with equal respect, and comprehending it under the bright manifestation of prayer. We certainly, therefore, are not degraded in receiving truth, like these worthy fathers, since we are all baptized under the same cloud, and receive of the same Spirit.

No; the Gospel has nothing stable, nothing veritable, or else it is really a charge—a good trust. "O, Timothy, keep that which is committed to thy charge! Hold fast the FORM of sound words."

Whosoever does not thus fear the obligation to teach in one only irreproachable way, is declared even by this *Word*, who is the sovereign Judge of his servants, to have an endless controversy of words, to have rejected the faith, and to be reproved by this knowledge. He vainly boasts his *reason*, who has never yet offered *this reasonable service* (τὴν λογικὴν λατρείαν) which the Apostle says is due to his God, when he *beseeches* the Romans to offer their *spirits* and their *bodies* for a *living sacrifice*.

NOTE.

We come now to the weighty matter of authority. Many declaim loudly against all authority; but does that detract from its value, or prove it useless? I think not. There certainly is some authority.

The analogy of faith is nothing more nor less than authority—the consideration of that which has always been true, that has always been received as such, the authority that the Bible has published, spread and rendered common among all Christians, which the Gospel has taught and presented to the Church universal, for the approbation of the universal Church. But who speaks of approbation, who of confession?

A Christian who would be alone in the world in his particular belief, would indeed have good *reason* to judge himself and to count himself rashly proud of his own understanding. This would truly be an isolated sense that he possessed, not common sense in the Christian Church. What we call *common sense* in earthly matters, in matters of faith is only an individual and particular interpretation. Here the customary expressions are neither correspondent nor synonymous. Christianity is not an isolated system; it is, on the contrary, one of reconciliation—it is a social system; the Christian is not a monad, but a part of the great whole which diffuses life and improvement among all the members. He is not merely one who believes, but one of the great number of believers.

When one is seeking salvation, at the commencement of the spiritual life, he should undoubtedly act and feel as if he were alone in the world. His relations with God are the same as if God had done all that he has done, and said all that he has said, only for him. Thus the Eternal Word causes the soul to feel its burden, and produces its effect; but when it concerns the piety of the individual, his perfection in faith, then has it reference to the whole, for this *is their common faith*, that *which has been given to the saints*, which unites, renders them members one of another.

There is an agreement in this faith which furnishes the believer a guiding thread—and he cannot take one step without holding it. There is a common understanding in the Church, or an unanimous consent which rules, concerning the particular sense; and that is the unity of the spirit; this is also a true authority.

The faith of every true Christian should correspond with that of all others, and this agreement is the analogy of faith.

Such an authority is not a yoke; it is a guaranty. Without it, one sails at random on the ocean of the Bible, as without a compass on that of this world. Were it possible to bring together the whole universal church to hear this, what it would declare to be true would undoubtedly be the truth, and thus it would unavoidably be brought under submission. Now in history we see the Church, as it appears to be that of all times and in all places. Here it is we find the summation of centuries. Those who were under its jurisdiction have unanimously acknowledged this is not a false agreement, but gives the weight of authority. This is what we can and must respect. This is no longer acting the severe theologian, but submitting to gross misconception.

We should not submit blindly to the opinion of men, it is true, because the Bible says, *truly every man is a liar*, from which we may infer that all men are liars, as Paul quotes from the poet, that all the Cretans are liars—but *all Christians are not liars;* for, 1st, Faith is not a human opinion; it has been given once to the saints: and 2dly, the Spirit of truth is with the Church, and not only *the Spirit*, the mind of Christ (1 Cor. ii. 6), but also the expression of this mind on the Word of truth, and not only the written Word, but a constant living Word. Our Confessions rightly say, the preaching of the Word of God is the Word of God. It carries not only *in* itself, but *with* itself, its own work and the declaration of its unchangeable stability.

What has always proved true for Christians, *is given* for truth. Denial is heresy. We do not teach according to our own understanding of God, manifested in the Gospel. We speak as we have heard (for faith cometh by hearing). We give as we have received (*tradere*). *I give you that which I also have received*, says the Apostle. Who shall be angry at such a *tradition*, and deny it a just title?

Thus we see orthodoxy exalted throughout all time by the voice of centuries; and reigning triumphant above all the contests which have divided the churches of the East and the West, the churches of Asia, Africa, and Europe, and even of the Reformed Church, and the sects which have been springing up around it. That which has been, is yet, and will be true above all others: orthodoxy has become a fact. Yet can one hope to possess this truth if he keeps himself beyond its reach?

Wherefore seek to make this authority obnoxious? What does it contain so repugnant to the nature of man? Do we not see these very individuals who become so passionate at the mere mention of the word authority, exercising it each in his own sphere, as pastors, as fathers, in the circle of their families, or of their external influence, the authority of age, even of that forbidding physiognomy, of gesture and appearance; speaking, for example, of the importance of religious education, they say, " These first impressions are never effaced, &c." And wherefore, if it is not that children, scholars, inferiors, receive with confidence and deference these opinions given with an air and show of authority? What inconsistency in those who cry up the use of reason, in matters of faith, in the sense of absolute independence! To reconcile all things by the opinion of the day, to avoid walking by a simple rule. This changing opinion, which appears to them a formidable power, has become a very different thing from simple authority (2 Peter ii. 19).

CONSCIENCE.

There is not a more important element among all those, which will increase the zeal of a minister of the Gospel, than conscience; but there is also no element which deserves to be better known. Shall we content ourselves, then, with common ideas with regard to it? It is worth the trouble of an examination.

There is necessarily something vague and ill-defined in the common acceptation of the word. It is in effect often mistaken for the point of a sentiment which it resembles, and often these metaphors are used in describing it: "Conscience! conscience!"

cries John and James, "immortal and celestial voice!" Again, with others it is by moral axioms, fixed principles, and uncreated laws, that they speak of it; it is an engraved table, say they, like that of Sinai. As a mute and defined, yet constant *witness*, they call upon it immediately, consult it at all times, question and make it speak like a *living* witness, which cannot remain unmoved; they call to it, trouble it, excite and endeavor to remove it. Is it, therefore, of no consequence to discover, or at least to become acquainted with this strange character, this mysterious agent? And if it be a power in man, should it not, at least, have a Christian name?

The commonly received ideas of CONSCIENCE, which obtain in life, and in ordinary conversation, are really unjust, and very incomplete, from which results a very imperfect development of the *moral sense*, that fails to lead man to his highest perfection. They speak of conscience merely as we have noticed them speaking of reason; yet it seems that it should be something by itself—a guide, a master, &c. We have seen formerly that the eye is not the light, but the organ through which light is seen; and, again, that the eye must be sound, and the light reach it, be admitted and not decomposed, in order to obtain and form just ideas of things. We here repeat it, and liken conscience to another of our senses. Not now the sight, but hearing which shall serve as a common point. There is a singular agreement between the precision of the first and the confusion of the second of these senses (considered psychologically), at the same time a delicacy, a sensibility, which distinguishes the hearing, by which it attains a relative perfection, while the sight is incapable of this same perfectibility,—yet its exactness and force confine it to a fixed point. There is, I say, a remarkable analogy between the two senses we have just observed, and reason, as compared with conscience.

Instead of speaking of conscience as a voice, it will be better to regard it as the organ by which this voice is recognized, which collects the sound, gives new shades to familiar perceptions—in fine, that a delicate conscience, like fine hearing, or a practised ear, will be the most exquisite organ, while a penetrating reason, like long, far-reaching sight, is, in other respects, the strongest of our faculties.

Conscience is less *the voice*, though it has long been represented thus, than *the locality* where it dwells, and where we must hear it. It is less the oracle itself, than the sanctuary where it speaks and gives its responses: but language confounds, by vague expressions, the Deity who inspires the temple where he resides, and the medium, the instrument, by which he communicates a knowledge of himself. And here we find the difficulty in what has already been said of conscience. For, in fine, we attribute it to God, when we say it is God whispering to man the claims of Judgment, when we say it is a tribunal established in man, or a judge, a guardian, a witness who watches his actions, an anticipated judgment, a present and lasting judgment, a prelude of the final; all these images revolving around the principal idea, render it obscure and indistinct.

This leads us into contradictions, and difficulties, deeper than those from which we would extricate ourselves, and makes us in practice feel sensibly the description of St. Paul (Rom. ii. 14), that at least *on one head*, conscience has something natural, common to all men—even to the savage. At length we come to the inquiry, what is this conscience of the righteous and the Christian ("void of reproach before God and man"), since the idea of conscience is only an idea of reproach, of profound guilt, which becomes more lively and intense, in proportion as it is enlightened and cultivated.*

For he who examines, who listens, who cleanses slightly his conscience, will have the fewest reproaches—while he, on the contrary, who watches more carefully, will become most susceptible to uneasiness and anxiety on this account. How pretend to have a conscience without reproach before God? Since that which escapes man, magnifies itself in the light of his countenance (Psalm xc.); and before men who never can read the conscience accurately, and should therefore abstain from it, what are we to understand by a conscience *void of reproach*, since no one has a right to force it to reveal that which is hid, and no one knows to draw the soul from its depths? The feeling that every one has, with regard to this, is, that he would not for all the world have his innermost thoughts brought to light or exposed to the judgment of the best disposed assembly or the most indulgent ear. I call every one here to witness! One feels, after all that has been said, the necessity of a more logical, and at the same time a more scriptural exposition. We have already given the principle in our definition. We know assuredly that it is rather the ear of the soul to hear, than the sound and the voice even; it is the most retired, the most secret, the most interior locality; as in the physical ear there are some chambers more interior than others. We say simply that God speaks in man. Man speaks from without, but God speaks from within.

---

* At least man, in his natural state, can have no other; and it is of this we now wish to speak. Take for example, modesty: why should modesty blush? Does not the word even (*pudor*) express shame? Is it not a sudden revelation, a subtle accusation, of a secret sympathy, an unknown correspondence with something hidden and impure within, of which one hardly believes himself capable? Can an angel feel it? No. Modesty shows that all evil is not from without, as would have been the case with simple, perfect innocence. Conscience gives the knowledge of sin, in whose presence evil should be held in check, yet which, turned aside from its original rectitude, cannot always tell when the Evil One approaches. "He comes, but has nothing in me."—(John xiv. 30.) It is true, say some, conscience approves us when we do well; but, certainly, that is doubtful. How can it prompt one to a secret approbation, when everything in its nature shows us the danger of indulging any feeling of complacency toward ourselves? And, after all, which is the most frequent, the most *conscientious* of the two—that which approves, or that which reproaches? Certainly the sphere of conscience is to reproach, and if it performs its duty, this is its most natural and most common office.

(See Imitat. of J. C.) *God speaks to the heart*, say the prophets, or rather, according to the original, *in the heart*, where it awakens a mighty echo.

Having placed this principle in advance, let us endeavor to give a scriptural and logical exposition of the nature of conscience, and then follow it out in its various steps.

1st. As in the faculty of vision, it is said that *the light lightens all men coming into the world*, and kindles in him the flame of intelligence, lays down the rules of these principles, founds the axioms, adjusts the measure of truth, so the natural oracle the conscience, speaks in the heathen himself, in the natural man, unconverted, causes him to hear a voice of reproach, enough, at least, *not to leave himself without a witness*, although the natural man gives little attention to this first degree of instruction, of divine warning which he hardly regards. But let us proceed—

If man becomes, by the gift of a positive revelation, *a worshipper in spirit and in truth*, he will enter most willingly and most joyfully into the mysterious place where this oracle resides, he will listen to it silently, he will tremble at its voice, and he will say before it as young Samuel was instructed by the High Priest—*Speak, Lord, thy servant heareth.*—(1 Sam. iii. 7, 9, 10. Heb. ii. 1., iii. 7, 15.)

2d. Then the oracle itself will become new (for all is new, under a new dispensation). " I will hear what He will say to those who love Him," says the Psalmist. "The merciful God will speak peace to them." This will be *a voice of mercy and of pardon*, instead of a voice of reproach, continual and pitiless. And St. Paul says three times in succession, that it is the Spirit which says— " To-day if ye will hear his voice, harden not your hearts." That this conscience is not natural, you can say nothing less. And this only can explain the gospel expression, *conscience of sin*, opposed to a *good conscience*, or *conscience without reproach*, that is, a satisfied conscience, renewed by God himself, or a sentiment acquired by a reconciliation. The Apostle does not say that he himself attempts to accomplish it, but to preserve and guard it when it has once been given him. St. Peter speaks concerning baptism as an answer before God. It is the testimony of faith, which is double, " when the Spirit witnesses with our spirit, that we are the children of God." We also render this testimony (John xv. 27.), " I know in whom I have believed, in the Lamb of God who taketh away the sins of the world," and who has power to justify those who receive it. St. Peter makes this a consequence of *the resurrection of Jesus Christ* (1 Peter iii. 21), for, having died for our offences, he is *raised again for our justification*. It is, in short, conscience *purified from dead works* (Heb. ix. 14), the conscience of justification.

3d. There is yet a more perfect conscience, or rather a third degree, relating to sanctification, upon which we must enter by a new way. There is a *Councillor*, as well as a judge, as well as a Saviour of souls. " Thou shalt hear," says the prophet Isaiah, " the voice of one behind thee, saying, this is the way, walk ye in it." This *Councillor* is he whom the Gospel, whom Jesus Christ calls by the beautiful name of Comforter, and to whom he delivers, commits and ever assigns the keeping of the *saved* soul, after having by the former act recovered it from sin, liberated it by grace, and delivered it by a full remission from the burden of sin. This also explains the expression of St. Paul in Romans (Rom. ix. 1). " My conscience also bearing me witness in the Holy Ghost." Here you see necessarily a privileged conscience, more, much more, than the obscure conscience of the heathen; more also than the enlightened conscience of a civilized man— more than one enlarged by education and the light of the age. Moreover, the doctrine of adoption not only establishes and affirms that the Spirit of God witnesses with our spirits, that we are the children of God ; but also that this spirit leads the children of God, and that " those who are led by the Spirit of God are the children of God." From that time, a Christian conscience receives not merely this first, and I may affirm greater witness of just or unjust actions, honest or dishonest, as we may say of all things, but it adds a yet finer tact, a new sense, a superior discernment almost heavenly, which St. Paul characterizes as very glorious, when he says, " the spiritual man judges all things, yet is himself judged by no man." For who has a right in this world, to judge the consciences of those who are justified, since one is even forbidden to judge of the carnal conscience ? The spiritual man is drawn by strange impulses to the will of the flesh, which is not subject to the Law of God, neither indeed can be. His aspirations soar higher, and his motives are not only purer and more elevated, but the movement which follows them, the active thought, the *movement of the Spirit*, is quite a different thing from that natural activity by which the human will is determined in the enterprises of this world. Who shall be able to judge of this life and principle?

4th. There are therefore two consciences. I see first a conscience of sin, then a conscience without reproach, that is, a conscience justified ; and then follows conscience, a councillor or guide. Finally, a good conscience, or witnessing by the Spirit, and " obeying the truth through the Spirit, with a true heart, without hypocrisy, keeping the mystery of faith in a pure conscience," such as the heirs of the kingdom God ought to possess ; and as the Apostle dares to affirm of himself—" We trust we have a good conscience, in all things willing to live honestly." (Heb. xiii. 18.) Finally, we may truly say, there is a good conscience, or a conscience planning rightly.

This regards equally the past, present, and future; and supposes already a certain degree of spiritual force, acquired, and rooted in the subject of grace. This is the established resolution of good, of holy resolution, and the solid, vigorous root of a new and powerful will. In vain does the sinner form plans of conversion and of a better life, while his will is yet ungrafted, like a good graft on a living tree, and while there stands against him a permanent accusation, which deprives him of strength and all true courage, and which also reduces him in spite of himself to remember the depths of iniquity which yet remain uncleansed—unremoved.

That conscience is the master-piece of grace, and constitutes the true renewal of the divine image in justice, and in true holiness. The foundation is wanting in the sinner, even in his best moments he has not even a velleity for good—he is altogether corrupt, from the head even to the feet. For though he may have something which men call sincerity, and which resembles it somewhat; this sincerity, which does not justify by itself, is then really the commencement of the kingdom of God—the invisible *Empire*, extending itself over the soul of the converted man; and when one can say he really belongs to God, from that moment integrity subsists before him and all his promises are realized.

This conscience corresponds with the simple eye. To a simple view of the only path of duty, the only right line, is joined an intention or simple wish to walk in it. Its root is like an undivided thread; and now there is no more of this division of the heart, so subtle, so condemned in the Word. "The man whose heart is divided, or double-hearted, double-minded" (James i.), "You who are double-minded"—by which he does not mean here gross hypocrisy,—but *division* between its own desires, secret and almost imperceptible, which yet remains with those who wish to be free, yet by this course dissipate all their strength, and paralyze their efforts, by their own carelessness or mistakes, and thus make life a perpetual inconsistency;

"O God, what cruel strife!
I find two wills within me," &c.

instead of all this, a condition truly miserable and worthy of pity—a movement, a momentary impulse (as there is one only faith and one only grace), to combat or to fly temptation, not only without an agreement with it, but without stopping even to consider the doubt; yes, without a particle of time for hesitation. It is God in the soul, with all that is jealous and absolute in his love, according to the summary of the law; it is faith operating by charity; it is the hidden mystery, to know "Christ in us, the hope of glory."

There is, therefore, something more than this *good and honest heart* necessary to receive the seed of God at the very commencement of the work of God. It is the crown of the new man—it is his *integrity*—it is the fulfilment of the wish of Paul, "THAT ALL THAT IS WITHIN YOU, *spirit*, *soul*, and *body*, may be preserved blameless;"—it is the fulness of praises of which David speaks in Psalm ciii.: "Let all that is within me bless the name of thy holiness!"

This, then, is the end of this unhappy division of the powers that God has created to desire good; and not only to *desire* it, but to *do* it; and of which Paul laments in the close of the seventh chapter of Romans, saying that he had *a will* to do well, but could not find the means of accomplishing it! This good conscience gives the true conductor, which shall ascend to the hill of the Lord, and attain otherwise inaccessible heights.

Now is mercy complete; it is not received in vain; all is accomplished; for God is obeyed. What though the external effect be not yet perfect, the will at least, the internal disposition to produce it, is entire, and avows itself boldly; not fearing to be proud to say to the Lord, " Try me," and is willing to be submitted to the fire which tries all things, inasmuch as he can endure the flames, who can look it steadily in the face, like the eagle, who, in its upward flight, fixes its steady gaze on the sun, through the power given him by its almighty Creator.

For holiness is equally essential to the children of God as to his angels: the sinner will therefore first speak of his goodness, of his love, of his mercy, in approaching the Lord, in tasting that He is sweet. But holiness—oh that he knew it, and desired to walk in it!

SOME OF THE PILLARS OF THE TEMPLE OF THE LORD.

The glory of the workman shines forth in his works. The genius of the artist appears in the characters that he knows how to sketch, to ornament, and sustain, than which, perhaps, nothing could be more perfect, because he has placed there something of his own spirit. You admire it as a choice specimen of human workmanship. The spirit of poetry charms you, and you have felt its power. Confess, then, candidly, have you never remarked some of those silent beauties with which the Book of God is ever clothed? It is, perhaps, one of the most singularly grand and original characteristics of the Bible, that those *men*, whom it does not call great men, who bear no resemblance to our heroes, it describes in passing, as if without design, with a kind of generous forgetfulness and divine negligence, yet imparting to them a glory which exceeds all who name themselves, in sketching some of their marked characteristics. It exceeds all that has ever been told by any other historian, or traced by any other limner. It exceeds, as one remarks, those sculptured by Plutarch. Human statuary! Stop and admire! Man of God, take thy pencil; thou hast only to copy, to repeat the image. Open thy repository; it is rich, it is vast, and in the first leaves equally with the last, shalt thou see beings passing from this world to that which is to come. Enoch, "the seventh man," foretold the coming of the great King, and from the beginning looked even to the end of the world to behold him, saying, " Behold, the Lord cometh with ten thousand of his saints, to execute judgment upon the earth" (Jude xiv. 15); and the man who, many centuries later, composed " the pleasant songs of Israel," cries out, " The chariots of God are twenty thousand, even thousands of angels: the Lord is among them, as in Sinai, as in the holy place" (Ps. lxviii. 17). Let us go on a little farther; yield an attentive ear, and listen to the funeral oration of a great people, who wept for him thirty days. His body cannot be found; God has hid it from them, lest it should become an object of worship. Upon none other of the sons of men has there been such an eulogy pronounced: " And there arose not a prophet since in Israel like unto Moses, whom the Lord knew face to face" (Deut.

xxxiv. 10), whose vigor was not abated (at a hundred and twenty years of age), and whose eye was not dim. He was truly one whom we may call an oak of justice, a plant of the Lord, to glorify him! Abraham had also seen his day, and had rejoiced in it: Abraham, father of nations, lord of the covenants, patriarch of the promises, representative of the true faith, he whom God called his friend, and from whom he did not conceal his plans. " Shall I hide from Abraham that thing which I do ?" But wherefore follow the succession of time, when He who has made it observes not its order? See you not that he annihilates all time to re-unite, to group these subjects of His royal kingdom? Though Noah, Daniel and Job were in it, they should deliver but their own souls by their righteousness. Seek the Lord, " That he may better judge of the greatness of His indignation, and the power of His dreadful anger;" hear now the protestation, even the oath of Him who, " because He could swear by no greater, swore by Himself." (Heb. vi. 13.) " As I live, saith the Lord, I will not show mercy to you." " For I lift up my hand to heaven, and say I live for ever. If I whet my glittering sword, I will make my arrows drunk with blood, and my sword shall devour flesh, &c." (Deut. xxxii 40, 41, 42.) The Judge of the world will say " *That these three men, Noah, Daniel and Job were in it* " (Ezek. xiv. 14, 20), and this is indeed a remarkable expression. But wherefore this group? Why this sacred trio? History of the Hebrews, unroll thy pages: sacred volume of the annals of this great people, teach us now, " For what nation is there so great, who hath God so nigh unto them as the Lord our God is in all things that we call upon Him for ?" (Deut. iv. 7.) Though Noah, Daniel and Job stood before me! They are too great for all panegyric. A few words from the Bible, one characteristic of each will express more than we could say; this is their due. Noah " the tenth " (we have seen the seventh man, for we consider as ages these men, these giants, these men of renown), Noah the tenth, the Prophet, the herald, the " prophecier of Justice," herald of judgments. He built the Ark, and by this Ark which he built by faith, he condemned the world! The world then perished in the flood—not one of the ungodly escaped; he had warned them, he had cried to them, he had published, threatened and preached, during the space of a hundred and twenty years, all in vain. Type of the future. So will it be in the end of this world, *as it was in the days of Noah.* And DANIEL, in the days of the captivity! Daniel a pleasant man, a man to be desired! From the commencement of his prayer, the word of deliverance has gone forth.. . . . the throne of heaven is moved—the archangel spreads his wings and prepares at that very hour, at that moment even, to leave the presence of Him whom he never ceases to worship and adore. Daniel, Belshazzar, chief of the Magi—Daniel, in whom is the spirit of the holy gods! What glory, what happiness, what honor! He has shut the mouths of the lions. . . . O, Daniel! thy God sees thee yet! He has declared to this king of kings and of nations who boasts himself, that seven times shall pass over him, and he shall be driven out with the beasts of the field, until he knows that the Lord reigns, and that His Kingdom ruleth over all. But I must hasten to the end of my journey. Job, the most powerful of the Orientals ... his reasoning with the great God, who deigns to reply to him from out the whirlwind. He only can silence Job, before whom his elders were as children and fools. Behold these three men, has there ever been any like them? Let us speak of the great king, who built, who consecrated a holy temple to the Lord, who fell upon his knees before all the congregation of Israel, and prayed and blessed the people with his hands raised to heaven. There are here yet greater than Solomon, of whom, however, we cannot speak. We will not speak of the giant slain by the youthful shepherd, the son of Jesse. We will say nothing of Nehemiah, whose countenance was sad when he thought of the desolation of the city of his fathers, and who, after a painful journey, was obliged to make by night the circuit of the city in a country surrounded by enemies. We will merely name Ezra, and his honorable title, Ezra *scribe of the words of the Law of the Lord*, with prayers and tears confessing the sins of the people.

Let us change the scene. Behold Moses and Elias on Mount Tabor; the Law and the Prophets united; the latter yet great by his challenge, his defiance and his victory over the four hundred priests of Baal. Besides these men, who are those three, so different in their appearance, and yet so closely related in their interests? They are Peter, James, and John, afterwards known as THE PILLARS. See these five witnesses of the double covenant, making by their presence here a moving pavilion, a tent prepared for a night, like the mortal life of man; like the tabernacle in the wilderness, raised in honor of Him, who, descending from the skies, walks upon the heights; goes from hill to hill, from the mountain of Capernaum, where he teaches, to Moriah, where he preaches; from Jordan where he is baptized, to the Mount of Olives, where he suffers; and to Calvary, where he expires, fulfilling the words of the prophecy. "How beautiful upon the mountains, are the feet of Him that bringeth good tidings; that publisheth peace; that saith unto Zion, thy God reigneth!" Glorious beauty, hidden loveliness, the perfection of love, of mercy, and truth shining from the cross.

The Holy One is dead, and no one regards it. But the Gospel is preached—witnesses are multiplied—the Holy Ghost accompanies their words, with the demonstration of the spirit, and with power. Look at them once more unitedly before they separate to preach the Gospel to all nations, beginning at Jerusalem. The disciple whom Christ loved, and who loved Christ. * * * * James and John, you were well called Boanerges—sons of thunder. Without doubt, your irresistible word, your powerful spirit, which vanquished all error, and silenced all falsehood, tells this which distinguishes you.

Cephas, Peter, rock—rock of faith, rock built upon the waves, which yet the tempest cannot shake! And Saul become Paul, incomprehensible man, standing alone from all the world (like Job of old) without the sacred college of the prophets. Hear him speak of himself as an untimely birth, as the least of the apostles, not worthy to be called an apostle, because he had persecuted the Church of Christ. Yet, he dares to add: "I have labored more abundantly than they all; yet, not I, but the grace of God which was with me." *The love of Christ constraining me.* And how did it operate? "In dangers oft; in dangers from false brethren; a day and a night in the deep," &c. (2 Cor. xi. 26).

Singular preaching of doctrine! Revealing *in detail* the Lord's Supper, at which he had not been present, but which he had *received from the Lord himself;* and presenting it in its most perfect development, and with all its mysterious excellence.—(1 Cor. xi. 23.)

Let us praise, says the son of Sirach, *let us praise these illustrious men,* &c.—Chap. li. In the midst of this glorious cortége, the august image of the Son of man shines forth: the root and the offspring of David, his Lord and his Son, the bright and morning Star, with a new and purer brilliancy. The messenger who prepared the way before Him, in the spirit and power of Elias, though holy from his mother's womb, and greater than all who had preached him, yet felt himself unworthy to unloose the shoe from his foot. What a man among such men, how wise among so many wise men, each of whom is *one of a thousand.* What a prophet in the midst of the prophets! Truly this is He of whom Moses spake to our fathers: "The Lord thy God will raise up unto thee a Prophet from the midst of thee, of thy brethren; and *whosoever shall not hear* this prophet, *shall be cut off* from the midst of the people." "This is my beloved Son in whom I am well pleased, HEAR YE HIM." God of God, Light of Light, ascending upon high—the Counsellor wonderful.

We have now seen some of the pillars of this holy temple; but is the temple itself empty? What is the temple without the Divine presence? Destroy this temple! He will raise it up! Is not His name Emmanuel! God with us! "Behold I will send you the Comforter." And now, pious souls, the Lord whom you love—the Angel of the Covenant that ever attends you will enter His temple, and will not wait. Behold! He comes, saith the Lord of Hosts.

FAITH

AND

KNOWLEDGE.

TRANSLATED BY M. M. BACKUS.

FAITH AND KNOWLEDGE.

'Εν τῇ πίστει ὑμῶν . . . τὴν γνῶσιν.
" Add to your faith . . . . knowledge."—2 PETER i. 5.

KNOWLEDGE and faith, as set forth in our text, are, in the opinion of the world, two opposite things, and mutually exclude each other. Faith in revealed verities, as one has remarked, is incompatible with that profound erudition of the human intellect, which probes the depths of the earth, measures the expanse of the heavens, and explores the still more mysterious realms of the spirit of man. The names of Bacon, Newton, Pascal, Leibnitz, Euler, and a host of similar spirits, have come into collision with, and more than once repelled, that singular assertion. You will nevertheless constantly meet it in the world, for there is not a single error which men are not incessantly struggling to rebuild in our midst.

It is not, however, to combat this error that we shall devote the present hour. Our design is to penetrate farther into the essence of faith, and into the domain of knowledge. We shall consider another faith and another knowledge; the faith of the heart, or the Christian life, and theology, or the knowledge of God.

In reality, if we step beyond the threshold and enter the sanctuary of divine knowledge, we will there discover the same claims set up, which we had just left behind in the world, applied, however, to other objects. Faith is there the new principle of life, and of holiness, which the word of the Holy Spirit develops in the hearts of the elect of God.

Knowledge, or theology, is the philosophy of that faith, the result of researches, reflection, and patient labor of the human intellect applied to divine things, and endeavoring to investigate and impart to them clearness, definiteness, and that systematic oneness, of which they are susceptible.

In this novel field the spectator is immediately struck with the decision of its incompatibility with knowledge; not, it is true, that certain historic faith, of which all theologians ought to a greater or less degree to be in possession, but the living faith of Christians. Unregenerate theologians direct against this doctrine the same attacks, and the same engines of war, as the wise of this world employ against the wisdom of God. There is not the slightest agreement, if you listen to those men, between a living faith and theology.

It must be acknowledged that there is some truth concealed under their assertions. The two things, faith aud theology, have been, and are still often separated by many ministers of the gospel. Among them are those who are uniquely theologians, intimately acquainted with the various branches of theological science, and able to explain the Christian system with the most methodical exactness, but in whose hearts the life of faith never had existence. On the other hand, there are some of their number who enjoy the faith of the heart, the Christian life, but are strangers to theology, and regard it as an undoubted science, but still a barren one, from which they may never hope to derive any personal advantage.

Your feet are exposed to both these by-paths of error. With a large number of theologians we have believed that it was unnecessary for the ministers of Christ at the present day to isolate these two things, and that their just combination would result in the greatest utility to the service of God. We have concluded, in accordance with the apostolic declaration, that the *pastor* ought to be a *teacher*. (Ephes. iv. 11.)

Let us then briefly investigate the relations in which faith stands to knowledge; let us indicate the necessity of the former, and the advantages of the latter, and at the same time lay down in our charts the sunken rocks which we should avoid.

FAITH.

And first, I address myself to those who, not having in their heart the living faith of Christians, may be harboring the imagination of supplying its place with theology.

It is impossible for a Christian, and by consequence for a minister, to exist without the life of faith. You may think that the scientific development of Christian doctrine will produce within you that living faith, without which you cannot exist. No, my brethren. The work of man cannot create the work of God. Theology is not the mother of faith, but faith is the mother of theology.

The cultivation of theological science has never produced a renovation of Christian life in the church. It is the simple preaching of Christian truths, it is that faith of the heart, that conviction, and those intimate experiences, which are expressed by the Apostle with a holy enthusiasm—" I believed and therefore have spoken" (2 Cor. iv. 13)—from which such renovations have ever taken their rise. If these are instances where theological instruction has been the means of producing the faith of the heart—and the number is by no means small—it was due not to the theological element, but the element of faith, which was found in that instruction. It was because the teacher was full of faith, and not because he was full of reflection, that he became a means of regeneration. Faith produces faith, but idea produces only idea. The purity, the definiteness, and the systematic arrangement of doctrines, has never given birth to spiritual life.

It is not a school, nor a theologian, to whom the minister or the simple believer in quest of faith ought to address himself. It is to the chief, to Jesus Christ. Seek life not in the apophthegms of knowledge, but in Him " in whom dwelleth all the fullness of the Godhead bodily," (Col. ii. 9.) Every believer, and consequently every minister, is called upon in his office of prophet, to ask immediately from Jesus Christ his own measure of grace. The quality of mediator between God and man no more appertains to the knowledge of the theologian, than to the hierarchy of the priest. It is not in any theological summary, nor in any common places,* in which men should search for faith; but in the Bible, immediately in the Bible, through the illumination of the Holy Spirit, promised unto all.

Let us advance another step. How far soever theology may be from producing life, it is nevertheless the Christian life which produces theology. It is faith which furnishes science with the media of knowledge, the ideas upon which it ought to reflect, and the elements which it ought to combine. For the true knowledge, which enlightens the eyes, is constructed not out of abstract ideas and dead elements, but out of living doctrines and principles, which are quickened into life by the Spirit of God.

There is another point farther on, which we may also reach. It is a living faith, which imparts to the spirit that rapture, that expansion, that depth, and that activity, necessary to set in motion the primitive elements, and thus give birth to a system with all its ramifications entire. An epoch dead in the matter of faith has never produced, and never will produce, a theology. The epochs which have been creative of knowledge have uniformly been preceded—history assures us of the fact—by a revival of Christian life in the Church. It was the upsoaring of faith which was the parent of those theological treatises that signalize the age of Augustine, of the scholastics of the thirteenth century, and of the Reformers.

If you would be theologians, cast yourselves into the current of living waters. It is faith which gives the impulse, without which no noble deed can ever be produced: that just truth, without which you will ramble in despair among vain systems; that life, without which your path will only lie through a valley of dry bones.

Test, then, the opposite system. Let the Christian life be only a principle of your theology, and then you will fall into the one or the other of two evils: for either you will cast yourselves, as thousands have done before you, upon the speculative distinctions of useless dialectics; or, choosing a negative tendency, and a hostile attitude, you will take up arms against what you ought to defend; you will exercise, in the sphere which is assigned to you, only a destructive influence, and instead of erecting an edifice to the living God, you will be amusing yourselves, as so many theologians, alas! have done, in destroying that which already exists, and rejoicing over its ruins.

* *Summa theologica* and *Loci communes*, were the ordinary titles of theological theories before and after the Reformation.

And what basis, gentlemen, would you construct for theology, if not the Word of God, and faith in the divine testimony wrought in the heart by the Holy Spirit? If theology has not that basis, it must of necessity repose either upon the transitory direction of the spirit of the age, or else upon the adventuresome speculations of the human reason. With only such points of support, knowledge will have strange wanderings, lamentable falls, and will soon be lost from view in those winding passages, the limits of which are overhung with the shades of night. In order that the tree of knowledge may prosper, it must, as David says, be planted upon the banks of the stream of the law of God; and it should uniformly and exclusively gather from that pure current its sap and its elements of life. Then it will send forth its fruit in its season; its foliage will not dry up; it shall flourish for ever. But if any strange elements should be absorbed by the roots, the same tree will soon change its color, will languish, will perish and die.

Or rather, plant the tree upon the declivity of Golgotha, in the shadow of the cross, and under the very eyes of the love of the crucified God, who is the wisdom of God and life itself. That which gives life to the most humble faith of the poorest believer, is the same as that which gives it the most sublime knowledge of the wisest teacher.

Faith is not only the creative principle of theology, but is also its renovating power. Knowledge—we have too many examples of the fact—can detach itself from the Word of God. At such times it goes astray; a fever of incredulity rages in the veins, and a crisis has entered upon its development. What will heal the disorder? What will restore the wanderer to the right path?

Statutes, laws, acts of power? Doubtless those who have been appointed to the oversight of education ought to guard against the influence of that which, instead of communicating life, gives only death. But any external force, arrests of justice, and human power, will never suffice for the cure of the malady. Restrain its action temporarily without, and it will only commit the greater ravages within.

What then shall save knowledge?

The life of the Church, my brethren, the simple faith of believers. That faith and that life existed anterior to all theology, and independently of all knowledge; they can never perish, and in them is found the energy which is to heal the nations. Upon theology they exercise a powerful reaction. The teachers, environed on every side with manifestations of the Christian faith, will, in spite of themselves, be drawn back, and that by an irresistible force, towards the focus of light and life. They will be constrained to abandon, one by one, all their perilous positions. Truth every day will gain greater power in the camp of the enemy, and will gradually concentrate an overwhelming opposing force. Knowledge itself, obliged to recognize the fact of her former detachment from that to which it ought to have been united, will elevate her standard again, and cover the errors of knowledge. It may be, for the case is not an extraordinary one, that it was scepticism in the Church which carried scepticism into theology. The faith of the Church will restore faith to theology.

That which has infected must heal; that which struck the blow will bind up the wound. The life and light of the Church are the sun of theology : when the sun is concealed, knowledge is overshadowed and perishes; when he shines forth anew, knowledge reappears in his train under the impulse of a new life.

Therefore, my brethren, in order that knowledge may be cultivated with success in a university, an academy, or a school, there is need of the presence of liberty, but first of all of piety ; there is need of ideas, but before them there is need of faith ; there is, in fine, need of knowledge, but antecedent to all else there is need of submission to the Word of God. Schools of theology, in order to prosper in a scientific form, ought to become sanctuaries. Far from them be every profane mocker—far from them all buffoonery, unseemly jesting, loose morals, and conformity to a world buried in sin. These would prove their destruction, both as temples of knowledge and as seminaries of the prophets.

The holiness of a school is the surest guaranty for the knowledge of a school.

"The Levites shall be mine," saith the Lord.

KNOWLEDGE.

Faith, then, is necessary to theology. But there is a second rock which we must lay down in the chart: that against which all those have dashed who have regarded theology as a sterile science, without application and without advantage to the Church.

Let us first then obtain a definite apprehension of what we now mean by the term *knowledge*. It is not that haughty knowledge which puffeth up, but an humble science, which is conscious of knowing nothing by itself, and of being bound to apprehend everything from the word. It is not a knowledge detached from God, but one which God himself accords to fervent prayers, to conscientious investigations, to serious and holy meditations, and all the works which are vivified and rendered efficacious by the breathings of the Holy Spirit.

The actual state of the world, and of the French nation in particular, demonstrates too forcibly the utility and necessity of this knowledge. Why is Christianity so little known, and its fundamental doctrines so grossly misconceived ? We will not hesitate to declare our own conviction of the cause. It is because, while other sciences have been taking a rapid flight, the science of theology has had no existence with us during the present generation, or at best has existed in an enfeebled frame.

There are perhaps certain epochs in the social and intellectual development of a people, in which it will suffice for the Christian life to animate the church. But that will not suffice in the present actual state of society. When man is fully developed in every function, it is man in his maturity which religion should embrace. She is large enough for the task, and there is nothing in the man which can escape her grasp. The faculty of cognition, which is within us, must find aliment enough of the kind it requires, and ample room enough for the development of its energies. The intellect comes from God, as well as the affections and the will. To pretend, as some have done, that it is sufficient for Christianity to speak to the heart, and that it can abandon the intellect without yielding any satisfaction to its demands, is to advance the same proposition as that the sun rises only upon a part of the creation of God; it is the same as to revolt against that order which has been established from on high.

It has become necessary for Christianity to defend her own position. She must maintain her own rank in the face of all human sciences. Theology must take up its residence in the bosom of Christian societies, and become, what the great regenerator of modern sciences, Lord Bacon, has called it, " the transcendental science."

Do not imagine that the existence of this science is useless for the salvation of souls. Wherefore is it, that in all countries where theological science is cultivated, as Germany for example, so much knowledge and intelligence is found among the laity, and so many true Christians, while with us they are so rare in the same proportion?

The existence of the science alone will explain the phenomenon. It has rendered men of wit and education attentive to the instructions of God. It has led them also to direct their eyes towards the branches of the tree which they are cultivating. Science has rendered the Word of God and Christianity honorable, even in the eyes of philosophers: some of their number have investigated it for the simple pleasure of its knowledge, but in that propitious moment Christianity has seized them, and the Word of God has proved their salvation.

Let us, then, lament, that while all sciences enjoy so much favor and so many worshippers among Frenchmen, the science of theology is still without monuments and without trophies— we should almost have said, without an existence and a name. Let us weep over the fact, that while all the branches of the tree of knowledge, under the shade of which our generation delights to repose, are full of vigor, and loaded with the richest fruits, still that branch which is the principal one of the tree, is fragile, desiccate, despoiled of its verdure, and barren of fruit. This immense vacuum is one of the most efficient causes of the humiliated condition of the faith.

The general opinion, however, tends in a contrary direction. You will meet not only men of the world, and adversaries of the faith, but even men and ministers of unquestionable piety, who pretend that every evil in the Church comes of theology.

Theology, say they, with its precise definitions, its subtle distinctions and its sententious systems, darkens the simplicity of the faith, dampens the fervor of the Christian life, and dishonors religion in the sight of all well educated men. Theology has proved the bane of Christianity. Happy days, when there was no theology! O. the simplicity of Christian doctrine in the primitive ages of the church! Would to heaven we might return thither!

This so much vaunted simplicity of the primitive ages, I will here remark, does not deserve to be all that is made of it. In a great number of instances it was the offspring of ignorance rather than of a strict attachment to the line of truth; it was the simplicity of infants, who knew but little, rather than that of men, who, having weighed good and evil, chose to attach themselves to the good. Thus that simplicity so much regretted by men, who are crying out for piety and not for knowledge, was far from being exempt from errors, and oftentimes very grave ones.

But let us come to that objection, which has been deemed worthy of signal repetition; namely, that this study is no protection against the waywardness of science and none against science itself. It must be confessed, that that is a false direction of knowledge which makes it come in collision with the simplicity of the faith. But it is only in the Christian life that true knowledge has any guaranties for its vigor and prosperity. Whenever it is developed independently of that life, it is soon seen to lose itself in vain formulas and in idle distinctions: it becomes a game of dialectics, which stifles in all who cultivate it the last respirations of life, and destroys in theology and religion all that consideration, which is their peculiar property.

This, however, is not knowledge: it is not a legitimate branch of the tree. It is a parasitical plant, which, in spite of its efforts put forth to confound its woody boughs and yellowish leaves with the true branch, will still be detected by the master of the tree as illegitimate and pernicious, and will be forced to disengage itself from its unnatural union.

The objection, then, turns in favor of that true science, which, emanating from the word of God, and intimately connected with the Christian life, flees from such vagaries. It is not a dry skeleton, which it would present to the world as the symbol of truth: it is a body, clothed with flesh, and filled with the Holy Spirit, and with the life that cometh from on high. It will not isolate any of the faculties of man. Addressing itself to his intelligence, it also addresses itself to his heart. That which you reproach it with lacking, is precisely that which, above all other things, it possesses in the most eminent degree; consequently it will be the very opposite of that, which your fears have represented it to be. Attacking every individual, it will gain over every individual to its cause.

Doubtless, says another objector, the science is useful to the world, for those without, as the Scripture says—but it is useless for the church.

Strange illusion! The legitimate science, such as we have described to you, will render the church the most distinguished service. It will maintain the Christian doctrine pure from all strange elements: and when the latter may receive contamination from any quarter, the former will be at hand as its refiner.

Such strange elements too readily penetrate, first, the Christian life, then the idea of Christianity, and at length knowledge itself. This is what took place in the first periods of the Church. Strange elements had gradually united themselves so intimately with the scriptural elements, and so effectually incorporated themselves with the faith of Christians, that it was almost impossible to distinguish the true from the false. Teachers and simple-hearted believers presented an inconceivable mixture of falsehood and truth.

The discernment of these diverse elements, the separation of the false from the true, is one of the most ennobling tasks of true science. It is one of the works to which she has been destined by God. Her piercing and unfailing eye discerns in that confused assembly that which is from God, and that which is from man. A true servant of the domestic head, theology is constantly dragging the net, which is cast into the sea of ages, and is constantly amassing, in the lapse of time, materials of every conceivable variety of character. With the torch of Revelation in her hand, she discovers and disentangles that which is corrupt from that which is pure: she stores away all that is good in chosen vessels, and flings away again all that is worthless.

And what she has once purified she will keep pure. She will watch with all the vigilance of a sleepless sentinel, that the pride of human reason and the vagaries of enthusiasm do not approach to injure the plant which she has preserved. As the officers who are placed in charge by the sovereign, to see that no vulgar ingredients be combined with the pure gold in the formation of the royal jewels, so a pure theology is charged by our Lord to maintain Christian doctrine, that jewel of God, pure from all human dross, and in the holiness and regal beauty which belonged to her upon her first descent from heaven.

We turn, however, to remind you of the advantages it offers to you, who are educated in her holy tuition, called to be one day the dispensers of her treasures. And what advantages has not knowledge to bestow upon the minister of the word? What service in particular has she not rendered to the very age in which we live? Of how great necessity is her existence at an epoch when there are so many objections, doubts, and controversies, not only in relation to this or that unimportant point but also to a point, which concerns the fundamental doctrines of salvation.

It is true knowledge—knowledge formed under the combined influence of the Holy Spirit and the word, and blessed from above —which will enable you to penetrate most deeply into divine revelation; which will capacitate you to find new treasures, unforeseen and veiled from the ordinary reader, and which, while they augment your knowledge, will also enrich your experience, and increase the efficiency of your ministry.

It is this which, giving importance both to the holy doctrines and the sad errors of times which are no more, making manifest the faith and disclosing the failings of the church, will explain to you what is and what ought to be, by what has been; and will supply to your youth all the riches of a tried experience. This it is, which will qualify you to penetrate with a keen glance the actual condition of the church; which will enable you to perceive the evils against which you have been forearmed; which will place you on your guard against exaggerations, hesitations, and all peculiar and individual determinations, to which your heart exposes you; and which, in the midst of the whirlwind of human opinions by which you are encircled, will communicate to your convictions, your views and your judgments, that perspicuity, that erect attitude and that immovable solidity, for which you will search in vain in your own selves.

It is this which will render you capable of discerning good and evil, what is useful from what is injurious, either in relation to the Christian church generally, or to the particular flock, which the Chief has placed under your direction; which will put you in a condition to keep a reckoning of times, places and circumstances, and which will clearly discover to you the end which you should propose in your career, the proper means of attaining it, and will impart to your ministry a real and enduring usefulness.

It is this which will assist you to avoid those rocks against which—alas! we have too many examples—the purest zeal, when it is unenlightened by knowledge, is liable to dash and go to pieces; and which, impressing upon all your works the characters of wisdom, reflection and discernment, will render your ministry honorable even in the eyes of the world.

It is this which will give you those qualifications so indispensable in a Christian minister, and so rarely found in combination; largeness without latitudinarianism; an exclusive submission to the word without bigotry; and which, rendering your convictions at the same time profound and expansive, strengthening your spirit, and enlarging your heart, will permit you to throw wide open the arms of charity and embrace all your brethren without leading you astray from the isolated focus of truth, and the unassailable central point of faith.

The knowledge which emanates from God will forearm you against that sad formalism which so often infects the evangelical minister, and transforms the services of Jesus Christ into a sordid trade. True knowledge will ever call back spirit, thought and life, in all your reflections and in all your works. It will not suffer your intellect to become a thing of manœuvre. It will constantly recall the truth, and the Spirit of God should be combined with every affair of human life, the breath from on high with those elements which the earth presents. It will recall to you the fact, that you are of the number of "wise men." It will make head against everything which could tend to your ruin, and as the organ of God, will prevent your intellectual perceptions from growing dull, and your spirit from yielding to habits of sluggishness.

The knowledge which emanates from God will save you from

rationalism. Why do so many young intellects plunge themselves into that heresy, and run with such avidity through all its various stages? Simply because they think to find in it food for their intellect and their reason. Vain attempts! For meanwhile their heart is drying up, their reason degrading itself, and their intellect is making to itself more straitened limits. It is Christian knowledge alone which holds in reserve all that of which their vague desires, sometimes the offspring of pride, but often of generosity, are in quest. To that knowledge, young Levites, address your inquiries. She has somewhat to answer from her oracle. Seek not in the wisdom of a day that which God offers you in the secret depths of His eternity. Knowledge will satisfy all your wants. She will show you in Christ all the treasures of a divine wisdom. She will put you in possession of a light, which is to that of rationalism what the sun in the heavens is to the will-o'-the-wisp hovering over a bog. Then discovering at once the meagerness of all the erroneous offspring of human wisdom, and the grandeur of the manifestations of the reason of God, you will cry out, as did the first of theologians, Augustine, when, after having long wandered in the labyrinth of systems, he at length found the true divine knowledge, "Alas! too slowly have I learned thee."

The knowledge which emanates from God will guard you against that false enthusiasm, which, entertaining certain sensations with great avidity, or tearing away certain ideas from the several groups to which they belong, abandons both of them to an unbridled imagination, where they boil and ferment until they break out into deplorable excesses—sometimes these will appear in theosophic speculations, sometimes in the disordered efforts of a vapory spirit, and sometimes in haughty pretensions to gifts and commissions, which no longer have existence, or to a fantastic condition of the church. Theological science will render you timely service in discovering to you all these errors. It will point them out to you in ancient times along with the sad fruits they there brought forth. It will discover to you their intimate connection with the corruption of the heart, and with deadly doctrines. It will at the same time enable you to sift the good from the evil in those ancient dogmas, and thus furnish you a shelter against a wonderful contagion.

The knowledge which emanates from God will put weapons in your hands to refute the vain sophisms of the times; to make successful attacks upon specious errors; to measure weapons, if it be necessary, with those who are practised in the use of arms of the intellect, with the wise in employing the weapons of knowledge—weapons, as we have already remarked, to which God has not assigned the office of changing the heart, but which nevertheless can often remove lamentable prejudices, and thus prepare the way for that joy of heaven, the conversion of a sinner.

But, it may be asked, is it required of us to prove the necessity of knowledge for the minister of Christ, as long as its necessity for every disciple, for every Christian, ought to be a truth of general recognition?

It is to all who have obtained an equal faith with the servants of Jesus Christ, that the Apostle Peter addresses the exhortation, "Add to your faith . . . knowledge." Doubtless there are departments of knowledge which are not absolutely necessary for every Christian, although it is very desirable for all to be possessed of them. But there is a Christian knowledge in which all ought to be making constant progress, according to their peculiar faculties and circumstances. Is not this demanded of those who are charged with teaching the natural sciences? And why should it not also be required of theologians, who are studying theology, that is, the science of God, of that God "who is above all, and through all, and in you all?" In an infected district, at the approach of a formidable pestilence, all seek to acquire some degree of medical knowledge. And should not the science which treats of the remedy by which man can escape eternal death, be regarded of sufficient magnitude and importance in the eyes of you all to deserve your earnest application? And where more important than for you, ministers of Christ?

What we have said will suffice, we trust, to demonstrate to all who will give it their serious attention, the necessity of not separating faith from knowledge, theology from piety, the shepherd from the teacher; and we have at the same time contributed to unfold one of the causes of the institution of this Theological School, both to those who, overlooking faith, speak only of knowledge, and to those who, overlooking knowledge, speak only of faith.

To study, then, my young friends, and to prayer: to prayer and to study! Let prayer first acquire for us the gift of the Spirit of God. Let us abase ourselves by true humility, before elevating ourselves by reflection and knowledge: for "if any man thinketh that he knoweth anything, he knoweth nothing yet as he ought to know." Like the air vehicles invented by the wisdom of man, we must first exhaust ourselves, before we will be able to mount into the elevated mansions of knowledge and contemplation.

Let faith be the key with which we approach the treasure, for the possession of which we are striving. For faith enables us to understand what the human intellect never could discover. The life which comes from God explains what meditation could never unfold. Faith is the eye with which we ought to be furnished, in order to penetrate into that unknown world of divine things which is the domain of theology. Faith is the true organ of the knowledge of God. It enables us to see the invisible, to comprehend the incomprehensible. "For what man knoweth the things of a man save the spirit of man, which is in him? Now the things of God knoweth no man, but the Spirit of God. Now we have received, not the spirit of the world, but the Spirit which is of God: that we might know the things that are freely given to us of God."

One thing more. Let holiness, let a life and conversation truly Christian, give us an intellectual perception, which can only be obtained with them. For, what is it that beclouds our spirit and darkens our understanding, unless it be sin? Lift the veil, and you will see. The more dead you are to sin, the more keen will be your eye, the more luminous your knowledge, and the more expanded your conceptions. Every Christian work, every self-renunciation, is not only a step in sanctification, but also one in knowledge and in theology. If the angels know more than we, it is because they are purer than ourselves. Darkness—that is sin: light—that is holiness. Let us press on, then, toward the light, in order to know Him who is light. "We shall see Him as He is; and every man that hath this hope in him purifieth himself."

Thus, then, disciples in the knowledge of God, we speak to you. "Pray, believe, be holy and blameless." But allow us to add to this, "Work."

Work, then, my young friends. Examine with care those two mighty instruments of sacred theology, the Old and the New Testaments: those two columns, at the base of which the simple seek protection, and which even to the experienced and far-sighted lose their mysterious heads afar in the clouds of heaven.

Review with discrimination all the facts, the teachings, the theories, the truths and the errors which history records for us, and even all the glimmering beams which philosophy throws upon the domain of knowledge, ever holding fast with an unfailing tenacity to the thread, which is the conductor of our holy faith.

Let us employ our intellect—explain, distinguish, and re-examine all the elements which science offers us. Let us fathom every point of doctrine, considered apart and by itself: let us sound it to its deepest significancy, and at the same time let us collect all the parts, apprehend their several relations and their affinities, admire their proportion, their unity and their magnificent harmony.

Let us by sanctified meditation elevate ourselves above the immense field which stretches before us. Let us consider science in all its phases. Let us place ourselves upon a holy mountain, from which we may discover all the country, which the Almighty has given us to conquer and possess. Let us trim our sails upon the stream, and, if needs be, trace the current in all its windings, re-mounting at one time to its source, and at another, following it to the end of its journey. Let us distinguish the primitive from the tributary waters, the principal from the accessory branches. Let us examine the marsh in which its pure water is defiled, because the original impulse of the current fails. Let us contemplate it when it glides sweetly with its fertile waters under the banks that are enriched with its gifts, and when it casts itself headlong with the roar of breaking waves. Let us study the tributaries, which bring to it their strange waters, and the various soils over which it rolls its waves, that we may clearly apprehend the elements which it imprints upon them. Of all these constituents is our present science formed; weighing all influences, and discerning all combinations, for the purpose of disengaging the Christian system, and constructing a sacred theology, which is the highest human science, because it is the science of God.

Observe, my young friends, the fervor with which those apply themselves who are studying either the material body of man, or his legislations, or the natural sciences. Students in theology, know and rest assured that you possess a still more beautiful field. Let the zeal of your contemporaries for the works of their vocation make you enter again into yourselves, and inspire you with a new ardor; yours is the study of God and man. Think of these things.

Take then this science, which is calling your attention, from the humiliating state into which she is fallen. Restore it to its primitive greatness. Be filled with an holy jealousy for its advancement; for upon whose aid can she count, if not upon yours? After reaching that point, having according to Scripture become "men in understanding," return according to the same Scripture to being "children in malice." Let our knowledge recall us to the faith of the simple; but to a faith more thoroughly strengthened, less exposed to change, and which, explored through all its windings, and examined in all its phases, can be defended at our hands with warmth, and distributed with wisdom, as sincere milk to babes, and as strong meat to them that are of full age.

THE

VOICE OF THE CHURCH ONE,

UNDER ALL THE SUCCESSIVE FORMS OF CHRISTIANITY.

TRANSLATED BY REV. R. SMITH,
OF WATERFORD, N. Y.

THE VOICE OF THE CHURCH ONE.

A DISCOURSE, PRONOUNCED AT THE OPENING OF THE THEOLOGICAL SCHOOL AT GENEVA.

WHAT astonishing labors—what untiring activities—what varied efforts, do men employ on earth! But time passes its level, for the most part, over their productions; while they imagine themselves to be building a tower which shall reach to the heavens, their proud works are confounded, after a few generations, with the sands of the desert.

There is nothing stable here, but Christianity. That alone is immovable, like its Author. It is this rock against which have broken, and are still breaking, waves ever new, without being able to shake it.

If, then, there is any one who wishes to give stability to his work on earth, let him connect it with Religion: it will receive from this connection an impress of immortality.

I am aware, gentlemen, that these are truths not generally recognized among men. There are two prevailing errors on this subject. There are those who find nothing unchangeable even in the essence of Christianity. "The Christian doctrine," say they, "is only a particular development of the religious sentiment. This form has succeeded to a previous one, and will, in turn, be succeeded by another. The Religion of Christ sprang necessarily out of the state of humanity in the time of the Cæsars, as a tree in Spring produces buds and flowers." Singular error of Rationalism; but which history refutes in the clearest manner. History shows that Christianity was not in accordance with the directions of the human mind, at the time it appeared, but in direct opposition to them. The wisdom of the world did not give Christianity birth;—it sought to crush it. Christianity was not the child of the times; it was, on the contrary, its adversary and regenerator: and as it was not from the dust of the earth that this precious fruit sprang, it cannot of course return thither again. Then did the Heavens give a treasure to the world, which successive generations ought to transmit uncorrupted from hand to hand. This is the treasure which we have received; which we are to hold with fear and reverence in earthen vessels; and we, in turn, must transmit it to our posterity, still unchanged and unchangeable amongst millions of men, "until the Heavens and the earth flee away, and there is found no more place for them."

But if we encounter, on the one hand, the triflers with Christianity, we meet, on the other, with those who would give to it *a uniformity of appearance in all ages.* There is something, undoubtedly, which never changes in Christianity, and that is its essence; but there is something also, which does change, and that is its appearance: and it is for want of properly understanding this distinction, that so many have erred in regard to the invariableness of Christ's religion. A man changes his *appearance* at different ages of his life: his essence, never:—he is still the same man.

The Christian Religion, at the time it came from heaven, was under the necessity, as is everything else in this world, of clothing itself in a human form. The external circumstances of different epochs must exercise an influence upon the successive developments of Christian truth. To such a form must succeed such another; nor could these forms be things altogether indifferent. Some have been better than others; but the same essential verities have been found in all past varieties, and will be, in all which are to come.

Gentlemen—the work in which we are engaged, and of which I am to give you some account to-day, is, in itself, a feeble, an humble work; but here is its glory, that it belongs to the work of eternity. If we attach ourselves to that which belongs to the *appearance* of Religion only, we can have no security for that which we labor to defend. The first revolution of society would sweep our work to the tomb. But if we address ourselves to the essence of Christianity, the cause to which we devote ourselves partakes of the perpetuity of the work of God. *We* may fail; and being mortal, we shall fail; our school may fail; but the cause to which it is devoted shall not fail, neither in this place, nor in all the earth. To that cause, according to the ancient oracle, "the gathering of the people shall be." Yes, Gentlemen, here lies the foundation of all our hopes; it is this which, by the grace of God, shall animate us in all our difficulties and trials: and it will be worth our pains to explain and defend, on the present occasion, this remarkable characteristic of the Religion of Jesus Christ—*The invariableness of its doctrines, under different forms;* or, *The voice of the Church one and the same, in all ages.*

If we search in the different periods of history for the human forms in which the truth of God has been clothed, we shall find a great number. It is necessary, therefore, to bring them together —to reunite and amass them. We shall obtain thus, in the last synthesis, FOUR PERIODS, or principal forms of Christianity.—The first is the *primitive,* or *the form of Life;* the second is *the form of Dogma;* the third, *the Scholastic,* or, *the form of the School;* and the last, *the form of the Reformation.*——The Church of Christ, to use a Scriptural illustration, is like an individual man. It has its youth, its maturity, its old age—and then, if we might so say, it has, without dying, a glorious resurrection.

Let us run rapidly over these four forms—so diverse, I had almost said, so opposite, in appearance—and see if we do not find, under each of them, the same unchangeable truths.

We shall hear the voice of Doctors. Undoubtedly, the declarations of no one single man are sufficient to satisfy us what was the faith of the Church; but if, on examining those Doctors who lived in countries the most distant from each other, we find, amidst great diversities of views, some doctrines on which they are all agreed, shall we not safely conclude that these doctrines have also been those of all the Church throughout the earth?

What, then, are the points on which to direct our present inquiry?

All Christianity, as well as all religious Philosophy, has respect, necessarily, to *three* principal points. It has respect, at first, to GOD; and then, to MAN; and then, to the RELATION between God and man; or, the scheme adopted by Deity to restore man to himself, which is REDEMPTION.

Let us now see what the voice of the Church has taught us, on these three points, in the different periods of Christianity.—There is,

I.—THE FORM OF LIFE.

In considering this form, we shall omit the time of the Apostles; since that deserves to be considered by itself. The primitive form, according to our plan, commences with the successors of the Apostles, and extends to the time of Arius. The character which distinguishes it, is that of *life*. The truths of Religion were not yet exhibited with that precision and system which distinguished them at a later period. The essential thing was *the life* which results from these truths, when properly received. They lived for Christ, in the midst of a world of idolatry; they died for Christ, in the arena and on the funeral pile, and without much discussing the nature of his person, or disputing about his work. Christianity was content to exist, and to know and profess that it existed, without enunciating and classifying all the parts in which that existence consisted. Just as a man is satisfied for a long time to have and enjoy being, without studying and explaining in what that being consists.

Certain Rationalistic Doctors strangely infer from this character of the primitive form of Christianity, that the Christian truths did not then exist, and that because there was no dogmatism, there were therefore no doctrines. But to reason thus, is to reason as strangely and falsely as would that inexperienced observer, who should maintain that the essential parts of a human being did not exist until the man had made a precise and rational analysis of them.

It results from this characteristic also, that the controversies of this period turn very little upon dogmas. The differences are in *tendencies* rather than *doctrines*. We shall meet with families presenting different aspects, rather than sects maintaining different doctrines. Let us trace these families a little, before proceeding to notice the doctrines which they all agreed to proclaim.

To the inspiration of the Apostles succeeded the simple Christianity of the Apostolic Fathers. It would seem that the ordinary course of nature had in this case been reversed, and that the ingenuousness and simplicity of infancy had followed the strength and maturity of the full-grown man. The Church, under the instruction of her Ignatius, her Polycarp, and many other faithful disciples, lived under the great idea of the speedy return of Jesus Christ: and behold the summary of her faith! "*A new creation must be accomplished in humanity, before the arrival of that solemn day.*" "There are," says Barnabas, "three constitutions, or three economies of the Lord;—*the hope of life* (the Old Testament), and *the commencement of life* (the New Testament), and *the consummation of life* (the Kingdom of heaven)."

But by little and little this direction towards the heavens seems to decline in the Church. A generation appears, which does not so deeply penetrate the spirit of Jesus Christ. They gather curious traditions concerning this terrestrial appearing of Christ. Some carnal Jews, who are still expecting a Messiah altogether human, brought in the grossest views under a Christian name. It seemed as if the Church was fatigued with her exalted flight and was beginning to seek the earth. Let us not be astonished at this. One always experiences languor and drowsiness after long watching and care.

But there now appeared on the limits of Christianity, and almost beyond it, a tendency directly the opposite of this. Oriental philosophy attempts to unite itself with the Religion of Jesus. It seeks to take away from Religion its practical character, and to convert it into systems, which lose themselves in the clouds. *Gnosticism* substituted for a salutary faith, a fantastic cosmogony, by means of which it proposed to explain that which is inexplicable, and to cultivate a theosophy, which would procure for man on earth the sublime contemplations of Heaven. The West recoils before these adventurous vagaries of the East. In Proconsular Africa, and among the Gauls, the *Tertullians* and the *Irenæuses* arise. These offer a Christianity simple, positive, historical—and propose to men that faith which nourishes alike the little and the great. Regarding philosophy as the source of Gnosticism, they begin to view with distrust the wisdom and scientific culture of the Greeks.

But this exclusive simplicity has also its dangers. The cultivated Pagans, not finding in the Christianity offered them, anything which responds to their intellectual taste, remain in the worship of their false Gods, or precipitately cast themselves into the adventurous systems of the Gnostics. Alexandria—situated on the borders of the Nile, between the East and West—remarks this: Alexandria, the grand mart of the Sciences—where the gospel is said to have been carried by the Apostle Mark—undertakes to mediate between these two tendencies of man, into which the world was divided. Pantænus, Clement, and Origen, found a *Christian* Science, and in that approach the East; but they found it on the *Scriptures*, and in that are nearer to the West:—(γνωσις ἀληθίνη— *true Science.*) Alas, it was not wholly so: and these Doctors, although they did not abandon the fundamental principles of Christianity, incorporated in their system the insidious germs of the two great heresies, which have since troubled a subsequent epoch and all the epochs.*

The School of Alexandria, by little and little, supplanted Gnosticism. But against that, in turn, are directed the arms of the severe and practical School of the west. A contest of a remarkable character arises between these two churches, or Schools rather, in the third century. But the opposite tendencies seem to balance each other, and thus contribute to the prosperity of Religion. Alexandria originates a Theological spirit in the church. She begins to systematize, to elucidate her doctrines. She prevents a gross *Anthropomorphism* from mingling with the celestial doctrines of Jesus Christ. The West is always bringing back to the simple and literal word of Scripture. It calls to mind constantly, that Christianity is a thing to be *felt*, proved in the heart, and exhibited in the life. It prevents the changing of these positive and salutary doctrines for vain and fantastic speculations.

Such, Gentlemen, are some of the successive phases of our primitive form of Christianity. But in the midst of all a spirit of life still animates the Church. It is the age of her youth. These Christians, delivered from the sins of Paganism, feel the transforming influence of the gospel, with more energy, from being able to compare what it has made them, and what they were before. This conflict with the world reminds them constantly of their vocation as soldiers of Jesus Christ. Everything in the Church now *lives*—everything *moves*. She aspires to the skies; she seems halfway ascended; and although the age of gold must be reserved for "the new heaven and the new earth," which she is expecting, the Christian Church presents, in these days of her youth and life, traits of beauty, that are absolutely celestial.

And what are the *doctrines*, which are professed by this new people, which the breath of the Almighty has created in the earth? They recognize *one living and true God.* They worship in God, not only the principle of all things (*The Father*), but the Redeemer also (*The Son*), and the sanctifier of fallen humanity (*The Holy Spirit*). They believed that the same God, who created man in righteousness, has redeemed him from sin, and does not cease to sanctify him until he comes to everlasting life. They knew nothing of the strange error, by which some would rob God of the work and glory of Redemption, by giving it to a creature.

The idea of *a Trinity in the Godhead* discovers itself from the very beginning of the primitive epoch, and never ceases to be proclaimed, in a manner the most distinct. How does the voice of these early soldiers of the Cross confound the bold pretensions of modern times! Hear it: CLEMENT OF ROME, a disciple of Paul,

* Arianism and Pelagianism.

renders glory to God in the following profession,—" One God, one Christ, one Spirit of Grace:" while *Polycarp*, a disciple of John, dying in the midst of the flames, ascribes eternal glory " to the Father, to the Son, and to the Holy Ghost."

JUSTIN MARTYR, a converted sage, who, in the time of the Antonines, poured out his blood for the cause of Christ, proclaims, " a unity in Trinity."—THEOPHILUS, Bishop of Antioch, about the same time, and in a manner still more explicit, professes " *The Holy Trinity.*"

A little afterwards, we find TERTULLIAN, a lawyer of Africa, now become a pastor of God's flock, proclaiming " a Trinity of one Divine Being, the Father, the Son, and the Holy Spirit!" and in another place—" Let us guard well the sacrament of our economy, ' a unity in Trinity,' recognizing *three*, the Father, the Son, and the Holy Ghost.—One in substance, one in estate, and one in power, became one God."*

And let us hear a Bishop of a city near our own, a city trampled by the fury of Christ's enemies in his day, and by other furies in our own—let us hear IRENÆUS, of LYONS, who had left the enlightened shores of Asia to bear the glad tidings of salvation to the barbarous Gauls—how does *he* defend the great doctrine of *God manifest in the flesh!* " Christ," says he, " united in himself God and man: if MAN had not vanquished the enemy of man (i. e. the Devil), he had not been properly vanquished: but, on the other hand, if GOD had not wrought salvation, we could never have been assured of possessing it."

We have thus passed, as yet, only some few scores of years, from the death of the Apostles, and we have found proclaimed by so many illustrious Doctors, this doctrine of Father, Son, and Holy Ghost, a doctrine of which Christ designed to establish a perpetual monument in the Church by the institution of Baptism. The first of all the Church's Teachers defend this most consoling doctrine of *God become Man.* The further we advance, the more do these testimonies increase: throughout, is most deeply engraven, both in the sentiments and worship of God's people, the eternal Divinity of the Son of God. Even one of the wisest of the Heathen sages could say of them, " These Christians meet together, to sing hymns to Christ, as being God."—But do we inquire now, what these Christians of the primitive epoch believed *concerning man?* They did not imagine, with certain Pagans and certain modern Doctors, that all evil proceeds from natural organization in man, and that this evil is not in opposition to the holiness of God!——Their sentiment was, that the first man, having, by disobedience, separated his will from the will of God, human nature has been abandoned to itself, and thus separated from God, has fallen under the dominion of evil.

Let us approach, for proof, the college of the Apostles: let us

---

* *Note by the Translator.*—The original authorities are referred to, and printed in full, in the notes to Dr. Merle's pamphlet; but it has not been deemed necessary to insert them here.

interrogate those who either surrounded or succeeded them. *Barnabas*, the companion of Paul, has these words: " Before we believed, the habitation of our hearts was full of corruption and sin; filled with idolatry, and a dwelling-place of demons." *Justin*, who had sought in vain, in all philosophy, a key to the history of man, finds it, at length, in the fall of Adam, effected by the seductions of Satan concealed in the form of a serpent. (See his Dialogue with Trypho, p. 306.)

The first man, according to the simple and practical *Irenæus*, is " like the case of one who, being incarcerated, propagates a race in prison." The profound *Tertullian* has already called the corruption of human nature " original sin." (*Vitium Originis*.) " The first man," says he, " infected the species descending from him, and rendered them partakers of his condemnation." *Cyprian*, Bishop of Carthage, understands the origin of sin in the same way. " The infant, at birth, has no sin," says he, " unless it be, in that it is descended, according to the flesh, from Adam, and has, by its birth, contracted the contagion of death."

And now, if we betake ourselves to the school of Alexandria and think to hear something more flattering to our pride from these philosophical Theologians, even there we shall learn from *Origen*, that " Adam turned from the straight way of Paradise, to take the evil ways of mortal life." In consequence, all those who, descending from him, have come into the world, are also turned out of the way, and become, like him, unprofitable." " Every man is corrupted in his father and in his mother: Jesus Christ alone was born pure." " It is impossible that man, since his fall, should regard God; he must be subject, at first, to the dominion of sin."

Thus Egypt, as well as Gaul, and Africa, with Asia, alike recognize man as a being fallen and impure.

And how is this fallen and defiled being to be reconciled to a holy God? What thought the Christians of this primitive epoch, of the means by which God saves? Let us interrogate those again who surrounded the Apostles. They will teach us those sacred doctrines of Grace, which were more fully explained at a later period. " The Son of God has suffered," says *Barnabas*, " that his sufferings might give us life. He offered in sacrifice for us, the vessel of his spirit (i e. *his body*)." Again, " Having learned to hope in the name of Christ, and having received the remission of sins, we are become *new men*, and *new-created*." *Hermas*—the same perhaps of whom Paul speaks—(Rom. xvi. 14)—says: " Before man receives the name of a child of God, he is condemned to death; but when this seal is applied, he is delivered from death and passes into life." " The law of God," says *Justin*, " pronounced a curse upon man, inasmuch as he could not fulfil it in all its extent. (See Deut. xvii. 26.) But Christ has delivered us from this curse, in bearing it on our behalf." Do we speak differently at the present day?

Irenæus sees in circumcision " a type of the saving blood of Christ, and in the tree of life, a type of the cross of Christ."

Elsewhere he declares "that man must no longer seek to purify himself by sacrifices, but by Christ's blood and his death." The Paschal Lamb, according to him, foreshadowed Christ, "who saves those that believe in him, by the sprinkling of his blood;" and the two goats—of which the one was sent away into the wilderness, and the other sacrificed to God—were a representation of the two-fold coming of Christ, the one for death, and the other for glory. He opposes to the disobedience of Adam, the obedience of Christ. "Christ reconciles the Father to us," says he, "in replacing, by his obedience, the disobedience of the first man;" and, pursuing his comparison of a man cast into prison by sin, and into captivity to the Devil, declares that "Christ has paid the ransom necessary for deliverance from this captivity."

In the same way does *Origen* represent the death of Christ as "that power which delivers man from sin." Indeed, the entire Church regards the sufferings of the Lamb of God as the means by which the way to the Father has been re-opened to the children of men. It is faith which renders man a partaker of this deliverance, and this communicates, at the same time, a divine life. "Called by the grace of God," says *Clement of Rome*, "we are justified—not by ourselves, not by our wisdom or goodness, or any works which we have wrought in the sanctity of our hearts; but by *faith*, according to which a sovereign God has justified men in all time. Do we live at ease, then, on that account? Do we cease to do good works? Far from it. We do good works with joy—even as God for ever works, and rejoices in his activity."

Behold, then, this holy Church of the primitive epoch. Hear how she speaks to us from the bosom of her griefs, and, as it were, from the height of the scaffolds where she suffered. She confesses her miseries, and embracing the knees of Jesus, calls him her "Saviour and her God." Who can misunderstand the profound accents of her sincere piety? How pitiable the occupation of those who would despoil her of these white robes, and clothe her with the tattered garments of a modern Infidelity! But this profane effort is, in the meantime, a homage rendered to the Church—the first Unitarians had recourse to the same expedient.

Vain are all these devices; for whoever will listen, shall always hear the voice of the primitive Church proclaiming, with one accord, these unchangeable truths.

II.—THE FORM OF DOGMA.

In our view of the primitive epoch of the Church—although we have gathered only here and there a sheaf from the vast harvest—we have already extended ourselves beyond the proper limits of this discourse. We have done so, because it is in this age alone that our adversaries are wont to hazard the controversy. They despair of other periods; and they make loud and violent complaints, if the faith, which they cannot but acknowledge, is to be found in them. We will not, therefore, greatly strive for a field, on which our foes proclaim in advance that they are vanquished and must abandon.

This epoch opens as the era of great Doctors, great truths, and great heresies. It was the period in which Christian Theology—of which the elements had been preparing in a preceding epoch—was carried, by illustrious men of God, to its highest point of elevation. It was the era of *Athanasius*, of *Hilary*, of *Gregory*, of *Basil*, of *Ambrose*, of *Augustin*, and of *Chrysostom;* the time of lofty spirits; the *age mature* of the Church. The last murders of the confessors of Christ have ceased—the memorable Council of Nice has been held—the epoch of *Life* is finished—the form of *Dogma* begins. Not that there was no longer any life in the Church; but that the characteristic of dogma is that which now prevails. Now man loves to have distinct ideas of what he believes; to methodize; to render reasons. The Church, no longer obliged to struggle with persecution from without, has more room to occupy herself with that which is within. She arranges the faith which she has long possessed.

The different tendencies of a former age, in the meantime, develope more and more; and, by a remarkable transformation, arrange themselves in opposing doctrines—just as the dispositions of youth, at first vague and indeterminate, are resolved into distinct characteristics, in the mature man. The *two great heresies* appear, conducted by *Arius* and *Pelagius;* but even these heresies became the means which God uses for the better establishment of the truth. The doctrines so clearly defined by the Church of this period will now be faithfully transmitted. They will be preserved and perpetuated amidst all the troubled barbarism of succeeding times. The Dogmatic form shall be, by divine grace, the shield of these truths in days of coming struggle and revolution, and the very hammer to break their way into minds of hardened barbarism. But while, in order to recognize truth more distinctly, they divide it into many *minutiæ*, it must be confessed they sometimes seem to lose sight of the essence—the life itself.

The East and West preserve, in the meantime, their peculiar characteristics. The East remains the country of lofty speculations—the West, that of practical questions. The East discourses concerning God—the West occupies itself more with man. The East produces an *Athanasius*—the West a *Pelagius* and an *Augustin*. But both in the one country and in the other, the truth is assailed, and obtains distinguished victories. Having passed the time of its youth, the Christian doctrine, like the just man, is put to trial, but was not to prove a second fall. It will resist seduction; it will remain firm.

The doctrine concerning God was first expounded now, and with great clearness; because it was the first upon which man had dared to lay a menacing hand. *Athanasius*, a distinguished Doctor of Alexandria, discovers, in the profound mystery of human redemption, the necessity of the eternal Divinity of the Redeemer. *Earth has no Saviour, if its Saviour be not God.* If *Athanasius* consecrates his life, and submits to so many exiles, to defend the identity of substance between the Father and the Son, it is not that he attaches so great value to a dialectic subtlety; no, he combats for the essence of Christianity itself, and for the salvation of souls. Christianity has for its object to re-establish man in communication with God. In order to this, there must be a Mediator. "But," said *Athanasius*, "if the Son of God be different in essence from God, then would there be need of another Mediator, to unite him with God. He alone can establish a real communication between God and his creatures, who has no need of a mediation for himself—but who *is himself* a part of the Divine essence. Now such is the Son of God. Were he a creature—be it the most excellent and exalted—he would, in interposing between God and man, instead of uniting, separate them one from another." (*Athan. Oratio contra Arian.*)

But let us hear the entire Church in the Symbols of her faith. "This is the faith universal," says she, "that we worship one God in Trinity, and the Trinity in unity—without confounding the Persons or dividing the Substance: for the person of the Father is one: that of the Son, another, and that of the Holy Spirit, another. But the Father, Son, and Spirit, are one same Divinity—one equal Glory—one co-eternal Majesty. Such as is the Father, such is the Son, and such the Holy Spirit. The Father is uncreated—the Son is uncreated—the Spirit is uncreated: the Father is God—the Son is God—the Spirit is God; but at the same time there are not three Gods, but one God. And the true faith is:—We believe and confess that our Saviour Jesus Christ, the Son of God, is God and man: God, of the substance of the Father, begotten before the world began; and man, of the substance of the mother, born in time—perfect God and perfect man—equal to the Father according to his Divinity—less than the Father according to humanity." (*Athanasian Creed.*)

A controversy of sixty years (from 320 to 381) was necessary to determine, explain, and defend this doctrine of the Divinity of Christ.

But new combats now commenced to determine another dogma. A little after *Athanasius* and those who followed with him, appeared another Teacher in the Church who seemed to have received a commission to explain and defend the true doctrine concerning MAN. This was *Augustin*. Already, indeed, had the truth on this subject been believed and confessed by those who had gone before him. "By the sin of one Adam," says *Hilary of Poictiers*, "all the human race has sinned." "We have all sinned in the first man," says *Ambrose*. "In him human nature has sinned." But it was when the great Doctor of the West arose; he under whose influence were to be found, during many ages, all who should have clear ideas of truth; it was when *Augustin* appeared, that all the depths of human impotency were developed.

This man had abandoned Manicheism, then Platonism—not finding in the one or the other that inward peace which he needed in the midst of life's tempests—and he seized with avidity on the Gospel, which dissipated his doubts, consoled his heart, and seat-tered light in all his ways. In these combats with sin and a vain philosophy, he had learned to recognize *in himself* all the corruption of the human heart; and here is the chord which henceforth vibrates in all his instructions. Pursued at once by the sublime ideal of sanctity, and by all the seductions of sensuality, he sees opened, by the shock of these conflicting elements, the deep profundities of his own heart—even as the tempests of the ocean will sometimes uncover the depths of the abyss. To perfect his opportunities, he now comes in contact with a man, who, without ideal, is placed in easy and ordinary circumstances of life, and who has formed thence, the most preposterous opinions of the morality of human nature.

Augustin enters the lists with *Pelagius*. But this is not a controversy between two men alone: it lies between principles—two leading tendencies of the human mind, which have appeared in all ages. *Augustin* sees the first man estranging himself from God: from this estrangement proceeds sin, and from this, the moral disorder of all humanity. Human nature, according to him, is a mass of ruin (*Massa perditionis*). The consequence, as well as the punishment of sin, in all his descendants, is the obligation to sin also (*Obligatio peccati*). Man has lost his liberty, and his power to do any good work. He can no more have anything, except as God is pleased to give it to him. If some come to have the faith of the Gospel, while others do not—the reason cannot be found in man; since all are equally incapable of any good: it is to be found in special act of God alone—in the secret counsels of the Almighty—in an election of grace. After a controversy of nearly thirty years—carried on in Africa, in Italy, and in Middle Gaul—the truth triumphs, and the doctrine of the total inability of man remains in the Church.

In the same spirit was *the doctrine of grace* explained and enforced by these great minds; and this brings us to the third point, which is to be examined. Already had it been said by the excellent *Hilary:* "Redemption is given gratuitously—not according to the merit of works, but according to the will of the giver—the choice of Him who redeems us."—" In this consists the grace of God—says *Augustin*—that He justifies, not by our righteousness, but by his own." But he insists above all, that the idea of grace excludes all merit, and all natural disposition in man to receive salvation. God is the *Alpha* and *Omega* with him—the beginning and the end of our salvation. " That which God begins by operating—says he—He ends by co-operating: Commencing—He operates, that we might be willing—and to finish, he now co-operates with those who have the will :— " *He that glorieth let him glory in the Lord.*"

Thus is the Christian science greatly advanced in this era. The doctrines of God, of man, of salvation, which the teachers of the first period had indeed seen in the Scriptures, are now sounded with greater precision and more profound research. Under the influence of the Spirit of God, Theology advances; for there is, gentlemen, such a thing as progress, even in Theology. What shall we say then of those, who, even at this day, would persuade us not only to abandon this advance, but to return to those errors which the Church has long since rejected? "Leaving the principles of the doctrine of Christ, let us go on to perfection."

III.—THE SCHOLASTIC FORM.

A new form succeeds to that which has supplanted the primitive. After ages of darkness, the East beheld a great intellectual movement in the eleventh century. This form has been called the *Scholastic* from *Schola*—the School. The School seeks to separate itself from the Church, which hath hitherto been supreme—to obtain action and authority, independent of the hierarchy. Certain liberal-minded men, who were in the beginning at least neither monks nor ecclesiastics, determined to establish schools altogether distinct from those which had hitherto existed. From these schools soon arises the University of Paris, the mother of Scholastic Philosophy. The general character of the scholastic form, then, is the *Spirit of the Schools*, we may say, of the *University*, or of *Science*. To apply philosophy to Christianity; to reduce Christian doctrines to systems; to show their connections, their internal proofs, and to measure them not only by the heart, but by the understanding; such is the tendency of the Scholastic form of Religion: so that if the first era may be called the form of *life*, and the second that of *doctrines*—the third is that of *system*. There is yet life—there are yet doctrines; but that which prevails is the systematic. It was then that each Doctor published his *system*—his *Summa Theologiæ*. It was the *age advanced* of the Church, which naturally succeeded to its youth and manhood. It is the age which loves to *arrange* what it had before *collected*. It meditates: it has little of impulse, but more of reflection. There were indeed men of great force in this middle era; but the prevailing disposition was to reflection and system.

Historical studies there were yet none: the exegetical were no more as esteemed; and yet the human mind was awaking with great force all over Europe. It needed a guide to direct it, and this guide was found in Dialectic Philosophy: and as Theology was the science of the age, the human mind adventured upon this field, under the auspices of their new leader. This tendency of the scholastic might lead to rationalism—to infidelity; but the good doctors of the age opposed to these the holy truths of Theology "The Christian (says *Anselm*, the father of Scholastic Theology) should come to understanding through faith, and not to faith through understanding. I seek not to comprehend, in order to believe; I believe, that I may comprehend." "And I believe even, because, if I did not believe, I should not comprehend." Immediately *Abelard* and his school avail themselves of the scholastic principle, and become the advocates of free examination. They wish first to comprehend, and then to believe. "Faith, say they, established by examination, is much more solid. It is necessary to meet the enemies of the Gospel on their own ground:

if we are not to discuss, we must believe everything, the false as well as the true."

In the meantime, whatever may have been the danger of these tendencies, and whatever the reproaches of the Church, we cannot accuse these doctors with having abandoned any doctrine of the Christian faith. We cannot, however, wholly absolve them. Scholasticism often disfigured Christian truth. Its tendencies and the times in which it appeared, necessarily led to this. Human reason never ventures without danger on those great truths which surpass created intelligence. The school of the middle ages, like that of Alexandria before, shook the foundations of the Christian system, in attempting to establish them. It had its great minds, and under its influence there was progress—I will not say of Religion, but of science, of Theology. The great men, who were the lights of these times, communicated much instruction to the scholars, who filled their schools, and who followed them by thousands, and into the descent, if necessary, where chairs of doctrine were established.

It has become common, with certain unbelievers, to brand Christian orthodoxy as an *invention of the middle ages.* This trite accusation does too much honor to the age in question: The Christian doctrine already existed. But let us interrogate some of the men of this age.

For their exposition of the *doctrine of Salvation,* let us hear *Anselm,* the most influential perhaps of all the Philosophical Theologians—*Anselm* of Canterbury, the second *Augustin* of the Latin Church, who knew so well how to unite the researches of Philosophy with the purity of the Christian faith. The system of Redemption is developed by him, in a manner to satisfy at once the understanding and the heart. "All rational creatures," says he, "are under obligation to submit their wills to the will of the great Creator. This law, the first man transgressed, and thus destroyed the harmony of moral order. Now the law of eternal righteousness demands, either that the human race should be punished, or that by some satisfaction, proceeding from humanity, that order should be restored. Without this, it would be altogether inconsistent that polluted man should hold communion with happy spirits. But man could not, of himself, accomplish this satisfaction. As human nature had been corrupted by one, so by one ought the satisfaction to be made.

"He, who should effect this, must be some being above creatures. He must be God himself; and in the meantime he must be human also, to the end that the satisfaction may be applicable to humanity. This could be none other, then, than GOD-MAN, the Mediator. This God-man must deliver himself up to death voluntarily, since he was not, as God, subject to death: and he must exhibit perfect obedience in the midst of the greatest sorrows. God would then owe to Christ a recompense; but Christ, as God, could need no recompense: he could therefore transfer his merits to the world, and demand for his reward the salvation of believers." Thus speaks *Anselm* in his Treatise—*Sur Deus homo.*

But what is remarkable—considering the common opinion formed of these men—is, that they insist much *on the sanctifying influence of faith*. "The sufferings of Christ," says *Peter Lambord*, the illustrious *Master of Sentences*—" deliver us from sin; for this immense sacrifice of divine love inspires us with love for God, and this love works our sanctification." "The just man, who lives by faith," says *Robert Pulleyn*, " is already sanctified within, and exhibits good works as signs of his faith and sanctification: faith first produces righteousness of heart, and righteousness of heart produces good works." *Alexander de Hales*, who was called the *irrefragable doctor*, speaks thus: " Man in his original state never opposed himself to God. He then had need only of *formative grace;* but now that there is something in him opposite to God, and which cannot be removed except by the power of God, man needs *transformative grace.*"

There are undoubtedly some differences between these great men, but these differences only show how firmly established they were in the essential truths of Salvation. *Anselm*, for instance, *Thomas Aquinas*, and others supposed that the sacrifice of Christ effected the salvation of man, in virtue of an intrinsic value (*ex insito valore*); while many other Scholastics, and *Duns Scott* in particular, contended that it was owing solely to the design and counsel of God. This was the difference; while all proclaimed that a man was a lost being, and saved alone by the death of the God-man Jesus Christ.

IV.—THE FORM OF THE REFORMATION.

Such is the testimony of these last ages, to say nothing of the *Wickliffs* and the *Waldos*, the forerunners of that great movement. which now began to appear in the world. The Church had had its youth, full of life and vigor, its manhood mature with strength and clearness, and its ripe age of reason and of system. But after the period of the schools the age of rationalism was past. Now the hierarchy sought to embrace all within its iron grasp: life, dogma, system, lay as under a funeral stone, and all the noble tendencies of the Church must die. Vain effort! She burst these bands of death, rolled back the stone of the Sepulchre, and came forth, a dead man restored to life! Let us salute her, under this fourth form, *the form of the Reformation.*

If the three preceding forms were those of life, of doctrines, of system, what shall be the characteristic of this? Gentlemen, the Reformation was the *re-establishment* of former things. But this re-establishment will not have respect to any one of the preceding forms exclusively; it shall be the re-uniting of the whole. Of these, which had before existed only in separate forms, it will now form an admirable *Triology*. Behold, our *fourth form*, an epoch of the Church. The Reformation takes the form of system, carries that back to dogma, and then crowns all with the characteristic of life. It unites the three wisdoms of preceding ages

She commenced with *the life*. *Luther* proved, through divine grace, the living influence of Christianity, as no preceding Doctor, perhaps, had ever felt it before. The Reformation sprang living from his own heart, where God himself had placed it. The era which passed during the time of the teacher of Wittemburgh, was, so to speak, *all life*. This is so true that the admirable work published by *Melancthon* (the Theologian of the Reformation), we speak now of the first edition of his *Loci Communes*—omits the doctrine of the *essence of God and the Trinity*. Not that he considered these doctrines unimportant; they are, on the contrary, the basis of his system; but because, in his own words, " it is more profitable to adore these mysteries, than deeply attempt to sound them."

But even here you will find that Christian life is built on Christian doctrine: and then accordingly, in the second period of the Reformation (that which produced *the confession of Augsburgh*, drawn up by Melancthon himself), these doctrines are presented, defined, and illustrated in all their force. The Trinity, total depravity, and above all, the doctrine of justification by faith alone, are there explained with a clearness and force scarce equalled in the epoch of dogmatism itself. You find *system*, also, in the harmonious distribution of all the doctrines of Christianity; and this characteristic appears above all in the third period of the Reformation, under the influence of Melancthon of Germany, and *Calvin* of Geneva. THE CHRISTIAN INSTITUTES of our Reformer will remain for ages one of the most beautiful monuments of the Christianity of *system*.

Would you know how strong is the testimony of this epoch to the immutable truths of the Gospel, hear the great Doctor of Wittemburgh on *the Divinity of Christ*. " If Christ," says he, " be not the true and essential God, begotten of the Father in eternity, and the creator of all creatures—*we are lost:* for of what avail were the sufferings and death of Christ, if he were only man like you and I? He could not, in that case, conquer Satan, sin, and death. We need a Saviour who is truly God over all: the conqueror of sin and death, of Satan and hell. In vain do the Arians tell us he is the most exalted of *creatures*. They wish in this way to screen their shameful error, that the people may not perceive it; but if we corrupt the Doctrine of Christ in the least degree, irreparable mischief is done. If you take away his proper Divinity, there is no deliverance for us from the wrath to come."

And what is the doctrine of the Reformation *concerning man*? It reduces to powder the subtleties of the Scholastics on this point, and presents the truth with an admirable clearness and simplicity. Luther, even before the publication of his famous Theses on Indulgences, published others concerning man; and here are some of the great truths, which, even at the morning of the Reformation, he declares himself ready to defend.

" That man has become an evil tree, and can neither will nor do anything but evil."

" On the part of man, there is nothing preceding grace but impotency and rebellion."

"There is no moral virtue without pride, or discontent (*tristesse*), that is, without sin."

"He who is destitute of the grace of God sins continually, though he should not steal, kill, or commit adultery."

But in what manner shall we speak, gentlemen, of the testimony which the Reformation gives to the *doctrine of grace?* It was by this doctrine that it overturned entirely the foundations of Rome.

The Reformation never suffers man to rest the hope of his salvation in anything done by himself or in himself. Christ is the only foundation: and faith, in his name, the only means of grace. Every other view leads either to pride or despair. Hear Luther: writing to his friend *Sphanlein*, he says, " Have you at length despaired of your own righteousness? And do you rejoice and confide in the righteousness of Christ? Learn, my brother, to know Christ and him crucified; learn to despair of yourself and to sing this song, ' Jesus, my Lord, thou art my righteousness, and I thy sin: thou hast taken that which was mine, and given me that which belonged to thee: thou hast become that which thou wast not, and caused me to be what I was not myself.' " Works," says he, " on one occasion, are not taken into consideration, when justification is the subject concerned. True faith, indeed, will never fail to produce good works, any more than the sun will fail to shine; but after all, it is not our good works which dispose God to justify us."

"Undoubtedly," says Melancthon, "renovation of heart must flow from faith; but if you inquire after justification, turn your eyes from this renovation and fix them on the promises—on Christ —knowing that we are justified only for the love of Christ, and not on account of our new nature. Faith justifies, not, as some suppose, because it is in us, as the root of a good tree; but because it lays hold on Jesus Christ, for the love of whom we are rendered acceptable to God." "We offer nothing to God," says Calvin, " but by his grace, we are become, as it were, all pure without regard to our works."

All the Reformers, while they differ on some points, are of one accord in this. In Germany, in Switzerland, in France, in Great Britain, in Italy even, and in Spain, they teach the doctrine of Justification by Faith alone.

But why do I enlarge? Have we not *the Confessions* of the Reformers, and do not the adversaries of our faith, as well as its friends, agree that this was pre-eminently the doctrine of the Reformation?

Gentlemen; there is yet another period—a *fifth* form, perhaps, now commencing for the Church;—a form unknown, mysterious, and of which the characteristics cannot yet be very clearly defined. Of one thing, however, we may be confident: one thing the past teaches, and that is, that the same great verities which have formed the foundation hitherto, will be the essence of the form which is yet to come. The salutary doctrines which have yet governed the Church, will not relinquish her helm now. This precious vessel shall not be abandoned to perfidious and ephemeral winds;—to the heresies of *Theodosius* and *Pelagius*—of *Arius* and *Socinus*. *Ce qui été sera!* That which has been, will be.

Further than this: the history of the past is a guarantee that the future shall re-unite all which was good in forms, that are now no more God will not permit anything to be lost, which was once in his Church, and for his Church. And this leads me to glance at an error of some well-intentioned Christians, who speak of returning to primitive Christianity, without caring for what lies in the way from that to the present times. The Church could no more disengage itself from the influence of the different forms through which she has passed, than a tree could despoil itself of the different layers with which each returning spring has clothed it; or the body of a full grown man get rid of the accretions of previous years.

For us, gentlemen, we will not indeed turn our eyes wholly to the future; but neither will we wholly reject the past. The past will be *in* the future. Life, doctrines, system, all will be united, and perfectly, in the form which is yet to be.

In the meantime there will undoubtedly be something to distinguish this new form from that of the Reformation; but who shall say what it will be? I will venture to say thus much,—that perhaps the principal characteristic will be *the missionary spirit*— the carrying to all the race of men, and to every individual, that which the preceding forms have preserved and produced. Did not the period of the Reformation unite the isolated good of three preceding eras, to the end that the new period might stretch out its hand, laden with these riches, and scatter them abroad over all the earth? Ought not these riches to become the property of all men, and in a manner they have not yet been? But I refrain from these suggestions—covered as they are with a veil of deep obscurity.

But one thing is certain and we ought to know it. We are, gentlemen, entering on a new era for science and for the Church: and ours is the generation which must give to this new era its first and most important impulse. There is much to do, and but few as yet to accomplish it. You, at least, my voice can reach. Destined, therefore, to open this new direction of piety and of science, form yourselves as scribes and teachers for the work. Understanding, that to conquer a strong infidelity will require a strong faith and extensive knowledge. Enrich yourselves with the past, to prepare for the future. Ye young men, who are yet to serve the Church of Him who has given his life for the sheep; and ye who are already established over the flock, understand well what it is, which a sound Theology will require. Profit by the instructions of history. Let her carry you beyond the narrow bounds with which prejudice or locality may have surrounded you—and leave the dull track where servile spirits are willing to drag themselves along. Live—not alone with the passing moment, but with other ages. History invokes them; history surrounds you with them, and makes you hear their grand and solemn testimony.

Will you reject the voice of all the Church, and of Jesus Christ himself, for the voice of a single teacher? Will you despise that glory which comes from God, and seek for that which comes from the present world? Pursue this wonderful chain, the first link of which is God himself, and which, forming itself through so many ages, has reached at length even unto us. Be unwilling to turn aside for some obscure heresy: be firm and faithful, should you find yourselves alone—alone in the Church, alone in the world—a confessor and a martyr for "God manifest in the flesh." Be not disheartened, but comfort yourselves in reflecting that you have God for your witness, and the company of all those illustrious men, whose voice you have to-day heard. History shows that Christianity has, in all ages, acted with force upon the minds of men; but shows at the same time, that it is by the same doctrines that this regenerating influence has been felt. The orthodox dogmas alone have had this power, whether on individuals or a people. All others have served only to amuse, and to ruin them. Never will you find life, where you do not truth. Are you willing then to be mere rhetoricians, and amused by high-sounding language; or do you desire to be the benefactors of your race, and save them by the power and wisdom of God? Attach yourselves, I pray you, to that which is saving—immutable—eternal: associate yourselves with a sacred host. Behold; what mighty efforts are now making in Switzerland and in France, in Germany and Holland, in Great Britain and America, to restore to the world a sound Theology and establish the throne of truth.

And thou, O God most High: by that light which causeth to see light—illuminate our minds, and open the portals of that science, whose unsearchable treasures are concealed in Jesus Christ!

A VOICE FROM ANTIQUITY

TO THE

MEN OF THE NINETEENTH CENTURY.

PROLOGUE.

BETWEEN THREE YOUNG MEN OF THE NINETEENTH CENTURY.

First Young Man.—Society is dissolving. Where is the link that once bound it together? Is there any one sentiment that governs it? Yes, one —and that is selfishness. Selfishness resulting in despair; and despair often in suicide! What can check this disease that is consuming us?

I.—Faith.

First Young Man.—Yes, faith. A noble sentiment, doubtless: but what faith? Shall it be that of the Sergeant who blew out his brains, crying, I believe in Victor Hugo, or——

I.—Faith in God.

First Young Man.—Does not everybody in France believe in God in one way or another? And yet France is not cured.

I.—Faith in God consists not only in believing that He is, but in believing also what He says. When we have faith in any one, we believe his word; now in France people do not believe what God has spoken.

First Young Man.—I can easily know what Cousin, Hugo, Lamartine or Chateaubriand have said, for their works abound among us. But pray, where shall we find what God has spoken?

I.—In the Bible; in *the Book*, the Book of nations, the Book of God.

First Young Man.—The Bible! Yes, I have heard of it, but must confess I have never read it and not even seen it. It is far from being generally diffused, like the Meditations of Lamartine, or Beranger's Songs. It is scarcely spoken of in France. Is it much known in other countries?

I.—The Book of God is translated into more than 150 languages; it is scattered among all tribes and nations of man. There are languages in which it is the only written book. The savages of distant islands come in crowds to lie down for days and nights before the humble missionary dwelling where it is being printed in their own tongue, that they may be the first to bear it away in fragments, leaf by leaf: and already has it begun to circulate among the three or four hundred millions of the Celestial Empire.

First Young Man.—It must be very ancient, to have travelled so far.

I.—When the first of its writers composed his books, Greece knew not yet her letters.

First Young Man.—But what has it been doing in the world? Has it produced effects comparable to those of the works of modern authors?

I.—When the world was sinking into decay, in the time of the Roman Emperors, this Book triumphed over the corruption of the South, and created a new world. And when the Barbarians had threatened to stifle our Europe in its new birth, this Book triumphed over the barbarism of the North, and created modern society. It is able to save us for the third time—and, even now, is converting the ends of the earth to the knowledge of the true God.

First Young Man.—Certainly if these things were known and understood, this Book would command more attention.

I.—It must be read; it must be found in every school and in every cottage; every Frenchman must own a Bible.

Third Young Man.—My dear friends of the city, you have been talking this half hour about religion, and you have not mentioned either church, bishop, or curate. It is not so with us in the country. We have a great respect for what you imagine to be no longer in existence. Know then, that in France we still go to confession, and still believe in the priest who alone has the right to direct us. Now, sir, the Church forbids the people to read this Book, whose cause you so valiantly espouse:

I.—How can the men of God prohibit the reading of the Word of God?

First Young Man.—What is that you say? An advertisement of this book, which I read in a paper, announced that it was published under the auspices of the Archbishop of Paris.

I.—The priests forbid the people to read the Holy Scriptures! As well might the king's ministers prohibit Frenchmen from reading the charter which they are bound to observe.

First Young Man.—Some ill-disposed minds would be ready to infer that the priests have special reasons for concealing the contents of that Book.

Third Young Man.—No matter: the Church is always the same. What the holy Fathers enjoined from the earliest ages, she enjoins still, despite the pretensions or the ridicule of the present generation. We ought to submit to what has been acknowledged from all antiquity to be true.

I.—But where do you find that the Church wishes to keep for her own use, the treasure which was entrusted to her to distribute generously to all?

Third Young Man.—If the early Fathers of the Church had wished us to read it, why is it not given to us?

First Young Man.—If this book is what you say it is, why has there been no appeal made to the present generation, to induce them to read it?

I.—(*To the first.*)—You, on the one side, demand an appeal to the men of our day. (*To the third.*) And you, on the other, desire to hear the voice of the ancients. If such an appeal and such a voice are heard, promise me one thing.

First Young Man.—What?

I.—Serious attention.

Both.—We promise.

A VOICE FROM ANTIQUITY.

Verbum autem Domini manet æternum.—St. Peter.

I.

Oh, Earth! earth! earth! *hear* the voice of the Almighty! God has spoken. He who in the beginning made the heavens and the earth, has caused his voice to be heard among men. His voice is powerful as the whirlwind that cleaves the mountains asunder, and rends the rocks from their base.

His voice is gentle and consoling; it penetrates the depths of the heart, and makes sunshine there. Oh man! thy Creator, thy Father, thy Friend, thy Saviour, thy God has spoken here below, and thou hast paid no regard to Him.

Thou hast listened to the voice of thy gay companions, to their tales, their jests, and their boisterous merriment, but thou hast given no attention to the words of thy God.

Thou hast listened to the voice of seducers, of those whose words were flattering, whose lips drop as an honey-comb while the poison of asps was concealed beneath;—of those who said, "Come with us"—but whose feet go down to death, and their steps take hold on hell; and still thou hast regarded not the message of thy God.

Thou hast listened in the haunts of business to the voice of those who buy, and those who sell, to the voice of stewards and of the servants of mammon—to the voice of thine own heart, which repeated evermore, "Give! Give!"—and yet thou hast had no ear for the words of thy God!

Thou hast listened to the voice of the courier as he swept by thee with the words, "a wonderful event has just transpired"—to the voice of friends who answer thy eager question, "what news to-day?"—to the voice of those who relate to thee the debates of statesmen, or the battles of soldiers—and yet thou hast disregarded the voice of thy God. All—all could gain attention from thee except thy Creator and Sovereign.

II.

Oh Earth! earth! earth! hear the voice of the Almighty! Could He forget thee who has given thee life? Could He who called thee into existence, fail to show thee the path of happiness? Must not He who formed thee, understand thee perfectly, and know certainly what is best for thee? Oh man! where wilt thou find a protector more powerful—a friend more tender than thy Creator, and thy God? To whom oughtest thou to listen if not to Him?

It was early spring time; all was calm. The silver moonlight streamed into a spacious hall, lately resounding with the voice of song and laughter; graceful forms had glided through the dance there, and sounds of deep melody had floated on the evening air. But the gay groups had separated; the silence of night had succeeded to the confused murmur of the festival; and thought awoke. The hearts of some among them said, "This is not happiness; we need something beyond this. The period of our life is as nothing in God's sight. There is a higher, an eternal happiness. Who will give it to us; who will show us the way to it?" And I seemed to hear a voice from Heaven answering—THE WORDS OF YOUR GOD! Oh sons and daughters of men! behold the guide to that better land—READ THEM.

It was summer; All was activity in city and field. The merchant was busy at his counting-house, the workman in his shop, the mother in her household, the soldier at his post, the laborer in his field.

There was a murmur like the humming of insects, in the heat of the day, but vast and deep, for it was the busy hum of men. And numbers among them said with hollow eyes and mournful voice, "Alas! true happiness is not found in the whirl of business. Who will tell us where to seek it?" And again I seemed to hear a voice from Heaven, answering, THE WORDS OF YOUR GOD —oh, children of men—will show you the path of happiness. READ THEM.

It was a day in autumn. The wind had stripped the trees, their dry leaves carpeted the earth, old men and women were reposing in the faint sunshine before their houses, while their children were at work, and each one thought to himself; Soon my last sun will rise; soon will the sharp blasts of death detach me from the tree of life, and lay me low, like these leaves, on the earth. Who will give me the assurance of immortality? Who will give me eternal life? And again I seemed to hear a voice from Heaven, answering, "Aged men, THE WORDS OF YOUR GOD can give it to you. READ THEM."

It was winter. Everything was dry, frozen, dead. It was the time when men assembling, incite each other to crime; but it was the time also, when God speaks powerfully to the soul. Conscience, that invisible witness, which each of us bears within, seemed awakened in many. Men and women, young and old, in the country, and in town, mourned over their faults. One voice in a tone of terror exclaimed, "I have sinned. The death which now reigns over all nature, dwells also in my soul; I do nothing but what is wrong; who can endure the day of the Lord's coming? Who shall stand when He appeareth? My sins, my sins, who will deliver me from them? Who will save me?" And I seemed to hear a voice from Heaven, saying, JESUS CHRIST! JESUS CHRIST will deliver thee. He has come to seek and save that which is lost. READ THE WORD OF GOD and thou wilt know thy Saviour, thou wilt possess salvation!

III.

"Hear ye this word which I take up against you, even a lamentation, oh house of Israel." There seems a spell cast upon men. Despite all solicitations they will not take this precious Book to their hearts, though the words of God are written in it.

It was offered to a woman with white hair, and shrunken hands and tottering limbs; "Ah, leave us in peace," she exclaimed, "do not trouble us with your Bibles;" and she shut her door against the holy volume and him who bore it. Ah, Lord! the children of this generation seek books of amusement, but they despise thy Word.

It was next presented to a man of haughty appearance, with a lofty glance and an air of dignity. He laughed in scorn at the offer; with a demoniac sarcasm and a fearful oath, that caused the Book to fall from the hands of the trembling listener, he went his way. Ah, Lord! the children of this generation feast on infamous books, but they despise thy Word.

Another approached. One would have taken him at the first glance for a truly venerable personage. His words were smoother than oil, but they left a sting behind sharper than any two-edged sword. Under the sheep's clothing, glittered the cruel eyes of a devouring wolf. "You must not read the Word of God," he exclaimed. Then he uttered blasphemy against it, and snatching the book from the hands of an old man who had found there the hope of eternal life and heavenly consolation, he threw it with sacrilegious hands into the fire; the flames arose and consumed it. I looked and behold! nothing but ashes remained of the oracles of Israel.

Ah, Lord, the children of this generation seek after cunningly devised fables and false doctrines; but they despise thy word. "You must not read the word of God," say they, and yet the voice of antiquity has spoken. The exhortations of the saints of the Eternal have been heard. All the teachers of the flock of Christ in the early ages of pure Christianity have entreated men to read the Holy Scriptures, and to listen to the oracles of the Almighty. But Christianity is sadly fallen, and neglects the voice of its early benefactors.

Oh proud and audacious tongue that dared to say, "Read not the word of God;" didst thou not fear lest the breath of the Almighty should smite thee into eternal silence, with a word! And you, ye sacrilegious hands, that snatched from the old man those oracles of truth, feared you not the paralyzing touch of death? O earth! earth! earth! hear the voice of God's people, of the teachers of the Truth, of the Fathers of the Church of Christ, of those who are now in the kingdom of Heaven with Abraham, and Isaac, and Jacob.

Christians! they speak to you from the stake and from the cross, to which they were condemned here below for the love they bore to Jesus. They speak to you from the height of Heaven, where they are reigning in glory now with their Redeemer. Listen to their voices; they are the voices of friends. They "fought a good fight" in behalf of this Gospel to which you owe every blessing you enjoy; the dedication of your little children to God's service; the peaceful repose of your aged parents; the intelligence of your mature age; the sweets of home-happiness; the arts of peace, and above all, *eternal life*.

Child of man, whoever thou art, man or woman, young or old, master or servant, layman or priest, wise or ignorant, rich or poor, listen! This cloud of witnesses calls to you out of heaven to take up the Book of God; to read it, to treasure its teachings in your heart, and to act them out in your life.

Come then—traverse with me the early ages of the Church, but first put off your shoes from off your feet, for the place whereon we tread is holy ground. He who calls himself, I AM, the author and finisher of our faith, is about to speak.

IV.

"In the beginning was the Word, and the Word was with God, and the Word was God. The same was in the beginning with God; all things were made by Him, and without Him was not anything made that was made. And the Word was made flesh, and dwelt among us (and we beheld His glory, the glory as of the only begotten of the Father) full of grace and truth." He called Himself

JESUS CHRIST.

Eighteen centuries ago earth was filled with rejoicings—God was made man! All who heard and believed the tidings received eternal life. Darkness fled before this light.

"Ah, we can no more hear Him! We can see Him no more! He has gone back to Heaven." Sons of men, you can yet hear Him; His word is in the midst of you; Why do you not read it? He who was from everlasting, and who for man's salvation veiled Himself in flesh, eighteen centuries ago, cast His far-reaching glance over ages to come. He saw that future generations would also sigh after eternal life, and He wished to open a way by which they too might be saved. Therefore, He gave them a commandment. Earth! earth! earth! listen to the command of Jesus Christ: "SEARCH THE SCRIPTURES, FOR IN THEM YE THINK YE HAVE ETERNAL LIFE, AND THEY ARE THEY WHICH TESTIFY OF ME."* Thus spoke the Lord Jesus.

---

* The Gospel according to St. John, v. 19, translated from the Vulgate by the Master De Saci, printed in 1759 by De Bret, ordinary printer to the King and clergy of France.

This is the first voice, and the greatest. Lord, enable us to understand thy words!

V.

SONS OF MEN! READ THE BOOK.

A certain man urged on the murderers of the first martyr, and kept their clothes while they stoned him to death. This man, as he journeyed at noon on the highway, was startled by the splendor of a supernatural light that burst upon him, and he fell to the earth. He heard a voice calling him by name, and answered, "who art thou?" The voice replied, "I am Jesus whom thou persecutest: rise up, for I will send you to the Gentiles to open their eyes that they may be converted." And this man became the chief laborer under God, in planting anew the tree of life in the desolate home of man. He was called ST. PAUL. Asia, Macedonia, Greece and Rome heard his voice, and a living spirit was infused into their dead bodies.

Men of this generation, he has instructions for you also. There are some who in their sad delusion say, "All Scripture is not good; it is not sufficient to teach us, to show us the way of salvation, to prepare us for good works." Listen to the words of St. Paul—"All Scripture is given by inspiration of God, and is profitable for doctrine, for reproof, for correction, for instruction in righteousness, that the man of God may be perfect, thoroughly furnished unto all good works."*

This was the second voice. Lord, enable us to understand these words!

VI.

SONS OF MEN! READ THE BOOK.

The Son had scattered the seed. The Holy Spirit vivified it, and Jews and Pagans, that long sterile soil, gave signs of life. Holy churches sprang up everywhere, like trees bearing flowers and fruit. Of the believers among the Jews, there were some who received the name of "noble," and the commendations of the Holy Spirit. They were the faithful Bereans.

And wherefore were they so honored? Because they searched the Scriptures daily, to see if these things were so; and believed nothing which their preacher told them, unless it corresponded with the teaching of God's Word. And yet these preachers were great apostles; they were St. Paul and Silas.

Children of the present day—imitate the Christians of Berea. Believe nothing that your preachers tell you, unless you find warrant for it in the Bible; and that you may be able to judge whether their teachings correspond with it, read it daily—read it much.

* 2d Epistle of St. Paul to Timothy, 3d chap., 16, 17 verses, Omnis scriptura divinitus inspirata utilis est ad docendum, ad arguendum, ad corripendum in justitia: ut perfectus sit homo Dei, ad omne opus bonum instructus.—(Vulgate.)

St. Luke says—They of Berea "were more noble than those in Thessalonica, in that they received the word with all readiness of mind, and searched the Scriptures daily whether these things were so."*

This is the third voice. Lord enable us to understand these words!

VII.

SONS OF MEN! READ THE BOOK.

Sixteen centuries ago, on the point where the Rhone and the Saone mingle their waters, there arose a great light. A son of the East, a disciple of Polycarp, who had himself sat at the feet of the disciple whom Jesus loved, crossed the seas, ascended the Rhone, and took up his abode in the city of Lyons, in which he became a minister.

All who lived on the banks of the Rhone, of the Saone, and farther still, were charmed with his teachings.

They abandoned their idols, and adored the Lord Jesus. The Saviour lifted up his pierced hand on them in benediction, and they began to live.

This man was called Saint Irenæus. (A. D. 177.)

Listen to the lessons which he gave on the banks of the Rhone and Saone 1600 years ago:

You say that the Scriptures are obscure and ambiguous. Irenæus says, "These things are placed before our eyes openly and without ambiguity in the different books of Scripture.† All these may openly and without ambiguity *be equally understood by all* ‡ They must be very stupid§ who close their eyes against so clear a revelation, and refuse to admit the light of the preached word."

This is the fourth voice. Lord, enable us to understand these words!

VIII.

SONS OF MEN! READ THE BOOK.

A man, in eager pursuit of science, but still under the yoke of heathenism, traversed Greece, Ionia, and Italy, and visited in these abodes of high civilisation the schools of the world's philosophers, hoping to find truth there.

---

* Acts xvii. 11. Hi autem erant nobiliores eorum, qui sunt Thessalonicæ, qui susceperunt verbum cum omni aviditate, quotidie scrutantes scripturas, si hæc ita se haberent. (Vulgate.)

† Aperte et sine ambiguo.

‡ Similiter ab omnibus audiri possint.

§ Valde hebetes—Tam lucidam. (Five books against all heresies, by St. Irenæus, Bishop of Lyons, Book II., chap. 46.) We do not give at length all the quotations in Greek and Latin from the Fathers, because they would occupy too much time and space, and would be without interest to a large class of readers. But a few are given to show the care that has been taken to have recourse to the original writings of the Fathers. All the passages alluded to may be found in an elegant work, entitled "The Select Library of the Fathers of the Church," by Mr. N. S. Guillon, Professor of Theology at Paris, Preacher in Ordinary to the King, &c., Paris, 1824.

In his journeyings he arrived at a city, famous for its splendor and wisdom, near the banks of the Nile. There he heard, for the first time, of the Lord Jesus, and there he believed. He received from the Redeemer remission of his sins, and brake his idols in pieces. A few more months passed, and he was himself spreading the light of truth through Egypt, Jerusalem, and Antioch.— Thousands of ministers of God were formed under his teachings. He was called Saint Clement of Alexandria. (A. D. 190.)

It is said by men of our day, " The spirit of the age and erroneous doctrines have misled great numbers; the Scriptures are no longer fit for them: they cannot understand them."

Hear what the Doctor of the Nile replies:

" Let him whose eyes are obscured by a bad education, and by false doctrines, hasten to the light, to the truth, to the Holy Scriptures, which will reveal to him what cannot be written. The Bible kindles a spark in the soul; it opens the spirit's eyes, that it may see; and like the gardener who grafts a tree, communicates to it something new."*

This is the fifth voice. Lord, enable us to understand these words!

IX.

Persecution was devastating the churches of Egypt. The populace rose in crowds against the Christians, and Severus crushed them with his sceptre.

A young man of sixteen years saw his father seized by a band of soldiers. He implored them to release him, but in vain. Leonidas was thrown into a dungeon. The young man determined to present himself before the heathen tribunal. He also would confess his Saviour—he would offer his life to those who murdered his brothers, while his father tried to shield them at the expense of his own. His heart-broken mother clasped him in her arms; and seeing him about to escape from her, she carried away his toga and tunic, and hid her son's garments that she might save his life. Then the young man, seeing that he could not share the death of his father, exclaimed, " At least, do not abandon, for our sakes, the name of our Lord Jesus Christ."

Leonidas died a martyr's death, leaving his wife a widow, his son without a protector, and six other children, still very young. The young man became a minister: he rose to the chair of Clement. And if Clement instructed a thousand, the son of Leonidas instructed ten thousand. He was called Origen. (A. D. 220.)

Men of our day—listen to the voice which charmed the eastern world. You say, " Who can explain to us these Scriptures? Shall men unfold their mysteries, and explain their hidden sense to us ? Shall we have a human tribunal ?"

The Doctor of the Church replies:

" My son, read above all, with *deep attention*, for this is requisite in order to speak and judge of them without precipitation. If

* Works of St. Clement of Alexandria, Stromatum, Book I., p. 274.

you persevere in the reading of the Bible with a fixed mind and with faith, knock, and whatever is shut will be opened to you by the porter of whom Jesus speaks in the Gospel according to St. John, chap. x., verse 3. Nevertheless, it is not enough to seek and to knock; that which is most of all necessary to enable us to understand heavenly things—is *prayer*. The Saviour enjoins it on us when he says, not only 'Seek and ye shall find—knock and it shall be opened unto you;' but also 'Ask and it shall be given unto you,'"*

Lord, enable us to understand these words!

X.

A certain bishop devoted his life to the preaching of the cross throughout Carthage, Africa, and all the West. Persecution ravaged the empire—and soon the venerable head of the bishop of Carthage was to be laid low on the scaffold. His persecutors were about to convey him to Utica, the birthplace of Cato, but he escaped from them, determined that if he was to die for his Master's cause, it should be among his own people—among the men and women, the aged and the young, whom he had taught, so that they might receive the last testimony which his words and his death could render to the glory of his Saviour. And when he learned that it was in Carthage, in the very bosom of his flock, that he was called to the crown of martyrdom—he cheerfully resigned himself into the hands of the proconsul. At the moment when the magistrate was pronouncing his sentence of death, his heart bounded, his eyes were raised to Heaven with a hopeful gaze, and he uttered these simple words. "God be praised!" He was called Cyprian. (A. D. 258.)

Before the murderous sword shall have stifled in death that voice of wisdom, speak, oh man of God, to the people that surround thee, and tell them how they may find the path to that heavenly home, towards which thy looks of love and hope are directed.

He did speak—and spoke for all ages. Listen to the voice of the martyr.

"God was pleased to reveal much to his servants, the prophets,† but how much greater are the revelations which His Son has given us,‡ those which the word of God, who inspired the prophets, has made known to us, with his own voice. He commands no longer that the way shall be prepared before him; but He comes Himself. He points out to us the way of life, and freely opens its entrance to us; and we who were lying in darkness, and in the shadow of death, are enlightened by the illumination of His Spirit, that we may be enabled to walk in that path under His divine

---

* A letter from Origen to his former pupil, Gregory of Nazianzen. Philocalia, chap. 13. (Collection of the Writings of Origen made by Saint Gregory and Saint Basil.)

† Multa et per prophetas servos suos, etc. (The Old Testament.)

‡ Sed quanto majora sunt quæ filius loquitur. (The Gospel.)

guidance. Oh brothers, well beloved! the teachings of the Gospel are the lessons of God Himself—these are the foundations on which our faith must rest, the helm which directs our vessel,* the citadel in which we find safety. They who in sincere faith receive these teachings on earth, will be guided to that glorious Home which God has prepared for those who love Him.

This is the seventh voice. Lord, enable us to understand these words!

XI.

Persecution raged against the Christians, but the truth of God spread faster and wider.

The blood of the martyrs was the seed of the Church. Then Satan, who was the spirit that animated the princes and priests of Paganism, inspired them with a new idea. "Let us burn," they said, "all the copies of the Scriptures; let us destroy the word of God : so shall we annihilate the source from which this religion flows, and Christianity shall be for ever banished from the earth."

This design bore direct evidence of its infernal origin, but Jesus was watching over His people and His cause from His throne of glory in the Heavens.

The priests of Jupiter and Bacchus demanded the Bible with loud outcries. The proconsuls caused the houses of Christians to be searched. Alas! alas! some poor timid wretches were cowardly enough to deliver up the book of God rather than face death in its defence. But others, faithful even unto death, refused to surrender it, and resigned their lives rather than their Bibles.

All the copies that could be collected were heaped up in the public squares and burned. The faithful saw from afar the rising flames, and stole mournfully and secretly by night to the spot where profane hands were committing to the fire the holy words which God has spoken. Tears flowed down their cheeks, and anguish filled their hearts, as they saw the oracles of Israel reduced to ashes. They were the priests of the dissolute Jupiter, of the impure Venus, of the reeling, drunken Bacchus, who then burned the New Testament. Men of the nineteenth century! who are they that burn it now?

"Shame, shame, everlasting shame," cried the Christians, "to those who delivered to unholy hands the sacred Word of God." They gave the name of traitors† to these cowards, and drove them from their Churches.

"Glory, glory, everlasting glory," sang the angels of Heaven, "to the witnesses for the truth and its defenders!" they are the Christian Martyrs.

"Have you the Holy Scriptures?" demanded the barbarous proconsuls of these holy men?

"I have," was the reply.

---

* Gubernacula dirigendi itineris. (Works of St. Cyprian. De Oratione dominica, in initio, p. 217.)

† Traditores.

"Where are they?"

"In my heart."

And they burned the defenders of the Word of God, in order to reduce to ashes even the living tables on which the finger of God had inscribed His glorious truths.*

This is the eighth voice. Lord, enable us to profit by these examples!

XII.

What man is this in the midst of the assembly of bishops, like a rock in the bosom of the ocean, who silences all those that deny that he who died on the cross was the true God, and who suffers repeated banishments for maintaining the supreme Divinity of his Saviour and mine?

He is called St. Athanasius. (A. D. 325.)

He speaks thus to Christians who have strayed into error. "If you would bring forward something beyond what is written, why do you dispute with us? We are determined to speak and to hear nothing in these matters but what God has revealed to us in Scripture."†

Then addressing the heathen who were seeking God, he said, "The Holy Scriptures are inspired by God and are sufficient to guide you into all truth."‡

This is the ninth voice. Lord, enable us to understand these words!

XIII.

On the banks of Vienne, a bishop feeds his flock, and within the walls of Poictiers delights the Gauls by his piety and the depth of his wisdom. He is called St Hilary. (A. D. 350.)

He turns towards the East, towards the magnificent city of Constantine, and addressing him, who from that majestic throne governs the world, he says—"Oh Emperor, you are seeking faith! Turn not in search of it to new and enticing books, but search the Scriptures, where alone its true foundation lies." Then addressing the Christian people around him, he said, "Let us read the things which are written, let us understand what we read, and then our faith will be perfect."

This is the tenth voice. Lord, enable us to understand these words!

XIV.

Who is this young man who studies in the flourishing schools of Athens, Alexandria, Constantinople and Cæsarea, and who, after having cultivated ancient letters, displays as bishop, all the treasures of wisdom and benevolence, and endeavors to restore peace between the contending East and West?

* Acts of Saturninus, of Dativus and others in Africa. Ruinart, Du Pin, &c.

† Works of St. Athanasius. De Incarnatione Christi.

‡ Ib. Oratio contra gentes.

It is Saint Basil. (A. D. 870.) He tells us, " it is right and necessary that each one should learn from the inspired word of God whatever is needful for his growth in grace, and to defend himself against the evils of human tradition." *

And wishing still more effectually to warn men against mere human treachery in divine things, the holy man adds, " it is want of faith, it is great pride, it is a heinous crime, to wish to take anything away from Scripture, or add anything thereto." †

This is the eleventh voice. Lord, enable us to understand these words!

XV.

Who is this that dares to bar the way against imperial majesty because its garments have been dipped in blood, and refuses to celebrate the Holy Communion in the presence of him, before whom Asia, Africa and Europe tremble, because he delivered up his subjects to the fury of his soldiery? From within the walls of Milan he summons the great Theodosius to bow before Him who alone is truly great and glorious. It is Saint Ambrose. (A. D. 380.)

He points both kings and people to the source of life. " Drink," he says, " of the two cups of the Old and New Testament, for from each of them you may drink of Christ.‡ Thus shall you drink of the blood by which you are redeemed. Thus shall you drink His words. The Old Testament, no less than the New, is all His word. We drink the Holy Scriptures, we devour the sacred Book, when the aliment of the eternal word descends into the veins of our soul and the powers of our mind,§ for " man shall not live by bread alone, but by every word that proceedeth out of the mouth of God."

This is the twelfth voice. Lord, enable us to understand these words!

XVI.

A recluse sits with his head bowed in deep study over the Book of God, in the birthplace of the Saviour. Around him from the fields of Bethlehem a multitude of disciples are assembled to learn the truths of Scripture, and from him the knowledge of the word of God is spread throughout the West. This is Saint Jerome. (A. D. 390.)

From his hermitage, he casts a mental glance over the children of that generation within the bounds of Rome, the magnificent, and writes thus to a Roman lady of high rank:

---

* Works of Saint Basil—Bishop of Cæsarea. Regulæ breviores, Responsio 95.

† Ibid, Sermo de fide, page 224.

‡ Utrumque poculum bibe Veteris et Novi Testamenti, quia ex utroque Christum bibis.

§ Bibitur scriptura divina, et devoratur scriptura divina, cum in venas mentis ac vires animi succus verbi descendit æterni. Works of Saint Ambrose, Bishop of Milan, in Psalm 1. Enarratio.

"Teach your daughter, from her earliest years, to love the Holy Scriptures better than gems and silks.* Let her learn from Job a lesson of patience and fortitude, and passing thence to the Gospel, let her never relax her hold on its blessed truths."†

Then addressing those who affirmed that the Bible could not be understood by all, the hermit of Bethlehem said :

"The Apostles have written, and the Saviour Himself has spoken in the Gospels, not that a few, but that all might understand."‡

Plato wrote for the learned few, not for the mass; and few indeed understand him. But these, that is the princes of the Church, the Prophets and Apostles of the Lord Jesus wrote not for the few, but for ALL.§

This is the thirteenth voice. Lord, enable us to understand these words!

XVII.

A young man of seventeen, just released from the faithful instructions of his pious mother, mingles with the heathen of Carthage in all the pleasures and disorders of that great city. But the pious Monica continued to pray, "Oh Lord, convert my son." The young Numidian is seduced by the deceitful religion of Manes: and soon after, his spirit is filled with enthusiasm for the philosophy of Plato. Still Monica continued her prayer—"Lord, convert my son!"

Next, he gave himself up with intense interest to the study of the art of rhetoric. The reputation of Ambrose attracts his notice. He enters the Christian temples of Milan in search of eloquence, and the words of the holy bishop break over his heart like the waves of the sea against its shores. And Monica, trembling with hope, prayed yet more earnestly—"Oh God, convert my son."

Her son, filled with anguish, ashamed of himself and of his dissipated youth—sought one day the solitude of his garden, that he might yield to his emotions unobserved. He threw himself down under a fig-tree; he wept bitterly; out of the depths of sorrow he cried unto the Lord. And a voice, soft and sweet as that of a child, stole on his ear, saying, "Take and read." He arose; a Bible was near him on a seat; and as he opened it, his eyes fell on these words, "Put ye on the Lord Jesus Christ." (St. Paul's Epistle to the Romans, chap. xiii. verse 14)—Peace flowed into his soul like a river; and a great light, like the sun of righteousness, shone in upon his understanding. He had found his Saviour.

He rose to the episcopal chair of Hippo; he became the torch

---

* Pro gemmis et serico divinas codices amet.

† Ad Evangelia transeat, nunquam ea positura de manibus. Works of St. Jerome, author of the translation called the Vulgate, used in the Catholic Church, Epistola 107, § 12.

‡ Non ut pauci intelligerent, sed ut omnes. Ibid. S. Hyeronymi in Psalm 87.

§ Non scripserunt paucis, sed universo populo. Ib. Comm. S. Hyeronymi in Psalm 87.

of the West, and all ages acknowledge him as the greatest of the Fathers. He was called St. Augustine (A. D. 396.)

In his time the Bible formed the subject of study and meditation among Christians of all ages, sexes, and conditions. What books are these which men are carrying on highways, in villages, in lanes, in the streets of cities, offering them to soldiers and to women, to young and old, to great and small ?

St. Augustine joyfully replies, " It is the Holy Scriptures which are thus publicly exposed for sale."*

A multitude of errors began to darken the horizon. The doctrines of Pelagius, of Priscillian, of Arius, of the disciples of Donatus, mingled in the spiritual kingdom like the fearful lightning preceding a night of storms. The Bishop of Hippo, calm as the luminary which receives its light from the sun, shed his safe and peaceful beams on all around.

With what weapon will you repulse these false teachers, oh son of Monica? and to what authority will you appeal, oh venerable man of God? He replies, " Who knows not that the canonical Scriptures of the Old and New Testament are contained within certain limits, and that they are to be preferred far above all the later writings of the bishops,† so that it is impossible to bring in doubt or question whether what is written be true and authentic ?‡ There are, undoubtedly, certain books of God, whose authority we all recognize; we believe them, and we obey them. There let us seek to identify the Church: by them let us discuss our cause.§ Let us cast away all arguments drawn from other sources. I cannot admit the authority of human documents as a rule of the Church, nor anything but the oracles of God."||

But what will the simple and unlearned, who shun controversy, find in the Sacred Word, servant of God? He replies, " The soul and the object of all Scripture is the love of Him who is the supreme good, and the love of His creatures, who are capable of obtaining happiness from him.¶ The legitimate effect of Holy Scripture is, first, to bring him who reads it to acknowledge himself in bondage to the love of this world, and a stranger to the love of God and of his fellow-beings, which the Word enjoins. The knowledge of the truth gives life, and excites in man, instead of his former presumptuous pride, humility and holy grief. Filled with deep sorrow, he is led to constant prayer, and in answer to it, receives, by the grace of God, joy and peace in believing. He does not sink into despair at the sight of his guilt, but is filled with an hungering and thirsting after righteousness. He flies from the

---

* Scriptura venalis fertur per publicum. Works of St. Augustine, Bishop of Hippo. In Psalm 36.

† Omnibus posterioribus episcoporum litteris esse præponendum.

‡ Works of St. Augustine, Bishop of Hippo. Epistola de baptismo contra Donatistas;. t. 9, p. 98.

§ Ibi discutiamus causam nostram.

|| Ibid. De unitate ecclesiæ, p. 341.

¶ Works of St. Augustine, Bishop of Hippo. De doctrina Christiana; L. I., c. 35.

allurements of worldly and perishable pleasures, and a love for that which is unseen and eternal is kindled within him."*

This is the fourteenth voice. Lord, enable us to understand these words!

XVIII.

SONS OF MEN! READ THE BOOK.

A hermit descended from the mountains near Antioch. He lifted up his voice in that metropolis of Asia, and ears and hearts were thrilled by his discourses. The imperial court soon resounded with his name, and he was called to the patriarchal chair of Constantinople, the new Rome, the capital of the world, which crowned with splendor the banks of the Bosphorus.

Who of all the children of men spoke like him?

A multitude hung upon his words; the poor were consoled; the great astonished; and the Gospel, by his indefatigable exertions, was carried to the barbarous gentile nations.

But suddenly a noise, as of approaching tempests, was heard in the palace of the Emperors. A desolating wintry wind sweeps howling from the magnificent dwelling of the haughty Eudoxia. He casts out the patriarch from his seat; he banishes him to the desert;—and there, an exile in a barbarous land, consumed by fever, as he is dragged onward by the satellites of the Emperor, he dies in the grasp of the soldiers, exclaiming triumphantly, "Glory be to God!" The people, charmed by his eloquence, had given him the name of St. Chrysostom (A. D. 400), or the Golden-Mouth.

Oh! if the patriarch of Constantinople could speak, at this moment, to the aged man by his fire-side—to the young man in his fields—to the noble in his palace—to the man of business in the midst of his sales and purchases—to the priest among his presbytery, and to the mother in her nursery—what would he say to you all, rich in this world's goods, who have all things, except the Word of God, or who have it merely as an ornament on the shelves of your libraries? Listen! The Golden-mouth says— "There are dice to be found in most houses, but Bibles in few, if any; and those who have them, are as if they had them not, for they keep them magnificently bound, and shut up in cases; and own them, not for the benefit they may draw from them, but to display their taste and opulence. It was not for the purpose of shutting them up in rich covers that the Holy Scriptures were given us, but to be engraven upon our hearts."†

What would the patriarch say to you, men of the world, who ask, "How can we be expected to read the Word of God? The multiplicity of our public and private affairs leaves us no time for such a purpose."

* Works of St. Augustine, L. II., c. 7.

† Works of St. John Chrysostom, Archbishop of Constantinople. Homil. Johan, 32 Savil. II., p. 686.

Listen to the Golden-Mouth. " Is not the very fact a reproach to you, that you have allowed yourselves to become so absorbed in earthly things, that you have no leisure left for the most important and indispensable of all? But we have witnesses who declare that to be merely a vain excuse. These witnesses are your gay social assemblies, your presence at the theatre, and at other public places, where you sometimes spend whole days."*

Listen, men in humble life, whether in the city or the country, to what the Golden-Mouth says to you—you who say, "We are poor, how can we obtain a Bible?" " Let me ask you," he says, " if you have not all the implements necessary for your occupation? And is it not in that case folly to allege poverty as an excuse, in a question of such immense advantage."†

To you who affirm that " the reading of the Holy Scriptures belongs to the clergy and the priests, and that laymen have nothing to do with them," the venerable patriarch says: listen to him of the Golden-Mouth—

" Let no one utter in my presence those cold and wicked words, ' I am a man of the world ; l have a wife and children ; it is not my business to read the Bible ; such an occupation becomes those who have renounced the world to lead a life of seclusion with God.' What sayest thou, oh man ! Is it not thy business to apply thyself diligently to the Scriptures, because thou art driven and tossed by ten thousand conflicting cares! Precisely the reverse ; it is much more needful for thee than for those of whom thou dost speak. Far from the field of battle, they receive few wounds, but thou who art always on the scene of combat, art incessantly wounded anew, and hast consequently need of many more remedies to cure thee. Let us not delay, then, to obtain a Bible, lest we meanwhile receive a mortal stroke. Let us not heap up gold, but let us collect Bibles : the very sight of that holy Book makes us shudder at our sinfulness. What then will it be, when, from a diligent reading of it, our souls shall have become living stones in the temple of our God?"‡

For you who say that the Bible cannot be understood by all; that it was made for the priests, and for the deeply learned; but that the mass, the artisans and laborers, cannot comprehend its sense ;—the patriarch has a word also. " The grace of the Holy Ghost has caused these holy books to be written by publicans, by fishermen, by tent-makers, by shepherds, by herdsmen, by the illiterate, for the express purpose that no person, however ignorant, might have recourse to that pretext for not reading them ; that the contents of the Scriptures might be intelligible to all, and that the laborer—the servant—the poor widow—the most ignorant of men, might draw instruction from them. Destined to be teachers of the whole world, these sacred writers, who were inspired by the Holy Spirit, have made known all things *in a clear*

---

* Works of St. John Chrysostom, Archbishop of Constantinople. Homil. Johan. 32 Savil. II., p. 686.
† Ibid., Homil. 9, in Johan.   ‡ In Lazarum Conc. 3.

and distinct manner, for the express purpose that each one might understand them for himself, without finding it necessary to have recourse to another. " I come not (to you)," said St. Paul, " with excellency of speech or of wisdom." (1 Corinthians ii. 1.) Take the Bible in your own hands—read; retain firmly what you understand; read over many times what seems to you obscure; and then, if repeated study fails to make it clear to you, ask the assistance of a more enlightened brother, or of a teacher. God, who sees your zeal, will not allow your efforts to be fruitless. *And even should no man make known to you what you seek, God himself will reveal it to you in his own good time and manner.*"

" Remember the 'Eunuch of great authority' under the Queen of Ethiopia. (Acts viii.) He read as he journeyed, seated in his chariot. He had no one to explain to him what he read; but God saw his zeal, and sent him a teacher. True, we have no longer a Philip, *but we have the Holy Spirit still who inspired Philip.*"

This is the last voice. Lord, enable us to understand these words!

XIX.

Thus spoke those holy men who stood foremost in the ranks of the Redeemer's service on earth, and who have now sat down in the kingdom of heaven with Abraham, and Isaac, and Jacob.

Who will dare to contradict what they have spoken? Who would blacken the memory of the confessors of Christ? Who would dishonor the ashes of his martyrs?

Soldier, who hast taken arms that thy countrymen may enjoy in peace the fruits of their labor; husbandman, who at night-fall dost leave thy fields and bend thy weary steps towards thy cottage home; artisan, who remainest in thy shop while thy companions are wasting their time and energies in folly; merchant, before the hour of business; magistrate, before the hour of duty; woman, in the quiet of the sanctuary of home: young man, dazzled by the illusions of the present; king, upon thy throne;—beggar, by the way-side; listen, all, to the counsels of the saints of the most High God; their wise admonitions reach you across the vast space of many ages. Read! read! read! the Word of God.

XX.

Lord, if another voice than thine or than that of thy servants appealed to me; if though, while upon earth thou didst say "*search the Scriptures*," other voices tell me, " shut them from sight, cast them away—burn them," what should I do, Lord?

And I seemed to hear a whisper escaping from the leaves of the holy volume before me, and swell into a strong voice " as the sound of many waters," saying, " THOUGH AN ANGEL FROM HEAVEN PREACH ANY OTHER GOSPEL UNTO YOU THAN THAT WHICH WE HAVE PREACHED UNTO YOU, LET HIM BE ACCURSED."* Galatians

---

* (Licet angelus de cælo evangelizet vobis præter quam quod evangelizavimus vobis, anathema sit. Vulgate.)

i. 8. And I replied, "What wilt thou say, then, oh Lord, to those who oppose the reading of Thy Word by Thy people; who forbid them to obtain it, who demand it from them when they own a copy, or order them to cast it into the fire?" And I seemed to hear again a solemn response from the pages of the Holy Scriptures before me in these words, "Wo unto you, Scribes and Pharisees, hypocrites, for ye shut up the kingdom of heaven against men; for ye neither go in yourselves, neither suffer ye them that are entering to go in!"*.

XXI.

There is a certain place, whether a city, a village, or a hamlet, I shall not say, in a country which shall be nameless. Its inhabitants despise the Word of God; they will not read it; they will have none of it: and every copy that could be found they have seized and torn up or burned.

What has been the consequence? Falsehood prevails there; hatred has engendered quarrels among neighbors; they eat the bread of wickedness, and drink the wine of violence: idleness has brought them to poverty; and famine stalks abroad in their streets. "Away with the noise of your songs," said the Almighty, "I will not listen to the music of your flutes. This people have fallen for want of wisdom, and their paths have gone down unto the dead."

There is another place—whether a city, a village, or a hamlet, I shall not say—in a country which shall also be nameless.

The young men there have sought for the Word of God; those of mature years, too, read it: the aged meditate upon it. A man clothed in black stands among them; he is venerable in his appearance, and benevolence illuminates his features; they call him *pastor*. He says, "My children, take the Bible—read it—it is the Word of God;" and they follow his precepts.

My heart bounded with thankfulness as I gazed on that happy scene; for I saw the people prospering, because the blessing of the Lord rested upon their dwellings. Their barns were filled with plenty, and their presses burst out with new wine. Their ways were ways of pleasantness, and all their paths were peace. The divine Word had become a tree of life to all who had laid hold on it; and all who retained it were richly blessed.

A soul lies surrounded with the terrors of death, with the sobs and tears of a family mourning in deep bitterness; the glory of life is passing rapidly away, yet that soul abides in unutterable peace, and seems a triumphant victor over the grave! How can this be? Because it has believed the assurance of the Gospel. *Jesus is* "*the Lamb of God who taketh away the sins of the world.*"

Why is this soul carried in the arms of angels, amidst innume-

---

* Væ autem vobis scribæ et Pharisæi hypocritæ; quia clauditis regnum cælorum ante homines; vos enim non intratis, nec introeuntes sinitis intrare. (Vulgate) Matthew xxiii. 13.

rable worlds, up to the bosom of God? Why does it see God, face to face, having awakened in His likeness? Because it has believed the Word of God which says, Jesus is "the way, and the truth, and the life: no man cometh unto the Father but by Him."

"Yes," says the Spirit, "blessed is the man whose delight is in the law of the Lord; and in his law doth he meditate day and night."

And all the saints and the angels in light reply: "He shall be like a tree planted by the rivers of water, that bringeth forth his fruit in his season; his leaf also shall not wither, and whatsoever he doeth shall prosper."* All celestial intelligences respond, "Amen!" And all unite in the ascription, "Glory be to the Father, and to the Son, and to the Holy Ghost, as it was in the beginning, is now, and ever shall be, world without end. Amen!"

* Psalm i.

LUTHER AND CALVIN;

OR THE

TRUE SPIRIT OF THE REFORMED CHURCH.

PREFACE.

This address was delivered June 6th, 1844, at the General Meeting of the Evangelical Society of Geneva. The Rev. Frederic Monod, deputy from the Evangelical Society of France, afterwards addressed the meeting, and in concluding spoke as follows: "I should not do justice to my feelings, if, before sitting down, I did not pray the committee of this Society to take into consideration, whether it would not be for the interest of the work of God in France, to have the address of our brother M. Merle printed separately, and circulated extensively among our churches. The evil pointed out in this address, is an evil which menaces—which advances on us more every day, and I know of nothing more suited to point it out, and consequently also to combat it." (*See Report.*) It is in compliance with this request that this address, which is not given in the Report, is published by the author in France,* and he feels himself constrained to add two remarks:—First, the following pages were never intended for publicity of this description; being nothing more than notes thrown rapidly together on the paper. Again, very far from exhibiting a new and particular idea, as some people have supposed, they verify or prove an ecclesiastical fact, a fact which has long been recognized by the most respectable authorities, as could easily have been shown, had it not been thought necessary to be sparing of quotations.

* The address was published in the original language in Paris. See publishers' Preface.—Tr.

LUTHER AND CALVIN;

OR,

THE TRUE SPIRIT OF THE REFORMED CHURCH.

Gentlemen :

The times are pressing. We must proceed to what is useful; and not lose ourselves in much speaking, but search, according to the apostolic precept, for what may truly contribute to the edification of the Church. It is this thought which induces me to bring before you the following question:

What is it, in our French reformed churches, that has characterized the year that has passed since our last anniversary?

It is, unless I am deceived, the manifestation anew of principles which have often been designated by the name of parties opposed to us, but of which from the heart we wish to speak in a friendly style, and shall therefore call them (making use of a name which is dear to us) the principles of Lutheranism.

Lutheranism and Reform* have distinctive characters; but they are not separated so much by errors as by diversities.

God willed that diversity, that the work of the Reformation might be complete. His powerful hand, intending from the beginning to cause immense bodies to move round the sun, endowed them with opposing forces, the one of which tends to take them away from the centre, and the other to draw them closer to it. From these apparent contradictions, he produced the course of the universe, and the admirable unity of the celestial system. It was the same in the times of the reformation. Opposing tendencies were necessary for that work; and these same tendencies it is which imprinted upon it such admirable unity.

> "In the garden of my master,
> There are flowers of ev'ry kind,"

sings a Christian author.† Shall we, gentlemen, only perceive

---

* It is almost unnecessary to remind the reader that the word *Reformation* applies to the whole work of the 19th century, and the words *Reform* and *Reformed* apply especially to the work of Zwingle and Calvin.

† Tersteegen.

there one flower? Ah! let us beware, careless gardeners that
we are, of tearing up indigenous plants whose nature is peculiarly adapted to our soil, to our climate, and of planting in their
stead exotics which require a different soil, and which may perish among our hands.

Yes, gentlemen, let us comprehend it well; there is not only
friendship—there is not only agreement between Lutheranism
and Reform—there is more than all that—there is unity.

There exists, above all, between them a profound unity, which
results from both being animated by the same living faith. They
believe equally in the complete incapacity of man to do good;
they believe in God manifested in the flesh; in expiation by his
blood; in regeneration by his Spirit; in justification by faith in
his name; in charity and good works by the power of his fellowship.

But it is not this unity of *identity* of which we wish now to
speak. We go much farther. We propose to show that Lutheranism and Reform are one even by their *diversities*, from which
we shall draw the conclusion, that in place of effacing the
greater part of these differences, and more especially those of
Reform, which we should defend, they ought to be carefully
preserved. Such is our thesis.

Yes, gentlemen, those individuals deceive themselves strangely,
who, knowing how to reckon the very different characteristics
which at the present day distinguish Lutheranism and Reform,
would cry out with painful surprise, "How then! friends fewer,
enemies more!" The body and the soul are very different in
their attributes, nevertheless they are but one single being. Man
and woman have quite opposite capacities and duties, and notwithstanding they are but one flesh. In Christ the human and
divine natures were certainly distinct, but nevertheless there is
only one Saviour. In the same manner, gentlemen, Lutheranism
and Reform, though very different, are but one unity.

Do they talk of their strifes? Ah! gentlemen, are there never
then strifes between the body and the spirit, between the husband
and the wife? Did none exist even in Christ between his human
and divine nature? "My soul is troubled, and what shall I say?
Father, save me from this hour!" cried his human nature, shuddering at the approach of the cross. Strife, but strife overcome, far
from being contrary to unity, is essential to it, at least upon the
earth. I believe, gentlemen, that with Lutheranism and Reform
the happy moment in which strife is overcome and unity triumphs
is neary arrived, if imprudent friends of the former do not seek
to bend the latter under its laws. Observe that Reform, which is
the friend of proselytism, does not proselytize in Lutheranism; it
loves it, respects it, and leaves it to its own strength, or rather to
God's. But, wonderful to be told! it is Lutheranism (certainly
neither that of Germany or Geneva), it is Lutheranism passive in
its character, which advances heedlessly, and apparently wishing
to deprive us of our patrimony, and to substitute itself in the place
of the tricentennial work of our reformers. To bring about unity,

is it then in reality necessary to slay one of the two members? That may perhaps be one method, but it is not ours.

Gentlemen, Lutheranism has great duties to discharge towards Reform, and we know too well the noble principles of the excellent men in Germany, its true representatives, not to be assured that it will not fail in its duty. If one of two allied and friendly armies were to be beaten and dispersed by the common enemy, whilst the other was resting on its arms, with its leaders and standards, would the latter take advantage of the moment when the former was rallying, but still stunned with the blow it had received, to impose its colors upon it? or would it not rather generously aid in recovering the ancient standard of its fathers? This is what we require from Lutheranism.

We do not require to inform you that we have not the slightest prejudice against Martin Luther. If in the history of the world there be an individual we love more than another, it is he. Calvin we venerate more, but Luther we love more. Besides, Lutheranism is of itself dear and precious in our eyes, and with reason. In Reform there are principles of which we should be afraid, were it not for the counter-balance of Lutheranism; and there are also in Lutheranism principles which would raise our alarm, were it not for the counter-balance of Reform. Luther and Lutheranism do not possess, even in Germany—even in Wittemberg—friends and admirers more ardent than we.

But if the question be placed before us: "Ought Reform to give way in France, in Switzerland, and elsewhere, to Lutheranism?" we answer without hesitation, Most certainly not!

Nevertheless, we think this is the question which has been placed before our Churches during the course of the past year.

Has this question been replied to everywhere as it ought to have been? We believe not. Reform is misrepresented even within Reform. Two centuries of persecution and humiliation have caused it to lose its fairest traditions; and principles to which it is opposed find pious and eloquent defenders. There are in its bosom distinguished minds that hesitate, that are irresolute at the moment of reveillé, and who, mistaking one voice for another, are about to undergo a strange transformation. After what is going on at the present hour, it might be said that Reform might well institute societies, and exercise a certain external activity; but if principles are involved, Lutheranism ought to supply them, so that it only remains to place ourselves under its tutelage. A banner of three centuries old is treated as a novelty and an innovation, and colors rejected by ten generations begin again to flourish here and there, in this Presbytery and in that Church; and this society even, composed as it is exclusively of the Reformed, is almost giving them its support. There are countries covered with eloquent ruins, sown with the sepulchres of the saints, where such things are going on, and where, unless they are arrested, the very stones will cry out.

Gentlemen, we believe firmly that the Reformed French and Swiss do not require to beg directions from a stranger Church, and, particularly, from a Church to which it is true they should be united in the same faith and charity, but which does not know them, and which, it must be said, notwithstanding notable exceptions, has often been found awanting to them in justice and impartiality. If Reform is to survive, it must live the life which befits it. In its own traditions it possesses abundance wherewithal to produce the most splendid inspirations, but unfortunately it does not appreciate them; and, in place of exploring the golden mine of its antiquity, though certainly with some difficulty, and with the sweat on the brow, it prefers receiving from hands eager to enrich it, a coinage already struck, but struck with the stamp and the arms of a stranger.

That the Reformed Church may apply herself to guard the principles which God has confided to her keeping, she must first know them. What are they, then? It is to the searching out of these that we shall devote this address; and we shall only adduce truths recognized these three centuries past, but which in our days seem to be forgotten.

A great mind, the penetrating genius of Montesquieu, already perceived the fundamental difference between Lutheranism and Reform, when he says in his Spirit of the Laws (*Esprit des Lois*), " Each of these two religions may think itself the most perfect: Calvinism believing itself more conformable to what Jesus Christ has said, and Lutheranism to what the Apostles have done." Doubtless, as much as to say that Reform has for its basis the word of God, and Lutheranism the acts and usages of the Church. This distinction has much profoundness in it, and, generally speaking, even truth.

But let us examine these differences more closely, without, however, attempting to enumerate them. Let us leave aside the specialties of doctrine, and in particular that free and eternal grace of God which is our most precious jewel. Let us neither speak at present of the election of the Father, nor of the manner in which the divine and human natures are united in the Man-God, nor of the nature of the Supper, nor of the doctrine of baptism, particularities the most generally known, and from which all others flow; and let us attend specially to what belongs to the Church, for it is the Church which is every day becoming the greatest, the most exciting question.

I. The Reformed Church lays down as the basis of Christianity the *Scriptural principle that the Word of God is the positive rule*, the *absolute standard, the only source of faith and Christian life*, whilst Luther lays down as the basis of his reformation a principle not less vulnerable, but quite different; *faith, justification by faith*.

We believe it was well that these two bases were established at the same time. The combined action of Lutheranism and Reform, in this instance, was admirable; that of Lutheranism, in particular, fills us with the profoundest veneration. Not only did Luther and his friends exhibit the fundamental doctrine of justification by faith in a manner still more marked than was done by Reform, but, we must assert boldly, if they had not done it there would have been no reformation. Why was not the great Reformation accomplished by the sects of the middle ages, who all started from the same principle as Reform? Undoubtedly for many reasons, but above all, perhaps, because they were not penetrated with sufficient power by that grand thought, that grand doctrine, of which, after St. Paul, Luther has been the most faithful promulgator.

The Reformation, and before it early Christianity, possessed two fundamental principles: one formal, the principle of Reform, one material, the principle of Lutheranism. Reform requires in addition, faith; and Lutheranism the Bible. But each of these two principles was confided separately and specially to the care of a faithful guard. These two distinct forces were destined to traverse the new world created in the sixteenth century; and here already let us with gratitude admire the most perfect unity in the diversity of the work of God.

We do not intend, however, to justify all the conclusions to which Luther carried his principle. Applying it to the Word of God with a hardihood which astonishes us, he declares in the Preface to his translation of the New Testament, that the Gospel of St. John, the Epistles of St. Paul, among others that to the Romans, and the First of St. Peter, are in truth the marrow of the Scriptures, because they treat especially of faith; he estimates the Gospels under the Epistles, and makes very little account of the Revelation of St. John, and pronounces, respecting an Epistle (that of St. James) a well-known saying, but one which I shall not repeat. Rationalism, which shakes or revokes all the canonical writings, has appeared, and in my opinion, could only appear in the Church of Luther.

Swiss and French Reform never had to reproach itself with such a disrespectful walk. On the contrary, detaching itself from the authority of the Church, it ran to the sovereign authority which the Church itself has always proclaimed, that of the Holy Scriptures. "Abandoning," says one of its chiefs,* "the decrees of the Popes and Fathers of the Church, I came to the source itself. My soul was there reinvigorated, and ever since, I firmly maintained this principle: the Holy Scriptures alone must be followed, and all human additions rejected."

"The Church of Christ," said the Bernese pastors, in the famous dispute which decided the Reform in that Canton in 1528, "invents neither laws nor commandments beyond the Word of God. For that reason, all human traditions, called ecclesiastical, are only binding upon us in so far as they are founded on and commanded in that Word." And in the middle of the seventeenth century one of the reformed, a member of the Church of England, Chillingworth, the chancellor of the diocese of Salisbury, the whole of whose opinions we do not wish to justify, but who

* Wolfgang Joner.

having been a Papist, understood well what ought to be the essence of Reform, uttered this beautiful expression—" The Bible, the whole Bible, nothing but the Bible, such is the religion of the Reformed Christians." In reality, gentlemen, let us remember that the Church of England is *Reformed*—not Lutheran. It is so not only by the name which it bears, but also by its admirable Articles of Faith, and above all by the marked homage which it renders to the Word of God.

This principle of Reform is older than Luther's views; for not only was it that of the primitive Church, that of Wickliff, of the Vaudois, and of many other true Christians; but it was also proclaimed at the beginning of the Reformation in 1518, by Carlstadt, who in the theses in which he attacked Doctor Eck, says, " The text of the Bible must be preferred not only to one or several doctors of the Church, but even to the authority of the entire Church."

Everything in the Reformed Church exhibits this great principle, the exclusive authority of the Word of God. While the confession of Augsburgh is silent upon the sole authority of the Scriptures, all the confessions of the Reformed Church are unanimous on this point.*

Whilst the Lutherans hold by the apocryphal books, and sometimes take their texts from them, the Reformed always distinguish them with care from the canonical books; fight, if it be necessary, decisive battles on their account, as has but lately been done by the British Bible Society, urged on by Scotland, that eminently Reformed country; and they regard it as a matter of the greatest importance to define exactly the extent of the Word of God, and to prevent any human words from creeping into it.

Whilst in the text of the Lutheran Bibles no distinction is made between words human and divine, in all our translations of the Scriptures, on the contrary, such words as are not to be found in the original text are printed in italic characters, so that the reader may be able to distinguish, as far as that can be done in a translation, between the word of man and the word of God. And it may be said that the version of the New Testament published some years ago at Lausanne, which is simply and purely a *fac-simile* of the text, is the product of the Spirit of Reform. Such a production could not, I believe, have been given forth by Lutheranism.

Reform has not, however, as some in our days have pretended, presented the Bible as a volume sufficient of itself, no matter what doctrine might be drawn from it.

" We are persuaded," says the Helvetic Confession, " that the sound knowledge of the true religion depends on the internal illumination of the Holy Spirit. We only regard as true and orthodox, those explanations which are derived from the Holy S   u   in conformity with the analogy of faith and the rules of
lcrept res

* Confess. Gallica, art. 5; Confessio Belgica, art. 5; Confessio Helvetica, art. 1 et 2; Confessio Anglicana, art. 6; Confess. Bohemica, art. 1; Westminster Confession (of Scotland), chap. i.

Nor is it any more true, as some have asserted, that Reform has no kind of tradition. There is not an age, nor a generation, whose voice Reform does not wish to hear and by which it is not ready to profit—only it places always the *great voice* above all the little ones; and in place of judging of the sense of Scripture by tradition, it judges, according to the principles of the Fathers, the truth of tradition by Scripture.

Such, gentlemen, is our First principle,

Reform is supremely the confession of *the Bible*.

There never is to be found among us an esteem of men, of the servants of God in the Church, which resembles, as it has been appropriately designated, a Lutherolatry.* Writings are never to be seen with us like those published in Germany, with the titles: *Luther a prophet—the second Moses—an Elias—a star—a sun.* We have no other prophet than Jesus Christ, and no other sun than the Bible. And whilst for a long time all sorts of relics of Luther were preserved, we scarcely know where the great Calvin dwelt; there is not even a little stone in our cemetery to mark the spot where his ashes repose, and four old trees, we saw five or six years ago, and which shade the ground where it is said the remains of this great servant of God were interred, have been cut down to give room! . . It is doubtless an excess, but it possesses great significancy. It recalls to our memory that Calvin forbade any monument to be erected to him, because he wished the Word of God alone to be honored in his Church.

Yes, gentlemen, the rock of the Word—such is the basis of Reform; we know no other. Let other churches boast of their ecclesiastical foundation; we, we shall only boast of our foundation in the Bible. And in that we believe ourselves more truly ecclesiastical than those who add to the divine rock the moving sands of human traditions. We shall not abandon this foundation at any cost; neither for the Pope nor for Luther. What do I say?—not even for our Reformers. Cursed be the day in which the Reformed Church shall glory in being the Church of Calvin or Zwingle. The Bible—the Bible—the whole Bible—nothing but the Bible.

We have seen at the beginning, that the principle confided to the Lutheran Church possessed in the days of the Reformation, an importance at least equal to that which God confided to the Reformed Church. Which of these two is the most important in our days? I dare not say, gentlemen. But I will say, however, that the principle of the Bible appears to me, at this hour at least, equally important with that of faith. In fact, what are the two great adversaries called forth to engage in the battle of the nineteenth century? *Evangelism* and *Churchism*. And how are we to put to silence Churchism with that cloud of human traditions and human works by which it is surrounded? By the Bible.

If we hesitate about the importance of the principle of Reform, shall we not be convinced by all those voices which at the present hour are calling out, The Church! The Church! and wish to put the visible Church above the Word of the Lord? Shall we

* French Lutherolâtrie, a word formed upon the same principle as *idolatry*.—Tr.

not be convinced by that proud pontiff who calls us *Bible* sectarians,* by that audacious *mouth, speaking great things,* as is said by Daniel the prophet, which has just uttered a cry from the depths of the magnificent halls of the Vatican, and who, stretching forth his arm with fear in the midst of his Apollos and Venuses, and of all those trophies of paganism by which he is surrounded, has just resounded throughout all Christendom that word of terror and alarm, The Bible! the Bible! What! gentlemen! would he who reveals secrets have declared to him in the watches of the night what was about to happen? would he have shown him the Bible at the gate of Italy? or above Rome, and already suspended in the air, the stone cut out without hands, which is destined to overthrow his ancient statue, and to lay it in the dust, in the midst of the ruins and debris which twenty centuries have strewn around it? Ah! gentlemen, if there ever was a time when Reform aught to remain firm to its principle, it is the time in which we live. To conquer by the Bible or perish; such is the futurity before us.

One thing among others, gentlemen, alarms me—the state of England. Very recently, about a month ago, while the meetings connected with each particular church (English or Dissenting), filled the vast extent of Exeter Hall to the door—for the first time the meeting of the Bible Society was comparatively thinly attended. I would not willingly deduce from that fact too dark canclusions; I know that there may be many different causes for it; but I confess that on reading the account of it, a shivering seized me, and I recalled to memory with sadness the words, *Ichabod! Ichabod!* Is then thy glory departed?

II. If the Reformed Church places the word of God in such a positive manner above all human writings, if it places it even above faith, it places, on the other hand, faith above the Church. One of the oldest doctors, Irenæus of Lyons, has already noted the grand antithesis, *where the Spirit is, there is the Church*—this is the principal reform; and *where the Church is, there is the Spirit*—this is the principle of Rome and of Oxford; and also, though in a less degree, that of Lutheranism. A distinguished theologian who occupies in the University of one of our confederate cities, the chair instead of Strauss, I refer to Doctor Lange, has recently revived this antithesis, by turning it into a formula thus: *the Church comes from Faith,* or *Faith comes from the Church.* We do not hesitate, gentlemen, to assert, that these propositions are both true in a certain sense, if the visible church be not confounded with the invisible; for there is a wonderful difference between Faith and the Church. But let it be remembered that while Lutheranism places the emphasis upon the second, and says specially that, since the foundation of the Church, God does not make Christians but by the Church; Reform, on the contrary, places the emphasis on the

* Encyclical Papal Address, the day after the Nones of May, 1844. [Portions of this notorious document were quoted extensively in the Journals of the day.—Tr.]

first, and says, that faith alone, the faith which God has put into the heart, creates the Church. Thus, Reform does not say, the Church which is the assembly of the faithful exists first, and then each believer; but that each believer exists first, and then the Church, which is the assembly of all. Lutheranism says, first the genus, and then the individual; Reform says, first the individual, and then the genus. I am quite ready to give reason for both; but I add, that our duty is to maintain the principle of Reform.

Wherefore, gentlemen? Because, if we say in an absolute sense, *Faith comes from the Church*, we establish by that the very principle which leads to the Inquisition, and which formerly created it. At the epoch of the Reformation, however, in a time when for ages preceding they had stretched upon the wooden horse, whoever would not receive his faith humbly from the hands of the visible Church, it was necessary the renewed Church should raise the opposing principle to a lofty elevation. Reform is therefore here in diametrical opposition to Rome and also to hyper-Lutheranism. I name thus that extreme Lutheran orthodoxy, which, in the days of the Calows and the Quenstedts, exaggerating the Lutheran principle, resuscitated the scholastic method, and raised the doctrines of the Church and of the means of salvation above all others; while, on the contrary, Reform, remembering that it is soul by soul that Christ saves his people, gives, has given, and will always give, the first place in Christian theology to what concerns the individual work, the regeneration, the justification, the conversion of the believer.

Thus, gentlemen, what distinguishes Lutheranism is the importance given to the Church, the whole Church, and most particularly to its ministers. It is not even entirely removed from that *sacerdotalism* which is the essence of Rome and of Oxford. The Lutherans are not afraid to give their pastors the name of priests; and in a celebrated *Practical theology*, by one of the Germans, whose memory is most precious to me, Claude Harm, the prevôt of Kiel, one of the parties is entitled the *Preacher*, another the *Pastor*, but a third the Priest.

Gentlemen, this much was still necessary for our unity. The individual element of Reform might have brought on a dissolution and a dispersion of the members of the Church, which would have been fatal to the whole body, had it not been restrained by the ecclesiastical element, that is to say, excuse the word, the *gatherer* of Lutheranism. In a like manner, the tendency of this last might have led to stagnation, petrifaction, and death, had it not been restrained by the active, spontaneous, vivifying element of Reform. It is the union of these two forces, the one centripetal the other centrifugal, which has launched forth a new world into the universe of God, and which sustains it in its place.

Shall we then abandon our position as we are summoned to do? God preserve us, gentlemen, from such a wicked attempt on the eternal decrees of his providence! Let us not look to one side only; I pray you let us look at both, and embrace the whole magnificence of the work of the Lord. If they be Lutheran, they are right, quite right, to appear Lutheran. Well then, but if they be Reformed, if they address the Reformed, let them not act, let them not speak as if they were Lutheran, as if they were speaking to Lutherans, and thus contradict, arrest, destroy the element of Reform, even in the bosom of Reform.

We shall not here enumerate all the excesses to which a too exclusive application of the Lutheran principle has led. Thence has arisen the usurpation of the clergy, the excessive authority of the pastor, or rather of the confessor (for among Lutherans each believer has a pastor to whom he gives this name), so that during the past century, these confessors, having become infidel, and the good Lutheran people being always humbly submissive, infidelity spread among these poor Churches with inconceivable facility. Some Lutherans have even asserted that we ought to keep strictly by the spiritual guide supplied by the competent ecclesiastical authority, even if he were a stranger opposed to the faith! Never will Reformed Christians recognize such a maxim. They will ever place the Bible above the pastor, and should there be a decided disagreement between the one and the other, then, rather than allow themselves and their children to be led on to infidelity, they will separate themselves from their pastor, and take refuge under the Word of Christ. In so doing, they will carry the Church with them, and leave together the sect and the pastor.

Further, gentlemen, from this *Churchism* arises the different meaning which Lutherans and Reformed attach to Church confessions of faith. The Lutherans regard them as rules of faith— *normæ normatæ*—" rules regulated" (by the Word); and they have even gone so far as to affirm that their authors possessed a certain kind of inspiration, a deutero-canonical inspiration as the Roman Catholics say, when speaking of the Apocryphal books. Among the Reformed, on the contrary, the symbolical books or confessions are only regarded as the expression of the faith of the Church. Our Churches do not say to those who present themselves to occupy their pulpits—*believe!* but they say—*do you believe?* as these two men dear to us, Cellerier and Gaussen, set it forth twenty-five years ago, in the true spirit of Reform, when reprinting the Helvetic Confession at Geneva. And here, gentlemen, although to another amongst us this privilege by right belongs, permit me, in passing, to lay with respect a flower upon the tomb of that faithful servant of Jesus Christ who was taken from us a few weeks ago, full of days, and whose glory it will remain to have been the first, after a century of infidelity, to raise in our native country the standard of the Gospel and of Reform.

I repeat it again. *The Church comes from faith*, before that *faith comes from the Church.*

Such is our watchword. And who will dare to assert that the moment has arrived when we ought to lower this banner and range ourselves meekly under a standard presented to us by others, and which even the papacy itself raised many centuries ago? If it be our brothers who believe that it ought to be done, we, we say it decidedly, we will not do it, convinced as we are, that even at the present hour, to maintain the principle of Reform is to save the Reformation.

But, it may be said, if the maxim that faith comes from the Church, taken absolutely, leads to the *Inquisition*, the maxim that the Church comes from faith leads to *separatism*.

We do not deny that that would result from the excess of the principle, and that this excess is seen in our days. But we deny that an abuse ever overturns a principle; no, the principle of Reform is not essentially separatist; it does not necessarily flow from it that Christianity should be divided into thousands of sects. Doubtless, it is a right possessed by the Christian, it is his duty, as was done at the epoch of the Reformation (and has been done since then), to separate himself from every community which does not confess Jesus Christ, God manifest in the flesh, the only justification of his people. But to make separation a duty, constantly to be renewed, is, according to Reform, to trample under foot a numerous class of passages of the Word of God; it is to call forth that which the apostle Paul orders to be rejected— " *strifes, seditions, heresies,*" Gal. v. 20.

" I say," thus speaks Calvin, " that we must not, under the pretext of minute differences, separate ourselves lightly from a Church in which the fundamental doctrine of salvation is preserved entire, and in which the sacraments are properly administered according to the institution of the Lord."—(Christian Institution, book iv., chap. i.)

However, if we must choose between uniformity and error on the one side, and diversity and truth on the other, Reform will not hesitate; it ranges itself always on the side of truth; truth is its grand aim.

III. But, gentlemen, and this third characteristic affords a triumphant answer to the reproach of separatism which is made against Reform, it has always been distinguished by the Christian liberality with which it has never ceased to stretch forth the hand of brotherly love to every communion which has preserved the doctrines of salvation. So that, whilst the spirit of sectarianism has in various degrees animated other Churches, Reform has always borne on its forehead the seal of true catholicity.

I shall not speak here of the sectarian spirit of Rome, nor of Oxford; these are facts too generally known; but history compels us to recognize this spirit even in Lutheranism. The Lutherans, like the Roman Catholics, have always wished, not to unite with Reform in the bands of brotherhood, but to absorb it.

Exclusiveness is a character of Lutheranism. Here at least it will be said, what becomes of your unity? Yes, gentlemen, even this exclusiveness is necessary to it. It is one of the wheels which must enter into the construction of the admirable machine prepared by the hand of the great Architect three centuries ago. *Exclusiveness* is essential to the Church. Who was more exclusive than he who said; " *No one cometh to the Father* BUT BY ME;" and again; "WITHOUT ME *ye can do nothing.*" The Church ought to have a holy jealousy for the eternal truth of God; for latitudinarianism is its death. The history of all ages has demonstrated this fact, and nothing could demonstrate it more clearly than the history of our own. This exclusiveness was what was confided to the charge of Martin Luther; and although he deceived himself by carrying it out, not only with regard to fundamental dogmas, but also with regard to the different ways of understanding the same truth, although it was against our Reform that his thunders were directed, I love, I admire Luther, even in his wanderings; and I see in him not a *furious Orestes,* as he was named often, even by Bucer and Capito, but a *Prometheus,* who, wishing that man should raise his looks to heaven,

—erectos ad sidera tollere vultus,

and in order to animate him, having stolen fire on high, was precipitated by his very elevation, and saw his entrails torn by cruel vultures. "*Let him that standeth take heed lest he fall!*" Luther believed that the corporeal presence of Christ was God's truth, and he went out of himself—for that truth.—Thou didst well, O great Luther! God teaches what thou didst not, to distinguish what is true from what is *not true*—what is essential, from what is secondary; God gives us, what thou didst not know, to treat with mildness those who differ from us in opinion! But God grant at the same time, as with thee, that the rights of the truth inspire us, and the zeal of God's house eat us up.

However, here again I cannot justify everything; for history is inexorable, and points out to us sad excesses. Here, gentlemen, is the most painful part of our task; for Luther is our father (I speak after the manner of men), a father whom we surround with the most profound veneration and the most filial affection; the true Lutherans are our friends, our well-beloved brethren—they are of those with whom we one day hope to sit at the table in the kingdom of God. If then their opposition cause us to give forth a groan, let it not, at least, create any bitterness in our heart. Let us rather remember that the violence of controversy, far from showing us to be enemies, is a proof of the intimate bonds which unite us to Lutheranism; for in all times, and on every subject, the more parties agree on essential points, the more are they borne away to disagreement on those which are secondary.

It was Luther, that great man of God, who marched here, as everywhere, at the head of his Church. When, as early as 1527, the Reformed requested brotherly love and Christian concord, he replied, "Cursed, even to the lowest depths of hell, be that charity and that unity." He himself relates to one of his friends, that in the conference, at Marbourg, convoked by the Landgrave of Hesse, for the purpose of uniting the Lutherans and the Reformed, Zwingle being moved, approached him, shedding tears before the whole assembly, and saying: "There are none on the face of all the earth with whom I so much desire to be *one*, as with the Wittembergians;" and that he, Luther, repulsed the Zurich reformer, answering: " Your spirit is not our spirit!" and refused to call Zwingle and the Swiss his *brethren!*

Since that time the sectarian spirit has never ceased to exist in Lutheranism. In 1553, when the unfortunate Reformed were driven from London by the bloody Mary, they were, at the instigation of Lutheran theologians, repulsed cruelly in the dead of winter from the walls of Copenhagen, of Rostock, of Lubeck, and of Hamburg, where they sought an asylum. "Rather a Papist than a Calvinist," said they to the people, " rather a Mahometan than a Reformed." And on a house in Wittemberg may be read: " The sayings and writings of Luther are the poison of the pope and of Calvin." They called their cats and dogs by the name of *Calvin;* and published books with titles such as this ; " Proof that the Calvinists have 666 errors in common with the Turks;" or this, " Short proof that the present (1721) attempt at union with the self-styled Reformed or Calvinists is in direct opposition to all the ten commandments, to all the articles of the apostles' creed, to all the petitions of the Lord's Prayer, to the doctrine of the holy baptism, to the power of the keys, to the holy Supper, and to the whole catechism."

In a Lutheran Catechism, of the beginning of the seventeenth century, we read this question: " Dost thou believe then fully that the Calvinists, in place of the living and true God, honor and adore the devil?"—answer; " I believe it from the bottom of my heart." A Lutheran doctor, still living, a man to be admired for his piety and his zeal, applied to the Reformed the passage from St. Paul; " Be not unequally yoked with unbelievers." And you know that the Lutheran missionary societies have recently broken off from Bâle, which, nevertheless, is nearer to Lutheranism than any other of the Reformed churches. What shall we say then in the face of these excesses ? We shall say with St. Paul; "they have zeal for God without knowledge;" and we shall add, smiling with Jerome of Prague, when he saw a peasant come loaded with a large bundle of wood, and place it at his stake: *Sancta simplicitas!** We shall also repeat; Nevertheless, nevertheless, the Lutherans are our brethren notwithstanding, and our well-beloved brethren !

Gentlemen, a spirit of conciliation, of union, of brotherhood, has animated our church in every age, and is, perhaps, its brightest ornament. Zwingle, Œcolampadius, Calvin, Farel never ceased to stretch forth the hand of brotherhood to Luther and to all his friends. Calvin did not even fear to say, that in his eyes Luther was far above Zwingle ;—*Nam si inter se comparantur, scis ipse quanto intervallo Lutherus excedat.*† And he writes to Bullinger, the 25th November, 1544; " I understand that Luther pours out atrocious

---

* Sacred simplicity.—Tr.

† For if these two be compared, you yourself know by how much Luther exce s.

invectives on you and on us all. I dare scarcely request you to keep silence. But I supplicate you at least to remember what a great man Luther is, by what admirable qualities he is distinguished, what courage, what constancy, what ability, what power of doctrine there is in him to beat down the kingdom of antichrist, and to propagate the knowledge of salvation. I say it, and have often repeated it, even though he called me *Satan*, I would not cease to honor him, and to acknowledge him as an illustrious servant of God." Gentlemen, behold these beautiful expressions. Let Reform never forget them! And they are expressions of Calvin, of that man who is represented to us as so irritable and so proud.

On several occasions propositions of peace, and projects of union, were brought forward on the part of Reform. The Swiss-French Reformed above all exhibited, in this respect, an unshaken perseverance. At the moment when the ultra-Lutherans, Westphal, Timann, von Eitzen, and many others, had made a violent discharge of their heavy artillery against the Reformed, Calvin and his friends appeared on the field of battle, in the midst of clouds of smoke, with the olive branch in their hand. The same year (1557) in which Theodore Beza and Farel visited all the Swiss towns to excite public sympathy in favor of the Vaudois, who had been cruelly butchered in the valley of Angrogne, these two Reformed doctors, extending their charity out on one side and another, entered Germany, and there exhibited a confession of faith of the Churches of Switzerland and Savoy, with the intent to unite the whole Reformation, by showing to the Lutheran churches that they also were brethren, companions in arms, in the war against antichrist. In 1631, the general synod of Charenton, near Paris, took the lead, and effected the union by passing a resolution, in which it was declared, "that the churches of the confession of Augsburg being one in opinion with the other Reformed ones in all the essential articles of true religion, the members of their churches may present themselves at the holy table in the Reformed churches without any previous abjuration." In our own days, it has always been from the Reformed that the propositions and efforts to re-establish a true union in the church have come.

And wherefore, gentlemen, is there this difference between Lutheranism and Reform? Doubtless it arises in a great measure, as far as regards Luther and the Lutherans, from the importance which they place in the corporeal presence of Jesus Christ in the Supper; from that unshaken attachment to what they believe to be the truth, an attachment which we sincerely respect; but it flows also, it must be said, from the difference which we have formerly pointed out. The *Biblical* tendency of Reform ought to induce every member of the Reformed Church to place little importance on ecclesiastical differences, much on *Bible truth*, and consequently engage him to stretch forth the hand of brotherhood to every church, to every individual who has the word of the *Bible*. It is thus that from good principles good consequences will always flow.

Gentlemen, let us be faithful to this spirit of true catholicity. Let us not cease to recall, both to ourselves and to our brethren, these words of the apostles: " one God, one Lord, one Spirit, one body." Such is the special mission of Reform.

IV. If Reform be possessed of great breadth, it is not less distinguished by true depth. It is not only a Reformation of the faith like Lutheranism, it is also a Reformation of the life ; and thus it is more universally Christian. Lutheranism is certainly free from antinomianism: Luther himself fought against it. Nevertheless, there is a great difference in the manner in which Lutheranism and Reform consider the law ; one of the principal of which is pointed out by a single and characteristic trait. In the Lutheran catechisms, the law, the ten commandments, are placed before faith, before the fundamental doctrines. Their use is to convince man of sin, and bring him to Christ. In the Reformed catechisms, on the contrary, the law (considered especially in the precepts of Christ and the apostles) is placed after faith, after the doctrines of salvation, as the expression of the gratitude of the child of God for the redemption given him by Christ. The law, according to Luther, only addresses itself to the unconverted, or at most to that portion of the faithful not fully converted. According to Calvin, it addresses itself also to the faithful, how believing soever they may be.

Luther accomplished no Reformation of manners ; he did not even attempt it. Not certainly because he did not consider it important. "How," wrote he to the Bohemian brethren, who exhorted him to establish a discipline similar to theirs, " how is it possible that we, who live in the midst of Sodom, of Gomorrah, and of Babylon, can make that order, that discipline, that pure life to prevail." Luther thought that the Reformation of manners ought to flow simply and naturally from the influence of sound doctrine.

Let us here remark again, gentlemen, how much the diversity of Lutheranism and of Reform is necessary to the unity, to the life of the Reformation. Who does not recognize a profoundly Christian truth in the opinion that faith itself will form the manners ? Was it not necessary that after ages, in which the discipline of the Church had been the cause of numerous vexations, and of superstitions still more numerous, there should be a protest taken against such fatal errors ? Was it not necessary that alongside of the power of Reform, which here tends to bind, there should be another power in the renewed Church, tending unceasingly to enlarge and relax ? Was it not necessary that, above all the exertions of man, and his efforts "to recall the wanderers and to watch over the heritages of the Lord," there should be a finger pointing to heaven, and a great voice proclaiming, " The good shepherd goes before his sheep, and his sheep follow him, because they know his voice?"

If, however, the one of these things was necessary, the other was no less so. The work of Christian vigilance, of pastoral superintendence, was confided to Reform; and, gentlemen, we are reformed.

Zwingle set out from this principle: " A universal re-establishment of life and manners is as necessary as a re-establishment of faith." Immediately, at Zurich, at Berne, at Bâle, ordinances for regulating manners were issued, the women of unchaste life were banished, the boarding-houses and the hotels were suppressed; aud when at a later period the pope, according to the ancient custom, requested troops from Zurich, the Zurichers offered him as a compromise 2000 monks or priests. Would to God we sent at the present day no other Swiss to Rome! In particular, they insisted on the manners of their ministers; " as the word of truth is grave," says the ordinance of 1532, " the life of its servant ought also to be full of gravity."

But it was in Geneva especially, that this principle was realized. Calvin, with the zeal of a prophet and the devotion of a martyr who submits himself unreservedly to the stern Word of God, exacted from the church under his care an absolute obedience. He strove hand to hand with the libertine party, and by the grace of God he remained the stronger. Geneva, formerly so corrupted, was regenerated, and displays a purity of manners, a Christian simplicity, which drew from Farel, after an absence of fifteen years, a shout of admiration, and these remarkable words: " I would rather wish to be the last in Geneva than the first anywhere else." And fifty years after Calvin's death Jean-Valentin Andreæ, a fervent Lutheran, having passed some time within our walls, said, on his return; " What I have seen there I shall never forget, and I shall ardently desire to attain it all my life. The fairest ornament of that republic is its tribunal of manners, which makes inquiry every week into the disorders among the citizens. Games of cards and chance, oaths, blasphemies, impurity, quarrels, hatreds, deceits, infidelities, drunkenness, and other vices are suppressed. Oh! but this purity is a beautiful ornament of Christianity! We (the Lutherans) cannot shed tears enough over that in which we are awanting. If the difference of doctrine did not withdraw me from Geneva, the harmony of its manners would have retained me there for ever."

This character of morality was not confined to Switzerland and Geneva; it spread into France, Holland, and Scotland, into every place where Reform penetrated. It still remains in some of these countries; and a German author, M. Göbel, after mentioning that a modern traveller, also a German, could not find in the Scotch churches, which he visited, a single instance of adultery or divorce, and very little impurity, exclaims: " Let them compare with that the horrible immorality of Germany; in the country as well as in the towns let them only interrogate the pastors, and they will be filled with astonishment and fear."

Alas! gentlemen, we have no longer any reason to be proud; these manners no longer exist. I do not say that there was not in this discipline an element fitted to bring on its destruction. On the contrary, I think that the part taken by the state in this order of manners necessarily induced its fall. I reject every kind of

Christian discipline exercised by magistrates and police; but I believe that they might have laid aside the civil power, and still preserved the strength of the watch, by charity and the Word of God.

They did not do so, and what is the result? Senebier said; " the prosperity of Geneva was for a long time the fruit of the wise laws of Calvin. The purity of our ancient manners was our boast; and it could be shown that one of the causes of our misfortunes is the diminution of their influence. Thus Rome was lost when her censors could no longer make themselves heard, and Sparta fell with the reputation of those who were charged with the care of making her virtue respected." If Senebier spoke thus in 1786, what shall we say at the present hour?

Ah! gentlemen, who could not understand what was said by Montesquieu, that the Genevese ought to bless, to celebrate the day of Calvin's birth, and of his arrival among them? But what was understood by the profoundest politician of the eighteenth century, the Genevese have not comprehended; instead of celebrating the birth of the Reformer, they celebrate and cause their children to celebrate the birth-day of a famous sophist, an ardent soul, a man of inimitable talent, but who sent to the foundling hospital the sad fruits of his libertinism! They are raising a magnificent statue to Jean Jacques, and they raise none to Calvin. "We shall do it in Edinburgh," said a Scotch doctor to me last year; " it is Edinburgh," added he, " which is now the metropolis of Reform."

Gentlemen, the re-establishment of faith and manners in Reform, that is the statue which Calvin, that extraordinary and modest man, would have desired. Will it not be raised to him? And if, as in Saxony in the days of Luther, a too strict rule be at present inapplicable, let us not the less remember, that whoever asks for the discipline of manners, is in the spirit of Reform, and that it is the most sacred duty, not only of the ministers, but of all reformed Christians, to strive that those who call upon the name of the Lord, be " *blameless and harmless, the sons of God, without rebuke, in the midst of a crooked and perverse nation,*" Phil. ii. 15.

V. This brings us, gentlemen, to the fifth character. Reform possesses, both in its principle and its course, something decided, of which Lutheranism is destitute. The principle of Lutheranism was, *to preserve in the Church everything that is not condemned by the word of God;* while that of Reform was, *to abolish in the Church everything that is not prescribed by the word of God.* Lutheranism is a Reformation of the Church, Reform is a renewal of it, or the difference may be indicated, if desired, by merely changing an *accent:* Lutheranism is a Refor*mat*ion, Reform is a Re-*form*ation. Lutheranism took the Church as it was, and contented itself with effacing its blemishes. Reform went to the foundation of the Church, and built its edifice upon the living rock of the apostles. Whilst Luther, when he heard what Carlstadt was doing, writes; " we must keep in the middle path," and rise up against those who overthrow the images, Carlstadt, the first Reformed, from 1521 boldly reforms the Church of Wittemberg, of which he was prevôt, abolishes in it the mass, the images, confession, fast days, and every abuse of popery. Zwingle, almost at the same time, acts in a like manner at Zurich. And for what was done at Geneva, I shall content myself with transcribing the inscription which was for nearly three centuries, from 1536 to 1798, fixed upon the walls of our Hôtel de Ville, and which expresses better than we can do the marked character of Reform. It ought to have been restored since the Jubilee of 1835, and placed in the Church of St. Peter;* but that has not been done. Here it is:—

"IN THE YEAR 1536, THE TYRANNY OF ROMAN ANTICHRIST HAVING BEEN OVERTHROWN, AND ITS SUPERSTITIONS ABOLISHED, THE MOST HOLY RELIGION OF JESUS CHRIST WAS RE-ESTABLISHED HERE IN ITS PURITY, AND THE CHURCH IN A BETTER ORDER, BY THE EXTRAORDINARY FAVOR OF GOD. AND AT THE SAME TIME, THE CITY ITSELF HAVING REPULSED AND PUT ITS ENEMIES TO FLIGHT, WAS FREED, NOT WITHOUT A MARKED INTERPOSITION OF PROVIDENCE. THE GENEVESE COUNCIL AND PEOPLE HAVE RAISED THIS MONUMENT, THAT THE MEMORY OF THESE EVENTS MIGHT BE PERPETUATED, AND THAT A TESTIMONY OF THEIR GRATITUDE TO GOD MIGHT BE HANDED DOWN TO THEIR POSTERITY."

What has been the result of this difference of character between Lutheranism and Reform?

Two very distinct courses, and which, we notice here again, have each their good side. The course of Lutheranism is defensive, successive; the course of Reform is offensive, conquering. To Lutheranism belongs the principle of resistance, of passiveness; to Reform the principle of movement and of life.

Gentlemen, is it necessary to remind you how important these two tendencies are to the prosperity of the church? Must I insist upon this, that in every well-constituted community, the immobility of principles must be united to the mobility of life?

There is not even a family in which two opposing tendencies are not to be found. The decided and imposing authority of the father must be accompanied by the more conciliating and more indulgent tenderness of the mother. The same in a political state, the conservative and the liberal element must always exist. An exclusive immobility leads to violence, to hatred, to revolution; has not Charles X. taught us this much? An excessive mobility leads to fickleness, *superficiality*, agitation, pride; is there not a nation which shows us this? These two elements are so indispensable to the life of the whole body, that if by any means you should destroy one of them, it would re-appear immediately after. In France, in 1830, the old conservatives being thrown out, those who, during fifteen years, had played the part of liberals, became conservatives themselves.

And what is necessary in the state, what is necessary even in every family, you do not wish in the church! You wish by some revolution to eject one of these elements! Impotent con-

* The Church in which Calvin preached.—Tr.

spirators!—even were you able to destroy the element of Reform, you would be compelled to become Reformed yourselves!

But, doubtless, Lutheranism suffered in the sixteenth century, for having pushed its principle to an extreme. Divided between the Bible and the church, between what it wished to take away, and what it wished to preserve, it had a difficult and uncertain course to pursue; its Reformation was never able to reach the extent to which its aim was at first directed, and Luther, whose character was so full of gaiety and joyous humor, spent at last days of sadness and full of sorrow. While Reform, having a precise and definite aim—the Bible,—nothing but the Bible, proceeded with power; and Calvin, Farel, Knox, Zwingle even, died with joy and in triumph. What death was that of Calvin, and what adieux were his!

Lutheranism, paralyzed from the beginning of its existence, saw, after the death of Luther, *conservation* changed, in its bosom, into *stagnation*.

The Lutheran princes, unfaithful to the glorious memory of the illustrious diet of Spires (1529), opposed all extension of Protestantism, and were but too well seconded by their theologians.

Now also, a new society, which we salute with affection and respect, the society of Gustavus Adolphus, faithful to this Lutheran principle, endeavors, it is true, to sustain the falling Protestant churches, but declares itself opposed to all exertion beyond recognized Protestantism, to all proselytism.

Such is not the case with Reform. It marches, it advances, it progresses, it gains everywhere. Our Evangelical Societies of Paris and Geneva, with their essentially proselyte character, and all our missionary societies, are the fairest fruits of the spirit of Reform.

But it is especially in the relation which these two churches bear to papacy that this distinguishing character is shown. Lutheranism, which is *offensive* towards Reform, remains *defensive* towards the pope; whilst Reform, on the contrary, stretching forth the hand of brotherhood to Lutheranism, takes openly and courageously the *offensive* against Rome. At Augsburg, in 1530, Melancthon said to the cardinals, that there was only a small line of separation between him and the pope, but that an immense abyss separated him from Zwingle!* Lutheranism, with which the visible church possesses so much weight, could capitulate with Rome. Reform, which only wishes the Bible, would run tilt against her. Wherever, also, superstitious fears exist of a conflict with papacy, wherever extreme circumspection prevails, the idea, for instance, that prudence forbids Protestants to stretch forth the fraternal hand to priests who reject the pope and confess Jesus Christ, there, perhaps, hyper-Lutheranism will be found, but not certainly the spirit of Reform.

Inspired by a holy love for souls and with a profound conviction

* Dogma nullum habemus diversum ab ecclesia Romana. Parati sumus obedire ecclesiæ Romanæ. (*Legato Pontifico Melancthon.*) Ambiunt (reformati) colloquium cum Philippo; sed hic hactenus recusavit. (*Brentius.*)

that Rome leads them to destruction, Reform, three centuries ago, seized the sword of the word, and began, with the papal power, a war of life or death. Notwithstanding the constant and violent opposition of the most powerful European monarchs, notwithstanding the redoubled efforts of that hierarchy which drew the world after it, Reform, like little David, advanced against this gigantic Goliath, with nothing in its scrip but the well-smoothed pebbles of the word of God, and it has conquered through the name of the Eternal of armies. Unquestionably, I am grateful for all that has been done by Christian princes, and especially by the immortal Gustavus Adolphus. But that was rather a matter of princes and perhaps the work of policy; with us it is rather a matter of the faithful, the work of faith. It was Reform which saved the Reformation in disastrous times, and it will still save it in the days in which we live.

It is true, that it has saved it at the expense of its blood. Whilst the Lutheran church scarcely possesses a single martyr, our churches count them by thousands, and their fidelity has acquired for them the respect and admiration of the best of Lutherans, the tender soul of the Spencers and Zinzendorfs. In Switzerland, in Scotland, in England, and especially in Belgium and France, the inquisition, the papacy, their poniards and their scaffolds have covered the soil of the Bible with the bodies of the slain. Reform has seen it, but it has not bowed its head. It has seen its children deliver up their blood with joy, looking to Jesus Christ, and it has held on its course.

A mandate, written in the name of a priest who styles himself Count of Lausanne and prince of the holy Roman empire (although the holy empire ceased to exist at the beginning of the present century), has dared to say quite recently in this city, "The pontiffs and priests of the Church (of Rome) have been continually and everywhere persecuted from the times of the apostles till the present day. The holy Pontiffs, the holy priests of Jesus Christ, laboring from the origin of Christianity for the conversion and sanctification of souls, have never employed any means that the gospel, conscience, and reason unite in condemning."*

This is in verity too strong, and a sigh escapes us. How then! you dare to hold such language in this city, in the midst of a population which is but formed, so to speak, from the debris which escaped from your wheels, your wooden horses, and your knives! We are accustomed to the effrontery of Rome, but we have never had such a specimen as this.

Forgetful people! from whom, tell us, came the bloody application of the passage, *Constrain them to enter*? By whose orders were shed those torrents of Vaudoisian and Albigensian blood, which inundated the middle ages? Who, if it was not your Pope, when in the night of August 24th, 1572, in the midst of nuptial rejoicings, the old Coligny had been butchered on his knees, and with him fully sixty thousand of the Reformed, who caused the bells of Rome to be rung, the cannon of the castle of St. Angelo

* Mandate of the Bishop of Lausanne and Geneva, May 17th, 1844.

to be fired, and medals to be struck? Who was it who, in 1685, overturned in France sixteen hundred temples, slaughtered thousands and thousands of Protestants, and forced the remainder to flee? In our own days, who is it that closes almost every Roman Catholic country to the preaching of the Gospel? Who constrains the poor inhabitants of the Zillerthal to quit the country of their fathers? Who in Austria makes laws against conversion to Protestantism? Who condemns to prison that *Maurette* who last winter contended with the priests charged to read your mandate from the pulpit? Who, two months ago, in a neighboring frontier village, distant a league from this, caused a poor peasant to be seized, thrown into a dungeon, and then condemned to the galleys, who had committed no other crime save that of reading the Bible? Who, not in the fourteenth nor fifteenth century, but a few weeks ago, condemned to *death* Maria Joaquina for having denied the duty of worshipping the Virgin and the doctrine of transubstantiation? And you talk of Rome as a *persecuted* church! And you say she never employed other means than those of conscience and gentleness! Forgetful people! go! go! when you persecute you are quite in harmony with yourselves. Persecution must be and in truth is one of your dogmas. No one shall take away that opprobrium from you, and no one shall deprive us of this glory. Your church is the church of executioners; ours the church of martyrs.

VI. I only take one other character from among all those that still remain. It is derived from the one we have just described; the difference which exists between our two communions as to the liberty of the Church and the State.

Luther was an humble and submissive monk, even according to his adversaries; and although he possessed great powers of speech, he kept always, in presence of the emperor and of his prince, within the limits of the most perfect obedience. And even in 1530, that same Luther, who in 1522 wrote a book "Against the state of the pope and the bishops falsely called spiritual," showed that he, as well as Melancthon, was quite disposed to recognize the bishops, if only the bishops would recognize the Gospel. Luther's reformation was essentially monarchical as regards the state, hierarchical as regards the church. The people never appear in it but to receive modestly what the authorities give them. Luther, in short, defined, it is true, the two swords clearly enough—the power of the state and that of the church; but after his day, and even while he was still living, the Lutheran princes, clothed with territorial episcopacy, absorbed all the ecclesiastical liberties and independence

Is it necessary, gentlemen, to remark, that Lutheranism possesses, in this character, an excellence which is peculiarly its own? The car which bears the human mind stood, in the sixteenth century, at the top of a rapid descent. Reform placed itself boldly in the seat; seized the reins with one hand, and with the other smacked its whip, and the car started. What was then required to prevent a fall to the bottom of the mountain, a terrible catastrophe? There was required, gentlemen (excuse a common word), a drag; which was Lutheranism. By this means its course would be swift but sure; and if the misfortune which was feared has happened, it is because Lutheranism and Reform, both the one and the other, lost, during the last century, their essential and intrinsic character; it is because the drag has been taken away, and the driver precipitated from his seat.

Here then is a new difference between Reform and Lutheranism; and it was not without reason that Bossuet said, before all the court of Louis XIV., " *The Calvinists are bolder than the Lutherans.*"

Reform, from its very commencement, was essentially democratic. Switzerland, where Reform developed itself, is an assemblage of little nations in which the people is sovereign. It was from the people that the Reformation emanated; and when the councils opposed it (as in Bâle, for example), it was the people who made it triumphant. Political rights and liberties trampled under foot by the papacy, lightly abandoned by Lutheranism, are zealously reclaimed by Reform. The reformation of the free German cities, now Lutheran, was the most brilliant act of their autonomy; but in making this lofty effort, they lost their energy and their liberty, and fell from that time under the influence or the power of formidable neighbors.

But, on the contrary, wherever Reform comes it preserves the ancient liberties, and adds others that are new. If the lot of Geneva, a free imperial city, be so different at the present hour from that of Augsburg, Nuremburg, and many other cities, formerly free and imperial as well as she, whence does it come, I pray? History shall supply our answer. Calvin, in 1559, at the time when Geneva expected to be besieged, put his own hand to the work to raise a new bastion. If Geneva was capable of maintaining its independence for three centuries against formidable enemies, it is due to that same spirit that animated Calvin. Everywhere this opposition between Lutheranism and Reform is to be met with. And in our own days, for example, when in 1830, at the time of the fall of Charles X., the Christians of France and other countries rejoiced, and the Christians of Germany were astonished and offended, it perhaps arose altogether from the one being Reformed, and the other Lutheran.

This opposition has for a long time, gentlemen, furnished Roman Catholics with a common field for invective against Reform. They are welcome to it. Let us just call to memory the constant agitations of the popish states, Italy, Spain, Portugal, Poland, Belgium, Ireland, France, and three days ago' the combat of Trient* (Valais). Let us recall to memory the inquietude, the restlessness, the sighs of the Lutheran states of Germany. Let us remember the powerful and fruitful liberties enjoyed at the present hour by the Reformed states, Scotland, Holland, England, America, and some cantons of Switzerland. And if in America the peaceful city

---

* Referring to the late revolution in the Valais.—Tr.

of William Penn, the city which was formerly that of brotherly love, be now stained with bloody excesses, whence does it arise? I do not say that the Protestants there are without blame. On the contrary, I grant that the *salt has there*, without doubt, *lost its savor*. But, nevertheless, it is impossible not to perceive that the disasters of Philadelphia are the act by which the papacy of Ireland heralds its invasion.

As respects political liberty the papacy is in a state of revolution; Lutheranism is in a state of fermentation; Reform is in a state of possession.

Let it not be said that if there are democratic sympathies in Reform, it is therefore unfavorable to monarchies. That were to make a strange anachronism, and to reason in the style of Louis XIV. Are not the greatest minds at present of opinion that democracy, under one form or another, is the futurity towards which the nations are tending. Now, Reform being possessed of light and strength fitted to guide and moderate democracy, as M. de Tocqueville himself alleges, is it not therefore, henceforth, requisite for the prosperity of states? To reject it now, would be the same as when a vessel is setting sail, and about to launch out into the great waters, to turn off its seamen, to dismiss its pilot, throw down its compass, and break its helm. "Let us moderate democracy by means of religion," says M. de Tocqueville. Reform is the golden bridle, powerful, yet easily managed, which the divine hand has prepared for the mouth of liberty. The real *pacific democracy* is Reform. You will find it nowhere else.

But if the reformed church gives liberty to the state, it arises from being itself possessed of it. The legislation and government of the church with it do not proceed from certain personages placed by office originally above the rest, but from the whole of the church, from the suffrages of the faithful, so that if any are raised above the others, it is only as organs and delegates of the church. Every necessary precaution is taken to prevent domination from creeping in. "Let the moderator have the presidency, but nothing more (say the ordinances of Schaffhausen), lest from a *democracy* it should become a *monarchy*."

Reform does not establish a church of the clergy, it establishes (but let us comprehend well the meaning of the words), it establishes a church of the people; not of the people of the world, but of the people of God; that is to say, a church composed essentially, though not exclusively, of all the grave and holy men, whose thoughts have been led captive to the will of Christ.

Finally, gentlemen, as to the independence of the Church, I do not assert the complete separation from the State; that is a question upon which I shall give no opinion in this address; as to the independence of the church, that is not less essential to our Reform. Zwingle who had never encountered the slightest hinderance from the state, who had, on the contrary, received from it every species of support, regarded the church, we must acknowledge, as a society inclosed within the state, protected, tended, and to a certain extent governed by the state. But if Zwingle had lived in a time when the state made war on Christian truth in favor of papacy and socinianism, do you think he would have made the church submissive to it? No, gentlemen, he would have separated the church from it.

In fact, already before the time of Calvin, the synod of Berne of 1532 established that the state ought not to interfere in religious matters, except as to what regards external order. "But as to what concerns the work of grace, that is not within the power of man, and is not held of any magistrate. The state ought not to meddle with consciences; Jesus Christ our Lord is the only master of them. If the magistrate mix himself up with the gospel, he will just make hypocrites."

But it was Calvin especially, the chief of our Reform, who claimed for the church autonomy, autocracy, and independence. He was not, like Zwingle, born a citizen of a Republic, but the subject of a monarchy, and as such he felt himself, less than he, an integral part of the state. The organization of a monarchy besides did not permit, so much as that of a republic, that confusion of church and state realized by Zwingle.

Luther was a German, Zwingle a Swiss; but nationality only occupied a secondary place in the great soul of Calvin; Christ and the church were all for him. He was neither a Frenchman, a Swiss, nor a Genevese; he was of the city of God. In quitting France, he sacrificed whatever he had that was most precious: and he never returned to the abode of his former idols to raise them anew. Undoubtedly he loved Geneva, the country of his adoption, but the great nationality reigned supreme over all lesser ones. Nothing was more insupportable to him than national egotism. Turning away from those narrow compartments in which each one wishes to encase himself, his eagle eye fixed itself unceasingly on the grand whole of the church. His colleagues of the cantons strove to form a national Swiss church, but even that attempt appeared too mean to his capacious mind; and passing beyond rivers and mountains, he aspired unceasingly after the church universal. He knew no nation but the nation of holiness, and no people but the people of God.

His principle even, which bound him to Bible and apostolical antiquity, carried him back to the first three centuries of the church, and caused him to regard the independence of the church as its normal condition. How, besides, when Calvin saw the state in France united to the Roman hierarchy and roaring like a ferocious beast against the humble Galilean confessors, would he not feel constrained to put the church beyond the reach of its assaults? Moreover, he did not only cast aside the oppression of Francis I. or Henry II., but also the protection of reformed magistrates, which filled him with lively apprehension. He perceived in the connection which existed between the church and the state at Zurich and at Berne, something servile which hindered the movements of the church and threatened its holy liberty. "I do not intend that we shall be so servilely bound," writes he in 1557 to Bullinger, who insisted on the authority of the magistrate. *Non puto tam serviliter nos constrictos teneri.*

Calvin then threw far from him the idea of causing the Church to be governed by the state, even by the state evangelized. He wished it to form a community *sui generis,* in which each member would have a certain share in the government. He made each church a little democracy, and from the reunion of all these churches a confederation.

Calvin's spirit, as to the independence of the church, was, perhaps, nowhere so powerfully manifested as in the canton Vaud (*Pays de Vaud*). The church, in that beautiful country, found itself between Berne and Geneva as it were between two mutually counteracting forces. The spirit of liberty and independence was blown towards it from the walls of Geneva by the powerful mouth of Calvin, whilst the military republic of Berne, wishing to maintain that strength in the state which for several ages constituted its greatness, applied itself with nervous arm to tighten firmly the bands and the forms in which the state intended to hold the church. Berne could not admit any part whatever of the public 'power to be withdrawn from the powerful hands of the state, not even in things religious. Thus, the Vaudean Church claiming the exercise of ecclesiastical discipline, the state was afraid if it granted that power, it would, in some sort, recognize the church's independence. The state was quite agreeable to have discipline, but intended to exercise it itself, and that by its own officers.*

However, Viret, Theodore Beza, and a great number of other ministers, maintained the principles of independence in the Pays de Vaud. The ties with Berne became more relaxed every day, and all looks were turned towards Geneva. The two great systems, brought into the presence of each other, rendered a crisis imminent. "A rupture was inevitable," says the wise Hnndeshagen, now professor at Berne, in his history of the conflicts of that church. Thus, gentlemen, in the sixteenth century, two hundred and fifty years before its emancipation, the independence of the church was on the point of conferring on the people political independence. But the beart was strongest. He descended roaring from his mountains; and Viret, Theodore Beza, Marlorat, Merlin, and about forty of their brethren, all friends of the liberty of the church, were compelled to flee from the country in which they had with so much joy announced the gospel of Christ, and go to enrich Geneva and the Reformed Churches of France with their piety and their light. The Free Church of Scotland has been able to remain even on the field of combat, but the *Free Church* of Vaud, crushed in its most noble members by the mailed hand of the powerful republic, was compelled to quit its smiling towns, its valleys, and its mountains—and the *bond Church* remained there alone. All classes of the pastors were shut up for two days under

---

* Reformation Ordinance of the Seigneurs of Berne (Voir Ruchat, 1837, vol. iv., p. 522, *Pièces Justificatives.*)

† The arms of Berne.—TR.

the bars and bolts of the castle of Lausanne, and no one could clear the gates of that prison, except by engaging to compear at the first citation. And at the same time the state deprived all classes of the right, in future, of convoking either class or conference. Vaud thus witnessed the complete triumph of the state over the church. *Order reigned at Warsaw.* That *order*, which succeeded one of the most memorable contests of Christianity, has continued for nearly three centuries; and the influence of the Bernese principles has during this lapse of time been so infiltrated into that beautiful country, that if here or there the eloquent voice of the Virets or the Bezas makes itself heard from the midst of the ruins, in order to claim the rights of the church of Jesus Christ, it is looked upon as a strange thing! These accents, three centuries old, are regarded as modern words, and as theories of the day.

Undoubtedly, gentlemen, there was still in Calvin's system some connection between the state and the church, but so little was it essential, that two years ago, since our revolution, some voices only required to recall to people's remembrance the principles of Reform, to bring it to the verge of being severed. Let us then understand perfectly, if there be at present in some minds a reverting to petty nationality, if there be some honorable Christians who preach blind submission, who oppose even what some citizens, some of the faithful, respectfully ask by petitions, the liberty which has been sworn to them, and which even the constitution of the country guarantees them; such a way of acting is an invasion of Lutheranism, even a false Lutheranism, and a considerable deviation from the Reformed principles.

Gentlemen, liberty in the affairs of the church and in those of the state; such is our antiquity; our custom; our tradition;—we are the conservators of them. To deprive Reform of this noble love of liberty would be to revolutionize it.

It is time to conclude.

"The catholic church," says Lange, "is the church of the priests; the Lutheran that of the theologians; the Reformed that of the faithful." We accept of this definition, remarking, however, what is certainly the idea of Lange, that even the catholicity of the Reformed church causes it to assign, whether to doctors or pastors, the place which belongs to them.

If it be required to find a motto for Reform, what, gentlemen, would you inscribe upon its banner? This is what I would choose:

Above:—

GRACE.

Below:—

CATHOLICITY, LIBERTY.

As regards the doctrine of *Grace*.

Grace in all its fulness, from everlasting to everlasting, from the first movement of the regenerated till the full accomplishment of his salvation.

Then, as regards the church, *catholicity* and *liberty*.

Catholicity. Unquestionably the Reformed church is possessed of that. A church which has never ceased to make the grand Christian union one of its most vehement desires, one of its most cherished aims. It possesses catholicity in a higher degree than the church styling itself Catholic, which has never ceased to cut off from its communion whoever was imbued with some truth and life, even a Jansenius and almost a Fenelon.

But if grace be the sun of Reform, and catholicity one of its poles, liberty is the other. Catholicity as regards the whole, liberty as regards the individual. Individuality and catholicity are equally essential to it, and to raise the one in opposition to the other is to cease to be Reformed.

Thus, gentlemen, in the day when the *Lord shall assemble his army in holy pomp*, in the day when the body of Christ shall reunite its scattered members, the Reformed church will come bringing as a gift to the New church these three things which shall endure; *Grace, Catholicity, Liberty*, What other church will be able to present so fair an offering?

Let us be then, gentlemen (this is my last sentence, the conclusion of this Address), let us be then intelligent, faithful, and unshaken sons of Reform; I do not say only in this school, only in Geneva, but in Lausanne, but in Neuchâtel, but in the whole of Switzerland, France, Holland, Scotland, England, Germany, America. The destinies of the church depend upon it.

Shall we forget our fathers, their principles, their struggles, their faithfulness, their blood? Whilst they took so much care to preserve Reform intact, in presence not only of the papacy, but also of all secondary shades of opinion, shall we lightly abandon the precious characters of their faith! Shall we walk up and down upon their graves, trampling their bones under foot and scattering their ashes?

Undoubtedly, Lutheranism has its task as we have ours. Undoubtedly, Lutheranism and Reform should march on hand in hand under the standard of Christ to the conquest of the world. But that we may render to our ally the service he has the right to expect from us, it is necessary we should be *ourselves*. And are we so?

Ah! gentlemen, he who addresses the awakening letters to the seven churches of Asia, makes us hear his voice. When he sees how many there are "whose hands are weakened and whose knees are out of joint," he cries to Reform; *Hold fast that which thou hast, that none may take away thy crown. Guard that good thing which has been confided to thee by the Holy Spirit dwelling in thee!*

Reform, gentlemen, is the church of the present time, *die Confession der Gegenwart*,* as Lange calls it. To Reform the Lord has specially committed the multitude of nations. Let it advance, then, freely, courageously in the world; let it there accomplish the holy work committed to it by the Eternal; and as the sixteenth century was signalized by a great separation, let the nineteenth be signalized through the prayers and the labors of Reform by a great union. *I will make thee a pillar in the temple of my God.*

* The Confession of the present time.—Tr.

PUSEYISM EXAMINED.

PUSEYISM EXAMINED.

GENEVA AND OXFORD

"Two systems of doctrine are now, and probably for the last time, in conflict—the Catholic and Genevan."
Dr. Pusey's Letter to the Archbishop of Canterbury.

GENTLEMEN:

I am in the practice, at the opening of the course of lectures in our School, to call your attention to some subject peculiarly appropriate to the wants and the circumstances of the times. Several such subjects now present themselves to our consideration.

And first of all, there is one which is appropriate to every year and to every day, it is that which concerns the very nature of this school. It has none of those temporal sources of prosperity, of endowment, and of power, which nourish other institutions; it can exist only as a plant of God; it can be nothing excepting just as the Spirit of God—like the sap—diffuses itself, without cessation, through the principal branches, and through even the least of its twigs; adorning the whole tree with leaves, with flowers, and with fruits. Gentlemen, Professors, and Students, we are those twigs and branches. Oh! that we may not be barren and withered branches!

There is another subject which begins greatly to occupy the most distinguished minds; it is the question whether the Church ought to depend upon the civil government, or ought to have a government of its own, having no dependence, in the last resort, but upon Christ and his Word. Without entering here into this important subject, I would indicate two opposite movements, which are at this moment simultaneously taking place under our eyes in the world; the one in theory, the other in practice. On the one hand, an admirable work, the production of one of the most profound thinkers of our age, Mr. Vinet,* leads some reflecting minds to acknowledge the independence of the Church; and, on the other, many people are uniting themselves with new zeal around the institutions of the government; so that there are all around us convictions and movements which seem to carry away the people of our day by contrary currents. It is thus that a student of Geneva has just written to us, that the refusal to grant to him the exemption from military duty which the law stipulates in favor of students in Theology, will oblige him to quit our school.

* Essai sur la Manifestation des Convictions Religieuses—Paris, 1842.

We will always respect authority, but we cannot refrain from remarking that if, as all parties maintain, there has been a radical revolution in Geneva this year, that revolution has not, assuredly, tended to establish among us that equality and that religious liberty, without which all other liberty is but a useless and dangerous plaything. However, it is in France above all that this movement is taking place. A French student writes to us, with regrets which have touched us, that he has united himself again to the Established Church. When young men, after having pursued in our Preparatory School those first studies which present so many difficulties, desire to secure to themselves, by certain measures, a future more easy; or even to abandon our Institution for the purpose of placing themselves in one sustained by government, from which Unitarian and Rationalist doctrines have been banished, we shall be happy to think that we have been able to prepare them in part, with the aid of God our Saviour, for the work of the ministry, and we shall follow them in their career with the same affection, and we hope, with the same prayers. But we ourselves, Gentlemen, will make no advances to the political governments; we believe that our sole resource is with the Government from above, and knowing the faithfulness of Christ towards those who seek only His glory, assured that there is a place for whomsoever He calls to preach His Gospel, we will ask of Him the confidence that we, teachers and pupils, ought to have in His love, and to make us all continue to walk *by faith* and not by sight.

The circumstances even of the Church in our country might also occupy our attention. Alas! we have played this year the part of Cassandra. In vain have we presented, as well as we could, the correct principles of Ecclesiastical Government; in vain, in particular, have we shown that the elders of the Church ought to be chosen by the people of the parishes assembled in their places of worship, with their pastors, after having invoked the name of God, and not by municipal councils, over which magistrates preside; our words for a moment heard, have in the end been in vain. We have seen among us, a very strange spectacle; we have seen ecclesiastics, men in other respects truly enlightened, and possessing undoubted talent, appear to fear their parishes, and employ their powerful influence to cause the rulers of the Church to be elected, not by the Church, but by the magistrates charged to watch over the maintenance of the roads and public edifices. And now that this election has been made, what do people say? surprising thing! Exclamations of astonishment and grief are heard, that the political bodies to which some have wished at all price to entrust the ecclesiastical elections, have made those elections political; the fall of the Church is predicted, men are now occupied with those who *are destined infallibly to share the spoils*,* and nothing can equal the zeal which has been employed to obtain this change, unless it be the grief which has been manifested when, as we predicted, its inevitable results have been discovered. Behold, Gentlemen, whither ignorance of the

---

* See the Courier of Geneva of the 24th Sept., 1842.

first principles of ecclesiastical government, on the part of those who administer the Church, whatever may be, in other respects, their illumination, their morality, their patriotism, inevitably conducts.

If we look beyond this School, beyond this city, into the religious world in general, there are, Gentlemen, other subjects which present themselves. It is thus that we see pious men, seduced, without doubt, by many truths mixed up with strange errors, receive a system come from a city in England,* according to which there is no more Church, although Jesus has promised (Matt. xvi.) that "the gates of hell shall not prevail against it;" and that there ought to be no more pastors and teachers, although revelation declares to us that Christ himself has established " pastors and teachers for the perfecting of the saints, for the work of the ministry, for the edifying of the body of Christ." (Ephes. iv. 11, 12.)

But, Gentlemen, there is another error; it is that which is found in the other extremity of the theological line, that I intend now to indicate to you. In the bosom of a University in England, that of Oxford, has grown up an ecclesiastical system which interests and justly grieves all Christendom. It is now some time since some laymen, whom I love and respect, came to me to ask me to write against that dangerous error. I answered that I had neither the time nor the capacity, nor the documents necessary for the task. But if I am incapable of composing a dissertation, I can at least show in few words how I regard it. It is with me even a duty, since respectable Christians ask it of me; and it is that which has determined me to choose this subject for the present occasion.

Let us comprehend well, Gentlemen, the position which Evangelical Christian Theology occupies.

At the epoch of the Reformation, if I may so speak, three distinct eras had occurred in the history of the Church.

1. That of Evangelical Christianity, which, having its focus in the times of the Apostles, extended its rays throughout the first and second centuries of the Church.

2. That of Ecclesiastical Catholicism, which, commencing its existence in the third century, reigned till the seventh.

3. That of the Papacy, which reigned from the seventh to the fifteenth century.

Such were the three grand eras in the then past history of the Church; let us see what characterized each one of them.

In the first period, the supreme authority was attributed to the revealed Word of God.

In the second, it was, according to some, ascribed to the Church as represented by its bishops.

In the third, to the Pope.

We acknowledge cheerfully that the second of these systems is much superior to the third; but it is inferior to the first!

* Plymouth. (Dr. Merle here refers to those who are called "Plymouth Brethren.")

" In fact, in the first of these systems it is GOD who rules.

In the second, it is MAN.

In the third, it is, to speak after the Apostle, " THAT WORKING OF SATAN, with all power, and signs and lying wonders" (2 Thess. ii. 9).

The Reformation, in abandoning the Papacy, might have returned to the second of these systems, that is, to Ecclesiastical Catholicism; or to the first, that is, to Evangelical Christianity.

In returning to the second, it would have made half the way. Ecclesiastical Catholicism is, in effect, a middle system—a *via media*, as one of the Oxford Doctors has termed it, in a sermon which he has just published. On the one hand, it approaches much to Papacy, for it contains, in the germ, all the principles which are there found. On the other, however, it diverges from it, for it rejects the Papacy itself.

The Reformation was not a system of pretended *juste milieu*. It went the whole way; and rebounding with that force which God gives, it fell, as at one single leap, into the Evangelical Christianity of the Apostles.

But there is now, Gentlemen, a numerous and powerful party in England, supported even by some Bishops (whose Charges have filled us with astonishment and grief), which would, according to its adversaries, quit the ground of Evangelical Christianity to plant itself upon that of Ecclesiastical Catholicism, with a marked tendency towards the Papacy; or which, according to what *it* pretends, would faithfully maintain itself on that hierarchical and semi-Romish ground, which is, according to it, the *true, native* and *legitimate* foundation of the Church of England. It is this movement which is, from the name of one of its principal chiefs, called *Puseyism*.

"The task of the true children of the Catholic Church," says the *British Critic* (one of the Journals which are the organs of the Oxford party), "is to unprotestantize the Church." "It is necessary," says one of these doctors,* "to reject entirely and to anathematize the principle of Protestantism, as being that of a heresy, with all its form, its sects and its denominations." "It is necessary," says another in his posthumous writings,† "to hate more and more the Reformation and the Reformers."

In separating the Church from the Reformation, this party pretends to wish not to bring back the Papacy, but to retain the church in the *juste milieu* of Ecclesiastical Catholicism. However, the fact is not to be disguised, that if it were forced to choose between what it considers two evils, it would greatly prefer Rome to the Reformation.

Men highly respectable for their knowledge, their talents, and their moral character, are found among these theologians. And, let us acknowledge it, the fundamental want which seems to have decided this movement is a legitimate one.

There has been felt in England, in the midst of all the waves

---

* Mr. Palmer. † Mr. Froude.

which now heave and agitate the Church, a want of *antiquity;* and men have sought a rock, firm and immovable, on which to plant their footsteps.

This want is founded in human nature; it is also justified by the social and religious state of the present time. I myself thirst for antiquity.

But the doctors of Oxford, do they satisfy, for themselves and others, these wants of the age?

I am convinced of the contrary. What a juvenile antiquity is that before which these eminent men prostrate themselves! It is the young and inexperienced Christianity of the first ages which they call ancient; it is to the child that they ascribe the authority of the old man. If it be a question respecting the antiquity of humanity, certainly we are more ancient than the Fathers, for we are fifteen or eighteen centuries older than they; it is we who have the light of experience and the maturity of grey hairs.

But no; it is not respecting such an antiquity that there can be any question in divine things. The only antiquity to which we hold is that of the " Ancient of days" (Dan. vii. 13), " of Him who before the mountains were brought forth, or ever He had formed the earth and the world, even from everlasting to everlasting is God." It is " He who is our refuge from age to age" (Ps. xc. 1, 2). The truly ancient document to which we appeal is that " Word which is settled for ever in heaven" (Ps. cxix, 89), and " which shall stand for ever" (Isaiah, x. 8). Behold, Gentlemen, *our* antiquity.

Alas, that which most afflicts us in the learned doctors of Oxford, is that whilst the people who surround them hunger and thirst after antiquity, they themselves, instead of leading them to the ancient testimony of the " Ancient of days," only conduct them to puerile novelties. What novelties in reality, and what faded novelties!—that *purgatory,* those *human pardons,* those *images,* those *relics,* that *invocation of the saints* which these doctors would restore to the Church.* What immense and monstrous innovation that Rome to which they would have us return!

Who are the innovators, I demand? those who say as we do, with the eternal Word: " God hath begotten us of His own will, with the word of truth" (Jas. i. 18), or those who say as do the " Tracts for the Times:" " Rome is our mother, it is by her that we have been born to Christ." Those who say as we do, with the eternal Word: " Take heed, brethren, lest there be in any of you an evil heart of unbelief in departing from the living God" (Heb. iii. 12); or those who say as do these doctors: " In losing visible union with the Church of Rome, we have lost great privileges,"† certainly the doctors of Oxford are the innovators.

The partisans of Rome, that grand innovation in Christendom, do not here deceive themselves; they hail in these new doctors advocates of Romish novelties. The famous Romish Doctor Wiseman writes to Lord Shrewsbury:

* Tracts for the Times, No. 90, Art. 6.
† British Critic.

",We can count certainly on a prompt, zealous, and able co-operation to bring the Church of England to obedience to the See of Rome. When I read in their chronological order the writings of the theologians of Oxford, I see in the clearest manner these doctors approximating from day to day our holy Church, both as to doctrine and good-will. Our Saints, our Popes, become more and more dear to them; our rites, our ceremonies, and even the festivals of our saints, and our days of fasting, are precious in their eyes, more precious, alas, than in the eyes of many of our own people."

And the doctors of Oxford, notwithstanding their protestations, do they not concur in this view of the matter, when they say: "the tendency to Romanism is at bottom only a fruit of the profound desire which the Church, greatly moved, experiences to become again that which the Saviour left her,—One."*

Such, Gentlemen, is the movement which is taking place in that Church of England, which so many pious men, so many Christian works have rendered illustrious. Dr. Pusey has had reason to say in his letter to the Archbishop of Canterbury: "upon the issue of the present struggle depend the destinies of our Church." And it is worth while for us to pause here for a few moments to examine what party we ought to prefer, as members of the ancient Church of the continent, and what we have to do in this grave and solemn crisis.

Gentlemen, we ought to profess frankly that we will have neither the *Papacy* nor the *via media* of Ecclesiastical Catholicism, but remain firm upon the foundation of Evangelical Christianity. In what consists this Christianity when it is opposed to the two other systems which we reject?

There are in it things essential and things unessential; it is of that only which forms its essence; of that which is its principle, that I would here speak.

There are three principles which form its essence; the first is that which we may call its *formal* principle, because it is the means by which this system is formed or constituted; the second is that which may be called the *material* principle, because it is the very doctrine which constitutes the religious system; the third I call the *personal* or *moral* principle, because it concerns the application of Christianity to the soul of each individual.

The *formal* principle of Christianity is expressed in few words:

THE WORD OF GOD, ONLY.

That is to say, the Christian receives the knowledge of the truth only by the Word of God, and admits of no other source of religious knowledge.

The *material* principle of Christianity is expressed with equal brevity:

THE GRACE OF CHRIST, ONLY.

That is to say, the Christian receives salvation only by the

---

* Letter of Dr. Pusey to the Archbishop of Canterbury.

grace of Christ, and recognizes no other meritorious cause of eternal life.

The *personal* principle of Christianity may be expressed in the most simple terms:

THE WORK OF THE SPIRIT, ONLY.

That is to say, there must be in each soul that is saved a moral and individual work of regeneration, wrought by the Spirit of God, and not by the simple concurrence of the Church,* and the magic influence of certain ceremonies.

Gentlemen, recall constantly to your minds these three simple truths:

The Word of God, ONLY;
The Grace of Christ, ONLY;
The Work of the Spirit, ONLY;

and they will truly be " a lamp to your feet and a light to your paths."

These are the three great beacons which the Holy Spirit has erected in the Church. Their effulgence should spread from one end of the world to the other. So long as they shine, the Church walks in the light; as soon as they shall become extinct or even obscured, darkness like that of Egypt will settle upon Christendom.

But, gentlemen, it is precisely these three fundamental principles of Evangelical Christianity which are attacked and overthrown by the new system of Ecclesiastical Catholicism. It is not to some minor point, to some doctrine of secondary importance that they direct their attention at Oxford; it is to that which constitutes the essence even of Christianity and of the Reformation, to those truths so important that, as Luther said, " with them the Church stands, and without them the Church falls." Let us consider them.

I.

The *formal* principle of Evangelical Christianity is this:

THE WORD OF GOD, ONLY.

He who would know and possess the Truth, in order to be saved, ought to address himself to that revelation of God which is contained in the sacred Scriptures, and to reject everything which is human addition, everything which, like the work of man, is justly suspected of being stamped with the impress of a deplorable mixture of error. There is one sole source at which the Christian quenches his thirst; it is that stream, clear, limpid, perfectly pure, which flows from the throne of God. He turns his lips away from every other fountain which flows parallel with it,

---

* The words which are used in the French are *adjunction de l'Eglise*, and are employed to express that additional or concurrent influence which the Church is believed, by the Puseyites, to exert in regeneration by her ministrations.—*Note by the Tr.*

or which would pretend to mix itself with it; for he knows that because of the source whence these streams issue, they all contain troubled, unwholesome, perhaps deadly waters.

The sole, ancient, eternal stream, is GOD; the new, ephemeral, failing stream, is MAN; and we will quench our thirst but in God alone. God is for us, so full of a sovereign majesty, that we would regard as an outrage, and even as impiety, the attempt to put anything by the side of His Word.

But this is what the authors of the novelties of Oxford are doing. " The Scriptures," say they, in the *Tracts for the Times,* " it is evident are not, according to the principles of the Church of England, the Rule of Faith. The doctrine or message of the Gospel is but indirectly presented in the Scriptures, and in an obsure and concealed manner."* " Catholic tradition," says one of the two principal chiefs of this school,† " is a divine informer in religious things; it is the unwritten word. These two things (the Bible and the Catholic traditions) form together a united rule of Faith. Catholic tradition is a divine source of knowledge in all things relating to Faith. The Scriptures are only the document of ultimate appeal; Catholic tradition is the authoritative teacher."

" Tradition is infallible," says another doctor;‡ " the unwritten word of God, of necessity, demands of us the same respect which his written word does, and precisely for the same reason—because it is His word." " We demand that the whole of the Catholic traditions should be taught," says a third.§

Behold, gentlemen, one of the most pestiferous errors which can be disseminated in the Church.

Whence has Rome and Oxford derived it? Certainly the respect which we entertain for the incontestable science of these doctors shall not prevent us from saying it: This error can come from no other source than the natural aversion of the heart of fallen man for everything that the Scriptures teach. It can be nothing else than a depraved will which leads man to put the Sacred Scriptures aside. Men first abandon the fountain of living waters, and then hew for themselves, here and there, cisterns which will hold no water. Here is a truth which the history of every Church teaches in its successive falls and errors, as well as that of every soul in particular. The theologians of Oxford only follow in the way of all flesh.

Behold, then, gentlemen, two established authorities by the side of each other—the Bible and Tradition. We do not hesitate as to what we have to do:

TO THE LAW AND TO THE TESTIMONY! We cry with the prophet: " If they speak not according to His word, it is because there is no light in them: and behold trouble and darkness, dimness of anguish; and they shall be driven to darkness." (Isa. viii. 20, 22.)

---

* Tract 85.   † Newman, Lecture on Romanism.
‡ Keble's Sermons.   § Palmer's Aids to Reflection.

We reject this Tradition as being a species of Rationalism which introduces, for a rule in Christian doctrine, not the human reason of the present time, but the human reason of the times past. We declare, with the Churches of the Reformation in their symbolical writings (Confessions of Faith), that " the Sacred Scriptures are the only judge, the only rule of Faith;" that it is to them, as to a touchstone, that all dogmas ought to be brought; that it is by them that the question should be decided, whether they are pious or impious, true or false?*

Without doubt there was originally an oral tradition which was pure; it was the instructions given by the Apostles themselves, before the sacred writings of the New Testament existed. However, even then, the apostle and the evangelist, Peter and Barnabas (Gal. ii. 13), could not walk uprightly, and consequently stumbled in their words. The divinely inspired Scriptures alone are infallible: the word of the Lord endureth for ever.

But, however pure was oral instruction, from the time that the apostles quitted the earth, that tradition was necessarily exposed in this world of sin, to be little by little defaced, polluted, corrupted. It is for this cause that the Evangelical Church honors and adores, with gratitude and humility, that gracious good pleasure of the Saviour, in virtue of which that pure, primitive type, that first, Apostolic tradition, in all its purity, has been rendered permanent, by being written, by the Spirit of God himself, in our sacred books, for all coming time. And now she finds in those writings, as we have just heard, the divine touchstone, which she employs for the purpose of trying all the traditions of men.

Nor does she establish concurrently, as do the doctors of Oxford and the Council of Trent, the tradition which is *written* and the tradition which is *oral;* but she decidedly renders the latter subordinate to the former, because one cannot be sure that this oral tradition is only and truly Apostolical tradition, such as it was in its primitive purity.

The knowledge of true Christianity, says the Protestant Church, flows only from one source, namely, from the Holy Scriptures, or, if you will, from the *Apostolic tradition*, such as we find it contained in the writings of the New Testament.

The Apostles of Jesus Christ—Peter, Paul, John, Matthew, James—perform their functions in the Church to-day; no one has need, no one has the power to take their place. They perform their functions at Jerusalem, at Geneva, at Corinth, at Berlin, at Paris; they bear testimony in Oxford and in Rome itself. They preach, even to the ends of the world, the remission of sins and conversion of the soul in the name of the Saviour; they announce the resurrection of the Crucified to every creature; they loose and they retain sins; they lay the foundation of the house of God and they build it; they teach the missionaries and the ministers of the Gospel; they regulate the order of the Church, and preside in Synods which would be Christian. They do all

* Formula of Agreement.

this by the *written* Word which they have left us. Or rather, Christ, Christ himself, does it by that Word, since it is the Word of Christ, rather than the word of Paul, of Peter, or of James. "Go ye, therefore, and teach all nations; lo! I am with you alway, even to the end of the world." (Matt. xxviii. 19, 20.)

Without doubt, as to the number of their words, the Apostles spoke more than they wrote; but as to the substance, they said nothing more than what they have left us in their divine books. And if they had taught by the mouth, as to the substance, differently or more explicitly than they did by their writings, no one could at this day be in a state to report to us with assurance, even one syllable of these instructions. If God did not wish to preserve them in His Bible, no one can come to His aid, and do what God himself has not wished to do, and what He has not done. If, in the writings more or less doubtful, of the companions of the Apostles, or of those Fathers who are called Apostolical, one should find any doctrines of the Apostles, it would be necessary first of all, to put it to the trial in comparing it with the certain instructions of the Apostles, that is with the Canon of the Scriptures.

So much for the tradition of the Apostles. Let us pass from the times when they lived to those which succeeded. Let us come to the tradition of the doctors of the first centuries. That tradition is, without doubt, of great value to us; but by the very fact of its being presbyterian, episcopal, or synodical, it is no more Apostolical. And let us suppose (what is not true) that it does not contradict itself; and let us suppose, that one Father does not overthrow what another Father has established (as is often the case, and Abelard has proved it in his famous work entitled *Sic et Non*, whose recent publication we owe to the care of a French philosopher);*—let us suppose for a moment, that one might reduce this tradition of the Fathers of the Church to a harmony similar to that which the Apostolical tradition presents, the canon which might be obtained thus could in no manner be placed on an equality with the canon of the Apostles.†

Without doubt,—and we acknowledge it,—the declarations of Christian doctors merit our attention, if it is the Holy Spirit which speaks in them, that Spirit ever living and ever acting in the Church. But we will not, we absolutely will not allow ourselves to be bound by that which, in this tradition and in these doctors, is only the work of man. And how shall we distinguish that which is of God from that which is of men, but by the Holy Scriptures? "It remains," says St. Augustine, "that I judge myself according to this only Master, from whose judgment I desire not to escape,"‡ The declarations of the doctors in the Church are only the testimonies of the faith which these eminent men had in the doctrines of the Scriptures. They see how these doctors received these doctrines;

* *Ouvrages inedites d'Abelard*, published by Mr. Victor Cousin. Paris, 1836. The Introduction of this work upon the history of Scholastic Philosophy in France, is a *chef-d'œuvre*.
† Nitzsch, Protestantische Theses.
‡ Retract. in Prol.

they may, without doubt, be instructive and edifying for us; but there is no authority in them which binds us. All the doctors, Greek, Latin, French, Swiss, German, English, American, placed in the presence of the Word of God, are altogether, only disciples who are receiving instruction. Men of the first times, men of the last, we are all alike upon the benches of that divine school; and in the chair of instruction, around which we are humbly assembled, nothing appears, nothing elevates itself, but the infallible Word of God. I perceive, in that vast auditory, Calvin, Luther, Cranmer, Augustine, Chrysostom, Athanasius, Cyprian, by the side of our contemporaries. We are not " disciples of Cyprian and Ignatius," as the doctors of Oxford* call themselves; but of Jesus Christ. " We do not despise the writings of the Fathers," we say with Calvin, " but in making use of them we remember always that ' all things are ours' (1 Cor. iii. 22); that they ought to serve, not govern us; and that ' we are Christ's,' (1 Cor. iii. 23), whom in all things, and without exception, it behooves us to obey."†

This the doctors of the first centuries are themselves the first to say. They claim for themselves no authority, and only wish that the Word which has taught them may teach us also. " Now that I am old," says Augustine, in his *Retractions*, " I do not expect not to stumble in word, or to be perfect in word: how much less when, being young, I commenced writing?"‡ " Beware," says he again, " of subjecting yourselves to my writings, as if they were Canonical Scriptures."§ " Do not esteem as Canonical Scriptures the works of Catholic and justly honored men," says he elsewhere. " It is allowed us, without impeaching that honor which is due to them, to reject those things in their writings, should we find such in them, which are contrary to the truth. I am, in regard to the writings of others, what I would have others be in regard to mine."‖ " All that has been said since the times of the Apostles ought to be retrenched," says Jerome, " and have no authority. However holy, however learned, a man may be, who comes after the Apostles, let him have no authority."¶

" Neither antiquity nor custom," says the Confession of the Reformed Church of France, " ought to be arrayed in opposition to the Holy Scriptures; on the contrary, all things ought to be examined, regulated and reformed according to them."

And the Confession of the English Church even says, the doctors of Oxford to the contrary notwithstanding: " The Holy Scriptures contain all that is necessary to salvation, so that all that is not found in them, all that cannot be proved by them, cannot be required of any one as an article of faith or as necessary to salvation."

Thus the Evangelical doctors of our times give the hand to the

---

* Newman on Romanism.   † Calv. Inst. Relig. Christ.
‡ Retractions.   § In Prol. de Trinitate.
‖ Ad Fortunatianum.   ¶ In Psalm. lxxxvi.

Reformers, the Reformers to the Fathers, the Fathers to the Apostles; and thus forming, as it were, a chain of gold, the whole Church of all ages and of all people, shouts forth as with one voice to the *God of Truth*, that hymn of one of our greatest poets :*

> Parle seul à mon cœur, et qu'aucune prudence,
> Qu'aucun autre Docteur ne m'explique tes lois;
> Que toute créature en ta sainte présence,
> S'impose le silence,
> Et laisse agir ta voix !†

What then is tradition? It is the testimony of History.

There is a historical testimony for the facts of a Christian history, as well as for those of any other history. We admit that testimony; only we would discuss it, and examine it, as we would all other testimony. The heresy of Rome and of Oxford,—and it is that which distinguishes them from us,—consists in the fact that they attribute infallibility to this testimony as to Scripture itself.

Although we receive the testimony of history in that which is true, as, for example, in that which relates to the collection of the writings of the Apostles; it by no means results from this that we should receive this testimony in that which is false, as, for instance, in the adoration of Mary, or the celibacy of the priests.

The Bible is the Faith, holy, authoritative, and truly ancient, of the child of God; human tradition springs from the love of novelties, and is the faith of ignorance, of superstition, and of a credulous puerility.

How deplorable but instructive, to see doctors of a Church called to the glorious liberty of the children of God, and which reposes only on God and his Word, place themselves under the bondage of human ordinances! And how loudly does that example cry to us : " Stand fast in the liberty wherewith Christ hath made us free, and be not entangled again with the yoke of bondage." (Gal. v. 1.)

All those errors which we are combating come from truths which have not been rightly understood. We also believe in the attributes of the Church of which they speak so much; but we believe in them according to the meaning which God attaches to it, and our opponents believe in them according to that which men attach to it.

Yes, there is *one holy* Catholic Church, but it is, as the Apostle says, " The general assembly and Church of the first-born, whose names are written in heaven" (Heb. xii, 23). *Unity* as well as *holiness* appertains to the invisible Church. It behooves us, without doubt, to pray that the visible Church should advance daily in the possession of these heavenly attributes; but neither rigorous unity nor universal holiness is a perfection essential to its existence, or a *sine quâ non*. To say that the visible Church must absolutely be composed of saints only, is the error of the Donatists and fanatics

---

* Corneille.
† Speak thou alone to my heart, and let no other wisdom, no other Doctor explain to me Thy laws; let every creature be silent in Thy holy presence, and let Thy voice speak!

of all ages. So also, to say that the visible Church must of necessity be externally one, is the corresponding error of Rome, of Oxford, and of formalists of all times. Let us guard against preferring the exterior hierarchy, which consists in certain human forms, to that interior hierarchy which is the kingdom of God itself Let us not permit that the form, which passes away, should determine the essence of the Church; but let us, on the contrary, make the essence of the Church, to wit, the Christian life—which emanates from the Word and Spirit of God—change and renew the form. *The form has killed the substance,*—here is the whole history of the Papacy and of false Catholicism. *The substance vivifies the form,*—here is the whole history of Evangelical Christianity, and of the true Catholic Church of Jesus Christ.

Yes, I admit it—The Church is the judge of controversies—*judex controversiarum*. But what is the Church? It is not the Clergy, it is not the Councils, still less is it the Pope. It is the Christian people, it is the faithful. " Prove all things, hold fast that which is good" (1 Thess. v. 21), is said to the children of God, and not to some assembly, or to a certain bishop; and it is they who are constituted, on the part of God, *judges of controversies.* If animals have the instinct which leads them not to eat that which is injurious to them, we cannot do less than allow to the Christian this instinct, or rather this intelligence, which emanates from the virtue of the Holy Spirit. Every Christian (the Word declares it) is called upon to reject " every spirit that confesses not that Jesus Christ is come in the flesh" (1 John iv. 1—5). And this is what is essentially meant, when it is said that the Church is the *judge of controversies!*

Yes, I believe and confess it,—there is an authority in the Church, and without authority the Church cannot stand. But where is it to be found? It is with him, whoever he may be, that has the external consecration, whether he possesses or not theological gifts, whether he has received or not grace and justification? Rome herself does not yet pretend that orders save and sanctify. Must then the children of God go, in many cases, to ask a decision in things relating to faith, of the children of this world? What! a bishop, from the moment he is seated in his chair, although he may be perhaps destitute of science, destitute of the Spirit of God, and although he may perhaps have the world and hell in his heart, as had Borgia and so many other bishops, shall he have authority in the assembly of the saints, and do his lips possess always the wisdom and the truth necessary for the Church? . . . , No, Gentlemen, the idea of a knowledge of God, true, but at the same time destitute of holiness, is a gross supernaturalism. " Sanctify them through the Truth" says Jesus (John xvii., 17). There is an authority in the Church, but that authority is wholly in the Word of God. It is not a man, not a minister, not a bishop, descended from Gregory, from Chrysostom, from Augustine, or from Irenæus, who has authority over the soul. It is not with a power so contemptible as that which comes from those men, that we, the ministers of God, go forth into the world. It is elsewhere than in that episcopal succession, that we seek that which gives authority to our ministry, and validity to our sacraments.

Rejecting these deplorable innovations, we appeal from them to the ancient, sovereign and divine authority of the Word of the Lord. The question which we ask of him who would inform himself concerning eternal things is that which we receive from Jesus himself: "What is written in the Law, and how readest thou?" (Luke x. 26.) That which we say to rebellious spirits is what Abraham said from heaven to the rich man; "You have Moses and the prophets, hear them." (Luke xvi. 29.)

That which we ask of all, is to imitate the Bereans who "searched the Scriptures daily, whether these things were so." (Acts xvii. 11.)

"We ought to obey God rather than men," even the most excellent of men. (Acts v. 29.)

Behold, the true authority, the true hierarchy, the true polity. The churches which men make possess human authority—this is natural. But the Church of God possesses the authority of God, and she will not receive it from others.

II.

Such is the *formal* principle of Christianity; let us come now to its *material* principle, that is to say, to that which is the body, the substance even, of religion. We have announced it in these terms:

THE GRACE OF CHRIST, ONLY.

"Ye are saved by grace, through faith," says the Scripture, "and that not of yourselves, it is the gift of God; not of works, lest any man should boast." (Eph. ii. 8.)

Evangelical Christianity not only seeks for complete salvation in Christ, but seeks it *in Christ only*, thus excluding, as a cause of salvation, all works of his own, all merit, all co-operation of man or of the Church. There is nothing, absolutely nothing, upon which we can build the hope of our salvation, but the *free and unmerited grace of God*, which is given to us *in Christ*, and communicated *by faith*.

Now, this second great foundation of Evangelical Christianity is equally overthrown by the modern Ecclesiastical Catholicism.

The famous Tract, No. 90, which I hold in my hand at this moment, seeks to explain in a papistical sense the Confession of Faith of the Church of England.

The 11th Article of this Confession says: "That we are justified by Faith only, is a most wholesome doctrine."

Behold the commentary of the new School of Oxford: "In adhering to the doctrine that faith alone justifies, we do not at all exclude the doctrine that works also justify. If it were said that works justify in the same sense in which it is said that faith alone justifies, there would be a contradiction in terms. But faith alone in one sense justifies us, and in another, good works justify us:

this is all that is here maintained! .... Christ alone, in one sense, justifies, faith also justifies in its proper sense; and so works, whether moral or ceremonial, may justify us in their respective sense."

"There are," says the *British Critic,* "some Catholic truths which are imprinted on the surface of the Scripture rather than enveloped in its profound meaning; such is the doctrine of justification by works." "The preaching of justification by Faith," says another doctor of this School, "ought to be addressed to Pagans by the *propagators* of Christian knowledge; its *promoters* ought to preach to baptized persons justification by works."—Works, yes: but justification by them, never!

Justification is not, according to these doctors, that judicial act by which God, for the sake of the expiatory death of Christ, declares that He treats us as righteous; it is confounded by them, as well as by Rome, with the work of the Holy Spirit.

"Justification," says again the chief of these doctors, "is a progressive work; it must be the work of the Holy Spirit and not of Christ. The distinction between deliverance from the guilt of sin and deliverance from sin itself, is not scriptural."* The *British Critic* calls the system of Justification by grace through faith "radically and fundamentally monstrous, immoral, heretical and anti-Christian." "The custom which has prevailed," say again these doctors, "of advancing, on all occasions, the doctrine of Justification explicitly and mainly, is evidently and entirely opposed to the teaching of the Holy Scriptures."† And they condemn those who make "Justification to consist in the act by which the soul rests upon the merits of Christ only."‡

I know that the doctors of Oxford pretend to have found here a middle term between the Evangelical doctrine and the Romish doctrine. "It is not," say they, "Sanctification which justifies us, but the presence of God in us, from which this Sanctification flows. Our Justification is the possession of this presence." But the doctrine of Oxford is at bottom the same with that of Rome. The Bible speaks to us of two great works of Christ: CHRIST FOR US, AND CHRIST IN US. Which of these two works is that which justifies us? The Church of Christ answers: The first. Rome and Oxford answer: The second. When this is said, all is said.

And these doctors do not conceal it. They inform us that it is the system against which they stand up. They declare to us that it is against the idea, that, when the sinner "has by faith laid hold of the saving merits of Christ, his sins are blotted out, covered, and cannot re-appear; his guilt has been abolished, so that he has only to render thanks to Christ, who has delivered him from his transgressions."—"My Lord," says Dr. Pusey to the Bishop of Oxford, "it is against this system that I have spoken"——Stop! Do not tear to pieces this Good News, which alone has been, and will be in all ages, the consolation of the sinner!

Gentlemen, if the first principle of this new School had for effect

---

* Newman on Justification. † Tract, 80.
‡ Newman on Justification.

to deprive the Church of all light, this second principle would have for its end to deprive her of all salvation. "If righteousness come by the law, then Christ is dead in vain. O foolish Galatians, who hath bewitched you, that ye should not obey the truth: receive ye the Spirit by the works of the law, or by the hearing of faith!". (Gal. ii. 21, iii. 2, 3.)

Men the most eminent for piety, have felt that it is the source even of the Christian life, the foundation of the Church, which is here attacked: "there is reason," says the excellent Bishop of Winchester, who, as well as several other Bishops, and particularly those of Chester and Calcutta, has denounced these errors, in a Charge addressed to his clergy, "there is reason to fear that the distinctive principles of our Church would be endangered, if men should envelope in a cloud the great doctrine which sets forth the way in which we are accounted righteous before God; if men doubt that the Protestant doctrine of Justification by faith is fundamental; if, instead of the sacrifice of Christ, the pure and only cause for which we are graciously received, men establish a certain inherent disposition of sanctification, and thus confound the work of the Spirit within with the work of Christ without."

The School of Oxford pretends, with Rome and the Council of Trent, "that justification is the indwelling in us, of God the Father and of the incarnate Word, by the Holy Spirit, and that the two acts distinguished from each other by the Bible and our theologians form only one."*—What then?

God, 1. remits to the sinner the penalty of sin; he absolves him; he pardons him; 2. he delivers him from sin itself; he renews him; he sanctifies him.

Are there not here two things?

The pardon of sin on the part of God, would it not be just nothing at all? Would it not be simply but an image of sanctification? Or should one say that the pardon which is granted to faith, and which produces in the heart the sentiment of reconciliation, of adoption, and of peace, is something too external to be taken into the account?

"The Lutheran system," says the *British Critic*, "is immoral, because it distinguishes these two works." Without doubt, it does distinguish them, but it does not separate them. "See wherefore we are justified," says Melancthon, in the Apology for the Confession of Augsburg; "it is in order that being righteous we should do good, and begin to obey the law of God; see here why it is that we are regenerated and receive the Holy Spirit; it is that the new life may have new works, and new dispositions." How many times has not the Reformation declared that justifying faith is not an historical, dead, vain knowledge, but a living action, a willing and a receiving, a work of the Holy Spirit, the true worship of God, obedience towards God in the most important of all moments. Yes, it is a living, efficacious faith which justifies; and these words *efficacious faith*—which are found in all our Confessions of Faith—are there for the purpose of declaring that faith

* Letter of Dr. Pusey to the Bishop of Oxford.

alone, without doubt, serves as a cause in the work of justification, that *alone*, without doubt, it justifies, but that precisely because of this it does not rest *alone*, that is to say, without its appropriate operations and its fruits.

Behold, the grand difference between us and the Oxford School. We believe in sanctification through justification, and the Oxford School believes in justification through sanctification. With us, justification is the cause and sanctification is the effect. With these doctors, on the contrary, sanctification is the cause, and justification the effect. And here are not things indifferent, and vain distinctions; it is the *sic* and the *non*, the yes and the no. Whilst our creed establishes in all their rights these two works, the creed of Oxford compromises and annihilates both. Justification exists no more, if it depend on man's sanctification, and not on the grace of God; for "the heavens," says the Scripture, "are not clean in his sight" (Job xv. 15), "and his eyes are too pure to behold iniquity" (Hab. i. 13); but on the other hand sanctification itself cannot be accomplished; for how could you expect the effect to be produced when you begin by taking away the cause? "Herein is love," says St. John, "not that we loved God, but that He loved us; we love Him because he first loved us." (1 John iv. 10, 19.) If I might use a vulgar expression, I should say that Oxford *puts the cart before the horse*, in placing sanctification before justification. In this way neither the cart nor the horse will advance. In order that the work should go on, it is necessary that that which draws should be placed before that which is drawn. There is not a system more contrary to true sanctification than that; and, to employ the language of the *British Critic*, there is not, consequently, a system more monstrous and immoral. What! your justification, shall it not depend upon the work which Christ accomplished on the cross, but upon that which is accomplished in your hearts! It is not to Christ, to his grace, that you ought to look in order to be justified, but to yourselves, to the righteousness which is in you, to your spiritual gifts!....

From this result two great evils.

Either you will deceive yourselves, in believing that there is a work in you sufficiently good to justify you before God; and then you will be inflated with pride, that pride which the Scriptures say, "goeth before a fall." Or you will not deceive yourselves; you will see, as the Saviour says, that you are poor, and wretched, and blind, and naked; and then you will fall into despair. The heights of pride and the depths of despair, these are the alternatives which the doctrine of Oxford and of Rome bequeathes us.

The Christian doctrine, on the contrary, places man in perfect humility, for it is Another who justifies him; and yet it gives him abundant peace, for his justification,—a fruit of the righteousness of God" (2 Cor. v. 21)—is complete, assured, eternal.

III.

Finally, we indicate the *personal* or *moral* principle of Christianity. We have announced it in these words:—

THE WORK OF THE SPIRIT ONLY.

Christianity is an individual work; the grace of God converts soul after soul. Each soul is a world, in which a creation peculiar to itself must be accomplished. The Church is but the assemblage of all the souls in whom this work is wrought, and who are now united because they have but "one Spirit, one Lord, one Father."

And what is the nature of this work? It is essentially moral. Christianity operates upon the will of man and changes it. Conversion comes from the action of the Spirit of God, and not from the magic action of certain ceremonies, which, rendering faith on the part of man vain and useless, would regenerate him by their own inherent virtue. "In Christ Jesus neither circumcision availeth anything, nor uncircumcision, but [to be] a new creature" (Gal. vi. 15). "If through the Spirit ye do mortify the deeds of the body, ye shall live" (Rom. viii. 13).

Now the doctors of Oxford, although there is a great difference among them on this point, as well as on some others—some going by no means as far as others—put immense obstacles in the way of this individual regeneration.

Nothing inspires them with greater repugnance than Christian individualism. They proceed by synthesis, not by analysis. They do not set out with the principle laid down by the Saviour, "except a man be born again, he cannot see the kingdom of God;" but they set out with this opposite principle: "all those who have participated in the ordinances of the Church are born again." And whilst the Saviour in all his discourses excites the efforts of each individual, saying: "Seek, ask, knock, strive to enter in at the strait gate; it is only the violent who take it by force;" the Oxford doctors say, on the contrary: "The idea of obtaining religious truth ourselves, and by our private inquiry, whether by reading, or by thinking, or by studying the Scriptures or other books, ... is nowhere commanded in the Scriptures. The great question which ought to be placed before every mind is this: What voice should be heard like that of the holy Catholic and Apostolic Church?"*

And this individual regeneration by the Holy Spirit, how shall it be accomplished, since the first task of Puseyism is to say to all, that it is already accomplished; that all who have been baptized have thereby been rendered partakers of the divine nature; and that to preach conversion again to them is contrary to the truth? "It is baptism and not faith," says one of these doctors, "that is the primary instrument of justification;"† and we know that with

---

* British Critic.   † Newman on Justification.

them justification and conversion are one and the same work. To prevent the wretched from escaping from the miserable state in which they are, would not be the best means to persuade a poor man that he possesses a large fortune, or an ignorant man that he has great science, or a sick man that he is in perfect health. The Evil One could not invent a stratagem more fit to prevent conversion, than this idea that all men who have been baptized by water are regenerated.

Still more, these doctors extend to the holy Supper this same magic virtue. " It is now almost universally believed," say they, in speaking of their Church, " that God communicates grace only through faith, prayer, spiritual contemplation, communion with God; whilst it is the Church and her sacraments which are *the* ordained, direct, visible means for conveying to the soul that which is invisible and supernatural It is said, for example, that to administer the Supper to infants, to dying persons apparently deprived of their senses, however pious they may have been, is a superstition; and yet these practices are sanctioned by antiquity. The essence of the sectarian doctrine is to consider *faith*, and not the *sacraments*, as the means of justification and other evangelical gifts."*

What then, a child which does not possess reason and which does not know even how to speak, a sick man whom the approach of death has deprived of perception and intelligence, shall they receive grace purely by the external application of the sacraments? The will, the affections of the heart, have they no need to be touched in order that man may be sanctified? What a degradation of man and of the religion of Jesus Christ! Is there a great difference between such ceremonies and the mummeries and charms of the debased Hindoos or of the African savages!

If the first error of Oxford deprives the Church of light, if the second deprives her of salvation, the third deprives her of all real sanctification. Without doubt, we believe the sacraments are means of grace; but they are only so when faith accompanies their use. To put faith and the sacraments in opposition, as the Oxford doctors do, is to annihilate the efficacy of the sacraments themselves.

The Church will rise up against such fatal errors. There is a work of renovation which must be wrought in man, a personal or individual work; and it is God who performs it. "A new heart," saith the Lord, will I give you, and a new spirit will I put within you." (Ez. xxxvi. 26.)

By what right would they thus put the Church in the place of God, and establish her clergy as the dispensers of divine life?

Then it would be of little consequence that a man had led a dissipated life, and that the heart remains attached to sin and the world; would not a participation in the sacraments of religion suffice to put him in possession of grace? We are assured that already sad consequences are manifested in the life of many of the adherents of Oxford.

* Tracts for the Times. Advertisement in Vol. ii.

The system of Puseyism tends to lull the conscience to sleep, by the participation of external rites: the Evangelical system tends to awaken it without cessation. The work of the Spirit, which is one of the grand principles of Evangelical Christianity, does not consist only in regeneration; it consists also in a sanctification, fundamental and universal. If, instead of permitting ourselves to be enfeebled by trusting to human ordinances, we have truly the *Spirit of Christ* within us, we shall not suffer the least contradiction to exist between the divine law on the one hand, and our dispositions and actions on the other. We shall not content ourselves with abstaining from the grosser manifestations of sin, but we shall desire that the very germ of evil be eradicated from our hearts. We shall love the Truth, and we shall reject with horror that sad hypocrisy which sometimes defiles the sanctuary. We shall not have in the communication of our religious convictions that reserve which Puseyism prescribes: " that which shall have been told to us in the ear, we shall proclaim on the housetops." (Matth. x. 27.) We shall not remain in a Church whose most sacred truths we trample under our feet, eating the bread which she gives us and lifting up the arm to strike her. From the moment that we shall have discovered that a doctrine is opposed to the word of God, neither dangers nor sacrifices shall prevent us from casting it far from us. The work of the Spirit will carry light into the most secret recesses of our hearts. " The King's daughter is all glorious within." (Ps. xlv. 13.) The King whom we follow has said to us: " I am the light of the world: he that followeth me shall not walk in darkness, but shall have the light of life." (John viii. 12.)

I repeat again in closing, Gentlemen, the three great principles of Christianity are these:

The Word of God, ONLY.
The Grace of God, ONLY.
The Work of the Spirit, ONLY.

I come now to ask you to apply to yourselves henceforth more and more these principles, and let them reign supremely over your hearts and lives.

And why, Gentlemen? Because everything that places our souls in immediate communication with God is salutary; and everything that interposes between God and our souls is injurious and ruinous. If a thick cloud should pass between you and the sun you would no longer feel its genial warmth, and might perhaps be seized with a chill. So if you place between yourselves and the Word of God the tradition and authority of the Church, you will no longer have to do with the Word of God; that is to say, with a divine, and consequently a powerful and perfect instrument; but with the word of man; that is to say, with a human, and consequently a weak and defective instrument, it will have lost that power which translates from darkness into light.

Or, if you place between the grace of God and yourselves the ordinances of the Church, the episcopal priesthood, the dispositions of the heart, works, *grace will then be no more grace*, as St. Paul says. The instrument of God will have been broken, and we shall no longer be able to say, that " charity proceeds from faith unfeigned" (1 Tim. i.); that "faith worketh by love," (Gal v.); "that our souls are purified in obeying the truth" (1 Cor. i.); "that Christ dwells in our hearts by faith" (Eph. iii).

Man always seeks to return, in some way, to a human salvation; this is the source of the innovations of Rome and of Oxford. The substitution of the Church for Jesus Christ is that which essentially characterizes these opinions. It is no longer Christ who enlightens, Christ who saves, Christ who forgives, Christ who commands, Christ who judges; it is the Church and always the Church, that is to say, an assembly of sinful men, as weak and prone to err as ourselves. "They have taken away the Lord, and we know not where they have laid him" (John xx. 2).

The errors which we have indicated are, therefore, practical errors, destructive of true piety in the soul, a deprivation of God's influence, and an exaltation of the flesh, although in a form that "has the show of wisdom in will-worship and humility" (Col. ii. 23). If they should ever obtain the ascendency in the Church, Christianity would cease to be a new, a holy, a spiritual, a heavenly life. It would become an external affair of ordinances, rites and ceremonies. This has been clearly seen by the servant of God, whom we have already quoted: "Finally," says Sumner, Bishop of Winchester, "I cannot but fear the consequences that a system of teaching, which confines itself to the external and ritual parts of divine worship, while it loses sight of their internal signification and the spiritual life, may have upon the character, the efficacy and the truth of our Church; a system, which robs the Church of its brightest glory, and, forgetting the continual presence of the Lord, seems to depose him from his just pre-eminence; a system, which tends to put the observance of days, months, times and seasons, in the place of a true and spiritual worship; which substitutes a spirit of hesitation, fear and doubt, for the cordial obedience of filial love; a slavish spirit for the liberty of the Gospel; and which, indeed, calls upon us to work out our sanctification with fear and trembling; but without any foretaste of the rest that remaineth for the people of God, without giving us joy in believing."[*]

The universal Church of Christ rejoices to hear such words. She beholds, with gratitude towards her divine Head, the firmness with which some bishops, ministers, and laymen of England meet this growing evil. But is this enough? Is it enough to retain, on the edge of a precipice, a Church and a people, hitherto so dear to the friends of the Gospel?

Oxford conducts to Rome; Mr. Sibthorp and others have proved it. The march of Puseyism regularly inclining, from Tract to

[*] Charge delivered by Ch. R. Sumner, D.D., Lord Bishop of Winchester, 1841.

Tract, towards the pure system of the Papacy, demonstrates clearly enough the end to which it tends. And even if it should not effect a total conversion to Popery—what signifies it, since it is nothing else than the Popish system (in its essential features) transferred to England? It is not necessary that the Thames should go to Rome to bear the tribute of its waters: the Tiber flows in Oxford.

England owes everything to the Reformation. What was she before the renovation of the Church? Blindly submissive to the Tudors, her forms of government, both political and ecclesiastical, were superannuated, without life and spirit; so that in England, as in almost all Europe, we might say, with a Christian statesman, that, " despotism seemed the only preservative against dissolution."* The Reformation developed, in an admirable manner, that Christian spirit, that love of liberty, that fear of God, that loyal affection for the sovereign, that patriotism, those generous sacrifices, that genius, that strength, that activity, which constitute the prosperity and glory of England. In the age of the Reformation, Catholic Spain, gorged with the blood of the children of God, fell, overthrown by the Almighty Arm, and reformed England ascended, in her stead, the throne of the seas, which has been justly termed the throne of the world. The winds which engulphed the *Armada* called up this new power from the depths.

The country of Philip II., wounded to the heart because she had attacked the people of God, dropped from her hand the sceptre of the ocean; and the country of Elizabeth, fortified by the Word of God, found it floating on the seas, seized it, and wielded it to bring into subjection to the King of Heaven the nations of the earth. It is the Gospel that has given to England our antipodes.† It is the God of the Gospel who has bestowed upon her all that she possesses. If in those distinguished islands the Gospel were to fall under the united attacks of Popery and Puseyism, we might write upon their hitherto triumphant banner: " ICHABOD, *the glory of the Lord has departed.*"

God has given the dominion of the seas to the nations who bear, everywhere, with them the Gospel of Jesus Christ. But if, instead of the Good News of Salvation, England carries to the heathen a mere human and priestly religion, God will deprive her of her power. The evil is already great. In India the Puseyite missionaries are satisfied with teaching the natives rites and ceremonies, without troubling themselves about the conversion of the heart; thus treading closely in the steps of the Roman Catholic Church. They endeavor to counteract the efforts of evangelical missionaries, and disturb the weak minds of the natives, by telling them that all those who have not received Episcopal ordination are not ministers.

If England prove unfaithful to the Gospel, God will humble her

---

* Archives of the House of Orange-Nassau, published at the Hague, by Mr. Groen Van Prinsterer, Counsellor of State.
† New Zealand.

in those powerful islands where she has established her throne, and in those distant countries subjected to her sway. Do we not already hear a faint rumor, which justifies these gloomy presentiments? The mother country sees her difficulties increase; unheard of disasters have spread fear and terror on the banks of the Indus. From the chariot of this people is heard a cracking noise, because impious hands have changed the pole-bolt. Should England forsake the faith of the Bible, the crown would fall from her head. Ah! We also, Christians of the continent and of the world, would mourn over her fall! We love her for Christ's sake; for His sake we pray for her. But if the apostasy, now begun, should be accomplished, we shall have nothing left for her but cries, groans and tears.

What are the Bishops doing? What is the Church doing? This is the general question.

If the Church of England were well administered, she would only admit to her pulpits teachers who submit to the Word of God, agreeably to the Thirty-nine Articles, and banish from them all those who violate her laws, and poison the minds of the youth, trouble souls, and seek to overthrow the Gospel of Jesus Christ.

A few Episcopal mandates will not accomplish this. We undoubtedly believe that no power can take from the Christian the right to " examine the Scriptures, and to try the spirits whether they are of God." But we do not believe in the supreme power of the Clergy: We do not believe that the servants of a church may announce to it doctrines which tend to overthrow it. Did it not please the Apostles, the elders, and the whole church, to impose silence upon those at Antioch, who wished to substitute, as they do now at Oxford, human ordinances for the grace of Christ? (Acts xv. 22.) Since when, does a well constituted Church speak only through isolated voices? Shall the Annual Convocations of the Church of England remain always a vain ceremony and an empty form? If their nature cannot be changed, shall not powerful remedies be applied to counteract great evils? Will not the Church be moved in England, as formerly at Jerusalem? Shall not the " elders and the whole Church" (Acts xv. 22) form a Council which shall, as tradition tells us they did at Nice, place the Word of God upon an elevated throne, in token of its supreme authority, and, condemning and cutting off all dangerous errors, render to Jesus Christ and his Word that sovereign authority, which usurping hands are on the point of wresting from Him?

But if the Church still holds her peace, if she allows her sacred foundations to be sapped in her Universities, then (we say it with profound grief) a voice like that of the prophet will be heard exclaiming: Woe to the Church! woe to the people! woe to England!

Gentlemen, there are two ways of destroying Christianity; one is to deny it, the other to displace it. To put the Church above Christianity, the hierarchy above the Word of God; to ask a man, not whether he has received the Holy Ghost, but whether he has received baptism from the hands of those who are termed successors of the Apostles, and their delegates,—all this may doubtless flatter the pride of the natural man, but is fundamentally opposed to the Bible, and aims a fatal blow at the religion of Jesus Christ. If God had intended that Christianity should, like the Mosaic system, be chiefly an ecclesiastical, sacerdotal and hierarchical system, he would have ordered it and established it in the New Testament, as he did in the Old. But there is nothing like this in the New Testament. All the declarations of our Lord and his Apostles tend to prove, that the new religion given to the world is "life and Spirit," and not a new system of priesthood and ordinances. "The kingdom of God," saith Jesus, "cometh not with observation: neither shall they say, lo here! or lo there! for behold the kingdom of God is within you" (Luke xvii. 20, 21). "The kingdom of God is not meat and drink; but righteousness and peace and joy in the Holy Ghost" (Rom. xiv. 17).

Let us then attribute a divine institution and a divine authority to the essence of the Church; but by no means to its *form*. God has undoubtedly established the ministry of the Word and sacraments, that is to say, general forms, which are adapted to the universal Church; but it is a narrow and dangerous bigotry, which would attribute more importance to the particular forms of each sect, than to the spirit of Christianity. This evil has long prevailed in the Eastern Church [Greek], and has rendered it barren. It is the essence of the Church of Rome, and it is destroying it. It is endeavoring to insinuate itself into every Church; it appears in England in the Established Church; in Germany in the Lutheran, and even in the Reformed and Presbyterian Church. It is that mystery of iniquity, which already began to work in the time of the Apostles. (2 Thess. ii. 7.) Let us reject and oppose this deadly principle wherever it is found. We are men before we are Swiss, French, English, or German; let us also remember that we are Christians before we are Episcopalians, Lutherans, Reformed, or Dissenters. These different forms of the Church are like the different costumes, different features, and different characters of nations; that which constitutes the man is not found in these accessories. We must seek for it in the heart which beats under this exterior, in the conscience which is seated there, in the intelligence which there shines, in the will which there acts. If we assign more importance to the Church than to Christianity, to the form than to the life, we shall infallibly reap that which we have sown; we shall soon have a Church composed of skeletons, clothed it may be in brilliant garments, and ranged, I admit, in a most imposing order to the eye; but as cold, stiff, and immoveable as a pale legion of the dead. If Puseyism (and, unfortunately, some of the doctrines which it promulgates are not, in England, confined to that school), if Puseyism should make progress in the Established Church, it will, in a few years, dry up all its springs of life. The feverish excitement which disease at first produces, will soon give way to languor, the blood will be congealed, the muscles stiffened, and that Church will be only a dead body, around which the eagles will gather together.

All forms, whether papal, patriarchal, episcopal, consistorial, or presbyterian, possess only a human value and authority. Let us not esteem the bark above the sap, the body above the soul, the form above the life, the visible Church above the invisible, the priest above the Holy Spirit. Let us hate all sectarian, ecclesiastical, national or dissenting spirit; but let us love Jesus Christ in all sects, whether ecclesiastical, national or dissenting. The true catholicity which we have lost, and which we must seek to recover, is that of " holding the Truth, in love." A renovation of the Church is necessary; I know it, I feel it, I pray for it from the bottom of my soul. Only let us seek for it in the right way. Forms, ecclesiastical constitutions, the organization of Churches, are important,—very important. " But let us seek first the kingdom of God and His righteousness, and all these things will be added unto us." (Matt. vi. 33.)

Let us then, Gentlemen, be firm and decided in the Truth; and while we love the erring, let us boldly attack the error. Let us stand upon the rock of ages,—the Word of God; and let the vain opinions, and stale innovations, which are constantly springing up and dying in the world, break powerless at our feet. " Two systems of doctrine," says Dr. Pusey, " have now, and, probably, for the last time, met in conflict; the system of Geneva and the Catholic system." We accept this definition. One of the men who have most powerfully resisted these errors, the Rev. W. Goode, seems to think that by the Genevan system, Dr. Pusey intends to designate the Unitarian, Pelagian, latitudinarian system, which has laid waste the Church, not only in Geneva, but throughout Christendom. " According to Romish tactics," says Mr. Goode, " the adversaries of the Oxford School are classed together under the name that will render them most odious; they belong, it is said, to the *Genevan School*.*

Certainly, Gentlemen, if the Unitarian School of England and Geneva were called upon to struggle with the semi-Papal School of Oxford, we should much fear the issue. But these divines will meet with other opponents in England, Scotland and Ireland, on the continent, and if need be, even in our little and humble Geneva.

Yes, we agree to it; it is the system of Geneva, which is now struggling with the Catholic system; but it is the system of the ancient Geneva; it is the system of Calvin and Beza, the system of the Gospel and the Reformation. The opprobrium they would cast upon us we receive as an honor; three centuries ago Geneva rose against Rome; let Geneva now rise against Oxford.

" I should like," says one of the Oxford doctors,† " to see the

---

* The Case as it is.

† W. Palmer's Aids to Reflection, 1841. This work contains some curious, and, without doubt, authentic conversations, which Mr. Palmer had at Geneva, in 1836, with different pastors and professors of the Academy and the Company. "*July* 26. The public professor of Dogmatic Theology told me, when I asked him what was the precise doctrine of the

Patriarch of Constantinople and our Archbishop of Canterbury go barefoot to Rome, throw their arms round the Pope, kiss him, and not let him go, till they had persuaded him to be more reasonable;" that is to say, doubtless, until he had extended his hand to them, and ceased to proclaim them heretics and schismatics.

Evangelical Christians of Geneva, England, and all other countries! It is not to Rome that you must drag yourselves, "to those seven mountains, on which the woman sitteth, having a golden cup in her hand, full of abominations" (Rev. xvii.); the pilgrimage that you must make is to that excellent and perfect tabernacle, "not made with hands" (Heb. ix.); that "throne of grace, where we find grace to help in time of need." (Heb. iv.)

It is not upon the neck of the "Man of Sin," that you must cast yourselves, covering him with your kisses and your tears; but upon the neck of Him with whom "Jacob wrestled, until the breaking of the day" (Gen. xxxii.); of Him "who is seated at the right hand of God in the heavenly places, far above all principality, and power, and every name that is named, not only in this world; but also in that which is to come." (Eph. v.)

Yes, let the children of God in the East and in the West arise, let them, understanding the signs of the times, and seeing that the destinies of the Church depend upon the issue of the present conflicts, conflicts so numerous, so different, and so powerful, for a sacred brotherhood, and with one heart, and one soul, exclaim, as Moses did when the ark set forward, "Rise up, Lord, and let thine enemies be scattered, and let them that hate Thee flee before Thee." (Num. x. 35.)

Company of Pastors at that time, on the subject of the Trinity, "Perhaps no two had exactly the same shade of opinion, that the great majority would deny the doctrine in the scholastic sense."—*August* 4. A pastor of the Company told me, "that of thirty-four members, he thinks there are only four who would admit the doctrine of the Trinity." The author was almost as much dissatisfied with the Evangelical as with the Unitarian ministers. He relates that one of the former said to him, on the 12th of August; "You are lost in the study of outward forms, mere worldly vanities: *You are a baby, a mere baby*, he said-in English."

THE END.

The Puritans and their Principles.

BY REV. EDWIN HALL.

PUBLISHED BY BAKER & SCRIBNER, 145 NASSAU STREET.

OPINIONS OF THE PRESS.

From the New York Observer.

THE PURITANS AND THEIR PRINCIPLES. By Edwin Hall. New York: Baker & Scribner. 1846.

Mr. Hall is the able pastor of the Congregational Church, in Norwalk, Ct. He writes with vigor, and in the midst of all his disquisitions, does not fail to sustain the interest of the reader. The work before us is the fruit of much research and thought, and will stand, in our opinion, as a noble defence of the character and principles of men' whose monument is civil and religious *liberty in the earth.*

This volume is richly worthy of a place in the library of every college, and of every man who wishes to understand the true greatness of the Puritans. We presume that it will be very generally sought after and extensively read.

From the N. Y. Evening Express.

They set forth the causes which brought the Pilgrims to these shores, their principles, and vindicate them from the aspersions which have been cast upon them. The subject is one of the greatest interest to any person who has any desire to know the history of his own country, and to be acquainted with the principles and sufferings of the most remarkable men that ever reached this continent.

From the N. Y. Tribune.

This is an interesting work for all who in our day adhere to the principles of the Puritans, or rejoice in a descent from the noble stock who were the champions of Freedom two centuries ago.

From the New Haven Courier.

The design of the work is to set forth the causes which brought the *Pilgrims* to these shores; to exhibit their *principles;* to show what these principles are worth, and what it cost to maintain them; to vindicate the character of the Puritans from the aspersions which have been cast upon them, and to show the PURITANIC SYSTEM OF CHURCH POLITY,—as distinguished from the Prelatic,—broadly and solidly based on the word of God; inseparable from religious Purity and Religious Freedom; and of immense permanent importance to the best interests of mankind.

The publication is intended to bring together such historical information concerning the Puritans, as is now scattered through many volumes, and cannot be obtained but with much labor and research, and an outlay beyond the means of ordinary readers.

From the N. Y. Commercial Advertiser.

The author enters with considerable minuteness into English ecclesiastical history prior to the persecutions of the Puritans, reviews the events which more immediately led to their emigration to this country, traces the effects of that step on the institutions and religious character of the people of both continents, and then enters into an analysis of both prelatical and Puritanical church polity, and warmly and eloquently defends the latter. The style of the work is vigorous and clothes a subject on which much has been already written with new attractions, combining succinctness of historical detail with elegance of diction.

From the N. Y. Courier & Enquirer.

Puritans and their Principles is the title of a very handsome octavo volume, by EDWIN HALL, which has just been published by Messrs. Baker & Scribner, at 145 Nassau street. Its purpose is to enable the public to judge concerning the character and history of the Puritans, which, as he contends, are now so perseveringly and so violently assailed; and he has discharged the laborious task with great zeal and ability. He says the utmost pains have been taken to caricature the principles, and to blacken the history of the Puritans; and as an evidence of this he cites the fact that very many persons at the present day believe that the famous code entitled the "*Blue Laws* of Connecticut," once actually had a place among the statutes of that colony;—whereas, in point of fact, they were the work of a Tory clergyman, and written expressly to blacken the character of the rebel colonists.

The volume exhibits proof of the industry and zeal of the author, no less than of his ability and devotion to the principles in defence of which he writes. As to the correctness of these principles, of course, we are not called upon to pronounce any judgment; but all who are interested in the subject, as indeed nearly all intelligent persons must of necessity be, may rely upon finding in this volume much matter, of fact and of argument, that will essentially guide their investigations.

The work is printed in very handsome style, and reflects great credit upon the newly established house by which it is published.

From the New England Puritan.

This is a neatly printed octavo, of between 400 and 500 pages, from the pen of one who has proved himself a master of his subject. It gives the history of the Puritans, embracing the most of its material and interesting facts; and also makes these facts subserve a defence of the character and principles of our ancestors. The work is ably and thoroughly executed, and it ought to furnish a part of the library of every descendant of the Puritans.

From the N. Y. Christian Intelligencer.

This is a beautiful octavo, of over 400 pp., handsomely printed. As it has but just reached us, we have given it, as yet, only a cursory examination. We regard it as a very valuable book. It contains a large amount of important historical matter, in a condensed form; precious under all circumstances, but especially useful in our times, when both Scripture and history are studiously distorted to prove the inventions of men superior in excellence to the institutions of God.

The book shows the causes which brought the Pilgrims to our shores; exhibits their principles; vindicates their character from unjust aspersions; and states their system of church polity, as distinguished from Prelacy. It enters into the history of the Puritans and their times; traces their progress from the discovery of one important principle to another; exhibits them in their sufferings, wanderings, and landing on the margin of this wilderness. The claims of Prelacy the author subjects to the severe test of the Bible, reason and history. It treats historically of England, before the times of Wickliffe; of Wickliffe and his times; of the reign of Henry VIII.; of Edward, Mary and Elizabeth; of the conflict of principle; of Puritan sufferings; of the judicious Hooker; of James I, and the going to Holland; of the voyage to America; of the Pilgrims at Plymouth; of the storm gathering in England; Charles I.; Archbishop Laud; founding of the Puritan churches; rise of the civil war; the Rule and Judge of Faith; on the alleged right to impose liturgies and ceremonies; on schism; the Church, its officers, discipline; Episcopacy; Apostolic succession, &c.,

From the Presbyterian.

The author presents, in his advertisement, a summary of his designs in this publication, which are " to set forth the causes which brought the Pilgrims to these shores; to exhibit their principles; to show what these principles are worth, and what it cost to maintain them; to vindicate the character of the Puritans from the aspersions which have been cast upon them, and to show the Puritanic system of church polity, as distinguished from the Prelatic." All this is accomplished with both zeal and knowledge, and the whole narrative, extending back to the early times of the Puritans, and embracing a most important period of ecclesiastical history, is full of absorbing interest, not merely to the descendants of the Pilgrims, but to every American Christian. We have met with no work, which, to our mind, presents so satisfactory, and yet succinct a history of the times and events to which it refers.

From the N. Y. Baptist Recorder.

The work of Mr. Hall was undertaken *con amore*,—his love of the Puritans is deep and unbounded. He has collected his facts from an extended course of reading, and expressed his thoughts in a style which, if not brilliant, is lucid and earnest. We hail with much pleasure all such contributions to our Historical Literature. We hope those who have read Dr. Coit will read Mr. Hall. Their conclusion will be that though the Puritans were mortal, and are justly chargeable with many inconsistencies and errors, they were still a noble race, the trace of whose influence is found in the best institutions of the world.

From the N. Y. Evening Post.

The object of the work, as he states in the preface, is to set forth the causes which led the Pilgrims to establish themselves on this continent, to exhibit the nature and value of their principles, and show the sacrifices at which they were maintained, to defend their character against the attacks levelled against it, and to vindicate the puritanic system of Church Polity.

The work is not historical merely, but in a good measure controversial, and the author wields the weapons of controversy with no little dexterity and vigor. The Puritans were a class of peculiarly strong and decided character—a character which impressed itself upon the age in which they arose, and the influence of which yet survives. The author is a warm admirer of this class, and defends their memory with zeal. He takes occasion to discuss the claims of prelacy at much length, not only in its historical but in its other aspects. We have no doubt that the work will be favorably received by the large religious denomination to which the author belongs.

From the Albany American Citizen.

We cannot forbear to express our conviction that it is a work of great merit, and has no common claims, especially upon the regard of those who have the blood of the Puritans flowing in their veins. Its historical details evince the most diligent research, and its vigorous and masterly discussion of important principles, shows a judicious, discriminating, and thoroughly trained mind. As the subjects of which it treats, have, to a great extent, a controversial bearing, it cannot be expected, that all will judge in the same manner of the merits of the book, but we think all who possess ordinary candor must agree that it is written with no common ability, and contains a great amount of useful information.

From the Hartford Christian Secretary.

After an Introduction, containing a glance at the condition of England before the days of Wickliffe, we are presented with a history of Wickliffe and his times, the reign of Henry VIII., and the rise of the Puritans, from whence we trace them in their conflicts, visit them in their prisons, follow them in their wanderings, and come with them to their first rude dwellings in the American wilderness. We behold the foundation here rising under their hands, until the wilderness became transformed into a fair and fruitful field. The principles of these noble men are exhibited and explained. The matter of Church Polity is discussed, and the claims of Prelacy are brought to the test of reason, of history, and of the word of God.

From the Christian Intelligencer.

We venerate the character and the principles of the Puritans of New England. Their history we have long since regarded as one of the most important triumphs of conscience and truth our world has seen. Our country will never cease to feel the blessed influence of their faith and principles; and we rejoice in the conviction, which is more and more confirmed by every year's observation, that the Puritan theology will spread itself widely over our land, and especially on the Sacramental question, will be the prevailing view of American Christians. We read with interest, accordingly, the accounts of the Pilgrim Celebrations, year after year, and wonder not that such enthusiasm should be manifested by those who claim lineal descent from the Pilgrim Fathers. That some things occur in connection with these occasions, which look very unlike the Puritans, it is mortifying to see. There have recently been some sad incongruities enacted. What, for instance, has fiddling and dancing and carousal, and all the paraphernalia of the ball-room, to do with Puritanism? If one of the good old Puritans should rise from his rest, and come to the door of a Pilgrims' ball—would he not more readily fancy that the sons of the Cavaliers were exulting in the riddance of them, than that the sons of the Pilgrims were celebrating the holy triumphs of a self-denying piety? There is, to our minds, very much that is wrong here. And then, how comes it that Unitarianism is so ardent in the Pilgrim Celebration? What fellowship has the Puritan system with Unitarianism? We were inclined to ask, where, on the last Pilgrim Anniversary, were the Orthodox ministers—the men who occupy the Puritan posts—of Boston? Have they given all into other hands—or do they seek other modes of showing their regard for the principles of their fathers, which they deem preferable to the formality of uncovering their heads as they pass the spot of hallowed memory? If there is any anniversary which should be kept with truly religious service, it is this; and every proper means should be employed, that the descendants of the Puritans should know in detail their fathers' history, and the principles for which they suffered.

In this view, Mr. Hall of Norwalk has done good service—but his work, in its benefits, goes very far beyond this. We noticed his book briefly, a few weeks ago, and now, after a careful reading, are prepared to speak more decidedly concerning it. We know of no work, which, in the same compass, gives so clear and satisfactory a view of the origin and progress of the principles of Puritanism. There are evidences of careful and patient research, and a comparison of the best authorities, in every chapter. The picture of the *Laudean policy* is one that has its counterpart only under the bloody Mary, or on the opposite side of the channel. We hope to be able to give the whole of this, that our readers may know more of the man, whose High Church views Puseyism sympathizes in, and whose execution it celebrates as martyrdom. The history of the successive colonies to New England is given with peculiar distinctness—and from the reading of it, we have derived a clearer knowledge of the several localities occupied. The style of Mr. Hall is vigorous, and his whole treatment of his subject manly. Our country congregations cannot fail of being well informed, with such courses of lectures as these.

As this work has grown out of the late outbreak of Prelatic exclusiveness—and especially in Connecticut—the author goes into the examination of the peculiar notions of Episcopacy. The controversy has called out several able works, and though this appears last, it loses nothing in interest, and is anticipated by nothing which has been published. In the chapters embraced in this part of the volume, there is a series of original and conclusive reasoning. A certain Mr. Chapin, as well as Bishop Brownell, comes in for his share of the showing up. In the concluding chapter, a curtain is drawn, and we are furnished with a view of some things worth seeing—note, for instance, the topics—" Episcopacy and Republicanism "—" Episcopacy in the American Revolution "—" Reproaches against the Puritans "—" The Table Turned." On the subject presented in this last topic, Dr. Phillips was led to say something in his late dedication sermon; the detail here given is amazing.

Mr. Hall closes his volume with a review of Dr. Coit on Puritanism, and exposes him fully. Every man of New England origin, who possesses any of the Puritan spirit, we should think, would make himself acquainted with this book. We commend it to every reader.

After these remarks concerning the book in general, there is one circumstance to which we would call special attention. Who has not heard of "the Blue Laws of Connecticut"—who has not felt aggrieved that good men should be concerned in their enactment? Behold, they are an *absolute fiction*—a mere Munchausen affair—according to Mr. Hall, the work of a Rev. Mr. Peters, an Episcopal clergyman, a Tory, who abandoned our country at the opening of the Revolution, and fled to England. Mr. Hall very justly expresses his amazement, that this man's fabrications should be brought out in a recent impression, with special commendation.